W9-CKK-165

Books and Monographs by Albert Ellis, Ph.D.

Published by Lyle Stuart:
Sex Without Guilt
The American Sexual Tragedy
The Art and Science of Love
Creative Marriage (*with Robert A. Harper*)
Reason and Emotion in Psychotherapy
If This Be Sexual Heresy . . .
Sex and the Single Man
The Origins and Development of the Incest Taboo
The Intelligent-Woman's Guide to Man-hunting
Homosexuality
The Art of Erotic Seduction (*with Roger O. Conway*)
Is Objectivism a Religion?
Murder and Assassination (*with John M. Gullo*)
Executive Leadership: A Rational Approach (Citadel Press)
The Sensuous Person: Critique and Corrections

Published by Others:
An Introduction to the Principles of Scientific Psychoanalysis
The Folklore of Sex
Sex, Society and the Individual (*with A. P. Pillay*)
Sex Life of the American Woman and the Kinsey Report
How to Live with a "Neurotic"
New Approaches to Psychotherapy Techniques
What is Psychotherapy?
The Psychology of Sex Offenders (*with Ralph Brancale*)
The Place of Value in the Practice of Psychotherapy
The Encyclopedia of Sexual Behavior (*with Albert Abarbanel*)
A New Guide to Rational Living (*with Robert A. Harper*)
Nymphomania: A Study of the Over-sexed Woman (*with Edward Sagarin*)
The Case for Sexual Liberty
Suppressed: Seven Key Essays Publishers Dared Not Print
The Search for Sexual Enjoyment
How to Prevent Your Child from Becoming a Neurotic Adult, (*with Janet L. Wolfe and Sandra Moseley*)
Growth Through Reason: Verbatim Cases in Rational-Emotive Therapy
The Civilized Couple's Guide to Extramarital Adventure
How to Master Your Fear of Flying

Sex and the Liberated Man

Sex and the Liberated Man

Albert Ellis, Ph.D.

Lyle Stuart, Inc.
Secaucus, New Jersey

First edition

Copyright © 1976 by the Institute for Rational Living, Inc.

All rights reserved, including the right to reproduce
this book or any portion thereof in any form

Published by Lyle Stuart, Inc.
120 Enterprise Ave., Secaucus, N. J. 07094
Published simultaneously in Canada by George J. McLeod Limited
73 Bathurst St., Toronto, Ont.

Address queries regarding rights and permissions
to Lyle Stuart, Inc.

Manufactured in the United States of America

LIBRARY OF CONGRESS CATALOGING IN PUBLICATION DATA
Ellis, Albert, 1913-
    Sex and the liberated man.

    Bibliography: p.
    Includes index.
    1. Sex instruction for men.   2. Rational-
emotive psychotherapy.   3. Single men.   I. Title.
HQ36.E32   1976   301.41'8'041   76-7000
ISBN 0-8184-0222-9

To
BROOKING TATUM
best damned editor I ever had

Contents

Foreword

This book, which I originally started as a revised edition of *Sex and the Single Man,* has now gone far beyond that aim and has finished up as practically an entirely new handbook of sexuality for males and their partners. And not only for single men, this time, but for mated ones, too. Hence, among other reasons, its new title. *Sex and the Single Man* remains one of my favorite books, of the more than thirty I have authored and edited—even though, originally, I did not place it high on the priority list of books that I intended to publish. Eventually, I would have got around to doing something like it, since my psychotherapeutic practice has always consisted largely of single men and women who have problems getting together with each other sexually and amatively, and I think I have helped thousands of them in this respect.

Not only have I dealt with their problems personally and intimately, in the course of innumerable individual and group-therapy sessions, but I have also presented hundreds of talks, seminars, and workshops on Creative Contacts and Relationships for Single People. These I've given at the Institute for Advanced Study in Rational Psychotherapy in New York, and at a large number of other growth centers and universities throughout the United States and several other countries. After all these years of therapeutic intervention in the single scene, I still feel surprised at the enthusiastic feedback I keep getting about my spoken and written work in this field.

My first major publication in the area of helping people with their sex-love relations consisted of *The American Sexual Tragedy,* which I brought out in the early 1950s. Although its predecessor,

The Folklore of Sex, made something of a stir and won considerable popularity in paperback in the 1960s, it not only seemed distinctly ahead of its time, but its publisher, Doubleday, largely disowned it and took its name off the title page before it reached the bookstalls. Publicity and advertising on the original edition also amounted to zilch, and the book got remaindered pretty rapidly.

Consequently, American publishers greeted *The American Sexual Tragedy* with little enthusiasm, let me desperately fart around with the manuscript for about two years, and drove me to give it, finally, to a small and almost entirely unknown publisher, Twayne, in order to get it in print. Again, although the second edition, published by Lyle Stuart, Inc., and Grove Press in the 1960s, had a fairly wide distribution, the original hardcover edition got pretty well ignored.

My first really popular sex book came out in 1958—the now widely known *Sex Without Guilt*. Along with the two books mentioned above (which, though hardly in high vogue with the general public, got steadily quoted in important literary and professional circles), this volume contributed strongly to ushering in what writers later started to call the sexual revolution. As I pointed out at that time, sexual liberalism has a long history and in the United States goes back to the Utopian socialists, the fanatical religionists, and the theoretical anarchists of mid-nineteenth century. The European tradition includes the romantic literati of the late eighteenth and early nineteenth centuries and the more professional and scientific sexual liberals, such as Havelock Ellis, Ellen Key, Sigmund Freud, Auguste Forel, Iwan Bloch, and Magnus Hirschfeld, who, from the 1890s onward, began to make significant assaults against Victorian puritanism.

The American sexual revolution, as Kinsey and his associates pointed out, began to take popular hold in the 1920s, largely because of technological advances like safe contraceptives, the automobile, and the anonymity of large-city living. But our practice in this respect tended to outrun our theory, and when I began writing about sex in the late 1940s, I largely made it my job to stress the latter and to give some up-to-date scientific backing to sexual liberalism. How well, in some respects, I succeeded! In the early 1960s, when popular women writers began to get on the revolutionary

bandwagon, I felt utterly delighted. For females who read *The Folklore of Sex, The American Sexual Tragedy,* and *Sex Without Guilt*
frequently said to me, "I can agree with some of the points you keep
making, and I especially like your egalitarian stand against the
double standard of sex ·morality and against the subjugation of
women. But don't you think you still take a largely male view,
which most women just will never go along with?"

Fortunately, two outstanding books by women changed a lot of
that. Helen Gurley Brown's *Sex and the Single Girl,* published in
1962, and Betty Friedan's *The Feminine Mystique,* brought out in
1963, showed that literally millions of modern women resented and
actively worked against the sex, love, marriage, and family restrictions placed upon them by the Judeo-Christian ethic and that in
increasing numbers they intended to do something about changing
this antifemale ethic. Women's liberation, a little slowly at first, but
then with increasing momentum, got under way!

The time seemed propitious for my own strong masculine voice
to augment that of Ms. Brown and Ms. Friedan, so that women
could see that many sensible, forward-looking men *wanted* them to
assert themselves sexually and amatively. Before *Sex and the Single
Girl* even reached the bestsellerdom that it highly deserved, I began
working hard on *The Intelligent Woman's Guide to Man-hunting*
(which I soon intend to revise as *The Intelligent Woman's Guide to
Mate-hunting.*) This book in many ways went far beyond Ms.
Brown's book and showed females why and how they could strongly
and sanely assert themselves to go after what they really wanted
sexually and emotionally. Today, many powerful voices, such as
those of Dr. Patricia Jakubowski, Dr. Janet Wolfe, Dr. Iris Fodor,
and the Boston Women's Collective, strongly advocate assertiveness
training for women. But in 1963, when *The Intelligent Woman's
Guide* appeared, virtually nothing of this sort existed; and I think I
can well give myself credit for a pioneering work.

At the suggestion of Lyle Stuart, I brought out, in the same year,
Sex and the Single Man, designed as a companion volume to *Sex
and the Single Girl* and *The Intelligent Woman's Guide.* I certainly
feel glad that I did! For although the original edition of *Sex and the
Single Man* contained some of the rampant male chauvinism that
then prevailed in Western civilization, it still struck several honest

and powerful blows for women's liberation, and I have felt consistent pleasure and surprise over the years at the great number of women who have read the book and told me how much they benefited from it. Not only did it help them to understand male attitudes and emotions, but it also helped them to loosen up many of their own sex-love prejudices.

Fine! But time still marches, and the sexual liberalism clearly apparent in *Sex and the Single Man* in 1963 could use some notable revision. Women's liberation, in theory if not yet that much in practice, has flowered considerably since that day, influencing much male as well as female thinking. The sexual revolution of the 1960s has continued to progress—with, expectably, some retrogressions and setbacks, but with some steady holding of the line. A large number of nonlegalized heterosexual and homosexual unions; a steady flow of X-rated movies; a much freer public use of previously banned four-letter words; the widespread sale of "pornographic" literature in highly respectable bookstores and newsstands; unusual gains on the part of gay-liberation groups; public toleration of (if not widespread engagement in) extramarital affairs and open marriage arrangements—these comprise some of the ongoing, and to some extent ever-increasing, fruits of what Lawrence Lipton called "the erotic revolution."

Meanwhile, the psychotherapeutic revolution has also made remarkable progress. My 1954 book, *The American Sexual Tragedy*, included a mind-boggling chapter entitled "The Folklore of Marital Relations," which spoke about "the Great Coital Myth" and which clearly advocated, as a replacement of this myth that penile-vaginal relations must remain sacred to heterosexuality, what Masters and Johnson (who began their sex researches at about that time) later referred to as the "sensate focus." What we now call sex therapy actually originated with the European sexologists of the late nineteenth cetnury and got developed in the United States by such authorities as Drs. William F. Robie, Alfred C. Kinsey, and G. Lombard Kelly. Spurred by their work, and by my own well-known 1953 article, "Is the Vaginal Orgasm a Myth?" Masters and Johnson hit the sexual scene with two block-busting books in 1966 and 1970 presenting fairly incontrovertible research data against the primacy of so-called vaginal orgasm and favoring what I called "noncoital" or "extracoital" sex play.

With the Masters and Johnson onslaught, sex therapy got under way. Although its behavior-modification and homework-assignment aspects—pioneered in the 1950s by Joseph Wolpe, Hans J. Eysenck, and my own early talks and writings on rational-emotive therapy—have received enormous and well-deserved endorsement, its cognitive-persuasive aspects have also got widely used, though much less publicized. For the Masters and Johnson sex-therapy methods, and virtually all the offshoots that others have developed from them, include an exceptionally strong informational and "antiawfulizing" element.

Psychiatrists like Alfred Adler and Paul Dubois emphasized this aspect of psychotherapy early in the twentieth century, but they largely fell into disrepute as the psychoanalysts came along to preempt the field with their "deeper" probing of presumably unconscious wishes and conflicts. When I originated rational-emotive therapy (RET) around the beginning of 1955, largely because I found some of its methods virtually necessary to the successful sex therapy that I had started to do several years previously, I abandoned the psychoanalytic ways of my early training and emphasized the rational-persuasive mode of treatment.

In the main, I showed people that they, and not their sacred or devilish parents, created their own emotional disturbances and sexual symptoms—such as frigidity and impotence—largely because they devoutly believed and stubbornly stuck to several irrational ideas. In particular, they escalated their desires, wishes, and preferences into absolutistic should's, ought's, and must's, and they especially demanded and commanded (in their heads and hearts, if not in their conscious philosophies): (1) "I *must* do very well and achieve greatly, and thereby win the approval of those I value; else I turn into a slobbish, pretty worthless person." (2) "You *must* treat me kindly and fairly; else you turn into a lousy, undeserving individual." (3) "The world *must* make things easy and nice for me and give me what I want without too much trouble or effort; else it rates as a horrible place and life hardly seems worth it."

Sexually speaking, these three perfectionistic, unrealistic demands get translated into: (1) "I must satisfy myself and my partner in a highly competent, outstanding manner; else I rate only as a thorough slob and a no-goodnik!" This irrational idea creates feelings of anxiety, insecurity, depression, and worthlessness and a self-spying

attitude that causes most of what we call sexual inadequacy, joyless-
ness, and withdrawal. (2) "You *must* love me thoroughly and help
me to achieve sex satisfaction and competence; else you amount to a
rotten person whom I can hardly bear to have sex with or to satisfy." This irrational idea creates feelings of anger, resentment, hostility, and depression and again leads to many kinds of inadequacy
and withdrawal. (3) "The world *must* provide me with quick, easy,
fully satisfying sex-love relations, and if it does not, it turns into a
horrible place where life hardly seems worth living." This crazy idea
produces intense feelings of low frustration tolerance, self-pity, and
depression, as well as inertia, withdrawal, inaction, and procrastina-
tion. Moreover, when the first two of these three irrational ideas
cause feelings of inadequacy and hostility, the third helps people to
harbor and retain these feelings, instead of working hard to change
them; thus, it seriously interferes with any kind of successful self-
management or psychotherapy.

Rational-emotive therapy clearly, quickly, and with maximum
efficiency shows people with sexual problems exactly what they tell
themselves to create these problems. Having important behavioral
and emotive components, RET gives them activity-oriented homework assignments to help them attack and undo their general and
sexual problems. It not only includes all the effective Masters and
Johnson sex-therapy procedures, but it normally goes far beyond
these and embraces a great deal of general antiawfulizing. It shows
clients that no matter how bad external conditions (including
mating conditions) become, *they* manufacture their own emotional
problems by awfulizing about these conditions. And it specializes in
antiawfulizing and anticatastrophizing procedures. After pioneering
by showing sex therapists how to accept and utilize masturbation,
RET now tries to extend therapeutic pioneering by making a con-
certed and vigorous attack on all forms of *must*-urbation!

When I first originated RET, most of the other psychotherapists
here and abroad felt horrified at its active-directive methods. These
people insisted that such methods could not possibly work (or that
they represented shallow and cavalier methods of symptom
removal) and that they'd better get replaced by more "depth-
centered" psychoanalytic procedures. How things have change in
this regard! Today, passively oriented, "listening" psychotherapies,

such as orthodox psychoanalysis and client-centered Rogerian procedures, gain less and less popularity, while intrusive, teaching, activity-oriented methods—such as transactional analysis, Gestalt therapy, encounter groups, and cognitive-behavior therapy—seem to
take over an increasing part of the therapeutic field. Good! To
change their self-defeating ways of thinking, emoting, and behaving,
people seem to require not only understanding, insight, and acceptance, but also instruction, practice, and the acquisition of social
skills. RET has led the field in this respect; and whereas *Sex and
the Single Man* included some of this pioneering, the present book
includes up-to-date, revised RET formulations and will help the
reader to help himself therapeutically even more than did the
original edition.

RET, as Dr. Donald Meichenbaum and other students of psychotherapy have kept pointing out, consists partly of semantic-
oriented therapy. It accepts the theories and practices of Alfred Korzybski and other outstanding general semanticists and continually
teaches people to avoid overgeneralizing, absolutizing, and what I
now call *must*urbating. More specifically, it tries to get them to
change the following semantic errors in talking to themselves and
others:

1. Instead of their saying, "I *should* not make a mistake," or "I
must not hate my womanfriend," we help them, in rational-emotive
therapy, to think and tell themselves, "*It would prove better* if I did
not make that mistake," and "I would in all likelihood find it *preferable* to stop hating my womanfriend."

2. Instead of their saying, "I can't stop worrying," or "I find it
impossible to control my sex feelings," we help them to change their
internal sentences to "I *haven't* stopped worrying yet, but if I keep
working at it in all probability, I *can*," and "I find it *exceptionally
difficult* to control my sex feelings, but that hardly means *impossible*."

3. Instead of people's insisting, "I *always* do badly *every time* I
try to court an attractive female," we try to help them change this to
"I *usually* or *often* do badly when I try to court an attractive female,
but that doesn't prove that I have to *keep* doing poorly in this
respect."

4. When men and women wail, "I would feel *awful* if my lover

left me!" or "How *terrible* I find rejection!" we try to help them think and say, "I would find it highly inconvenient if my lover left me," or "I would view it as distinctly disadvantageous if I got rejected," or "I would feel deeply disappointed to lose such a friend."

5. When rational-emotive clients proclaim, "I *am* a *bad person* for acting so incompetently," or "I *am* a *worthless individual* for treating my mate so badly," we show them how to say, instead, "I find it highly unfortunate when I act incompetently, but my poor behavior by no means make me a bad person," and "I behave immorally and wrongly when I treat my mate so badly, but *I* cannot get legitimately rated, either as a worthwhile or as a worthless individual, for any of my actions."

6. When people say, "I *am* no good at lovemaking," we help them to say, instead, "Up to the present time, I have not done so well at lovemaking. But that doesn't mean that I cannot do much better in the future."

7. When men say, "She is a castrating woman, and I can't stand her!" we try to show them that they could more accurately say, "She sometimes acts castrating (while other women act less threatening); therefore, I do not like to remain in her presence. But since she also has other traits, I can not legitimately view her as a rotten person just because she sometimes acts castrating."

8. When clients claim, "I *need* love!" we attempt to get them to think, instead, "I *want* love very much, but I do not absolutely *need* it and can survive and feel reasonably happy without it." When they say, "I *must* have a wife who doesn't spend too much money, and couldn't bear it if I had one who acted like a spendthrift," we help them to believe, "I would very much *desire* or *like* to have a thrifty wife, and I'll find it damned inconvenient if I don't have one. But I certainly can stand it!"

9. When people say, *"That* makes me anxious," or *"You* made me angry," we help them see, instead, "I *made myself* anxious about that," and "I angered myself about your behavior."

10. When clients use language like, "I'm OK, you're OK," we show them that they can preferably say, instead, "I choose to remain alive and to feel that I have the right to enjoy myself, even though I do many wrong things; and I also accept your aliveness

and your right, as a human, to exist and make yourself happy, even though you may at times act poorly and perform deeds that I don't like. I don't have to rate or give a report card to myself, you, or anyone."

As the above examples show, RET stresses a semantic approach to understanding and minimizing human disturbance. To help in this respect, *Sex and the Liberated Man* uses a form of language called E-prime by its developer, D. David Bourland, Jr. After Alfred Korzybski recommended that we avoid the "is" of identity and the "is" of prediction, Bourland implemented his recommendations by showing that if we avoid all usage of the verb, *to be—is, am, are, was, were, be, been* and *being*—we eliminate a good deal (though not all) of the inaccurate overgeneralizing that this verb encourages. Thus, if we say "The rose *is* red," we strongly imply that (1) redness constitutes the "natural" or usual identity of *all* roses; (2) this particular rose has *total* redness; (3) it will *always* remain completely red; (4) it has some intrinsic *essence* of redness; and (5) if it did not have redness, we could not legitimately call it a rose. To avoid this kind of overgeneralizing, we can more accurately say, "The rose has redness," or "The rose has a red quality," or "The rose appears red."

With the encouragement and editorial help of Robert H. Moore, a staff member of the Florida branch of the Institute for Rational Living, Inc., at Clearwater, I have therefore written this book in E-prime. Although Bourland and a few others have written articles in E-prime, practically no books seem to exist in this mode. With Bob Moore's help, I recently published an E-prime version of the revised edition of *How to Live with a "Neurotic"*; and Dr. Robert A. Harper and I also brought out our book *A New Guide to Rational Living*, devoid of *to be* usage. The present book seems to hold the honor of appearing as the first sex book ever written in E-prime. I hope that it will prove the precursor of a host of similarly written tomes!

A final introductory word. Most of this book consists of new material. It goes beyond *Sex and the Single Man*; and only about 25 percent of it continues and updates that original volume. Much knowledge on sex has accumulated since I wrote the original book for men; many social attitudes have changed significantly. All men by no means feel or work toward male liberation today, but an increasing number do. Several good books—especially Warren Farrell's *The Liberated Man*—significantly help in this respect.

As Farrell trenchantly notes, "becoming a liberated man, then, is achieving new freedoms—freedom beyond proving onself; beyond worrying about appearances, on the playing field or in the office; in earned degrees or in job titles; in clothes, status, or swagger. It is getting beyond condescension and contempt toward women, needing to be in control and have an answer to all problems at all times; beyond specializing, needing to become expert, being the sole breadwinner, the victim of male bribes—ultimately a security object."

And that goes, of course, for sex. A sexually liberated man also achieves new freedoms—including freedom from proving himself in bed, from showing that he can outdo any other man with his immense and incredibly expert genitals, from seeing women mainly as pieces of ass, and from self-denigration in case he fails to live up to others' or his own unrealistic expectations. While my original version of *Sex and the Single Man* did its best to release males (as well as their female partners) from the society-imposed shackles of century-old erotic purnitanism and ignorance, this updated and greatly expanded volume, *Sex and the Liberated Man*, will hopefully continue that goal and press still further: to the releasing of males from their self-imposed fetters of sexual machismo and male chauvinist pigdom. Well, we shall see!

Albert Ellis, Ph.D.
Institute for Rational Living
              and
Institute for Advanced Study in Rational Psychotherapy
45 East 65th Street
New York, N.Y. 10021

Introduction to
"Sex and the Single Man"

For a man there exist three near certainties in life—death, taxes, and women. Which proves the worst? We can view the man who thinks he can handle women as an optimist or a superoptimist.

This book deals with sex and the single man. This means that it deals with the single man—and *women*. It will also consider some of the nonheterosexual aspects of bachelorhood, such as the problems of masturbation and homosexuality and the important relationship of the man *to himself*.

Largely, however, this book tells you, the presumably male reader, how to meet, get involved with, have satisfactory sex relations with, and perhaps marry a suitably selected person of the other sex. Not, of course, that you *have* to do so. As a respectable, independent member of the human race, you do have other choices.

You could, for example, consort only with other men or become a Trappist monk or live happily (though probably not too sexually) with a bird dog.

If you make any of these choices, take it—with my blessing. But if you *do* want to get along successfully with women, I've designed this book to tell you how. And it *will* tell you—it will give you the *knowledge*, at least, that will enable you to relate with females better than before.

Suppose you dote on homosexual rather than heterosexual relations. So you do. In the old days, you would necessarily have got diagnosed as a disturbed person. Today, many authorities still think this, but many others, including most members of the American Psychiatric Association, think otherwise. Anyway, though I have not written this book particularly for you (any more than I specifi-

21

cally address it to women), you will find a lot of material in it that also applies to you. Just read it selectively and substitute *male friend* for *woman friend* in some of its passages. Female readers, too, can often do likewise.

Will knowledge suffice? Does *knowing* how to make it with the members of the other sex automatically enable you to do so?

No; decidedly not. In addition to know-how, you'd better have several other things to aid good sex-love relationships with females —specifically: intelligence; emotional stability; experience and practice; sympathy *for* and interest *in* women; and good luck!

Without a fair degree of intelligence and emotional stability, all the knowledge in the world will not help you understand females. Without experience and practice, you probably won't succeed at anything, sex included. Without genuine sympathy for and interest in women, you will antagonize them and defeat your own best ends. And without some measure of good luck—without your possessing, for example, the right age, or body build, or sensitivity, or talent, or something else that just happens to appeal to a particular woman who interests you—you won't get what you want, even though you have other ample blessings.

This book will not appreciably increase your intelligence quotient nor provide any kind of good-luck charm. But assuming you have a reasonably good mind and feel prepared to use it, this volume will give you pertinent knowledge about people, show you how to achieve more emotional stability, aid you to get sex practice, and help you relate.

A hell of a lot for one volume to attempt? Undoubtedly; but you can't kill a book for trying. And although the material presented here may seem easily stated and cavalierly arrived at, don't fool yourself. More than thirty-five years of intense preparation have gone into compiling it, during which I have read and digested thousands of books and articles on sex-love relations, done primary research in the psychology of sex and love, intensively worked with thousands of psychotherapy and marriage-counseling clients, written hundreds of articles and published more than thirty books on sex, love, marriage, the family, and allied fields of living, and personally (and without editorial assistance!) got involved in a dozen major and countless minor relationships with women.

On this last count, I enjoy telling a story of what happened to me many years ago when I did research at the library of the Academy of Medicine in New York City. After I had finished my work one day, as I stopped to view a medical exhibit in the library, I ran into my personal physician. Although this man had known me for a long time and had intimate knowledge of my physical condition, he had never bothered to ask what kind of work I did, whether I had married, or similar personal questions. I think he thought I worked as an accountant or as some other type of conventional businessman.

Surprised, therefore, to see me in such medical surroundings, he asked, "What the devil brings *you* here?"

"Research," I retorted. "I come here almost every day to do research."

"Research in *what?*" he half-snorted.

"Sex," I said.

"Oh?" he ejaculated, almost unbelievingly. Then he smiled and made a beautiful comeback. "Well, I certainly hope you get in some laboratory work!"

Ever since then—doctor's orders, you know—I have done my best to fulfill his hopes. And I include the results of my first-hand (not to mention -lips, -tongue, and -genitalia) sex research in this and several of my other books.

The present book, then, stems from extensive clinical, experimental, and personal investigation of (what I still prejudicially see as) a highly fascinating field of human endeavor. It attempts to answer the most important questions that almost any unmarried male in our society will have. With the use of the information in this book *and* some intelligence *and* a little luck, you may well have a sex-love ball.

Sex and the Liberated Man

CHAPTER 1

What Price Sexual Abstinence?

MILLIONS OF WORDS written and declaimed during the past several centuries have attempted to prove sexual abstinence not only perfectly harmless to the young male (and female), but actually a beneficial form of (non-) behavior. What do these words really prove? That their authors thought like asses.

To begin with, as modern sex research has shown, no such thing as sexual abstinence tends to exist in the human male. Although the theory of sex sublimation, stoutly propounded by no less an authority than Sigmund Freud, still holds credence, normal males just don't follow it. W. S. Taylor showed in a classic monograph that not even highly ethical, clerically minded college boys refrain completely from sex activities. When they stop one form of sex (such as premarital intercourse), they simply find other sex outlets, such as masturbation, petting to orgasm, or homosexual affairs.

Alfred C. Kinsey and his associates went far beyond Taylor's original investigation of sex sublimation and studied the sexual outlets of more than six thousand males of all ages, from many walks of life. They discovered that the average male's number of sex outlets remains surprisingly constant, so that he merely substitutes one form of sexual behavior for another and practically never stays abstinent.

When a young man has no sex whatever for any considerable period of time, he may do himself considerable harm and practically never do himself any good. Not that he will probably die of sexual abstention, but he may easily wish he would!

The results of prolonged avoidance of orgasm in the male? I shall discuss some of them in this chapter.

27

Impairment of Physical Health

Although some low-sexed individuals can remain abstinent for long periods without any physical consequences, many of us can't. We don't get tuberculosis, and we hardly die from abstaining, but we do develop various ailments, most of them minor but practically all of them highly unpleasant.

In a pioneering book, *Sexual Continence*, a famous sex author, Dr. William J. Robinson, pointed out that the normal male often develops numerous physical complaints, including headaches, gastric upsets, congestion of the pelvic region, and high blood pressure when he has no sex life. Abraham Myerson believed that attempts to suppress sexuality on the part of a highly sexed male may "throw his visceral responses into a sort of confusion as well as create within him the most dramatic and dramatized conflict."

Here follow some other views on the physical harm that may ensue if a male, particularly a young, virile one, suppresses all overt sexuality.

Dr. C. David Cawood: Prostatic congestion, or abacterial prostatitis, constitutes a disease that can result from "many types of unfulfilled irritative symptoms, low back pain, perineal discomfort, testicular aching, and early morning discharge."

Dr. LeMon Clark: A great deal of discomfort in the testicles stems from sex engorgement and congestion. If this congestion gets "repeated at fairly frequent intervals through a period of many months, it may actually bring about a chronic congestion of the prostate which might give you some trouble. When orgasm and ejaculation do not take place after prolonged sex arousal, after a period of time one may get more and more uncomfortable."

Many people still wrongly believe, with such outstanding advocates of abstinence as Gandhi, that complete chastity improves physical and mental functioning and enhances and prolongs life. As Dr. Isadore Rubin has pointed out, this seems an unfounded view, since no evidence of any kind exists "that abstinence will improve health or lengthen life." If anything, the contrary appears much more true!

Impairment of Psychological Health

In regard to psychological health or mental functioning, a great deal of evidence exists that complete abstinence from sex: (1) rarely occurs; (2) does *not* lead to successful sublimation—as Freud wrongly contended and as I and many others have solidly refuted; and (3) frequently contributes to distinct emotional harm. Many authorities—such as René Guyon, Lester Kirkendall, and Walter Stokes and David Mace—have indicated that all kinds and degrees of nervousness and more severe emotional trouble may easily afflict normally and highly sexed individuals who force themselves to refrain completely from sex satisfaction.

Here we have some typical comments on this important point.

Dr. Hugo Beigel: "In young people abstinence [may] increase sexual desire and evoke an abundance of sexual imagery. This may result in inability to concentrate, irritability, insomnia, extreme nervousness, or more serious complications, the extent of the disturbance depending on the individual's drive intensity, temperament, and environments. These conditions may so [distract] some people that they cannot work."

Sigmund Freud: Unrelieved sex tensions lead to a physical buildup and to eventual anxiety neurosis. To ward off this kind of disturbance, "nothing but adequate activity (orgasm) would [prove] effective; for, once it has reached the required level, the somatic sexual excitation gets continuously transmutted into psychical excitation; the activity which will free the nerve-endings from burdensome pressure and so abolish the whole of the somatic excitation present, thus allowing the subcortical tracts to reestablish their resistance, must absolutely [get] carried into operation." Also: Hysteria gets "frequently caused by the voluntary suppression of the sexual life."

Wilhelm Reich: Only one thing remains "wrong with neurotic patients: the *lack of full and repeated sexual satisfaction*. . . . The severity of any kind of psychic disturbance [occurs] in direct relation to the severity of the disturbance of genitality."

Dr. Walter F. Robie: "Neurosis, instability, irascibility, relative impotence, [constitute] common symptoms of excessive repression." I have got thoroughly convinced "from an enormous experience in dealing with the sex lives of men and women, that prolonged sexual abstinence not only [proves] detrimental to both, so far as [concerns] the sex function itself, but that such abstinence renders one easier prey to ordinary diseases, and that, sooner or later, under such conditions, some neurosis inevitably [results]."

A spurious causation may, of course, arise here. Since sexual asceticism and severe emotional disturbance tend to go together, we may too easily conclude that the former causes the latter—when, in fact, the latter frequently causes the former. Modern psychological thinkers rarely agree with early psychoanalysts that sex blockings directly cause emotional impairment; they tend, instead, to follow the more moderate views of Alfred Adler, Karen Horney, Erich Fromm, Leon Salzman, and other authorities that general disturbance leads to sex problems, rather than vice versa.

I have strongly upheld this view and presented evidence favoring it in many of my writings—especially *Reason and Emotion in Psychotherapy, Growth Through Reason,* and *Humanistic Psychotherapy: the Rational-Emotive Approach.* Consequently, I would take extremist views on the psychic harm caused by abstinence—such as those held by Freud and Reich—with a huge bucket of salt. Nonetheless, abstinence born of puritanical taboos has for centuries created and still importantly continues to wreak much damage in those —who remain legion!—who have strong vulnerabilities to psychological insult. Foolish social rules, as Alex Comfort has demonstrated, don't fully *make* people anxious, but they certainly contribute—especially arbitrary rules favoring or compelling abstinence!

An interesting connection between abstinence and emotional disturbance arose in the life of Gandhi. In his autobiography, Gandhi tells us that when, at the tender age of sixteen, he had intercourse with his young wife, a servant knocked at his door, announcing his father's death. "So all had ended! I had but to wring my hands. I felt deeply ashamed and miserable. I ran to my father's room. I saw that, if animal passion had not blinded me, I should have [got] spared the torture of separation from my father during his last moments." A few months later, Gandhi's wife had a premature child, who died. He severely condemned himself again, and as a result of his guilt he adopted a policy of abstinence for many years.

Then, to make matters worse, Gandhi's second son, Manilal, committed the unforgivable "sin" of losing his virginity to a woman when he had not yet reached his twenty-first birthday. Even though his extreme censure of his older son, Harilal, for remarrying after the death of his wife had previously led to bad results (Harilal turned alcoholic and feuded with his father bitterly for many years), Gandhi vigorously damned Manilal, decreed that he must never marry, went on a penitential fast, and took fifteen years to relent and allow Manilal to contract a marriage.

I think that this represents a good example of a basically and easily disturbed individual who made himslf terribly guilty quite unnecessarily, used sexual abstinence as a punishment, then probably helped get himself more disturbed by remaining abstinent and kept having aberrant views and feelings about sex. The more abstinence gets used in this way, I would hypothesize, the more the individual will upset himself emotionally.

Impairment of Sexual Adequacy

In many (though not necessarily all) humans, complete abstinence seriously interferes with sex performance and may render an individual temporarily or permanently impotent or frigid. Hirschfeld, after studying the results of abstinence during World War I, concluded: "We have every reason to assume that the abstinence enforced by the war resulted in all forms of sexual neurosis. Particularly the most important of these neuroses, ejaculatio praecox (premature ejaculation)."

Wilhelm Reich, studying the effect of continence on marriage, concluded that although the demand for abstinence might possibly make the adolescent male submissive and therefore capable of remaining monogamous once he married, "in doing so it creates the very sexual impotence which in turn destroys marriage and accentuates the problem of marriage."

Henri-Frédéric Amiel, drawing from his own sex experience, wrote, "I seem to have lost my sex. My general softening comes perhaps from my complete abstinence."

And St. Augustine, after trying sexual abstinence for some time, reported, "I now neither seek nor desire anything whatever of this sort [sexual intercourse]. Only with horror and loathing do I even remember it."

After making a comprehensive review of the effects of abstinence, Taylor concluded that "physically, also, despite many misleading arguments to the contrary, it seems reasonable to conclude with modern authorities that prolonged sexual abstinence often produces, in men, weak erections and premature ejaculations, impotence, prostatic and testicular disorders; in women, chlorosis, dysmenorrhea, shrinking of the breasts, and congestion of the ovaries; and in both sexes, insomnia and metabolic and nervous disorders. Abstinence after habituation to intercourse especially conduces these disorders. In short, sexual abstinence (like probably any continually unsatisfied urge) considered solely in its direct individual effects, exists usually if not always as an evil."

Impairment of Social Values

Not only does continence prove physically, mentally, and sexually injurious to numerous individuals who attempt (usually unsuccessfully) to practice it, but it also has grave social disadvantages. J. D. Unwin, one of the greatest prudes of this century, despite his espousal of sexual inhibition, has written, "Fashion [led] new converts to found religious houses, soon filled by male and female votaries of celibacy. This happened among the Anglo-Saxons at the end of the seventh century and again in the tenth century, and among the Normans in the twelfth century. By their voluntary acceptance of compulsory continence the women who first entered these houses proved themselves to [constitute] the very ones who, fruitful, would have bred a generation of energetic sons. If you examine the records of the events which took place in Western Europe between the seventh and thirteenth centuries, you will find that after the acceptance of this type of Christianity a society soon ceased to manifest the same energy as before. It does not matter whether Anglo-Saxons, Danes, Normans, Franks, or Venetians; their social energy varied according as they permitted or did not permit the custom of voluntary sterility."

From quite a different standpoint, Freud also noted the dysgenic influence of abstinence: "Let us add that together with the restrictions on sexual activity in any nation there always goes an increase of anxiety concerning life and of fear of death, which interfere with each individual's capacity for enjoyment, and do away with his willingness to incur risk of death in whatever cause—showing itself in a diminished inclination to beget offspring, thus excluding any people or group of such a type from participation in the future."

General Disadvantages

Clearly, sexual abstinence by no means wreaks harm on *all* individuals. Great numbers of females in our culture refrain from any kind of sex play, including masturbation, without any noticeable handicaps or ills; and a small, though still sizable, number of males at least refrain from petting or coitus without ending up in the bughouse. But these remain minorities. The *average* person—especially the average *male* person—feels highly uncomfortable and disadvantaged by complete abstinence, to such an extent that in spite of all social mores and laws, he rarely adheres to it for any length of time. Premarital sex, for example, has got rigorously banned by many groups for many ages. But the evidence clearly shows (as summarized, for example, in Lawrence Casler's *Is Marriage Necessary?* and in my *Case for Sexual Liberty*) that sticking with this kind of ban gets so difficult for most of the people most of the time that they often flout it.

Some general or summary statements against prolonged continence include the following, from outstanding authorities.

Dr. James Leslie McCary: "No empirical evidence . . . indicate[s] that sublimation of biological drives can really get accomplished. As a matter of fact, a conscious attempt to sublimate sexual urges can result in such psychological malfunctions as frigidity, impotence, inability to concentrate, irritability, and insomnia, or in such physical problems as premature ejaculation, difficulty in achieving erection, prostatitis, ovarian and vulval congestion, and decreased sex drive."

Henry Miller: When our desires get "thwarted or suppressed life [turns] mean, ugly, vicious and death-like."

We can perhaps best sum up this short survey of the harmful effects of sexual abstinence by quoting from two authorities who made intensive studies of the subject many years apart. Writing in 1924, the great sexologist Dr. William J. Robinson noted, "In the vast majority of men and women continence produces unpleasant and undesirable effects. . . . In some people however continence after maturity produces distinctly unfavorable results; sometimes purely physical, sometimes purely psychic, but usually a combination of both. In some cases the symptoms [prove] very grave, and in a certain percentage the condition brought about [stays] incurable. . . . To say it in one sentence. Sexual abstinence in the majority of both men and women [remains] abnormal and undesirable."

Decades later, the sexologist and psychologist Dr. Hugo G. Beigel concluded his own intensive survey of the results of abstinence with this statement: "The gratification of the sexual drive [proves] a necessity for the normally developed human, and the disregard of this necessity over a long period of time [will] likely break the life impulses and thus affect not only happiness but also physical and mental health."

To the question, then, "What price sexual abstinence?" we can unhesitatingly answer, The price seems too damned high! Naturally, complete sexual abstention has *some* advantages. It can, for example, save time (assuming that the abstainer does not remain continually *pre*occupied with the acts with which he does *not* occupy himself!). It eliminates certain dangers, such as incurring venereal disease or getting a woman pregnant. It avoids entangling alliances (such as marriage), which may have their own inconveniences. But almost all its advantages you could just as well—nay, much better —achieve if you avoided heterosexual relations but regularly resorted to masturbation.

Its disadvantages, moreover, remain enormous. For only the unusually low-sexed individual, or one fanatically devoted to some nonsexual cause that consumes practically all his time and energy, can *easily* remain abstinent. The normal human, particularly the normal male, works his guts off (sometimes literally!) to remain totally inactive sexually. He continually forces himself to brush aside incipient and full-blown sex thoughts and fantasies, to convince himself over and over that he *should* remain inviolate, to rigorously keep away from easily available temptations, and, almost obsessively-compulsively, to keep his mind and his body from automatically returning to sexual enticements.

Almost always, as indicated above, he will more or less fail in his abstinence endeavors. In fact, he will not merely fail occasionally, but find that he frequently lapses into sex activity of one kind or another. And when he does lapse, he will tend to go off on a series of sexual binges, rather than minor, occasional interludes. Even when he succeeds in remaining abstemious, he will almost always feel *anxious* about his continued success. And when he fails, he will tend to damn and punish himself for his slips.

Finally, as we have also just seen, if the abstinence-minded individual somehow manages to succeed in his puritanical aim, his very success will involve its own failure, since he will in the great majority of cases injure himself physically, emotionally, sexually, and/or socially. He won't, I again concede, die of his self-imposed sexual constraint—at least, not very often! But neither will he *live* with it, in any true sense of the word.

The price of sexual abstinence, then, almost always proves exorbitant. When, in very rare cases (as when you have some serious illness and your physician bans any sex activity), you require total abstinence, you can stoically accept it or, as I teach my clients, gracefully lump it—just as you can any necessary evil. But *voluntary* abstinence remains an *un*necessary evil. Accept *that* misery, and you seem off your rocker! You'd better see a psychologist, fast, than keep afflicting yourself with that kind of nonsense.

A client of mine, whom I shall call Malcolm B., maintained that he found it better to refrain completely from sex because he wanted to devote all his spare time to studying the stock market, and sex thoughts and acts would only interfere with this great interest.

"But wouldn't your not having any sex lead you to get somewhat obsessed with sex thoughts and fantasies?" I asked. "And would not this kind of obsession detract even *more* from your interest in the stock market?"

"Oh, no. I feel ready to put up with that kind of thing," Malcolm replied. "I can easily handle my fantasies."

"No doubt," I said. "But won't they *still* prove rather time consuming? And won't the effort you have to take to squelch them detract from your absorption in the stock market?"

"No, the sex itself would take still more time and energy," he insisted.

By this time, I got quite suspicious. "How so?" I asked. "Let's suppose you did engage in some kind of sex. How often would you do so every week, on the average? And how much time would you consume on each occasion?"

"Oh," Malcolm answered rather vaguely, "a good deal of time, I guess."

"You mean that if you dated women and got them to go to bed with you, it would take at least five or ten hours a week?"

"Well, wouldn't it?" asked Malcolm, somewhat belligerently and defensively.

"Yes, it might, but you can use various methods of achieving sex satisfaction other than petting or having intercourse."

"What do you mean?"

"Well, masturbation, for example. You don't mean to tell me, now, *that* would take you five or ten hours a week, even if you did it every day."

"Oh, I would never do a thing like *that!*" Malcolm exclaimed.

"You wouldn't? Why?"

"Well . . . uh . . . I just wouldn't."

I saw that my suspicions proved well founded. Malcolm had created his objection to the time-consuming aspects of sex as a pure rationalization. Actually, as I soon induced him to admit, he thought *any* kind of sex act wicked, that he would merit worthiness and specialness only if he refrained from every form of sex. Like so many others who attempt to remain completely abstinent, he grew disturbed by demanding he perform perfectly in all significant areas, by loathing himself when he fell a few degress below this level of perfection, and by compensating for his assumed worthlessness by acting "better" than other males in sexual areas.

Where other self-downing people like Malcolm try to perform as the most potent of Don Juans (or even as the most frequent masturbators) and thereby "prove" their superiority over others, he took the overcompensatory road of sexual "purity" and tried to excel in that respect. After we had worked several months at intensive psychotherapy, and he no longer needed to excel over all other males but could accept himself in his own right, he recognized his obsession with continence and "purity" as a symptom of emotional disturbance and began to have quite enjoyable masturbatory and heterosexual outlets.

Not that *all* totally abstinent males turn out disturbed. A few physically low-sexed individuals can remain normally and harmlessly continent. If you fit in this class, you have nothing to worry about. Sex—and, for that matter, marriage—may just not seem your cup of bouillon. But if you feel highly sexed—if, for instance, you continually experience arousal and excitement—and if you *still* feel that you must remain completely abstinent, then you'd better get, pronto, to the nearest psychotherapist and find out why. You may refrain from overeating very sensibly, but to refrain from *any* eating constitutes sheer lunacy. Abstaining from all sexuality, when you feel young and physically healthy, equals abstaining from happy living. He who puts his sex urges behind him, viewing them as aspects of satanism, would better put aside enough funds for prolonged psychological treatment!

CHAPTER 2

The Art and Science
of Masturbation

ALTHOUGH WE HAVE remarkably liberalized our attitudes toward masturbation during the last fifty years, writers on sex rarely take a completely objective, nonmoralistic attitude toward this touchy subject. Complete public endorsement of self-stimulation prevails only among some widely scattered primitive peoples; and when raised in any civilized nation we find it almost shocking to read about the unusual freedom experienced by such peoples.

Thus, Linton tells us that among the Marquesan Islanders, "The child found early in life that it got nowhere by yelling, for if the adults [got] busy, they just let it cry. However, if the child [turned] too troublesome, an adult might quiet it by masturbating it. The masturbation of female children began very early; in fact from the moment of birth there existed systematic manipulation of the labia to elongate them, as elongation was considered a mark of beauty."

According to Elkin, among the northern Arapaho Indians of Wyoming, "Much of the Arapaho humor, told only among the men and often for the purpose of genital rubbing, revolved about the unusual and unexpected in the love quest. It frequently related to sodomy, in nonhuman form, and masturbation, in which the young men seemed to have engaged rather often, in a spirit of good-natured sport."

Laubscher tells us that among the Tembu people of Africa, "Masturbatory manipulations of the penis [prove] quite common and may receive a playful rebuke, but do not [get] viewed at all seriously. They [get] merely considered as the playful activities of children."

38

Devereux notes that among the young Mohave Indian males "Masturbating and urinating competitions occurred frequently. In masturbating competitions both the shortness of the time required to cause ejaculation and the distance to which the sperm projected [got] taken into consideration. Urinating competitions consisted of urinating figures and letters on the ground."

So much for some of the "uncivilized" primitives. In our own "higher" civilization, attitudes toward masturbation appear infinitely primmer. Menninger notes that "even today few authors [seem] brave enough and honest enough to make the flat statements that masturbation never harms a child and that the child whose sexual life evolves without a period of masturbation exists as an exceptional and, one may say, an abnormal child." He also points out that even psychoanalysts tend to view masturbation as self-destructive because it represents a preoccupation with the self, based on aggressive feelings toward others. He fails to acknowledge this psychoanalytic concept as largely a biased view, not based on any factual evidence, since only a small minority of individuals masturbate because of their hatred of others.

As Lester Dearborn notes, "No other form of sexual activity has gotten more frequently discussed, more roundly condemned, and more universally practiced than masturbation. . . . The superstitions regarding masturbation have not [suffered] entire annihilation, for we find in a few of our modern writings an insistence upon classifying it under the heading of perversion. Whenever modern religious leaders feel under the obligation to discourage masturbation, they now [rarely] refer to any horrible consequences but rather consider it a religious offense. The Catholic Church, for example, deals with it dogmatically as a sin. This attitude also [gets] held by some Orthodox groups and by certain fundamentalist Protestant bodies."

As Morton Hunt points out, ever since the 1960s and the widespread publication of unexpurgated editions of books by Henry Miller, the Marquis de Sade, D. H. Lawrence, and other "sexy" writers, there has occurred "a liberation of sexuality from a two-millennia-long tradition of Judeo-Christian asceticism, a liberation so sweeping that nearly everyone can now think about, talk about and read about sex as freely as they can about food, politics or money and most people have [turned] grudgingly tolerant, even if not warmly approving, of many forms of sexual behavior they would formerly have regarded with loathing or even righteous indignation."

Yet in his large-scale study of sexual behavior in the 1970s, Hunt makes this almost astounding conclusion: "Most persons who masturbate remain more or less guilt-ridden about it, and nearly all of them [appear] extremely secretive about their masturbating and would [feel] horribly embarrassed to have anyone know the truth."

Two more items on shame and guilt about masturbating. In studying the incidence and the treatment of foreign bodies in the female genitourinary tract, many of which got placed there because the patients had masturbated with devices that got sucked into their urethras or vaginas, Drs. Haft, Benjamin, and Zeit had a good deal of difficulty determining exactly what had happened to these patients and how to advise them about their ailments, because most of them felt great embarrassment in coming for treatment or discussing with their physicians what they had done.

Finally, in a recent intensive study of masturbation, Arafat and Cotton discovered that about 90 percent of college males and 61 percent of college females admitted to current masturbation. But in spite of their high educational level, 44 percent of the males and 24 percent of the females who did not masturbate gave as their reasons for refraining that they considered autoeroticism a waste of energy, immoral, producing cheap feelings, and leading to guilt. Of the majority of respondents who did masturbate, 11 percent of the males and 24 percent of the females stated that they felt depressed after they masturbate; 13 percent of the males and 10 percent of the females had guilt feelings; 4 percent of the males and 7 percent of the females feared going insane through masturbation; and 5 percent of the males and 1 percent of the females felt perverse. This seems almost incredible for college students during the closing decades of the twentieth century. But true!

Objections to Masturbation

In my books *Sex Without Guilt* and *The Art and Science of Love,* I have examined various objections raised against masturbation and shown their invalidity. Let me again briefly consider these objections, particularly as they apply to the single adult male, to see if they hold any water.

Supposed Immaturity

People claim that although masturbation may remain perfectly normal for adolescents, it denotes immature behavior for older males, who should completely forgo it for other, presumably heterosexual outlets. Nonsense! As every study of masturbatory activity has shown, not only youngsters, but most unmarried individuals, particularly males, practice it as their main—yes, *main*—sex outlet. How senseless to call autoerotic activities names when humans practice them so universally and harmlessly!

This includes married people, too. Beigel noted that "among the married men, between 21 and 25 percent supplemented their marital relations by this means at one time or another." And he found this practice "entirely harmless and perhaps even helpful in some instances."

Studies by Kinsey and his associates and by Yankowski not only showed self-stimulation widespread among males and females, but as Gillette pointed out, "Active incidence of masturbation among men over fifty [proves] generally higher than among any other post-adolescent group. Among females, masturbation appears as widespread in adulthood as in adolescence."

Morton Hunt, in his large-scale study of American sexual behavior, also found that adolescence hardly constitutes the time when masturbation reaches its highest peaks, since "as young adults, single males and single females masturbate considerably more frequently than formerly."

Dr. Hobart H. Sewell, a well-known psychiatrist, wrote in this connection, "People masturbate from soon after birth to shortly before they die. Masturbation [exists as] an acceptable variation within marriage today . . . for some couples, learning how the other partner masturbates can [prove] both exciting as well as useful in enhancing their knowledge of each other's sexuality."

We'd better acknowledge, of course, that autoeroticism *may* prove childish or compulsive when you have the choice of several other modes of sex activity and find that you can enjoy *only* this one or when you use masturbatory fantasies and activities to reduce your feelings of anxiety. But this pathological use of masturbation seems relatively rare, and the great majority of people who masturbate regularly or irregularly show, by mere virtue of this activity, no pathology whatever. We probably can't say the same for most people who never bring themselves to orgasm!

Supposed Antisocialness

Autoerotism often gets considered an asocial or antisocial habit, because those addicted to it presumably tend to withdraw from social life. No evidence whatever backs this hypothesis; the facts actually show that some of the most extraverted and highly socialized individuals masturbate steadily. Certainly, *some* males may masturbate rather than face their anxieties about engaging in heterosexual relations, but this hardly proves *most* or *all* masturbators socially anxious. The vast majority of people who masturbate seem to do so because they find it much easier, in this antisexual world we live in, than to court another person successfully and have mutually satisfying affairs.

Not the difficulty of getting along *socially*, but of making it sexually with others, leads them to masturbate. Our antisexual customs, moreover, actually *create* social difficulties, since they make it so difficult for males and females to get together sexually, and to succeed in their relationships with each other, that many of them tend to develop social inhibitions. So our rules against sex, including those against masturbating, help make these individuals more asocial or antisocial than any amount of masturbation could possibly do.

Emotional maturity, moreover, largely consists of your striving, as a human, to remain alive and to enjoy yourself during your lifetime, while bringing on yourself a minimum amount of needless pain and misery. It includes your getting along, as well as you can, with yourself and others and avoiding needlessly self-defeating behavior, particularly short-range pleasures, such as smoking and drug addiction, which may well lead to future pain and death. Masturbation, although it certainly proves immediately gratifying, also has many long-range gains—it helps you to discover what *you* really like sexually, to imagine interpersonal relations with others that you and they would want to achieve, to train yourself to enjoy sex in a maximally satisfying way. These comprise distinctly self-interested, but hardly antisocial, goals; and evidence shows that, particularly in the case of females, these goals usually aid heterosexual (and homosexual) arousal and orgasm. How, then, can we look upon this kind of masturbatory experience as *im*mature?

Mary and John Ryan take a dim view of masturbation because "Anyone capable of moral decisions can understand the difference between treating oneself and others as persons or as things. The normal adolescent can certainly see, for example, that reading 'girlie' magazines [constitutes] a means of stirring up sexual excitement for its own sake as an impersonal source of pleasure; what [seems] wrong [doesn't include] the pleasure but the purpose—clearly not a loving one. This way of evaluating the morality of sexual behavior would seem to offer very convincing arguments against masturbation, as a clear instance of seeking self-centered, unloving sexual pleasure."

John D. Latendresse, adding a supposedly existentialist point of view to the Ryans' Catholicism, makes a somewhat similar view: "Whereas the masturbator [gets] involved with the surface feelings of his body, and the construction of images, the man with his beloved [makes himself] occupied with an inner knowledge of himself, through her body. In the union in which the partner [gets] used as a non-person, as in masturbation, one must work towards orgasm, raking up images to sustain the effort."

These critics of autoeroticism do not see that masturbation actually tends to involve people in imagining themselves having sex with *others* and rarely proves as narcissistic as it may at first sound. Moreover, it gives them sex practice, which, again, enables them to get along more successfully later in their interpersonal relations.

Again, as we know from recent research in sex fantasizing, even when you have sex with another, you tend to get highly aroused and come to orgasm, on many occasions, through your focusing and imaging about (1) the bodily parts of these others or (2) the arousing features of third parties whose presence exists only in your head.

In all kinds of sex, therefore, you basically remain self-involved; you focus on what feels exciting to *you* and on your *own* sensations. As Dr. Lonnie Myers has aptly indicated, this holds particularly when you approach orgasm. Before you reach this point, you may get very involved in your sex partner, and even primarily think of

her. But as you ascend toward orgasm, your own sensations and
feelings tend to take over, true *intimacy* gets temporarily lost, and
you probably wouldn't reach climax at all if you didn't focus almost
exclusively on yourself for at least a few moments. Interpersonal sex
does not differ too significantly from masturbatory sex in this
connection; we wrongly *assume* that it does.

For those individuals who really *do* get more absorbed in themselves than in any partner, and who would rather masturbate than
have heterosexual or homosexual relations, we might well say that
they lose something by this kind of self-centered approach. But they
may not act more unusual or disturbed in this respect than those
who prefer to sing or play the piano by themselves, without any
kind of accompaniment. If they really enjoy masturbation more
than interpersonal sex, and they do not get driven to it because they
feel afraid of relating to or failing with others, that seems quite unusual, and most of us would look upon them curiously. But why not,
if that seems their bent? Why do they *have to* like having sex with
others more than they like having it with themselves?

Supposed Lack of Emotional Gratification

Masturbation, people say, does not produce full emotional or
sexual gratification. Havelock Ellis, for instance, noted that "in the
absence of the desired partner, the orgasm, whatever relief it may
give, must [get] followed by a sense of dissatisfaction, perhaps of
depression, even of exhaustion, often of shame and remorse." With
all due apologies to the great sage of sex, this sounds like claptrap.

Certainly masturbation leads to depression and remorse—*when*
you do not wholeheartedly accept it as a good and beneficial act,
when you erroneously *view* it as unsatisfying, or when, again, you
act so childish that you absolutely refuse to accept a lesser, and
available, sex satisfaction instead of an ideal, and presently unavailable, one.

No sex act, in fact, including heterosexual coitus, can give ideal
or full emotional or physical gratification at all times to all persons,
simply because humans exist as unique individuals and continually
differ *from themselves* from day to day (as well as from each
other). Objective observation reveals literally millions of people

who at least *at times* obtain *more* emotional and physical gratification from masturbation than from any other kind of sex. Only (as noted above) when these individuals *always* enjoy autoerotism more than intersexual relations do they act oddly.

Even more millions of people practically never enjoy masturbation as much as they enjoy heterosexual activities; but when they find masturbation the only kind of sex available, they do enjoy it with full emotional and physical impact. Still other individuals derive no emotional feelings, in the sense of love for another person, from masturbation; but since when must they find love *necessary* for full sex enjoyment? It seems desirable, yes; preferable, in most instances. But sex engaged in without love (or even friendship) can certainly amount to one of the most satisfying of human pursuits. Let us not sell it short because it doesn't prove ideal.

As for the allegation that masturbation constitutes, in its own right, a severe deviation or emotional problem, or that it inevitably leads to various forms of disturbance, I might well quote the statement of Dr. J. L. McCary in this connection. "Indeed, those who do not practice masturbation, or have never done so, are far more likely suffer from an emotional or sexual problem than those who have masturbatory experience."

Supposed Leading to Sexual Inadequacy

Some people allege that masturbation leads to impotence in the male or frigidity in the female. This allegation has no factual evidence to support it. On the contrary, I have found in my clinical practice that impotent males tend to engage in considerably less autoerotism than potent ones. And the Kinsey research group discovered that although approximately 33 percent of females who did not masturbate before marriage felt unresponsive in intercourse during the early years of their marriage, only about 15 percent of females who did masturbate felt equally coitally unresponsive. In treating both males and females for sexual inadequacy, I often find that inducing them to masturbate to orgasm helps them to overcome their sexual inadequacy.

As Professor Douglas Sprenkle points out, control over your sexual response tends to prove greater in masturbation than in coitus—and some therapists therefore prescribe self-stimulation as a part of a treatment program for learning to control fast ejaculation. You can, of course, condition yourself to ejaculate quickly through masturbation, in order to bring on pleasure more quickly. But such conditioning would often accompany your worrying about the wrongness of masturbation—and your therefore wanting to get it over as quickly as possible.

Supposed Excessiveness

Many so-called authorities hold masturbation dangerous because it easily leads to sexual excess on the part of the masturbator. This allegation is directly contradicted by the findings of Kirkendall, who studied the masturbatory activities of young males and showed that they usually have considerably more sexual potential than they actually use. Moreover, as I have pointed out in previous writings, you will find it almost impossible to masturbate to excess, unless you turn practically psychotic—because erotic response depends upon a remarkably foolproof mechanism. When you reach the limit of your physiological endurance, you no longer respond sexually. In fact, you will more likely act foolish and go beyond your normal sex limits when you engage in heterosexual intercourse than when you masturbate, since in the former instance you may feel obliged to satisfy your sex partner even though your own desire has faded.

To illustrate that "excess" rarely stems from autoeroticism, Professor Sprenkle cites the case of a prisoner in a German concentration camp during the Second World War. His captors forced him to masturbate every three hours, twenty-four hours a day, for two years. But upon his release, physicians could not find any evidence of physical damage. When he later married, he had excellent potency and fathered a child.

Similarly, evidence lays to rest the myth that masturbation leads to energy loss and fatigue and that athletes must therefore not engage in it before an important game. Dr. Wardell Pomeroy notes, in this regard, the case of a national track record set within an hour after the athlete masturbated. And Dr. William Masters has pointed out that athletes can perform at peak efficiency if they allow themselves sufficient time to relax after a sexual experience. How much times does this take? One to five minutes!

Supposed Unnaturalness

Few writers on sex these days put down masturbation as an "unnatural" practice because it obviously precludes procreation. Not so long ago, however, a presumed authority, James R. Sauls, wrote that it does not remain "entirely normal to have oneself as his sex object, since normalcy in sex [rests] always in relationship to the primary function of sex, reproduction. It [remains] clearly impossible to reproduce and continue the human race by self-loving." True! But although *one* purpose of sex involves the continuation of the human species, almost all sexologists today agree that its *main* purpose involves pleasure, joy, the facilitating of human relating, and the happy maintenance of the life of the individual rather than of the human race. Especially in today's world, when overpopulation seems much more of a problem than human extinction, masturbation provides one of the best ways of helping the individual—and the race as a whole!

Advantages of Masturbation

As you can see from the foregoing discussion, the main objections raised against autoeroticism turn out, upon closer examination, specious and nonsensical. At the same time, the indubitable advantages of masturbation frequently get ignored in our literature. What constitute some of these reasons? Let me list a few salient ones.

1. Self-stimulation consists of a harmless, exceptionally repeatable sex act that virtually never interferes with the desires, activities, or rights of others.

2. It keeps you completely free from the dangers of venereal infection, pregnancy, abortion, illegitimacy, and other difficulties that may go with intersexuality.

3. It serves as a fine and effective apprenticeship in erotic fantasy that often proves good for later relationships.

4. It has a most calming effect on your sex urges and emotional excitation if you want quick relief from erotic tension.

5. It involves a minimum of monetary expense.

6. It requires much less expenditure of time and energy than do most forms of sex.

7. You can practice it in many circumstances and under many conditions where you can't very well engage in heterosexual or homosexual activity.

8. It makes no demands whatever on any of your sex partners.

9. It encourages all kinds of sex experimentation that will very likely help you discover what kind of sexuality you have (and have not!), what you really want, and how to satisfy yourself maximally in masturbatory and other kinds of sex pursuits.

10. You can easily intersperse it with various nonsexual occupations that you want to perform.

11. It ordinarily requires few preliminary steps or paraphernalia.

12. It involves few or no hygienic precautions or later ablutions.

13. You can proceed with it when you feel sick, have taken to your bed, or live under other conditions that normally preclude other forms of sex.

14. It contributes to your physical health and to your personality development.

15. It can serve as a precipitant of relaxation and sleep.

16. It serves as one of the most intensely enjoyable, as well as frequently available, acts known to most humans.

17. It promotes a healthy, affirmative attitude toward your body (as well as your imagination) as a major source of comfort and satisfaction.

18. It provides, if you work at improving it, a source of confidence in your ability to behave competently and enjoyably.

19. It gives you a pleasant source of distraction from many of the hassles of everyday living.

20. It provides a challenge by the use of which you can help make yourself unguilty and unashamed of your hedonistic pursuits and pleasurable performances.

21. It gives you a chance to think for yourself, to fight against foolish taboos that you imbibed during your youth, and to develop a spirit of sane rebelliousness against needless, personal-sabotaging rules.

Do these advantages of masturbation seem products of my own prejudices? In some ways, yes, for I have frankly favored masturbation myself, since my teens, and consider myself greatly benefited and little harmed by it. Just to show you, however, that my permissive attitude toward autoeroticism, once somewhat unique among writers in the field, has also received endorsements from some other outstanding authorities, let me quote:

Boston's Women's Health Book Collective: "Masturbating can [exist as] a useful part of a person's sexual development. Besides helping you learn to enjoy your body, it can also teach you what techniques [prove] best for arousing yourself, so that you [can] show your sexual partner how to arouse you."

Dr. Charles Brown: "Whether you beat, pull, jack, or jerk [off] it [constitutes] masturbation—or one of the few solitary pleasures left to man. Masturbation [remains] a good preparation for robust sexuality. So, enjoy."

Student Committee on Sexuality at Syracuse University: We find "masturbation a normal way to express sexual desires. Whether married or single, old or young, male or female, when you enjoy masturbating, then it [proves] good. As long as you enjoy it, it makes little difference how often you do it. No matter how often you masturbate, you will cause yourself no physical harm."

Sex Information and Education Council of the U.S.: We find "sexual self-pleasuring, or masturbation, a natural part of sexual behavior for individuals of all ages. It can help to develop a sense of the body as belonging to the self, and an affirmative attitude toward the body as a legitimate source of enjoyment. It can also help in the release of tension in a way harmless to the self and to others, and provide an intense experience of the self as preparation for experiencing another. Masturbation, and the fantasies that frequently accompany it, can [show themselves as] important aids in maintaining or restoring the image of one's self as a fully functioning human."

David Cole Gordon: "Masturbation aids people's fundamental drive for unification of mind and body, of union with his and her fellow human, and of humanity with the world. The most intense moment of unification occurs during orgasm, especially when experienced through masturbation."

Betty Dodson: "Masturbation holds the key to breaking this socially approved bondage [of women] simply because it reverses the whole process of repression. With sexual independence, we gain control of our bodies and stand up straight and strong. By making no secret of our masturbation, we challenge those who have a stake in our repression, who perpetuate the conspiracy of grim silence. By openly advocating masturbation and debunking myths about it, we [get] less intimidated and more confident about ourselves and our bodies. . . . Masturbation [represents] our primary sex life. It [constitutes] our sexual base."

My conclusion from this material? Not that self-stimulation seems better or more desirable than intersexual union. For some people some of the time, it does, but for the most part, it doesn't. As long as heterosexual and homosexual intercourse remain as intrinsically enjoyable as they seem for most people, they will not get totally or even mainly replaced by masturbation. Most men and women would much rather copulate with other people once a week than masturbate daily, and I fully believe that they will continue to feel this way for some time to come.

Your choice, however, doesn't rest between whether you'd better masturbate or have heterosexual relations, but whether you may, at various times, do *both*. The answer seems obvious to any sane and thinking person. When interpersonal sex seems truly unavailable, or when it would require your going far out of your way to obtain it, can you find any reason why you should not *then* masturbate? If you don't do so in such circumstances we may suspect you to have some disturbance.

As I say in the concluding paragraph of my chapter on masturbation in *Sex Without Guilt,* "We would find it difficult to conceive of a more beneficial, harmless, tension-releasing human act than masturbation, spontaneously performed with (puritanically inculcated and groundlessly held) fears and anxieties. Let us, please, now that Kinsey and his associates have stoutly reaffirmed this fact, see that our sex manuals and sex education texts unequivocally say it in plain English."

Techniques of Masturbation

Although almost innumerable books exist on coital techniques, exceptionally few consider in detail the attitudinal and physical methods of achieving autoerotic satisfaction. Betty Dodson's paperback volume *Liberating Masturbation* constitutes one of the rare volumes of its kind, and she had unusual difficulties compiling the material for the book and finally getting it published. It deals, moreover, almost exclusively with female masturbation and with liberating women's attitudes more than with showing them exactly what to do.

The following section will largely include techniques of self-stimulation. Techniques of "masturbating" your partner to arousal and orgasm get dealt with later in this volume. If you want to know something more about bringing yourself to sex fulfillment, read on!

Self-fulfilling Attitudes

In his article "Autoeroticism: A Sociological Approach," Dr. Edward Sagarin highlights some of the negative attitudes toward self-stimulation that have existed for centuries and that still continue. He notes that if you really want to enjoy this kind of activity, you'd better release yourself from most of your inhibiting puritanism. How true! Women, especially, tend to think that they have no right to pure sex pleasure and that they must not take advantage of their own bodies; but so do millions of men!

First and foremost, then: Look forward to masturbation joyously, eagerly. Fully convince yourself that *any* pleasure you can give yourself, as long as it does not lead to subsequent pain or sabotage, has legitimacy. You come into the world for no special reason, and the universe doesn't really care whether you live or die, achieve great pleasure or pain. But you, if you act wisely, will make your existence as enjoyable as you can. You will decide that you have an inalienable *right* to pleasure yourself—as long as you do not unduly infringe on the rights of others to please themselves.

See masturbation, therefore, as good, great, even marvelous. Convince yourself that the universe utterly permits, nay encourages, it and that your biology strongly predisposes you toward it. Let yourself see that although it may bring about less pleasure than other forms of sex, it normally proves far better than no sex at all.

As Jody Hannaken points out, "When a guy does bang his prong he'd [better] 'go' with complete abandon, reaching inside himself as well as outside, to express or relive sexual activities and desires. It all adds up to a healthier, hornier session, with side benefits of really throwing to the wind frustrations and deep-seated urges or repressions."

And as Dr. Charles Brown indicates, "Enjoying oneself sexually does not have to play second fiddle to any form of solitary pleasure."

So *look for,* actively *seek out* masturbatory satisfactions. As in any other endeavor, try to *maximize* your pleasure in this respect. Don't think you *have* to get the best autoerotic joys in the world; but feel determined that you *want to* reach some summits.

Fantasies

Although authorities often state that many animals masturbate, and therefore we can consider this act "normal," human masturbation seems unique in the animal kingdom, in that it almost invariably includes thinking, imagining, and emotion. Young children may masturbate mechanically, for sheer physical gratification. But older children and adults almost always arouse themselves and bring themselves to orgasm with distinct ideas and fantasies. Otherwise, they rarely get aroused or satisfied; and some of them have orgasmic failure.

To masturbate well, then, think your goddamned head off! Don't *desperately* try to get aroused and satisfied; but determinedly and experimentally discover what seems highly exciting to *you* and use that kind of thinking and imagining. For years, sexologists (including Kinsey) believed that men easily and naturally fantasize about sex, while women much more seldom do. Evidence by Nancy Friday, Barbara Hariton, J. Aphrodite and other investigators tends to show that women, too, can easily have fantasies similar to those of males and that many fantasize to good effect.

What kind of fantasies can you use in this respect? Virtually any kind that work! Lester Dearborn indicated that even bizarre or "sick" fantasies appear legitimate—so long as you do not actually carry them into practice to any considerable or compulsive degree. Thus, you can put yourself, in your head, into various masochistic or sadistic scenes. But don't, in real life, go on to actual bloodshed! Also, if your sex fantasy reinforces some of your self-defeating *general* ideas, watch it and try to change it!

Suppose, for example, you see yourself, while masturbating, getting scorned or shit upon or raped against your will. If this idea reinforces your notion that you rate as a worthless individual who *deserves* to have sex (or any other pleasure) only when others put you down, you'd better try for some other fantasy that helps you give up this nonsense. You unguiltily deserve orgasm and ecstasy just because you exist and want to feel happy—and not because you do great things or because you lower yourself in some manner.

Fantasies also may prove compulsive and therefore limiting. If you can see yourself *only* in one way in your fantasy—for example, having sex with an animal—and refuse to let yourself get aroused when you use other fantasies, you arbitrarily limit yourself. You might, therefore, try to broaden your range of fantasizing, employ more variety, and train yourself to use, at least from time to time, other fantasies as well.

With these exceptions, fantasies generally remain harmless and can, even when bizarre, lead to excellent results. Sometimes, just *because* they seem bizarre, they add novelty, strangeness, or interest to your sex life.

How do you get fantasy material? By making it up in your own head or by using things that have actually happened or that might happen. The more varied your sex life, the more you can use various aspects of it in your imagination—imagining yourself, for example, screwing someone you have previously screwed or having oral relations with someone you know but have not had oral sex with.

Literature serves well in this connection—erotic or pornographic works, nonfictional presentations that excite you, films or dramas you have seen, stories that other people have told you about their sex lives. Whatever works, try!

Sexual Focusing

A form of sex thinking or attending that somewhat resembles fantasy but also has distinct differences consists of focusing—usually on your own sensations. While you masturbate, you can focus on your own sensual and sexual feelings and actually bring yourself to arousal or orgasm by doing this quite intently. Women especially use focusing to arouse and satisfy themselves, but men do it much more than they think they do, since they usually intersperse it with actual fantasy and may do more of the latter than the former. If you will attend to your own sensations, you can heighten them by this kind of concentration, and that can make all the difference between coming and not coming.

Can you voluntarily emphasize sexual feelings? Of course you can—just as you have the ability to relax your various muscles and put yourself to sleep. Physical pressure and friction will at times bring you to climax, but intense sensations produced by these means can also get heightened by your focusing on your body and your sex organs, just as you can focus on a painfully throbbing finger or a headache and make it more painful. So practice sexual and genital focusing, and your masturbatory (and copulatory) movements will tend to feel more effective and orgasmic.

Persistence

For some strange reason, people often believe that sex arousal and satisfaction should come quickly and easily. Drivel! Frequently, you can bring yourself to excitement and orgasm *too* quickly, before you have much of a chance to enjoy yourself very much. But at other times, you may take a fairly long time either to get fully aroused or to reach a climax. Persist! Not that you *have* to come. You don't. But lots of times, instead of giving up and wrongly concluding that you can't make it try a different position, another movement, a new image, or a more intense continuation of the same thing you have thus far done to little avail. Surprise, surprise!—your genitals may start swelling and erupting. Many tasks that at first appear uncompletable—hitting a tennis ball over the net, for example, or playing the piano well—later turn successful. Masturbatory play may well get included in the same category. If at once you don't succeed, try, try again!

Sounding Off

Sex with another person often gets enhanced by your or his or her accompanying sounds. If you talk in a sexy manner or moan and sigh and groan as your excitement mounts, you frequently turn yourself and your partner on. Fantasies themselves can come into play mutually—you tell your partner yours, and he or she relates to or adds to these or goes off on his or her own kick. Similarly with masturbation—sex talk can add to the proceedings. As Jody Hannaken has written in this regard, if you masturbate "in a place where you can do it, *talk* it up, man! Even all by yourself. Holy, fucking shit! Spit out those delicious cock and cunt words, right out loud if you can. It makes a juicy jack-off! And sigh and moan and groan. Express your lusty joys with the pleasures in that wonderful, proud prick. Use all of your [self] to help that beautiful thing happening along, instead of just whipping all kinds of pressures back into your precious cock by beating it to death."

Just as you may employ sex literature, so you may use sex sounds. Music, the noises of two or more people making love, other recorded sounds that you find personally arousing—go to it, if you will, in these connections. Try what you will—even if others won't!

Scenic Aids

Some people get distinctly turned on by the sight of their own bodies. In women, this often requires self-training, as Betty Dodson points out, since women frequently put down their own bodies, especially their genitalia, and consider them ugly and disgusting. Such individuals could well use hand mirrors and other devices to see themselves more fully when they masturbate, and train themselves to like their bodies—or to turn what Ms. Dodson calls "cunt positive." Seeing photos of themselves, especially in sexual positions or with their genitalia very visible, also may help.

Erotic art involving others has its great advantages too. For years —probably centuries!—males have had their pinups and have often used them largely for masturbatory purposes. But women and couples, too, have done the same thing, as witnessed by the ancient Chinese practice of giving brides and grooms well-illustrated "pillow books" to help them with their sex lives.

What sends you in this respect? Find out! Paintings, drawings, photos, sculptures, films, videotape (including tapes of your own copulating or masturbating)—whatever works, use! Also, of course, watching others in the flesh. If you can get a partner or partners who will do something sexual while you masturbate, this may prove much more exciting than less live presentations. Not easy to arrange, in many instances, but not necessarily impossible!

Mutual Sex

Technically, masturbation does not include another individual's manipulating your genitalia until you come to orgasm, since that constitutes petting or noncoital sex. But it does include your masturbating in the presence of another, and perhaps when that other stimulates you in some nongenital way. Thus, as a male you can have a partner hold or kiss you, while you take care of your own genitalia. And as a woman, you can do the same—and often to great advantage, since many women get turned off if another person manipulates their genitalia and they have to keep instructing this other to go faster, go slower, make this motion, try it that way, etc. So if you can conquer your feelings of shame at masturbating in another's presence—which you can damned well do if you really work at it —you may add a vector to your masturbating that you can hardly surpass. Watching or joining in with another person sexually while you focus on massaging your own genitalia may prove one of the most exciting moves you ever make!

Physical Movement

Speaking of moving, many individuals find it good to masturbate while simulating coital or other sexual positions. Not only do they move their hands aptly and strongly while bringing themselves to climax, but they also move their genitalia or other parts of their bodies. Some of them simulate actual coitus—for example, males who lie on their bellies and "fuck" their hand, a bed, or some other object. Others lie on their backs, sit, or stand, and still actively move their pelvic regions, thighs, or other parts of their bodies while masturbating. What do you prefer? Experiment! Find out!

Lubrication

Great numbers of people, especially those who masturbate for long periods at a time, find it best to use lubrication—such as Vaseline, oil, K-Y jelly, soap, saliva, or other lubricants. For one thing, such lubrication often makes masturbation closely resemble coitus.

For another, it avoids excessive and painful friction. Again, it may provide a sensuous quality that otherwise they find lacking. Whatever the reason, it can distinctly add to sex satisfaction. The famous sex writer Rey Anthony has noted that "leaving the sex organs unlubricated [remains] no more natural than leaving the teeth unwashed, or the hair uncut or uncombed." Many people will not agree with this—since they find sex without lubrication quite satisfying. But if you find Ms. Anthony correct, look for the right kind of lubrication that works best for you.

Variety

Almost all sexuality feeds on a certain amount of variety, and a position or a technique that really excites you today may turn into a routine, unstimulating performance tomorrow. Masturbation sometimes proves an exception to this rule, since some individuals really seem to enjoy almost exactly the same procedure day after day; and, as a matter of fact, without it, they can hardly climax at all. But most of us don't fit this category. We like the same old jacking-off technique, but we like other methods, too. And the old favorite often gains new gloss when we forgo it for a while and substitute different methods.

As Dr. Alex Comfort puts it, in *More Joy*, "A male should consciously look for new techniques: try with your left hand if you normally use the right (you'll feel surprised at the difference), use the foreskin if you normally retract it—if circumcised, try wetting or oiling the glans and rubbing only that. A woman should similarily try things she hasn't normally tried—the clitoris alone, if you use the whole-hand method, and vice versa. The object [remains] to enjoy and to learn more about the responses of which you [prove] capable."

Speed and Pressure

What works for you, works! You may like very speedy stimulation of your genitalia or very slow or somewhere in between. You may desire great pressure, medium pressure, or low pressure. Sometimes you will prefer one mode; sometimes, another. Don't go by what others adore—or by what they think you *should*. One of the great advantages of masturbation, as against having your genitalia

massaged by a partner, consists of your having the greatest leeway
to vary procedures as befits your sexual mood—to start fast, then go
slow, then speed up again . . . or whatever!

A partner, especially one who gets more aroused as sex proceeds,
tends to get so involved that he or she speeds up or resorts to greater
pressure, often quite unconsciously, in rhythmic consort to his or
her own arousal. Not so good—at least, in many instances. By controlling your own speed, rhythm, pressure, etc., you remove this difficulty and get closer to what you really want. Also, of course,
relieved of the watchfulness of a partner, and your normal desire to
come fairly quickly so as to put this person to relatively little trouble, you will not tend to monitor yourself too closely and interfere
with your own satisfaction. As in reading, listening to music, and
various other pursuits, solitude sometimes truly pays off!

Sensitive Zones

All penises and all female genitalia hardly have the same sensitized zones. Most males seem to feel most sensitive on the underside
of the penis, about one inch behind the head or prepuce. But not
all! Most females tend to bring themselves to orgasm by massaging
the clitoral area, specially the sides of the clitoris, as Masters and
Johnson have shown. The shaft itself, and the head of the clitoris,
often remain too stimulatable for these females. But not always! At
times, they want direct stimulation of the clitoral shaft or head. At
other times, they crave massage of the inner labia or the entrance to
the vagina. Occasionally, they want deep penetration—as with a
penis or artificial phallus.

What constitute *your* sensitive genital zones? How can you tell,
without experimenting? And how will you know unless you try different areas, with various kinds of procedures, at different times?
Answer: You most probably won't!

Positions for Masturbation

As in the case of intercourse, positions for masturbating vary—
and you have several basic choices and a good many minor variations on each major theme. You might think that people who bring
themselves to orgasm, particularly those who have done so for
twenty or more years, would have explored all possible positions

and finally hit on those which prove most satisfactory. Well, frequently they haven't!

For one thing, partly for reasons connected with privacy, they use convenient places that limit their techniques. Thus, boys frequently masturbate in the bathroom—where they have little chance to lie on their backs or bellies. And women often masturbate at work, by rubbing their thighs together—an effective but still limited position. Relatively few individuals seem to try almost all possible places and positions, even when they live by themselves and have almost unlimited possibilities.

Does place or position really matter? It certainly may! In my own case, I have found that squatting in the bathroom, taking a shower, and jerking off in bed can give quite different sensations and that each of these positions may prove most desirable at certain times. Other positions—such as lying prone upon a bed and rubbing against the sheets—work, all right, but rarely as well as the three mentioned above. If you plot and scheme, as well you may, to determine the most comfortable and satisfactory positions you choose for eating, sleeping, reading, and working, why not use your imagination to figure out, and your reason to evaluate, the best positions you may employ for autoeroticism? Why not get comfortable as you make yourself come!

Timing

Most people seem to take a minimum of time masturbating, and their game seems to include the goal of discovering the great heights of pleasure they can achieve in relatively few minutes. Fine—if that truly consists of the way you want it. Sex hardly amounts to the acme of human existence, and the more efficiently you learn to masturbate, the more time and energy you may save for other worthwhile pursuits.

But some things, including self-stimulation, would better not always get rushed! Climaxes that you achieve too readily may prove quite shallow, almost joyless. And climaxes themselves may amount to only half the fun. Some people truly enjoy the masturbatory process more than the end of that process—groove on what Albert Moll once called tumescence, rather than contrection. Bringing yourself close to, but not quite up to, orgasm may keep you immensely involved, titillated, and almost ecstatically on edge. Getting yourself to the point of ejaculation several times, then allowing your organs to relax, then making yourself maximally excited again—this may seem your real sexual thing.

Not that prolonged masturbation hasn't got disadvantages. It takes a hell of a lot of time. It may prove too preoccupying. It may get so arousing that your final climax seems anticlimactic. It may in some instances lead to too much engorgement of the genital region, with possible physical trauma. But it also may have none of these liabilities. One person's method of joyously beating his or her meat equals another person's poison. What makes *you* joyous—or poisoned?

Mechanical Devices.

Men and women have employed mchanical devices for masturbatory purposes from the beginning of human history to the present. Males have frequently used hollowed-out objects of various sorts, such as melons, bottles, pipes, jars, and rubber or plastic appliances. Women have employed cucumbers, candles, sausages, ears of corn, bananas, bottles, tubes, mercury balls, etc. Both sexes have used smaller objects, such as hairpins, bobby pins, and pencils, for urethral stimulation, and both have used a wide variety of small and large objects, including hairbrush handles and necks of bottles, for anal masturbation.

Nothing unusual here—except that when objects get inserted in the urethra or the anus, they may find themselves sucked into the bladder or the lower intestine; and urologists, proctologists, and other physicians not infrequently get called to remove such objects, which can lead to minor or serious damage. Obviously, therefore, if you decide to resort to mechanical devices for masturbatory purposes, you'd better use your common sense regarding what you do and how you do it. You normally wouldn't eat by putting a sharp knife in your mouth, and you'd better use at least as much caution about what objects you stick in your genitalia!

In a famous chapter on "Varieties of Autoerotic Phenomena," in his *Studies in the Psychology of Sex*, Havelock Ellis outlines some of the main appliances used by men and women for masturbatory purposes. In addition to the usual ones applied directly to the sex organs, he also refers "to the effects that, naturally or unnaturally, may [get] produced by many of the objects and implements of daily life that do not normally come in direct contact with the sexual organs." Thus, he shows that children and adults masturbate by friction against the corner of a chair or some other piece of furniture, by making large knots in their underclothing to rub against their genitalia, by sitting and putting their genitalia against the heels of their shoes, by riding hobby horses, real horses, or bicycles, by using swings, by climbing ropes or poles, by working hard at sewing machines, by tightly lacing their corsets or other garments, and by using various other objects to stimulate themselves.

In regard to masturbation in both men and women, however, mechanical instruments and objects rarely get used only in their own right. They tend to *represent* something else, in most cases—symbolize the genitalia, the body, or even the personality of a partner. If a male, for example, employs a roll of toilet paper for masturbatory purposes, and even oils it so that it resembles a vagina more closely than it normally would, he tends to *think* of it as part of a female.

As Eduard Lea sagely notes in this connection, in R. E. L. Masters's book *Sexual Self-stimulation*, "When we look historically and anthropologically at the widespread use of penis substitutes, and to some extent of vagina substitutes, it does seem likely that these [get] employed much more for the psychological than for the physical stimulation they provide. Rarely does the crude masturbatory instrument provide stimulation the equal of that which the fingers afford. What these instruments may give, then, that the fingers cannot, [comprises] the sense, however faint, of an *other* —a sex partner and an act that involves *something more* than just one's own body. With varying degrees of success the imagination builds a human other upon the slight foundation of the masturbatory object—and loneliness [gets] that much assuaged."

The one outstanding sex invention of the last few thousand years consists of the electric vibrator. Many different kinds of instruments powered by electricity may get used for sex purposes—an electric toothbrush, for example. But the vibrator, ostensibly devised to massage the scalp or body, proves most useful and harmless in connection with specific sexual manipulation. When correctly applied to the genital area, it provides both sexes, especially women, with an exceptionally rapid and exciting form of stimulation that virtually no manual technique can provide. And in many instances, particularly when the individual has difficulty coming to orgasm, the vibrator promptly and uniquely brings it about. Once achieved in this manner, as Dr. LeMon Clark showed a good many years ago, orgasm may then get brought on by nonmechanical methods.

Do vibrators have their disadvantages? Probably yes—for some people some of the time. I have known a few women who got addicted to them, in the sense that vibrators proved so enjoyable and easy to use that these women didn't want to take the trouble, thereafter, to achieve orgasm in other ways. Dr. J. L. Rosenberg, who has given much thought to masturbation and definitely endorses it, opposes the use of vibrators because he feels that they create too much excitement "from outside" and that therefore, the users do not allow themselves to generate "enough inner excitement." For some individuals this may prove true; but for others, particularly women who have enormous difficulty coming to orgasm by regular means, vibrators give phenomenally good results. Moreover, training oneself to get "inner excitement" may seem just great in theory but prove wasteful, and just not worth it, in actual practice.

Although great for females, vibrators and other mechanical devices may hardly work for males. Regular vibrators, such as those designed for massaging the scalp or the face, can sometimes get strapped to the underside of the penis (using, for example, a rubber band to keep them in place) and may then bring on a powerful, and usually swift, climax. Devices also exist, obtainable in sex stores or by mail, like the Accu-jac or the Auto-suck, which you can place over the penis and which, when turned on, give what amounts to an electric cock-sucking job. Most men find these devices far from ideal, but if you want to experiment with them, you may find them worth the cost and the trouble.

The same thing goes for life-size plastic or rubber dolls, available for both sexes. I have not yet found anyone who uses these with great satisfaction, and I doubt whether they will ever become terribly popular. But tastes differ widely, and if you do decide to use any kind of gadget whatever, you don't have to make yourself feel ashamed of doing so.

When you have no shame about sex and masturbation, you feel free to explore whatever devices seem good for you and, at times, for your partner—you can use practically all masturbatory devices for interpersonal sex as well. You can use them, for example, on yourself with your partner looking on, and perhaps holding you or doing something to you sexually while you masturbate. Or you can use them with her, in a similar manner. Or you can use many "masturbatory" instruments for regular heterosexual (or homosexual) purposes. Thus, you can get a double dildo and put one end of it in your partner's vagina and another end in your anus and have sex with her that way. Or you can use a French tickler—a condom with "feathers" on the end of it—to satisfy your woman partner, instead of her using a dildo with similar "feather" (or rubber) protruberances on it to satisfy herself.

The less ashamed you feel, the more you can experiment with mechanical devices for sex purposes. Women, for example, can experiment with the three basic types of vibrators—a penis-shaped device that vibrates, a hand-held vibrator that has three or four rubber instruments on the end of it, and a vibrator that straps onto the hand and makes one's fingers vibrate, so that they can in turn massage the genitalia in a pulsating manner. Usually, they will find the second of these units the best, but experimentally, they may decide otherwise. So may you, as you employ various mechanical devices.

Warning!—not all devices prove safe and useful. A plastic or metal coronal extension, which you place on your penis to help stimulate your female partner, may pain her or actually rip up her genitalia. And even French ticklers may prove useless, since they follow the male fantasy that a female's vaginal walls have great sensitivity and must get stimulated to give her maximum pleasure. Her stimulation, in point of fact, largely remains clitoral, even during intercourse, so such devices may not help in the least.

Sex catalogs, these days, contain many kinds of gadgets for pleasurable purposes, and over the years, new inventions will doubtless get added to the list. I recently looked through one of the largest catalogs and saw, for male satisfaction, anal stimulators, an electric vagina, inflatable dolls (with deep-throat mouths *and* usable vaginas!), artificial vaginas filled with foam, vaginas filled with water, etc. For the female masturbator, I saw electric driven *ben-wa* devices (vibrating pellets to place in the vagina), vagina stretchers, remote-control vibrators (so that a woman can masturbate while typing or doing other work!), and special soft-rubber stimulators to get slipped over a vibrator or around the base of the penis. For members of both sexes, I found a "love machine" that "comes complete with two different simulated penis extensions for women *or* with our 'vibro-master' attachment for men. Can also [get] used with hollow extensions like our 'super-penis.' " This love machine seems to consist of a veritable fucking machine that "accurately duplicates stroking motions of sexual intercourse or oral sex."

I also saw advertised a strange device from Brazil called a "restimulator"—a pneumatic chamber placed between the external sexual organs of a married couple. "This chamber, as a result of the working of the apparatus, fills and empties with air in a rhythmic sequence. It causes the union and the separation of the two bodies which lie on each other in a horizontal position; this [gets] done in a continuous and moral manner as required by nature to this end."

(Note well!—*don't* bother writing me to ask for the sources of these mechanical sex devices. I got them from catalogs of sex shops that no longer seem in business. Try your local sex shop or mail-order house!)

As noted above, Dr. LeMon Clark has pioneered in experimenting with and recommending electric vibrators and other mechanical sex aids—after he got the idea, originally, from his mentor Dr. Walter F. Robie. But other authorities have come out in favor of them too. Dr. Hugo Beigel found that a vibrator worked beautifully for a couple he saw in sex therapy. One of the great American sexologists, Dr. Isadore Rubin, wrote several articles favoring sex devices. Frederick Massey, like Dr. Rubin, pointed out the dangers of some devices but also showed how useful "sex toys" can prove it. In *The Cradle of Erotica*, Allen Edwards and R. E. L. Masters discussed several mechanical aids to sex and showed how people have employed them in many lands for centuries. They remark, "The ways of the world [remain] a wonder to behold and to contemplate!"

Paul Tabori gives something of a history of the use of mechanical devices for sex purposes and shows how they existed in the Middle Ages in Japan, England, and France. He notes, "Another striking proof that men and boys used an artificial penis for anal masturbation [we find] in a comedy by Cratinus (who, with Eupolis and Aristophanes, [reigned as] the chief representative of the Old Attic comedy at Athens). In this he speaks of the '*olisboi* of Narcissus.'"

G. and C. Greene show how instruments that aid people in masturbatory and interpersonal sadomasochistic relations get sold in modern New York. "In the larger urban centers it [seems] surprising the number of stores stocking umbrellas and sticks which also have a smaller selection of canes, whips, and cravaches. In New York the justly famous and splendidly named Uncle Sam Umbrella Shop boasts two emporia where, among the racks and rows of umbrellas and sticks, a wide variety of sound s-m instrumentalia can [get] inspected before purchase by the *aficionado*."

An original kind of sex "instrument" got devised by an anonymous correspondent to *Forum* magazine. "My wife and I enjoy the many delights of fellatio and cunnilingus, and I have recently overcome a problem which [kept] shortening these happy interludes. Whilst adopting the 69 position, I had great difficulty in breathing and frequently had to 'come up for air,' which lessened the enjoyment for my wife. After a great deal of thought, I procured a nose snorkel which I made from an ordinary swimmer's snorkel, a dissected Guy Fawkes mask and plenty of sticking tape. Held in place by elastic, it enables us to spend many happy hours at our favorite hobby." As the editors of *Forum* wryly remark, "Patent pending, we presume?"

As usual, mechanical devices have their limitations—especially when used in disturbed ways. Dr. Warren J. Jones, Jr., who generally endorses the use of vibrators and other mechanical aids to sex, writes, "I have seen two or three guilt-ridden wives on emergency consultations in a state of decompensated depression after their spouses discovered the power of the vibrator and proceeded to use it compulsively without regard to the wife's feelings."

How true! Any kind of sexuality, including normal intercourse, can get performed compulsively. I, too, have seen several women who felt they kept getting driven "up the wall" by their partners' compulsively insisting that they achieve orgasm in various ways, as well as several males who compulsively kept trying to achieve orgasm themselves and felt utterly desperate when they did not succeed.

Ralph Cremmons, for example, wrote an article, "23 Lays in 23 Days," in which he showed how he started screwing a new woman every night for six nights in a row and then decided that he would go on like that as long as he could. When, after much effort, he reached the peak of eighteen women in eighteen nights and it looked as if he had struck out and would miss out on any woman for the nineteenth night, "I just got quiet and finished my drink. I only had an hour left and the bars closed soon, so I just hung my head at the bar and got real sad. It [felt] like the world ended. . . . Nothing seemed left. I thought of suicide. Go out right, after eighteen straight different screws. Then I kept getting sadder and sadder. I realized that nothing mattered to me anymore but to screw someone different every day."

Too much of a good thing can get obsessive-compulsive! And compulsion, as I show later in this book, constitutes a large part of sex disturbance. So try, if you want, all kinds of sex and all kinds of mechanical devices to aid you in your masturbatory and interpersonal practices. But not compulsively! Not desperately! Learn to want strongly without direly needing. Then your experimentation can remain sexy—and sound!

Some final words on masturbation. Humans remain inevitably *human.* They use all kinds of mechanical devices in sex (and even in love); but they use them *imaginatively,* and they *invent* partners for themselves while so doing. Their "animalism" gets embedded in a uniquely human context.

To make yourself more enjoyably human, teach yourself—with, I would naturally recommend, rational-emotive procedures—to do away with practically all your sexual (and nonsexual) shame, embarrassment, and humiliation. Stop gratuitously upsetting yourself by your own self-downing.

For *you* invariably bring on feelings of shame and self-denigration by convincing yourself of two points, at least one of which turns out wrong: (1) "This act that I have committed appears mistaken, foolish, or immature"; (2) therefore, I must rate myself as an

idiot, a fool, or a rotten person." Although the first of these views
may certainly have some sense to it, the second never does. *You*, by
performing a mistaken, foolish, or immature act, can only remain a
person who acts wrongly. You can never, except by word-magic,
make yourself into a *foolish or bad person*. To down, and later try
to correct, your acts may prove very wise. To down *yourself* for
doing such acts amounts to an overgeneralization that interferes
with, rather than aids, your correcting your poor behavior.

Remember this in regard to practically every sex act that you perform—particularly in regard to masturbation! For although your
autoeroticism may at times seem wrong—meaning, productive of
less enjoyment or more disadvantages than you could obtain by
other forms of sex—*you* never amount to a louse for engaging in it.
Always remember that!

A final note. As this book went to press, in the last quarter of
the 20th century, the Vatican in Rome, through its Congregation
for the Doctrine of the Faith, issued one of the most reactionary
statements in its history, calling a virtual halt to all the liberal
Catholicism of the last few decades. Unequivocally condemning
masturbation and allied sexual "sins," this statement said: "Whatever the force of certain arguments of a biological and philosophical nature, which have sometimes been used by theologians, in fact
both the magisterium of the church—in the course of a constant
tradition—and the moral sense of the faithful have declared without hesitation that masturbation is an intrinsically and seriously
disordered act. Even if it cannot be proved that Scripture condemns
this sin by name, the tradition of the church has rightly understood
it to be condemned in the New Testament when the latter speaks
of 'impurity,' 'unchasteness' and other vices contrary to chastity and
continence." Whatever your religious views, you can hardly imagine
a more regressive doctrine than this! My advice? Fight it—with
every pulse of sexuality that you have in your mind and body!

CHAPTER 3

How to Avoid Guilt Without Sex

IN OUR COUNTRY there seems much more guilt without sex than vice versa, in spite of my own and others' efforts over the past several decades to help make it otherwise. Our females obviously feel exceptionally guilty about many of their sex activities—and even many of their sex thoughts—and our males do not fall far behind them in self-blame.

"Does any of this sex guilt prove justifiable?" you may ask.

No, not an iota, say I.

"But do not *some* of the sex things people do today seem wrong? And shouldn't they at least feel guilty about *those* things?"

Yes to the first; and No, definitely no, to the second of these questions.

"That seems confusing. If some of the sex deeds people perform prove bad or wrong, why shouldn't they feel guilty about performing them?"

For the very good reason, I contend, that *no one* need *ever feel guilty about anything he or she does.*

"No one should ever feel guilty about anything! Why, wouldn't that bring about a state of total anarchism—or even satanism—when you say that?"

Not in the least. I ask for a state of true self-discipline and sanity.

"I don't get it. Explain!"

All right. Gladly.

Guilt as an Emotional Disturbance

Let us take the case of one of my psychotherapy clients, Norman S., who came to see me because he had gruesome nightmares almost every night, felt a near panic state during most of each day, and

68

experienced almost total impotence with his womanfriend, Lynn. During my first sesssion with Norman, we quickly determined that he felt very guilty because he had no intention of marrying Lynn, and he felt he kept unfairly leading her on by continuing to have sex with her. He believed himself a bastard, moreover, for devirginizing her, when he didn't really love her.

"Apparently," I said to Norman S., "you mightily blame yourself because you have done two terrible wrongs to this woman—taken her virginity and kept seeing her when you knew you would not marry her. Correct?"

"Yes, I feel terribly guilty about both these things," he replied. "If she only had had other men before me, it wouldn't matter that much. But even then I'd hate myself for continuing to lead her on as I do."

"Okay," I said. "First let's look at your acts to see whether they prove really wrong. Take your devirginizing this woman. What do you think wrong about that?"

"Well . . . uh . . . I don't know. I just think it wrong. After all, I had her first, you know. And . . . well, it just seems wrong."

"But you said before that if you had *not* had her first you would have had her without qualms. Right?"

"Yes; that wouldn't have bothered me at all."

"Then what magic does devirginization add to—or perhaps subtract from—her? If you had had her *second,* you'd feel fine about her (and about intercourse with her). This means, presumably, that if *anyone else* has her, now that you have taken her virginity, he can also feel fine about her (and about intercourse with her). True?"

"Uh . . yes, I guess so."

"So neither your having her first nor anyone else's having her first seems to change her or change intercourse with her. Obviously, then, her devirginization has not changed her or done her any harm. Why, then, should *you* feel disturbed about taking her virginity?"

"Mmmm. I see what you mean. I wouldn't look down on her, or refuse to see her, if she had already lost her virginity when I met her; so why should anyone else look down on her, or refuse to have sex or love with her, now that I've taken her virginity? She stays really unchanged by having me sexually, or having anyone else. Hmm."

"No, she obviously has not changed. And yet you seem to think

that by your devirginizing her she *has* changed—and for the worse
—and that you get labeled as a bastard because you created this
bad change in her."

"I guess I do."

"Would you prefer it, then, if you had *not* slept with her, that she
remain a virgin forever? Do you think virginity itself a fine state?"

"Hell, no! As I said before, I would have liked her better, from
the start, if I hadn't found her a virgin. And I certainly don't think
that virginity *helps* any woman."

"Then how have you turned into a heel for devirginizing her?
Looks to me like you've sort of, in your own view, done her a favor,
and you perhaps might praise your act, rather than condemn it!"

"I never thought of that!"

"No, you didn't. But couldn't you? Or do you fear that someone
else—some other man—who comes along next in her life won't like
her loss of virginity, and she will *then* regret its loss, and *that* will
make you a bastard for taking it from her?"

"Well, that *could* happen, couldn't it? The next guy she goes with
could feel upset about her loss of virginity."

"Yes, he could. But he could also feel upset, if you had *not* slept
with her, about her remaining a virgin. Or he could get upset about
her not having red hair, her not possessing a fortune, her not having
had the right kind of sex with you, and a million other things. Will
you worry about all those possibilities?"

"No, of course not. But *she* could feel upset, now, about giving
me her virginity, when I won't marry her."

"True; she certainly could. But did you promise to marry her
before she slept with you? Did you induce her to surrender only
because you would stay with her forever?"

"Oh, no. Not at all. I acted honestly with her, right from the
start, and didn't even tell her I loved her when we first went to bed.
So she can't accuse me of *that* kind of thing."

"Very well, then. You acted honestly with her, and she went to bed
with you because, for one reason or another, *she* wanted to do so.
Maybe she just wanted to have the sex or lose her virginity or take
the *chance* that she would marry you or something else. But you
hardly twisted her arm—or her leg. She fornicated *voluntarily*.
Right?"

"Yes, quite right. Come to think of it, I'd say now, she even seemed a little overeager. Perhaps she thought it high time to give up her virginity. Or perhaps she merely loved me and wanted to cement our relationship. Anyway, I had no trouble getting her into the sack."

"Which means that even if she *now* regrets having gone to bed with you and *now* blames you for taking her virginity, she avoids self-responsibility for having had sex. She did it with her eyes open —and because of what *she* thought *she* would gain thereby. And now, if you leave her, she has gambled and lost. But does that constitute *your* responsibility or wrongdoing?"

"Mmm. No. I guess not. She knew perfectly well what she was doing, thought that she would gain by it, and would better assume responsibility for her act, if she now regrets it."

"So what seems *your* wrongdoing in all this, even assuming that *she* made a mistake and now sees that she made it?"

"None, I guess."

"Obviously you have nothing to feel guilty about. Now let's go on to your second element of self-damning. You continue to have sex with this woman, even though you know you won't marry her, and she apparently believes that you may. You thereby, by an error of omission if not commission, keep misleading her—inducing her to believe that you will marry her when you know that you won't. Correct?"

"Yes."

"Which means that you deliberately keep information from her that, if she knew about it, might well induce her to change her attitude toward you and perhaps get rid of you as a sleeping partner."

"I feel sure she would. She wants me sexually only because she loves me and wants me to marry her. And if she finds out I'll never do so, she'll break off immediately."

"All right, so you pretend you love her more than you do and thereby deprive her of the freedom to make up her mind about sleeping with you on the basis of full evidence. This kind of lying, where you needlessly and deliberately deprive another person of her freedom of action and thereby potentially harm her, seems distinctly unethical, does it not?"

"Yes. I know it does. And therefore, I feel guilty about doing it."

"Oh, no, you don't feel guilty for *that* reason!"

"But I do. I know I keep doing the wrong thing, and I naturally feel guilty."

"What do you mean *naturally?* You *artificially* keep making yourself guilty. Because (a) you do the wrong thing, as you said; and more importantly, because (b) you've got an idiotic philosophy that compels you to damn yourself for doing the wrong thing."

"But shouldn't I blame myself when I definitely do wrong? Shouldn't I feel guilty?"

"No. Why *should* you? You'd better have a sense of wrongdoing; a clearheaded admission that you behave unethically and that you will do your best to change and to do less wrong in the future. But that doesn't equal having the sense of guilt that you now have."

"I don't get it. What difference exists between what you call my having a sense of wrongdoing and what I call my guilt?"

"All the difference in the world. A sense of wrongdoing, or of responsibility to oneself and others, consists of two sane internalized philosophies: 'I behave wrongly, mistakenly, or erroneously in performing'; and 'therefore, let me see how I can work at performing better in the future!' "

"But don't I keep saying exactly that to myself?"

"No. You keep saying *one* of these sane sentences, but then you end up with a completely different, and quite insane, sentence. More concretely, you say to yourself, 'I behave wrongly in not telling my womanfriend that I will never marry her'; and 'therefore, I turn into a louse for behaving wrongly and leading her on like this.' "

"But don't I achieve lousehood for acting this way? Wouldn't *anyone* in my place?"

"No. You certainly behave as a wrong (as we already said), fallible human. And we need not in the least condone your deed or call it right or good. We assume it remains wrong. But a fallible human who does a wrong deed does *not* turn into a louse (or a pumpkin!), except by arbitrary definition. He remains just what we said—a fallible human who does a wrong deed. Period. And if and when he corrects himself, and no longer behaves badly, he will stay a fallible human who no longer does *this* wrong deed but who, you can bet, will soon enough, *because* of his fallibility, do some *other* wrong deed."

"You mean that no matter how many times I correct myself, and keep trying to behave well, I will still tend to make mistakes again and to behave badly?"

"Well—*won't* you?"

"I . . . uh . . . Yes, come to think of it, I guess I will. I'll always behave more or less wrongly—unless, of course, I turn into a perfect specimen."

"Right. And you'll never, at least as long as you remain human, do that. Only angels seem to behave perfectly. And I've met no angels yet."

"Nor I, I have to admit."

"Then why keep striving so idiotically to prove yourself the first?"

"Do I *really* try for that?"

"Not consciously, perhaps, for consciously you know full well you won't achieve angelhood. But unconsciously, as your behavior —your guilt—shows, you keep demanding perfection, demanding that you don't make certain mistakes. And then when you do make them, you measure yourself against your impossible, perfectionistic ideals and see yourself as a louse. And instead of seeing yourself as an individual who *now* makes mistakes, but who could correct them if he tried, you view yourself as an absolute skunk, a no-good rotter who *must* keep failing, failing, failing."

"So I seem to keep making a logical error. I see that as a human, I won't avoid making *some* mistakes and will have a hard time avoiding this one, so I overgeneralize and wrongly conclude that I must make *all* mistakes, including this one."

"Yes. Overgeneralization lies at the core of virtually all human disturbance. And you take a valid point—that a fallible human like you finds it *hard* to correct his mistakes—and falsely generalize this into the 'fact' that you find it impossible. Or, as I said before, you take the observable point that you do wrong and make it into the unprovable point that this wrong act makes you a total sinner, a no-goodnik."

"What makes my point unprovable?"

"Because it remains definitional. No factual proof or disproof of it exists. No such thing as a human sinner, louse, or no-goodnik exists, any more than there exists such a thing as a devil, hobgoblins, or gremlins. A sinner really means someone who remains *hope-*

lessly wrong; a louse, someone who must *always* act bad; a no-goodnik, someone who makes mistakes and cannot possibly *ever* correct them.

"But we have no way, of course, of proving that a person, how-ever many times he or she made mistakes in the past or makes them present, *cannot* possibly make fewer mistakes in the future; and no way of demonstrating that an individual who does wrong *deeds* makes himself or herself wrong and worthless and cannot possibly ever behave well again."

"Lousehood, then, seems just another overgeneralization, doesn't it?" he asked.

"Yes, a generalization carried to such ridiculous extremes that it seems impossible to actualize. For it would prove just about impos-sible, even if we wanted to do so, to construct a human who abso-lutely, positively *could* not ever do well just because he or she has done badly so far. Our knowledge about humans, in fact, proves just the opposite—that they frequently *can* change themselves remarkably and do much better in the future than they have ever done in the past. Some of them, indeed, have managed to make such drastic changes in their modes of behavior as to produce a virtual miracle."

"You mean people like Nathan Leopold, for example?"

"Yes. Leopold perpetrated one of the worst crimes in human his-tory: for a thrill—not, mind you, for political motives, for philo-sophic ideals, or for anything but a thrill. With his partner in crime, Loeb, he helped kill an innocent young boy. Certainly he committed a great crime. Yet some thirty years after he committed it, and during a life mostly spent in the penitentiary, he somehow managed to change his ways drastically, so that for the rest of his life there remained little likelihood of his committing any other crimes. He lived as a warm, useful, helpful person.

"So this man, whom almost everyone felt 'justified' in thinking of as a hopeless criminal in his youth, evolved into a fine, upright citi-zen. Just one of many cases that show that no hopeless, irreparable human 'lice' exist—just billions of wrongdoers, virtually all of whom, with proper care and treatment, *could* theoretically develop into do-gooders instead."

"You seem to show, then, that even if I remain dead wrong about not telling my girlfriend that I won't marry her, I don't make myself a louse for acting wrong."

"Yes. You do wrong. And if you want to live healthfully and sanely, try to correct your mistake, tell her the truth, and take the consequences. But feeling guilty about what you do—denigrating yourself as a human because you do wrong—will not help you to change. In fact, it will quite probably make you focus so much on your lousehood that you won't have the time and energy to devote to changing."

"Does my real problem, then, consist of *change,* rather than *guilt?*"

"Right! Moral codes seem useless unless they help us to *change* our behavior for the better. If they only 'help' us to feel guilty, or to devalue ourselves as humans, they prove senseless—and basically immoral."

I continued to talk in this vein; my client finally saw that he had nothing to feel guilty about, even though he behaved wrongly. Once he stopped condemning himself for his acts, he faced the music, told his woman friend, Lynn, that he had no intention of marrying her, and broke off his relationship with her on amicable terms. He later got involved with a woman more to his liking, whom he finally married.

Similarly, I contend and have stated in several of my books that we can't legitimately damn or blame anyone for *anything.* We all, goodness knows, make plenty of mistakes and commit our fair share of misdeeds, including needless harm to other humans. And we'd better acknowledge that as bad and not excuse it as good. Nor can we avoid taking any responsibility for our immoral acts, since, to some degree at least, we normally *could* control ourselves and *could* refrain from doing them. Nonetheless, we remain fallible, but unbad *people* who do these bad *acts.* We cannot, as our fiction and drama unfortunately keep telling us we can, accurately get labeled as villains or scoundrels, for a *villain* or *scoundrel* presumably deserves to get damned for his or her misdeeds; and *damnation* seems an unprovable concept.

Sex as "Sin"

Most of the so-called sex wrongs, moreover, amount to nothing of the sort. They exist only as definitional misdeeds. Thus, millions of people *think* masturbation, premarital sex relations, adultery, and sex deviations wicked or perverse. But as long as these acts get committed between adults who voluntarily and straightforwardly engage in them, what proves *truly* wrong about them?

Certainly, your Aunt Matilda may feel upset if she discovers that you have masturbated or have copulated with the nineteen-year-old woman next door. But that remains Aunt Matilda's problem; and if the woman next door gets upset about your fornicative relationship, she can always stop it. Aunt Matilda or the woman next door (or the abstraction of these individuals that we call "society") will feel hurt in these instances because they insist on *hurting themselves* by maintaining puritan attitudes and downing themselves for failing to live up to these "ideals." *You,* whatever they may say, do not truly hurt them—although you may, if you masturbate or fornicate obsessively-compulsively and thereby keep yourself away from potentially more rewarding pursuits, possibly sabotage your happiness.

Actually, because most of the people in this culture take their Aunt Matildas too seriously, we tend to have much more guilt without sex than vice versa—particularly among the unmarried part of the populace. As I have shown in *The Folklore of Sex* and *The American Sexual Tragedy,* and as several other studies by Chesser, Ehrmann, Hunt, Kinsey and his collaborators, Masters and Johnson, Reiss, Sorensen, and others have indicated, arbitrarily condemning harmless sex acts as wrong or immoral results in two kinds of disturbance—people guiltily refrain from the banned sexual behavior or they engage in this behavior guiltily.

For the most part, males tend to feel guilty sexually and consequently "enjoy" a considerable amount of masturbation, fornication, adultery, and other banned sex acts in a self-blaming way. But as Arlington has incisively noted, millions of them force themselves to stay away from activities that they would otherwise engage in either because they feel too guilty or because such activities prove difficult for them to find.

In other words, we actually have a considerable amount of guilt without sex in Western civilization. Instead of having sex and enjoying it, or even having it and not enjoying it, lots of people do not have sex—and *still* feel guilty about it! For these people can, of course, *think* about sex; and with their thoughts and feelings they create a focal point for self-deprecation and end up feeling woefully ashamed.

Eradicating Sex Guilt

I take the still heretical viewpoint that sex, *per se,* rates as good and that sex without guilt rates even better. I also think that sex with guilt seems pretty bad and that guilt without sex seems much worse. Consequently, I spend a good deal of my time showing people how they can get rid of their guilt—and enjoy sex more. Some of the rules I teach in this respect include:

1. Sex, on the whole, proves unusually beneficial and remarkably harmless, unless you deliberately make it otherwise. You will find it hard to imagine any truly injurious sex activities among sensible, consenting adults.

2. Physically or emotionally harmful sex acts do exist, but they seem rare and easily avoided. Forcing another person to have sex relations with you, for example, or taking advantage of a minor who cannot very well give true consent, or behaving dishonestly, and thereby unfairly taking advantage of a partner—these remain examples of antisocial acts, which we may judge immoral or wrong. But as long as you do not obsessively damn yourself for such misdeeds, but quietly and determinedly work at eliminating them, you can normally stop this kind of antisocial sex behavior.

3. Many so-called sex perversions—such as oral-genital, anal-genital, or noncompulsive homosexual relations—do not prove perverse but exist as healthy human sex behavior. We cannot label them as immoral or abnormal, except by arbitrary (usually biblically inspired) fiat. Enjoy them, if you will, and do not permit anyone to propagandize you into believing them wrong. If laws against such acts exist in your community, then you'd better obey these silly laws or see that you disobey them most discreetly. But do not think of various forms of extravaginal sex acts as perverted. Rather, people who completely avoid them, as I said in *The American Sexual Tragedy,* may show disturbance.

4. Some obsessive-compulsive, fetishistic, or compulsively per-

formed sex acts, such as obligatory homosexuality, compulsive voy-eurism, or obsessive preoccupation with sex thoughts, may represent disturbances. But individuals who engage in such behavior do not behave wickedly or immorally just because of their disturbance. Instead, they behave self-defeatingly, and we'd better help rather than condemn or punish them.

5. We may call a sex act truly wrong by exactly the same rule we use for a nonsexual act—if it needlessly harms or takes unfair advantage of another human. If it only proves self-harming, then it is wrong in the sense of its indicating self-defeatism or neurosis. But we cannot label it immoral (antisocial) in the usual sense in which we employ this term.

6. When you find that you have committed a distinctly wrong (antisocial) sex act, you can say to yourself: (a) "I have done this deed and will assume full responsibility for having committed it"; (b) "I definitely did wrong in performing it"; (c) "Anything that I can do, I can also *not* do; therefore, I can find it possible *not* to per-form this wrong act again"; (d) "Now let me figure out exactly what I'd better do (or not do) to avoid this same mistake in the future"; and (e) "Once I have figured out a better mode of future activity, let me work and practice, and work and practice some more, until I get so proficient at not doing this misdeed that I will have little chance of committing it again."

7. After you have done a wrong sex act, don't confuse the *act* with your*self,* damn (or devalue) yourself for doing it, keep repeti-tively blaming yourself for it, or deliberately punish yourself for having committed the misdeed.

8. Keep in mind that your main goal in life, in the seventy-five or so years that you have to exist on this earth, can consist of enjoy-ment. Yes, peculiarly enough—*enjoyment.* You can pursue this enjoyment, preferably on a long-range rather than a short-range basis. You can make it largely nonsexual rather than sexual. You can enjoy involved, serious, complex things rather than the playboy aspects of life. But frankly acknowledge that you don't *have* to achieve something wonderful during your lifetime, to do great ser-vice to others, to change the course of the world. Merely try to enjoy yourself!

In the course of enjoying yourself, and protecting yourself against harm, you will often find it useful to make sacrifices, to act nice to other people, to put off present pleasures for future gains, and sometimes to place other interests before your own. You will also often find that you do enjoy, in a nonmasochistic way, behaving kindly or lovingly to certain other people—such as to your woman friend, your wife, your parents, or your children. But in the main, you can have these as secondary aims.

You can keep as your main goal discovering what *you* experience as most pleasing, most satisfying, and then doing those things, if feasible, no matter what others may think. Naturally, act sensible about how others take to your goals and aims, and don't unduly antagonize them—especially when they have some power over you. But don't, by any means, largely live for what others think of you, for that seems the way of overconformity and self-downing.

In summary, if you can *think* about the things that precede or accompany your guilt, discover your own philosophic assumptions with which you make them bother you, and forcefully and consistently challenge and dispute these assumptions, you will stop feeling guilty about anything you do—particularly sex acts. For what happens to you at point A (an Activating Experience or Activating Event) doesn't upset you at point C (an emotional or behavioral Consequence). Rather, your irrational Belief system, at point B, creates your upset.

Thus, suppose that at point A you flatly lie and tell a woman that you can't have children, and you thereby induce her to copulate without contraception and risk making her pregnant. At point C, you feel extremely guilty, especially when you learn that she has not had her regular period. Your guilt feeling does not stem from the *fact* that you have unethically lied (for obviously, many other males have done the same immoral act and *not* felt guilty about it), but, first, from your rational Belief (B) "I acted wrong in lying to her, and I deem that most unfortunate." This rational Belief (rB) tends to create the appropriate negative feelings of sorrow and disappointment about your unethical behavior. But more important, your guilt stems from your irrational Belief (iB), "I find it *terrible* that I acted wrong. I *should* not have behaved that way! I turn into a *rotten person* for doing what I *shouldn't* have done!"

What makes this second set of Beliefs irrational? Several things:

1. It doesn't prove *terrible* (or *awful* or *horrible*) for you to have acted wrong or immoral, because *terrible* usually means (a) bad or unfortunate *and* (b) *more than* (more than 100 percent) bad or unfortunate. To label your behavior *terrible,* therefore, defines it as *inconceivably* bad, or beyond human limits. *Awful* acts equal *subhuman* acts, beyond the reach of empirical reality.

2. To say that you *should* not have behaved wrongly or unethically means (a) that you unwisely and undesirably acted this way and (b) that therefore you absolutely *should* or *must* not have so acted. Although statement (a) remains provable (in terms of rules of conduct that humans set for themselves to live peacefully and happily in a social group), (b) remains unprovable, because it assumes an unalterable law of the universe that says that you *have to* follow accepted human rules of conduct. Obviously you don't— else you could not have behaved wrongly (against these "unalterable" rules) when you committed your unethical act!

3. You hardly turn into a rotten *person* for committing a wrong or rotten *act.* For a bad *person* means someone who proves innately or intrinsically bad, who would have to *consistently* or *always* do extremely immoral deeds, and who deserves perpetual damnation and punishment (according to some immanent law of the universe) for doing these deeds. All these propositions remain unprovable.

In other words, when you devalue your*self,* your *person,* or your *essence* because of your wrong or immoral deeds, acts, performances, or characteristics, you illegitimately or magically overgeneralize. For although you do your misdeeds and usually prove *responsible* for them, and in that sense you *behave* wrongly, the total organism (or person) that we call *you* remains too complex for a global or final rating. *You* perform thousands of acts during your lifetime. *You* consist of an ongoing, everchanging *process. You* includes a conscious, decision-making, potentially self-altering aspect (often called your will or intentionality) that can considerably modify your "personality" (or your other characteristics). Your complete "youness" can therefore not get accurately rated, evaluated, or given a report card—even though many of your performances can. *You* emerge as neither good nor bad; and it amounts to a serious mistake to monolithically rate your highly pluralistic (and continually developing) existence. But your feeling of guilt (or shame or self-downing) means that you have globally labeled your entire *self,* your total *worth,* as "bad," just because you responsibly recognize the wrongness or immorality of *some* of your behaviors.

Your feelings of guilt, moreover, frequently do not help you to *change* your obnoxious behavior. To return to our example, if you induce a woman to have sex with you by lying to her, you can responsibly *acknowledge* your unethical act and strive to *change* it. You can decide, "I have behaved badly. I will now admit my poor behavior to this woman and help to make restitution for it (especially if I made her pregnant). And I feel determined to do my best to stop repeating this kind of lying, unethical deed in the future."

If you act in this manner, you desist from your immorality and start to behave more responsibly. You then feel ethical or moral— and *able* to act responsibly in the future. When you feel guilty, or self-downing, you concomitantly tend to believe, "How could a total turd like me possibly act *un*turdily hereafter?" Guilt, or lack of confidence in your *self,* helps you believe that you can hardly do *anything* well—including behaving responsibly.

Admit it, then—you make no goddamn saint. You have very human sex desires, and they often lead you to stupid, even antisocial, acts. That remains too bad; but only too bad. Not terrible, horrible, or awful. The world won't come to an end because of it. And unangelic you doesn't get transformed into a louse, a rat, or any other low-down animal. You still remain human. Fallible, yes; wrongheaded, of course; imperfect, you can bet your life! But *all* humans stay fallible, wrongheaded, and imperfect.

If this constitutes your basic sexual (and nonsexual) philosophy, and if you can use this philosophy to work at—yes, *work* at—behaving a little less fallibly, a trifle less wrongheadedly, during the course of your life, you will do the best a human can do. If this does not emerge as your fundamental, deeply held viewpoint, you will guiltily (and angrily) suffer. So think about it; work on it; if necessary, get psychological help in connection with it. Okay: On your mark . . . get set . . . *think!*

CHAPTER 4

The Sexuality of Women

IN ORDER TO understand how best to have sex-love relations with women, you had better know something about women's sexuality. This may not prove easy, for even experts in this field often disagree violently. In this chapter, I shall attempt to present some of the major knowns and unknowns in this respect and to give at least some useful insights into the sexual psychology of women.

Supposed Sex Differences between Men and Women

For many years, almost all writers on sex have assumed significant differences in the sexuality of men and women. For the most part, they have stressed that women experience less imperiousness in their sex drives, that they often have very little interest in sex for sex's sake, that they take considerably longer to get aroused, that they do not especially enjoy intercourse, that they desire sex less often than males, that they can easily live without having orgasms, that they do not respond as well to erotic materials, and that their sex desires fade away sooner than do those of their male partners.

Can we accept these kinds of statements about women's sexuality as true? By no means! Some of these statements have a grain of truth, others ring true only for some of the women some of the time, and still others have exceptionally little evidence in their support. Various biases exist in the observation and recording of women's sexuality, especially when this gets done by male researchers; and getting at the facts behind the biases does not prove very easy.

Some points we may make about the seemingly real sex differences that exist between males and females include the following, but they all seem fairly tentative and liable to modification, since new evidence keeps coming in.

1. Sexuality in the human female relates with various hormonal factors, getting affected by estrogen, progesterone, androgen, and other hormones. If a woman has a hormonal imbalance, particularly if she has a serious deficiency of androgen (the male hormone), she may well lose her sex desire and orgasm capacity.

Many female researchers, such as Judith Bardwick, Dee Bailey, and June Reinisch, point out the important physiological and cultural factors that produce significant male-female differences in sexuality.

2. Women may respond somewhat more slowly sexually than men, but the difference proves slight and may result largely from a failure in communication. As Shirley and Leon Zussman point out, "Although traditionally presented as the expert, no man can possibly know what a woman likes, where she wants to [get] touched, what she needs for sexual arousal, from one moment to the next, from one occasion to another, unless the female feels free to tell him verbally or to guide his hand as they caress each other." If men make themselves better, more communicating lovers, their partners may respond almost as quickly as they do sexually.

3. Women frequently have very strong sexual urges, and a small percentage of them seem consistently to have stronger urges than do men, as Kinsey and his associates pointed out. As Dr. Paul Jay Fink notes, men will consequently find it crucial that they "not underestimate the sexual excitability of the woman, and not deal with women in a chauvinistic way, implying that men [remain] the only sexual creatures. Women have strong sexual urges and should have them encouraged by their partners rather than dampened."

4. Even when highly sexual, women frequently don't emphasize having an orgasm as much as do men; they can enjoy sex immensely without a climax. Some women do not seem to follow this rule; they require an orgasm practically every time they copulate, make sure that they somehow get it, and feel exceptionally deprived and displeased when they don't. But many women can have great sex without orgasm and not seem to mind very much.

5. Although in their younger days women in our society frequently favor love and romance over direct sexuality in their relationships, they later may change in this respect; and since males may change in the opposite direction, the two may get closer in their sex-love goals.

6. For both biological and sociological reasons, males in our society get more easily aroused than females by visual or psychic stimuli, and as Dr. Robert Arnstein indicates, arousal proves "more rapid for the majority of men than . . . for women so that men more quickly and frequently identify sexual desire." Also, men tend to focus specifically on genital and women on more diffuse sensual satisfaction.

7. In some ways, as Masters and Johnson have shown, women frequently have a greater capacity for sex enjoyment than men, in that they can enjoy petting for a longer period of time without having to wind up with orgasm and in that they can finally have, in a single session, three, four, or more orgasms, whereas most men can have one or two in an equal period. This capacity of women for multiple orgasm, and sometimes for ten or more orgasms in a fairly short period, seems to have a biological origin, though of course, it can get significantly affected by social and emotional factors.

8. Women frequently require a good deal of foreplay in order to get aroused sufficiently to come to orgasm. Some women *at times* get aroused immediately; and a few women *often* feel ready for sex, even for intercourse, right away. But many of them most of the time want a good deal of foreplay, whereas many men want intercourse quickly. Moreover, once intercourse starts, men can frequently have an orgasm within a minute or two, though most women cannot.

Consequently, as Dr. Alfred Auerback writes, "Recurrent dissatisfaction leads to less sexual interest for the woman. Currently only 40 percent of women consistently [prove] orgasmic."

Mind, however—the relative low interest and orgasmic achievement on the part of the women follows from their not feeling satisfied and not from their intrinsic inability to experience satisfaction. So the sex "differences" here stem partly from or escalate from the male's original misperception of female sexuality or from his unwillingness to go along with what women really seem to want.

9. As Wardell Pomeroy shows, largely following the original Kinsey findings, young women have different desires and experiences than do young men. By the time they reach fifteen, almost all boys have orgasm, whereas only half the girls, by this age, get sexually aroused and only a quarter come to climax. The boys, moreover, tend to have two or three orgasms a week by the age of fifteen, and the girls who do have it come to orgasm only about once every

two weeks. Males tend to reach sexual maturity at about thirteen and reach their sex peaks by nineteen, whereas females develop much more slowly and reach their peaks in their late twenties.

When they have sex with each other, therefore, their sexual experiences differ somewhat widely, and they may have great difficulty understanding each other.

10. As Pomeroy also notes, sex holds less importance to females "than their public image or reputation" in our culture. "Boys, by contrast, [seem] not so concerned about their sexual reputation; they may even [feel] proud if it [proves] an extensive one. But girls [feel] painfully conscious of what other people think of them, and especially what other girls think."

Obviously, not all teenage females fit into this category, but even in our relatively liberated age, significantly more young women than young men do.

Dr. Julia A. Sherman agrees with Dr. Pomeroy that "girls date for social reasons, not sexual reasons."

11. Dr. Sherman also points out this common difference between the sexes: "Inexperienced girls have little conception of the emotions their casual caresses arouse in boys. Even when they [get] explicitly told, there [exists] a tendency not to appreciate the full strength of the reaction they set off. Many times males assume that females invite a sexual interaction when they [do] not, at least not at the level of awareness."

I may add to Dr. Sherman's statement the equivalent observation that many males I have talked with, especially sexually excitable ones, have great difficulty seeing that women do not feel exactly the way they do about sex; they keep reading into their female partners indications of reaction and arousal that largely seem fictional. When I inform them that many (though of course, not all) women have little direct interest in sex and that they largely engage in it for emotional reasons, the males just will not accept that fact. Because *they* want sex for sex's sake, they think it only "natural" and "normal" that all women feel the same way.

12. Women frequently seem able to enjoy sex without orgasm and to suffer few consequences. Wallin and Clark did a study of orgasm as a condition of women's enjoyment of coitus in the middle years and found that of women reporting no or few orgasms during intercourse, 17 percent enjoyed coitus "very much" and 28 percent

more enjoyed it "much." They also found that 11 percent of the women who never had orgasm with their husbands still usually got complete relief from sexual desire. A similar study of males would hardly turn up the same high percentages!

13. Dr. Sherman also notes that many women "never experience more than a mild sexual excitement" but that they nonetheless find it generally pleasant to have sex. Women who do get quite aroused sexually, on the other hand, can also experience groin pain, nervousness, and other kinds of discomfort when they do not achieve orgasm.

14. One of the most comprehensive studies of female sexuality ever done consists of Dr. Seymour Fisher's *The Female Orgasm*. Among the vast amount of information included in this study we find the observation that the typical woman estimated that her husband wanted to have intercourse about one more time a week than she did. Here again we have some evidence that males may show a higher sexuality, in terms of more desire, than females—especially since Dr. Fisher's sample consisted largely of orgasmic women who have relatively little difficulty getting aroused and coming to climax.

Like the authorities cited in the preceding paragraphs, Fisher again found that 60 percent of the women in his sample did not experience orgasm consistently and about 5 percent have never experienced it at all. But he, too, noted that "whether women experienced orgasm or not, [they still overwhelmingly considered intercourse] a highly gratifying experience."

Special Kinds of Sexuality in Women

The foregoing findings and considerable other information that researchers and clinicians have gathered for the last century about women's sexuality tend to indicate that females in our culture (and perhaps in most other cultures) seem to differ distinctly from males in some respects but that this difference by no means equals inferiority. In some ways, as indicated above, women actually seem superior, in that they can often achieve more orgasms, have more intense sex feelings, enjoy more sensuality, and can maintain a fairly steady level of sexuality once they achieve their peak desires and performances during their twenties.

Males, though originally driven to sex more than most women, gradually and consistently decline after their early twenties and in many instances feel relatively unsexy by the time they reach their forties.

Some of the uniquenesses and advantages of women's sexuality include the following:

1. Jessie Potter, a sex therapist, notes that women tend to see sexuality as "much more than genital contact. Men would [feel] able to offer so much more if sexuality [didn't get] defined in terms of the penis." Several other members of the round-table discussion on female sexuality, chaired by Barbara Nellis, in which Ms. Potter participated, seem to agree with her enthusiastically. Terry Garrity ("J."), in her revolutionary book *The Sensuous Woman*, also shows how amazingly sensual women feel and how they can enhance their (and their partners') sexual activities by cultivating sensuous pursuits.

2. Betty Dodson, in this same panel discussion and in her outstanding booklet on female masturbation, accurately indicates that we cannot view women's sexuality only through their responsiveness to other partners. Like men, they also have a great ability to enjoy themselves masturbatorily, and many of them unusually excel and outdo themselves in this form of sex.

Says Ms. Dodson, I used masturbation as "a primary technique . . . once I had made a decision that I [would feel] responsible for my own sexuality and that I wanted to [feel] orgasmic with more than one person. . . . My strongest, most consistent orgasms come from masturbation. Now, I can have outstanding orgasms with partners, but over a long period of time, I am my best lover."

3. Women's sexuality can actually at times get linked up with pregnancy and childbirth—so much so that these conditions themselves can lead to highly sexualized and orgasmic experiences.

4. As pointed out above, cuddling can give a woman an enormous amount of pleasure, some of which we may definitely call sexual. Men can easily mistake this kind of female holding for a sexual overture and think that their partners want coitus along with it—which may or may not prove true.

The Wide Range of Women's Sexuality

All human sexuality differs widely from individual to individual. The Kinsey researchers showed that both men and women may vary enormously, so that some otherwise "normal" individuals want to have sex relations a few times a year, whereas others want to have them a few times every day in the year. Women perhaps outrange men in this respect, since some women can literally have sex for hours at a time and enjoy thirty or more orgasms in the process, whereas others can happily go without sex for years and yet enjoy it when it finally does come along.

I frequently tell the story, in this respect, that Kinsey personally told me many years ago, when I spent a sixteen-hour day with him at his Institute for Sex Research at the University of Indiana. One of the thousands of women he had interviewed in his famous pioneering study of sex had not had any sex relations, including masturbation, until her early twenties, when she married and had intercourse with her husband virtually every day in the week, culminating in orgasm. A few years later her husband died (not of too much sex!), and for the next ten years she went back to a completely abstinent life—no masturbation, no sex of any kind. She had no trouble returning to this state of abstinence. Then she remarried and had intercourse with her second husband virtually every day in the week again, culminating in easy and satisfactory orgasm.

With a humorous glint in his eye, Kinsey asked me, "Can you imagine any male duplicating that kind of record?"

I had to admit that I could not. For even a low-sexed male, once he gets aroused and has steady orgasms, would rarely give them up if he refrained, for whatever reason, from heterosexual or homosexual activities. At least he would tend to masturbate! The fact that some women—though perhaps not many—could easily go from no sex, to steady sex, and then back to no sex again shows how different they can feel from men.

Perhaps an outstanding difference between males and females, therefore, consists of the fact that women range so widely in their sexuality. Some, though few, seem almost exactly like men in their urges and satisfactions; others seem almost diametrically opposed. As Wardell Pomeroy notes, many young women remain "simply uninterested in sex itself and . . . not aroused by pictures, books or by what they see in the movies. They do not, however, necessarily [feel] apathetic about boys. They may like boys and want to date them and enjoy their company, but sex has not yet become a part of their conscious lives. At the other extreme [exist] a small number of girls who [get] more easily aroused even than boys."

I sometimes feel tempted to make two main categories of women —those who strongly desire sex and those who don't. This seems an overgeneralization, since there probably exist many types in between. But the generalization still has some truth, and I note with interest that the old East Indian love book the *Koka Shastra* makes a similar distinction. In Alex Comfort's translation, "A woman who [acts] strong as a man, who can take plenty of blows and scratches and who actively desires intercourse, will likely [prove] passionate—in a woman of cold temper the reverse [holds], and intermediate characteristics suggest an intermediate disposition." Here sexuality gets linked with general personality traits, and some such connection may exist, although modern studies, such as those of Seymour Fisher, have not shown any close correlation in this respect.

Will Harvey points out a kind of antithetical finding—that women who show themselves relatively poor bedmates may excel the good ones in many other character traits. "A man who marries one of these women [seems] a fool to feel any great neglect because she may not [prove] a superwoman in bed. He has [got] blessed with the most faithful companion, dedicated mother, and one-woman fan club that anyone could ever ask for." This phenomenon may result from the fact that a relatively unsexy woman sees that she'd better use her other good traits as bargaining power and therefore *makes herself* good in the ways that Harvey outlines. Anyway, the point he posits often does hold true.

David Shope presents some evidence that nonorgasmic women may show sexual and nonsexual characteristics that differ significantly from orgasmic ones. He found, for example, that orgasmic women "reported more satisfaction with both their general adjustment and their sexual adjustment to their mates." He also found that they considered themselves more free of sexual inhibitions and that they felt considerably *more* interested in increasing their sexual responsiveness than the nonorgasmic women said they felt. Oddly enough, the women who did not have orgasm had little interest in achieving more arousability.

Dr. Leah Schafer, in an unusually detailed and intensive study of women's sexuality, also emphasizes the wide range of sexuality in different women. "Some women seem to have strong sexual drives, some deny their sexuality and apparently can 'live without it,' and some women, perhaps, just do not have very much sexual drive. Kinsey suggests that 'the capacity to get aroused psychosexually evidently depends on something more innate than the culture . . . there appears a limit beyond which psychosexual capacities cannot [get] developed within an individual's lifetime.' "

If you, therefore, want to get anywhere sexually with a woman, and both arouse and satisfy her, you had certainly better not place her in any general or abstract category. She remains her own person —quite different from many or most other women. She doesn't *have* to show sexiness, or great orgasmic capacity, or consummate skill in bed, or anything else. You always have the choice of trying to teach her some new tricks—but preferably while accepting that she may not prove amenable to learning them.

As Dr. Julia Sherman indicates, "Generally speaking, [you'll find] it necessary to ask each individual woman what she likes and wants and to listen to what she says. Men frequently have the ability to disregard what women say and often pay little attention." *You* don't have to cherish and cultivate this ability!

Cultural and Learning Factors in Women's Sexuality

As I have noted so far in this chapter, on biological and physiological grounds women differ significantly from men and from each other in their sexuality. But environmental and cultural factors play a major part in such differences too, either helping to exacerbate real differences or, in some instances, even creating differences where few or none originally existed. From time immemorial, societies—largely, of course, male-dominated societies—have insisted that women *should* operate in certain sexual, childbearing, child-rearing and familial ways. And, alas, women have often followed these fascist-like rules and have "proved" their "femininity" by accepting the societally taught roles.

Consequently, many women who probably have highly sexed "natural" tendencies have trained themselves to respond "properly," "chastely," or in a "ladylike" manner. But conversely, especially in recent years, women who do not feel greatly turned on to sex have made great efforts to turn themselves on to act "sensuous," and to achieve multiple orgasms, largely because they believe that *this* represents truly feminine or normal behavior.

Some of this pressure for sexual-social conformity by females has arisen from professional or "scientific" sources. Sigmund Freud made a huge error by assuming that since some women at first mainly feel clitoral sensation and achieve orgasms through manipulation of their external genitalia, and since some of these same women later find themselves able to experience considerable pleasure and intense orgasms through penile-vaginal copulation, the latter mode of sexuality equals a "mature," or "adult," mode and the former remains "immature," or "neurotic." Hogwash! A small proportion of women may interfere with their achieving orgasm during intercourse because they block themselves with puritanical ideas, and others may interfere by perfectionistically demanding that they absolutely *must* achieve "vaginal" orgasm. But most women who have difficulty achieving or who never come to climax through intercourse may well have this tendency for quite normal physical reasons, and not because of any severe disturbances on their part.

As we have noted, women differ widely in regard to their sexual propensities, and no "right" way or "feminine" way exists for all of them to behave. Many "natural" tendencies of women have got highly exaggerated in the sex and psychological literature. The Kinsey investigators, for example, finding that women do not respond to the same kind of erotic or pornographic materials as males, assumed that this followed from their slighter tendency to use sexual fantasy. But Barbara Hariton, J. Aphrodite, and other investigators have found that women frequently use the same kind of imagery as men and that they bring themselves to arousal and orgasm by its use.

As Nancy Friday said in the round-table discussion on female sexuality chaired by Barbara Nellis, "A number of women who reported their fantasies for my book talked about transforming themselves. One woman said she tranformed her dull life into some kind of Hollywood scene with wine buckets, and she would get herself to such a pitch that she would get on top of her husband and in her fantasy yell to herself, 'Go ahead, you deserve it. You deserve it, baby, go ahead.' "

To test the hypothesis that women and men differ significantly in their sexual responsiveness, Proctor, Wagner, and Butler of the University of Washington had males and females anonymously indicate what an orgasm feels like and had judges identify the sex of the individual giving this anonymous response. They concluded that individuals who concern themselves "most closely with sexual behavior [prove] unable to distinguish the sex of a person from that person's written description of his or her orgasm. Neither psychologists, medical students, nor obstetricians-gynecologists had significant success in this task . . . The results raise serious questions about the assumption that orgasm as experienced by males [equals] something different from orgasm experienced by females."

Manfred DeMartino, in two major studies of female sexuality, found that women have sexual urges, arousal patterns, and responsiveness that closely resemble those of males. Schmidt, Sigusch, and Schafer, in a notable article "Responses to Reading Erotic Stories: Male-Female Differences," retested the original Kinsey hypotheses the females feel far less responsive to nontactile stimulation than males, using subjects of all educational levels and ages. They found few or no sex differences. In commenting on this finding, Dr. Paul H. Gebhard, one of the main Kinsey investigators, admitted that the original Kinsey study wrongly concerned itself with sexual stimuli that get *suddenly* presented.

He noted, "Both Masters and Johnson and the Institute for Sex Research have demonstrated the essential equality of males and females in terms of response to tactile stimuli, and I suspect that if culturally produced variables can [get] identified and analytically partialed out, males and females will prove very similar, if not identical, in their inherent capacity to respond sexually to visual stimuli."

Another study at Temple University indicated that married women today tend to feel just as sexually experimental as married men and that therefore extramarital affairs increasingly prevail among younger, well-educated wives. A study by Izard and Caplan at Vanderbilt University showed women to have less sex arousal, interest, and joy and more disgust in regard to reading erotic passages, but the absolute magnitude of these differences proved slight.

Barbara Seaman in *Free and Female* and Mary Jane Sherfey in *The Nature and Evolution of Female Sexuality* review various studies and conclude that male-female differences in sexuality result largely from societal influences and from the biased observations of male clinicians (especially Freud!) and researchers. Dr. Sherfey takes the unusual position that women's sexuality has almost unlimited possibilities, from the biological point of view, and that as soon as cultural limitations on females get lifted, they will tend to outperform males considerably.

My own conclusion? Distinct differences in male and female sexuality exist and will probably continue to exist, but they get considerably exacerbated by cultural prejudices. In some ways, such as desire for sex (rather than sensual or loving) contact, males seem more interested than females, and in other ways (such as desire for and ability to have multiple orgasms), women appear distinctly "superior." Differences among individual females seem greater and more significant than differences between the two sexes. Preconceptions and bigotries about "significant" male-female sexuality differences prove pernicious. If you have any biases in this connection, you had better work hard to give them up!

Women's Sexuality and Women's Liberation

In recent years, the women's liberation movement has exerted a powerful influence in questioning antifemale biases and uprooting the concept that women have low-sexed, inferior, or abnormal desires and responsiveness. Partly because of women's liberation, female attitudes toward sexuality have changed considerably and still keep changing. Women like Kate Millet, in her book *Sexual Politics,* have notably unmasked some of the antifemale biases of men, including their sex biases. For example Ms. Millet insists that the novelist Henry Miller uses his penis as an instrument to degrade women and uplift men, and that other male writers and artists frequently do the same.

Although Ms. Millet probably exaggerates—as most crusaders for a cause tend to do—she seems to have more than a grain of truth in her accusations. As Julius Fast points out in *The Incompatibility of Men and Women,* Norman Mailer's vitriolic attack on Kate Millet in *The Prisoner of Sex* tries to vindicate himself and Miller, but actually succeeds in sustaining some of her theses. Fast did his own survey of male attitudes toward women and concluded,

"What did the men who answered our questions say about womanliness? *A woman [proves] womanly when she has a man. When she [feels] wanted. Sex fulfills her. [Getting] made love to by a man.* It [appears] basically true. She [gets] considered a woman only when she services men."

Other observers also point out that women's liberation has only limited acceptance in the Western world so far and that male-chauvinist attitudes persist. Warren Farrell, upholding the concept of antisexist male liberation, indicates that men had better give women true sex freedom, or else they will not have it themselves. But he points out how they still restrict women in many ways.

Susan Lydon notes, "Freud's insistence on the superiority of the vaginal orgasms seems almost a demonic determination on his part to finalize the Victorian's repression of feminine eroticism, to stigmatize the remaining vestiges of pleasure felt by women, and thus make them unacceptable to the women themselves." She also observes that our modern sex manuals dictate prudery and restraint under the guise of frankness and sexual liberation and that they put new pressure on women to have superduper orgasms.

In *The Sensuous Person,* I show how some of the most popular sex authorities, such as Terry Garrity ("J."), David Reuben, and Robert Chartham, have a number of puritanical, antifemale attitudes in their writings and how they foolishly demand that "any woman can"—meaning that any woman can turn herself and her lover on sexually and reach the summits of satisfaction in practically every instance.

Wardell Pomeroy shows that in our society we insist that a woman learns "to respond in the bedroom while she maintains a ladylike appearance the rest of the time." And he seems to go along with this woman-downing attitude somewhat when he notes that "armed with all this knowledge, I [feel] convinced that a girl will come to understand she must [turn into] something of an actress in life."

Alexander Lowen does much worse in this respect by insisting that women must achieve so-called vaginal orgasm in order to achieve true "femininity." He follows the nonsense of Dr. Marie Robinson in this respect, who antiliberationally espouses the "power of sexual surrender" for women and feels that only through surrendering to males will they achieve the sacredness of vaginal orgasm. Under the guise of helping women go "back to nature," attain "a higher consciousness," and achieve "knowledge, power, Christian love and romantic love," Lowen states that "the emancipation of woman [remains] a hollow victory when . . . obtained by the denial of her essential nature as the vessel that holds the mystery of life." This doesn't seem far removed from the Nazi children-church-home philosophy that proved so inimical to women in Hitler's Germany.

The fight persists. Male supremacist attitudes creep into all kinds of sex and reproductive relations with women. As Barbara Seaman has shown, even male gynecologists, who know a great deal about women and help them in significant ways, often "persist in treating their patients more like slaves than like free human[s]." But things do change, and women's liberation continues to make inroads. As this progresses, women seem to feel more released to let themselves go sexually and to cut down some of the differences that exist between them and men. As Robert Bell notes, "as more and more restrictions [get] removed from the woman and she [feels] encouraged to achieve personal sexual satisfaction, it seems logical that she will increasingly desire greater frequency of sexual intercourse. This [gets] confirmed by empirical evidence."

I, too, predict that as liberation attitudes increase, women will tend to act in a more "masculine" way—but will also act in their own unique sexually feminine ways and will not feel ashamed of doing so.

Periodicity and Female Sexuality

To some degree female sexuality varies with hormonal changes, so that many (and, as usual, not all!) women feel much sexier at certain times of their menstrual cycle and less sexy at other times. Dmowski, Luna, and Scommegna state that "several studies indicate that in some women periods of increased sex desire occur near the time of catamenia [menstruation], when estrogen is at the lowest level. . . . Other women report a sharp rise in frequency of intercourse and orgasm toward the middle of the cycle, a decline during the luteal phase, and a second rise toward the end of the cycle."

Shirley and Leon Zussman agree that "some women report that

they sometimes have increased sexual interest and activity during various phases of the menstrual cycle." Dr. R. B. Greenblatt concurs.

J. A. Kenny, studying pregnant and breast-feeding women, found that most of the mothers reported that their sex behavior remained the same during as before pregnancy except for the third trimester, when desire, frequency, and enjoyment decreased. Desire returned for most of them by the fourth week after childbirth, and most women reported their sex interest after weaning about the same as before.

Sexual periodicity to some degree seems to have a valid existence, but Mary Brown Parlee has reviewed this scientific literature on the premenstrual syndrome and found that although such a syndrome may well exist—certainly many women spontaneously attest to phenomena that support it—"as a scientific hypothesis the existence of a premenstrual syndrome has little other than face validity." Solid facts to support various cyclical behaviors in women do not yet exist, and we could well use more solid evidence in this connection.

So-called Nymphomania

Men seem to like to write about the existence of "nymphomania" in women. Literally scores of books and articles keep getting published in this connection, many of which seem to have as their main purpose the titillation of male prurience. As I showed in a book *Nymphomania: A Study of the Oversexed Woman*, which I wrote with Dr. Edward Sagarin, we frequently falsely tend to call a highly sexed woman a nymphomaniac and to do so pejoratively. Actually, very few real nymphomaniacs tend to exist, and when they do they can get more legitimately diagnosed as females who compulsively drive themselves to sex activity, largely for nonsexual reasons. Thus, most of them feel that they have to engage in a great deal of sex in order to feel loved, or to conquer one man after another, or otherwise to prove themselves. Although we had better not view them as "bad women," we can see their compulsive sexuality as a product of their disturbed attitudes and feelings.

Some authorities, for example Dr. J. D. Chapman, believe that instead of proving a hot-breathed little package of feminine pulchritude, a nymphomaniac actually remains "by all standards and characteristics, *frigid*" becuse she invariably fails to achieve release of sexual tension and seldom experiences orgasm. Although I sometimes find this true, I also find that many so-called nymphomaniacs remain in the normal range of sexuality and that others actually rate at the top of that range.

As D. Gordon notes in one of his cases, "One very successful career woman, who had made a fortune in commercial art, confessed to a friend who asked why she did not get married, 'I prefer not to. I like the arrangement of my life. Several men I have known over the years call me every so often and come to my apartment and spend the night. Then I don't see them again for a few weeks. That [seems] fine with them, and with me. I live my own life, and they live theirs, and no one asks any questions.' "

As Gordon remarks, "They use her, and she uses them, for the purpose of sex. She [lives], to a certain degree, like a call girl except she does not get paid for sex and asks from the men that they satisfy her sexually, which a call girl does not."

I, too, have talked with a number of women like this, and find that they have unusually high sex drives, which they find easier to satisfy with many different partners than with a single lover or husband. I don't think of them as nymphomaniacs, since they do not feel compulsively driven to have sex but merely have it in a permissive, preferential manner.

On the other hand, Gordon points out that some women get addicted to sex "to escape facing deeper emotions—anger, fear, jealousy, depression." They feel that these might destroy them if they had to admit such emotions. Instead, with their frantic pursuit of sex, they deny they have such emotions.

This, of course, happens with some nymphomaniacs, just as they feel driven to their hypersexuality for other disturbed reasons. This does not mean, however, that a woman cannot feel both highly sexed *and* driven to compulsive relations, for she can. In fact, the likelihood exists that most nymphomaniacs have strong natural urges and that *therefore* they "pick" this addiction, rather than some nonsexual compulsion.

Clitoral and Vaginal Orgasm

Freud and his followers have assumed that women experience two different kinds of orgasm, clitoral and vaginal. Many women report feeling these two different types of climaxes, and say that the former feels relatively light and shallow, whereas the latter, the vaginal orgasm, feels profound, real, and deeper. But does this feeling mirror reality? Women frequently "feel" or "know," for example, that they absolutely cannot enjoy sex without love; and yet, one day, they miraculously do. So what does their feeling really prove?

Masters and Johnson presumably settled this question when they discovered that: (1) women who receive so-called vaginal orgasms —or what I many years ago more accurately labeled *orgasms during intercourse*—actually have their clitoral regions manipulated during coitus, and this direct or indirect clitoral massage, rather than the penile-vaginal contact itself, brings on the orgasm; and (2) the physiological effects during both "clitoral" and "vaginal" orgasm appear identical, so that in both cases a woman experiences the same kind of heartbeat, respiration rate, flushing, loss of arousal, etc.

These findings presumably proved what I pointed out when I stated in my well-known paper "Is the Vaginal Orgasm a Myth?" which I published in 1953: Orgasm remains orgasm, however achieved, and if women would only accept that fact they would have relatively little trouble in coming to climax.

That seemed to settle that. But it didn't. The notion of a special or different kind of vaginal orgasm, fairly distinct from clitoral orgasm, has never got entirely laid to rest; in fact, recent evidence tends to show that in some respects it may exist.

Dr. J. D. Chapman notes in this respect, "It would appear that some investigators who claim no such thing as vaginal orgasm [occurs] do not completely understand the anatomy of the female pelvis. The clitoris has an abundance of sensory nerve fibers—the nerve supply [emerging as] the same as that of the penis, since the two [get] derived from the same source and by the same mechanism embryologically. The vagina, on the other hand, has few sensory fibers, but does have an abundance of nerves whose function [remains] proprioceptive . . . sensitive to pressure. The end receptors [get] called 'genital corpuscles.' These receptors respond to pressure and call forth sensations. Thus, the clitoral response [exists] to touch and the vaginal to pressure."

In her study *Women and Sex,* Dr. Leah Schaefer remarks,

"Although Masters and Johnson claim that the *physiological* phenomenon of orgasm [stays] always essentially the same, regardless of the source of stimulation, these women perceived striking differences in the sensations of various kinds of climax experiences."

The most comprehensive studies of this question of so-called clitoral and vaginal orgasm have occurred under the direction of Dr. Irving Singer and Dr. Seymour Fisher. Singer reviews the literature in great detail and concludes that two different kinds of orgasm exist—the first, a vulval orgasm (often called the clitoral orgasm) and the second a uterine orgasm (often called a vaginal climax). He writes, "There [seems] reason to believe that vulval orgasms [comprise] consummations in which the sensuous predominate while uterine orgasms have a special dependency upon the passionate. A priori, none of these modes of satisfaction—whether terminative or nonterminative, passionate or sensuous, uterine, vulval, or blended—[proves] necessarily preferable to any other."

Seymour Fisher made a more empirical study of orgasmic women and also found that they reported so-called vaginal and clitoral orgasms and that they often had different sensations with each. Oddly enough, however, he found that the clitorally oriented women had some distinct advantages over the vaginally oriented ones. "Contrary to the Freudian position, which sees the vaginally oriented woman as the epitome of maturity, I found that the clitorally oriented women [proved] considerably less anxious. The vaginally oriented women suffered more from generalized, free-floating anxiety. Our findings [showed] a direct contradiction of the Freudian notion that the clitorally oriented woman [rates as] immature, can't accept herself as a woman, and so on."

Quite a finding! Another surprise from the same writer: "When we asked women that if they could choose only clitoral or only vaginal stimulation a great majority selected clitoral. The stereotype has [remained] that most women achieve orgasm mainly through penile intromission. The harmfulness of the myth [appears] evident in the great numbers of women who think themselves abnormal and seek therapy because they [experience] 'only' clitoral climaxes."

My own conclusion: Although many women seem to experience only clitoral orgasm—through direct stimulation of the clitoral region or by its indirect stimulation during intercourse—a minority, perhaps 20 percent, can have a different kind of orgasm, of vaginal orientation, either instead of or in addition to orgasms of clitoral orientation. Some of these latter women have more intense and "satisfying" climaxes, but most don't. The average female has primarily clitoral orientation all her life and might just as well have it, since it does not bring significant physical or emotional disadvantages (unless she *views* it negatively) and it has some distinct advantages.

But women differ widely in this, as in other, sexual respects. Putting them all in a similar mode and contending—as writers such as Marie Robinson, Alexander Lowen, Wilhelm Reich, Rachel Copelan, and John Somme tend to do—that women should or *must* experience particular kinds of orgasm, such as that achieved through intercourse, leads to highly pernicious results. Similarly, contending that all women *must* achieve clitoral climax, as a few writers imply, has great and iatrogenic disadvantages.

Your partner has an individuality in her own right. She may or may not rise to climactic heights by penile-vaginal intromission. She may never get all-consuming, total orgasms as do some women. She may not even achieve any pronounced orgasms whatever. So? Your and her job, as cooperating partners, remains the discovery of what she *can* experience, in whatever way she can feel it. Look for *her* possibilities and forget about any abstract or overgeneralized views of what she *should* or *has to* achieve.

Women's Disturbances and Sexuality

Many psychotherapists, particularly psychoanalytic theorists and practitioners, such as Sigmund Freud, Wilhelm Stekel, Wilhelm Reich, and many other "authorities," have assumed that a clear-cut relationship exists between sexuality or nonsexuality and emotional disturbance. I have taken a dim view of this position ever since I found, in my own experience with women, that some of the freest, sexiest, and most orgasmic women I have encountered have displayed exceptionally severe emotional disturbance; and, as I report in my book *Suppressed: Seven Key Essays Publishers Dared Not Print,* some of the sanest women I have known have hardly enjoyed sex or have had relatively little pleasure with it.

More generalized support for my personal findings has come from more objective studies. As noted in the last section, Dr. Seymour Fisher found that clitorally oriented women, who according to Freudian and Reichian theory have severe disturbances, tend to feel considerably less anxious than vaginally oriented ones. Dr. Julia Sherman, in reviewing the literature on sex, also notes that non-orgasmic women can remain otherwise healthy and that "one cannot assume that coital orgasm [represents] the most salient of a woman's needs."

Dr. Leah Schafer, in her study of women and sex, also reported, "Not all women with social-emotional problems had accompanying sexual response problems, nor did all women with sexual response problems have social relationship problems. This fact and the unanimity of orgasmic response suggest that sexual responsiveness and emotional stability do *not* [emerge as] necessarily mutually dependent."

At the same time, a connection *may* exist between emotional disturbance that somewhat contradicts the usual psychoanalytic hypothesis. Dr. Helen Singer Kaplan, in her book *The New Sex Therapy,* points out that in cases of sexual inadequacy, a general emotional problem often comes first and then leads to the sexual problem. Correct! Karen Horney, Erich Fromm, various non-Freudians, and I have noted this for quite a number of years.

The classical psychoanalytic position tends to claim that the individual first gets disturbed sexually—has an Oedipus or Electra complex or gets hung up on some pregenital phase of existence, such as anality or orality—and then feels anxious, depressed, or hostile. I have rarely, even during the period when I practiced psychoanalysis for several years, found this true.

Instead, I find that people usually first construct some general irrational ideas—for example, "I *must* succeed and prove my competence in all important ways," or "I *have to* win the approval of every member of the other sex with whom I get emotionally involved"—and then, as a result of holding these ideas, they tend to get hung up sexually and fail to get aroused or satisfied. Once their sex disability arises, they view *that* through the dismally tinted glasses of their original irrational ideas—for example, by insisting, "I *must* get full and powerful erections," or "I absolutely *have to* achieve several powerful vaginal orgasms every time I have sex"—and then they develop two disturbances for the price of one. In other words, they feel disturbed *about* their first disturbance and thereby notably exacerbate it.

This happens, of course, to many women. They have general feelings of anxiety, worthlessness, depression, or hostility. Then they develop distinct sex hangups. Then they feel anxious or worthless about their sex problems. Then they get even more seriously disturbed. So the general rule I follow consists in assuming that the sexually hung-up woman well may (but doesn't *have* to) have a negative philosophy or general set of irrational ideas and that she'd better get some help in discovering and eliminating these notions. But many low-sexed or "inadequate" women have little or no general disturbance, and many highly sexed and "swinging" women have considerable emotional hangups.

Each individual had better get seen and treated in her own right, and not by some arbitrary psychological standard of sexual or general "health."

Other Considerations

Let me list some other observations about the sexuality of women.

1. It seems probable that a correlation exists between high energy levels in women and their sexual performances. Dr. Leah Schaefer found that of the thirty women in her study who exhibited 100 percent orgasm capacity, "every woman showed a great deal of life energy—in her striving to achieve happiness and success, and in her constant struggle to defy and defeat many of the negative forces of her past."

2. If you want to satisfy a particular woman sexually, discover how *her* interests and capacities run. Usually, women have increased chances of reaching orgasm if they have foreplay of about twenty minutes and active intercourse for from ten to twenty minutes. Your particular partner may reach her orgasm in more or less time. But prepare yourself for some amount of effort in this connection.

3. Some women may have an increased likelihood of orgasm if they strengthen their pubococcygeal muscle—one of the main muscles in the vagina. They may do this by concentrated exercise, in the

manner recommended by Dr. Arnold Kegel. Such exercise most probably offers no panacea for inorgasmic women, but it may help in many cases.

4. As will be noted in the chapter on physical methods of arousal, women's erogenous zones vary widely. In general, however, Fisher found a remarkable consistency in that the women he studied could easily get aroused by stimulation of the clitoris, the area near the clitoris, and the inner lips of the vulva. On the other hand, relatively insensitive or nonerogenous parts of their bodies included the interior of the vagina, the breasts, and the outer lips (labia majora) of the vulva.

5. Women's dependence on their love objects often contributes mightily to their sex arousal and satisfaction. When they feel that the man they care for and have sex with will stick around and keep loving them, they tend to let themselves go more and enjoy sex to a greater degree. To some extent, however, the ease or ability with which they have consistent orgasm may relate to endogenous factors, such as hormonal supply, and remain fairly independent of the amative relationship a woman has with her mate.

6. Even the most highly sexed and freest women frequently have to work to reach orgasm. As Will Harvey noted, "Most of the young women I've known had to work at achieving a climax—I mean physically work at it each time. They couldn't just lie back and let it happen, no matter how relaxed they [felt] or how hard I worked. They had to participate—move, clutch, gyrate, thrust—in cycles of varying intensity until finally it hit them."

I agree. Many women with whom I've gone to bed had no trouble whatever in getting aroused and reaching orgasm. But this many still only amounted to a minority!

7. Like men, women incessantly *talk to themselves* while having sex. They frequently spy on themselves and worry about their own reactions—or lack thereof. And they often ask themselves what their partner thinks of them and whether he finds them satisfactory. Self-talk can help them if they use it sexily. But if they use it, as they often do, for worrisome, self-rating purposes, it can prove deadly.

8. Women's self-talk during sex frequently gets sparked by their perfectionism or unrealistic expectations. They devoutly believe that they *should* outdo Cleopatra or *must* have the greatest love affair

that ever existed in human history. They have, to use Karen Horney's term, an idealized image of themselves as sex-love partners that can hardly get fulfilled, and they consequently render themselves anxious and depressed. If you, as a partner, show your womanfriend that she *doesn't* have to measure up to any kind of perfection and that you can easily accept her *with* her failings, you may help her feel and act much better sexually.

9. Do women have much interest in the size of a man's genitalia? In most cases, not that much. As Masters and Johnson, Kinsey, G. Lombard Kelly, and other authors have shown, the nerve endings in the vagina fortunately occur in the vestibule, or first inch or so of this organ; consequently, a man with a very small penis can sometimes satisfy a woman sexually as well as a man with a much larger penile endowment.

But don't kid yourself here! For various reasons, some women like or require a fairly sizable sex organ. Some have large vaginal orifices and feel little contact unless entered by a large penis. Others want their cervixes touched, since that kind of pressure adds to their enjoyment of intercourse. Others find that a male with a long or a wide organ will fill their vaginas in such a way as to exert additional friction on the inner lips and consequently on the clitoral area, leading to increased excitement and orgasm.

As Jessie Potter, a grandmother and a sex therapist, said during a panel on female sexuality chaired by Barbara Nellis, "People keep saying size makes no difference, but to make that an absolute [rates as] crap. If a woman has had a lot of kids, size does make a difference. Sometimes doctors do an operation on women to tighten up the vaginal walls after a lot of childbirth. For countless women, size probably makes a great psychological difference. For instance, a very large penis may [seem] scary. But to say size makes no difference either way [proves] just not true."

What can you do about the fact that you just may not suit a woman that you want in the size of your genitalia? Damned little, as far as changing things goes! You can, of course, use your tongue and your fingers to the best possible advantage—and you'd better! But if this does not suffice, you may best turn to selectivity. Fortunately, not every woman wants a man with either a small or a large penis. Though one particular woman may reject you anatomically, the great majority probably won't. Don't put yourself down if you seem deficient to some females—and keep trying for one who will find you more than enough!

10. Although I have emphasized throughout this chapter that some women can go without orgasm completely or have it only occasionally and still enjoy sex, most of them do much better with it than without. The more effort you make to satisfy any steady sex partner and to give her fairly regular orgasms, the better she will probably function sexually and nonsexually. So give it a try—and reap maximum rewards from your relationship with her.

How to Satisfy an Intelligent and Sexually Liberated Woman

Men frequently want to know how to get along better with a so-called liberated woman or with an intelligent woman who doesn't consider herself a member of women's liberation. These usually include women who seem to feel rather independent, who want male companionship but will not sell their soul to get it, who act fairly assertive in going after what they want (and refusing what they don't want), and who try to enjoy sex and love relations for their own sake and not in order to make themselves feel like "worthwhile" people.

In regard to highly intelligent women, Manfred DeMartino has done the most comprehensive study to date, in his detailed research on members of Mensa (a society whose members literally have to test in the upper 2 percent of the population in IQ). His findings tend to show that his subjects proved quite "sexy" by usual standards but that their sexuality tended to differ significantly from that of males in several significant ways:

● They frequently engaged in masturbation but often found it undesirable, an unavoidable necessity, and too lonely.

● They had positive attitudes toward sex mainly when they felt it went with emotional or loving feelings.

● They had to get stimulated, to achieve orgasm, by petting, clitoral manipulation, or kissing before or during intercourse.

● They engaged in deliberate and persistent sex fantasy to a lesser degree than did an equivalent sample of males.

● They had about four orgasms in their best twenty-four-hour period—about the same number as males had in their best twenty-four hours.

• They obtained their greatest number of orgasms from masturbation or direct clitoral stimulation.

• They found the idea of participating in group sex appealing in only 18 percent of the cases.

• They engaged in extramarital affairs in 39 percent of the cases studied but did not do so out of an intense desire for variety. Rather, they had extramarital affairs because they felt seriously frustrated by passionless husbands, because of curiosity, or for reasons of emotional involvement.

• They largely reported that they required more time than their mates to get sexually stimulated, that they got thoroughly aroused only when they received a high degree of emotional acceptance from their partners, and that they had to work hard at achieving climaxes.

Noting these facts, I present several rules for satisfying highly intelligent women in the epilogue that I wrote for DeMartino's book:

1. Understand the attitudes of women and see them in their own light and not in the way you might *like* them to think and act.

2. Treat them as individuals. Experiment until you find what *your* partner considers most pleasurable.

3. Focus largely on the *emotional* relationship you have with a woman and treat her as a *person*.

4. Minimize your male egotism and stay with a woman for her and your enjoyment—not to give yourself a high ego rating or deify your "manliness."

5. Take your time sexually and pay considerable attention to foreplay—to simple holding, caressing, and petting.

6. Use a sufficient amount of sex variation and employ your imagination as much as you employ your sex organs!

7. Don't act lazy, but recognize that the "easy" way to sex often proves the most unrewarding in the long run.

8. Don't overemphasize sex or orgasm. You don't *have to* screw every day in the week, and you don't *need* to have an orgasm or to bring your partner to climax every time you have sex.

9. Often, make postcoital involvement as important as precoital or coital technique. As one of DeMartino's subjects reported, men often "leave too soon after they [get] satisfied. It spoils the afterglow and makes me feel used instead of loved." Don't leave a woman's arms or bed precipitately!

Do women's liberationists differ significantly from other intelligent women? In some ways, yes, for they have a definite point of view to follow, and they attempt to follow it in their sex-love lives. In some ways, however, they have their limitations in this respect. Somewhat like the couples who would like to practice open marriage but get held back by their intense feelings of jealousy and insecurity, their bark often turns out much different from their bite.

This goes for young women in general in our society. As Leah Schaefer notes, they "engage in more sexual *activity* than their elders; however, I have found that the feelings attached to this activity [emerge as] not much freer of guilt, confusion, or contradictions than the feelings of their parents' generation."

Inteviewing women at a women's-liberation conference, Elaina Zuker found that "most of the women said they still preferred to have emotional attachment to their sex partners. Many said they felt 'cheap' or 'promiscuous' otherwise. But some stated that they [could] 'get it on' with no emotional involvement whatsoever. As one woman explained, 'Variety without attachment—that [remains] *my* idea of a good sex life.'"

Another outcome of women's liberation amounts to the belief that females do not have to ape male sexuality or to make themselves "free" in exactly the same way that men would. As Shere Hite points out in *Sexual Honesty by Women for Women,* "There has rarely [arisen] any acknowledgment that female sexuality might have a nature of its own, which would involve more than merely [posing as] the logical counterpart of male sexuality."

Polly Kellogg, writing on "Sexual Behavior in the Human Female: A Feminist Critique," also notes that male sexuality doesn't equal female sexuality and that men wrongly try to approach women as they would like to get approached, with immediate genital stimulation. But genital stimulation, she says, comprises only one-third of women's sexuality—the other two-thirds consisting of physical stimulation of the whole body and generalized emotional stimulation. She takes the Kinsey researchers to task because "unfortunately, the authors never explore the basics of women's sexual preferences for emotionality" and never investigate emotional variables, such as giving encouragement, receiving encouragement, understanding another's emotions, feeling understood themselves, doing and receiving favors, smiling, humor, etc. They also don't explore variables that combine emotional and physical stimuli, such as expressive eye contact, tender facial stroking, leaning on a lover to express desire for closeness or comfort, getting leaned on, holding or cradling a lover in a comforting way, getting so held, etc.

If this holds true, and women have a different kind of sexuality than men in certain ways and seem likely to keep looking for what *they* really want—and not for what males or for what their society *thinks* they should want—you had better keep in mind certain modes of behavior when you go with a woman who believes strongly in the women's liberation position. For example,

1. Treat your partner as a person and not as an inferior. She may well have her "weaknesses," including her hyperemotionality. But she also has her distinct advantages as a woman, and you had better refrain from putting her down in any way.

2. Don't use your greater physical strength, economic power, or other influence to blackmail or coerce her. Try to get her to want to do what you would like her to do and not to submit because she dares not buck you.

3. Try to see things from her personal and female frame of reference. Just because you do not understand some of her aspects fully —such as her ease of crying or her insistence that certain things get done—try not to view these aspects as "stupid," "weak," or "irrational." When seen from a human, rather than from a "masculine," point of view, her behavior may well have its real advantages.

4. Make an effort to see sexuality in a sensual-emotive, rather than a purely genital, framework. Don't view it narrowly in terms of excitement and orgasm.

5. Watch your language! Don't refer to females as *girls*, but as *women* or *people*. Don't always use the term *he* when you mean *he or she*. Try to give women truly equal status in this world, in every possible verbal and active way.

6. Try to remain as honest as you can in your dealings with women. You don't have to feel ashamed of having purely sexual feelings and of wanting female companionship mainly for the fun of rolling in the hay. But don't pretend that you want it for highly emotional or mating purposes, when you really don't. Love easily creates illusion, so lean over backward to let a woman know your real feelings about her—both the tender and the harsh, the quick and the dead.

7. Try to discover your partner's main sexual feelings and wishes, however different from yours they may seem, and take the time and trouble to satisfy her as well as yourself. Intelligent selfishness means enlightened self-interest, and if you really get absorbed in satisfying the women in your life sexually, you will usually find that they amply reward you in turn with some enlightened self-interest of their own.

Let me conclude this chapter with a pertinent statement from the writings of Janet Barkas, a highly knowledgeable and competent sexologist and editor. Men who welcome "the new wave of expression from liberated women will find, though the going must [seem] rough at first, that their partner's awakened sexuality and fulfillment [proves] an exciting addition to their relationship, resulting in intensified experiences. And, inevitably, the outcome of these struggles to [turn into] 'new' men and 'new' women will [prove] worth the effort."

Ms. Barkas seems right on the ball. See if you can help fulfill her prophecy!

CHAPTER 5

The Art of Sexual Persuasion

Webster's New World Dictionary defines the word *seduce* in this way: "To persuade to engage in unlawful sexual intercourse, especially for the first time; induce to give chastity." The essence of the art of seduction consists of first convincing yourself of the wrongness of this definition. For it mistakenly states and implies that sexual intercourse and the surrender of chastity have to register as wicked or unlawful.

Precisely this implication, in fact, keeps millions of females from having premarital sex. They erroneously believe—although there no longer exists any evidence to support this belief—that if they engage in heavy petting or copulation, they will do an immoral, socially and legally banned act; thus, even though they would often like nothing better than to give up their chastity, they steadfastly refuse to do so because of this belief system. Or—just as importantly—millions of potentially seducible females today do not personally view anything wrong with premarital sex participation. However, they think that their male companions believe this, and their fear of what they think these males believe mainly keeps them chaste.

Not that these women seem entirely wrong. There do, alas, exist males who asininely believe that women who surrender their virginity before marriage, or who pet to orgasm, prove "bad" or "whorish" and that in no circumstances should they marry such females. Even a minority of intelligent, college-level males believe this claptrap. And noting or sensing that they believe it, the females who go out with them naturally stay far away from sex intimacy, rather than risk the censure of this type of fascist-minded fellow.

All this, peculiarly enough, makes it relatively easy for the truly

110

liberal-minded male to persuade most intelligent and educated fe-males in our society. For if such a free-thinking person thoroughly feels that chastity does *not* constitute a good state, that he would *never* marry a virgin, and that a woman who remains sexually "pure" has something of a hole in her head, he will more likely get his female companions to bed than if he has the opposite set of beliefs.

A host of modern commentators, have shown that people today accept premarital and extramarital sex far more than they did a few decades ago. Good! Why should you and your partner stay in the sexual dark ages?

Psychological Techniques of Persuasion

The art of sexual persuasion today largely consists of the art of believing, as wholeheartedly as you can, that voluntarily entered sex relations remain good, right, and proper in virtually all circum-stances and that a woman's refraining from sex hardly proves admi-rable, sensible, or respectable. You'd better not only feel sex good at certain special times—as when people get married or engaged or fall in love—but sincerely feel it good in its own right, whether or not these other conditions exist.

Let me emphasize, again, the importance of your really believing in the goodness of sex and of holding this belief thoroughly and unconsciously, as well as in the top layer of your consciousness. For if you merely pretend to yourself and your female companion that you think sex great and that you have no negative feelings toward women who participate honestly and actively in it, you will sooner or later communicate your feelings to your companion, and she will usually tend to feel guilty about what she does with you and to with-draw from you sexually.

How can you acquire a truly open-minded attitude about sex, if you don't really have such an attitude right now? By thinking—and thinking quite hard and long. For if you do think hard, instead of parroting the views and feelings of others around you, you will soon see that, when mutually entered into and cooperatively carried out, sex almost always brings more good than harm.

You or your partner can certainly *make mistakes* sexually. You can, for example, have intercourse with a person whom you don't love and thereby relatively waste your time. Or you can carelessly have sex relations leading to unwanted pregnancy. Or you can enter into an adulterous relationship that involves inconvenient (and occasionally even illegal) complications. But such sexual mistakes remain precisely and only that—mistakes. They do not amount to horrors or acts of unalloyed wickedness.

Otherwise stated: The sexual aspect, *itself,* of a given mode of behavior never makes it wrong or mistaken—only the stupid or unthinking *way* in which you perform this behavior may prove wrong. Thus, your act of copulation doesn't cause harm when you screw promiscuously—for you may well find that act, in itself, quite enjoyable and good. Your manner of performing intercourse, however, may lead to self-defeat, because it may preclude your having *more* sex-love satisfaction on a selective basis. Promiscuity, moreover, can prove just as unwise nonsexually as sexually. Thus, your promiscuously accepting jobs that you do not really enjoy (but that perhaps temporarily pay well) or your promiscuously remaining friendly with males with whom you have little in common seems just as senseless as your promiscuously having sex with women.

By the same token, *you,* as a person, never rate as bad, no matter how mistaken your sex acts. If you get women pregnant, your *behavior* certainly seems stupid and antisocial. But *you* cannot legitimately get labeled as hopelessly stupid or antisocial, since, as a result of this experience, you may change tomorrow and most scrupulously employ contraceptive techniques. Similarly, if your companion lies to you about some significant aspect of her life, you can view her *behavior* as reprehensible but not legitimately view *her* as louse or a no-goodnik because of this behavior. Next month, particularly if you try to help her get less disturbed and more reliable, she may behave very truthfully.

To see sex sanely, try to view sexual acts in exactly the same light as you would view nonsexual affairs. Don't condemn a woman for erotic inexperience or fickleness any more than you would damn her for inexperience in business or unreliability. Preferably, don't blame *her* at all, even though you may consider many of her *acts* unwise or mistaken. If you take *this* kind of an objective, unblaming attitude toward sex and toward women, they will tend to view you as one man out of hundred, one who will have a rare advantage when it comes to getting them to bed.

The second attitude to cultivate for successful relations with women consists in respecting them as *persons*, rather than just as bodies. Not that you have to give up frankly admiring the female form. As Hugh Hefner has noted, if God exists, He would have created the beautiful female form, as well as everything else in the world. So why see feminine pulchritude and sexiness as instruments of the devil? Female breasts and hips and thighs and genitalia appear good—damned good! Let's have no nonsense about this.

But few women, and particularly few intelligent women, like your viewing them *only* or *mainly* as fleshpots. They also want acceptance for what they consider *themselves:* for their interests, their attitudes, their conversation, their companionship, their lovingness, etc. And most of them often resent the male who wants *only* to get them to bed, and then quickly turns over and goes to sleep or gets up and leaves.

You generally find the way to the female form, therefore, through the heart and the mind. You usually have to please the *woman* rather than merely arouse her physically. And very often, you'd better get her to like your general personality and not merely to dote on your looks or appreciate your sex technique. This does not mean that every female you meet has to love you madly and think that you truly feel enamored of her, before she will let you undo her underpants. Most of the time, you can honestly let her know that you don't intend to sacrifice your life for her, and she will willingly pet heavily with you or go still further. For she knows full well, in many instances, that she doesn't feel deeply moved by you, either, and that perhaps if both of you do enjoy sex greatly, a more lasting and deeper involvement will spring up. Possibly she even knows that she will never love you, nor you her, but she does find you sufficiently attractive to give her a few hours of sex pleasure, and only that interests her at this moment.

Nevertheless!—even the highly sexed, quickly bedded woman usually wants you to *like* her, *enjoy* her, feel *friendly* to her. And the faster she discovers that you really *do* have some nonsexual as well as sexual interest in her, the faster she will tend to think of you as a potential sex partner. You won't, of course, *always* find this true. Some females actually seem to want to take lovers in whom they have no nonsexual and only sexual interest in them. But these women remain very few and far between.

In addition to finding you interested in them, most females want to feel nonsexually interested in *you* before they engage in sexual intimacies. I have often found that two or three hours of showing a woman how well I can converse, of confiding various things about myself to her, and of acting my unconstrained *self,* will make her more sexually receptive than any amount of properly applied sexual technique. But again, not always. In some instances *no* amount of conversation will do the trick, and *only* making sexual overtures to a woman, and finally arousing her physically, will tip the scales in your direction. But more times than not, you will have to *talk* the bright, sophisticated female into feeling receptive—not necessarily by direct persuasion, but by indirect conversation, which may have little or nothing to do with sex.

Not that direct persuasion itself proves useless. Frequently, no! Literally millions of women today seem to *want* to get persuaded to jump into bed with their male companions. They think that they can *probably* have intercourse with a male whom they know only slightly, but they don't quite feel sure of what he will think of them in case they do. Therefore, they require that he give them a good many reasons why they'd better go to bed with him and why he will *not* despise them afterward. They may have heard all these reasons before, and even largely believe them before he begins to recite them. But they still want him to reassure them that they can rightly let him explore their genitalia.

You can even persuade many women who *don't* want to get talked into having sex. Some have exceptionally poor reasons for not indulging, and you can logically undermine such reasons. Females may believe, for example, that you will look down on them after intercourse, that you will not use proper contraceptive methods, that you would never marry a nonvirgin, that most women today do not have premarital sex relations, and so on. Unhesitatingly try to rip up such mistaken views!

Not only will this kind of persuasion help you to have sex at any given time, but it will likely make it easier for you to have it on succeeding occasions. Physical methods of approach, on the other hand, may work only temporarily, since a highly aroused woman may copulate with you now, but may build up all kinds of resistances to repeating this performance later.

Calm, consistent, forceful depropagandization, on the other hand, usually has a much deeper and longer-lasting effect. It has a more generalized result, as well, for the woman you persuade to think well of sex today will often remain a more willing bedmate for some other fellow tomorrow. Likewise, the person he persuades or unbrainwashes when he sees her will tend to have liberal attitudes and behavior when you see her. The more you employ straightforward and sincere counterpropaganda against puritanism, therefore, the more you help to make the general female culture more sexually liberal.

Will the line work that you want to have sex relations with a woman for *her* good? Very rarely—for you damned well lie. You may want to help a woman out sexually, particularly if she senselessly hangs on to her virginity, to her own physical and emotional detriment. But let's face it—you hardly have that as the *only* reason why you want to roll her in the hay, and you may as well admit this. Acknowledge that you expect to enjoy sex with her immensely and that *you* want it for your own pleasure. But you can indicate that you want to see her enjoy herself, too. Then she won't see you as hypocritical.

What verbal line can you best use for persuading a woman to have sex? Generally, no "line" at all. Give her, if you will, all the sane and sober arguments you can muster, but give her arguments in which you truly believe, not ones you have merely dreamed up for this occasion, for this "victory."

Don't tell her, for example, that you simply can't stand not having sex with her and that you'll turn into a mental and physical wreck if you don't. Tell her, more honestly, that you will *dislike* the discomfort of her not giving in to you sexually, but you'll still bear it and live. And don't tell her that every woman you know goes to bed very easily with guys, when they don't. Tell her instead that, of the females you know who let down the sex barriers, almost all of them soon have a ball and lose their guilt feelings, whereas most of those who continue sexually constrained have indefinitely prolonged conflicts and dissatisfactions. Try to convince her, not that she *must* suffer if she remains virginal, but merely that she *probably* will.

As one of the best persuasive methods for getting a woman to go farther sexually than she originally intends, convince her that you don't necessarily want her to have actual intercourse with you but that you want her to have some form of mutually satisfying relations that will result in orgasm for both of you. Most women in our society remain infinitely more afraid of intercourse than of any other form of sex—and with at least some reason, since they can get pregnant through intercourse. Moreover, they fear that intercourse will prove painful, that they will fail at it, that it will seem messy, that it will mean technical loss of virginity, etc. So much gets made of this *special* act in our culture (and in most other cultures) that literally millions of females will fairly willingly do everything *except* intercourse.

Many others, moreover, have actually tried penile-vaginal copulation and found it unsatisfying. It often remains less enjoyable for these females and less inducive to orgasm than various other methods of sex. The so-called vaginal orgasm in a woman seems largely a myth, and many females find that they can more easily attain full climax by extravaginal methods (particularly by manipulation of the clitoral area) than by intercourse.

You can easily see, then, why females who hesitate to have coitus will not hestitate half so much to pet to orgasm. And if you, as a woman's potential lover, will convince her that you do not necessarily require intercourse and that you do want to satisfy her and yourself by noncoital methods, you have a much better chance to induce her to engage in sexual intimacies with you. Moreover, once you start petting heavily, she may later change her mind and decide that she does want to copulate. Further, if she does not want actual intercourse, you can fully satisfy her and yourself if you get rid of your prejudices about the sancity of intercourse and if you try almost everything in the book *except* penile-vaginal congress.

The rest of the art of sexual persuasion, from a verbal standpoint, largely equals the art of conversation and friendship. Hundreds of books have been written in this connection—such as Dale Carnegie's *How to Win Friends and Influence People*—and I'd strongly advise you to look over some of these writings and put them to good use. Also read *The Art of Erotic Seduction*, which I wrote with Roger O. Conway and which has helped large numbers of males to get going strongly for themselves and for the women they want to go to bed with. The usual kind of seduction, we point out in this book, shows little real consideration for a woman and has many serious disadvantages for her and for you. We therefore recommend what we call modified seduction, which we define as: the process of persuading an initially unwilling female to engage in sexual activity (not necessarily intercourse) for the purposes of (1) your own immediate and future enjoyment with her; (2) her sex-love satisfaction; and (3) the hope that she will get so fulfilled by having an affair with you that she will have a more positive attitude toward sex and feel eager to seek it on her own initiative (with you or other males) in the future.

This form of seduction, as you will note, not only proves useful and beneficial with a new woman whom you may encounter, but you may satisfactorily employ it with one with whom you have previously had sex but who may now feel reluctant to continue having it. You may also employ it with a regular sweetheart, fiancée, or mate who appears sexually reluctant from time to time.

Conforming to this definition, Roger Conway and I point out some basic seduction dos and don'ts. Among the dos, we think that you, as a male, had better attract favorable attention from females whom you want to seduce, show very definite interest in them as people, deal with them quite gently and patiently, do your best to minimize the sex antagonism that frequently exists between men and women (and that women's liberationists accurately tend to emphasize), try to behave as helpfully as you can toward your potential sex partners, and gain as much knowledge as you can about yourself, about women, and about sex.

Among the don'ts of modified seduction, Conway and I indicate that you would better not try to seduce an incompetent or inadequate woman, behave dishonestly or break a trust, use any degree of force or threats of force, buy sex with words of love that you do not mean, use a "line," act judgmental, go by your preconceptions of whether a woman will or will not go to bed with you, overcautiously try to avoid getting emotionally involved with a woman, or think that you have to live with or marry a woman who has treated you well sexually or proves great in the saddle.

Let me give a few more preliminary rules about trying to get a female into bed.

1. Don't behave compulsively about fucking. It won't kill you if you don't go to bed with a woman quickly; at worst, you'll only find

it frustrating. Many women, these days, will help you to get an orgasm in some way or other when they see that your cock goes up. But even if they don't, you'll merely suffer some real inconvenience. If you insist on getting to first base, not to mention home plate, fast, your partner will see that you have extremely low frustration tolerance, that you will probably show it in many other ways as you continue the relationship with her, and that she needs to get close to a baby like you about as much as she needs a pet gorilla.

Certainly, if you want to do so, let her know that you have an erection and that you would feel much better, physically and psychologically, if she helped you come to orgasm. But you don't *have* to! Your prick won't fall off if it doesn't spurt its load into her hand, mouth, or vagina. And don't forget—if necessary, you can always masturbate.

2. Go easy on trying to induce guilt in a partner who does not satisfy you sexually. Many females will feel obliged to have sex with you if you point out how much you will suffer from not having it. Trying to invoke guilt in them will therefore get you somewhere—this time. But will you really find this worth it? Emotionally blackmailing a date to spread her legs when she really doesn't want to may easily boomerang and help you get what you immediately want at the expense of ruining the future relationship, and maybe especially the future sex, with her. Watch your short-range hedonism in this respect!

3. Also, watch your goddamned ego! If you *must* have a woman quickly and feel glorious about the conquest when you do, that usually means that you have an ego problem—that you only accept yourself and consider yourself worthy of living and enjoying *when* you succeed at something, such as getting sexual favors. How, may I ask, does *that* make you a worthwhile or noble person? It doesn't! If you *want* to get to bed with a woman quickly and you feel quite *disappointed* or *sorry* when you don't, fine. But if you've *got* to make it bedwise on the first night and you feel *awful* and *downed* when you fail, watch it! You have made the game of *rating yourself* important and vital; and sooner, rather than later, you'll probably put yourself down for failing at sex or something else.

4. As noted, women screw best when they *want* you sexually. Oddly enough, most of them want you sexually for nonsexual rea-

sons. When aroused, they feel charmed by *you*—by your talk, your manner, your intelligence, your consideration, your interest in them. Even when sexually excited, they frequently won't do much about it unless they feel that they want *you*. And even when unaroused, they will often give you the greatest time in the world sexually when they like you nonsexually and think that you make a good companion or friend.

Don't go by your own feelings in this respect. As the old saying goes, "A stiff prick has no conscience." You would probably screw a gnu if your cock went up in its presence. But not most of your female companions! To get them to bed, therefore, you'd better try to win *them* and not merely their genitalia.

5. Consider carefully whether you will play the dumping-on-women game. Various authorities on sex, such as Will Harvey and James Dean, not to mention Casanova, have claimed that if you throw women off-balance and show them that you really *don't* care for them and that they hardly seem worthy of kissing your feet, they will frequently deify you.

Unfortunately, this often proves true. The worse you treat certain females, the more their dire need for your love increases and the more they will do virtually anything, including sexual things they really don't want to do, to keep you around. Therefore, Dean dogmatically concludes: "WOMEN NEED TO [GET] DUMPED ON. . . . I'd *love* to treat them as equals, demanding nothing that I did not also give, affording them the same courtesies I want afforded me. No way. They [prove] incapable of accepting parity. They must [get] manipulated and maneuvered, played upon like violins, treated constantly as the emotionally immature creatures that they [remain]."

True? Partly. Loads of self-denigrating, disturbed women fit this category, and if you look, you can easily find them. But personally, I'd advise you not to look. For when you do dump on women and they come through for you, they also strongly tend to: (1) remain overdemanding and desperate about getting and keeping your approval; (2) feel terribly angry, as well as self-hating, when you don't give them exactly what they want in return for sex favors; (3) fail to enjoy sex-love relations in their own right, but "enjoy" them mainly as part of the I've-got-to-prove-that-I-don't-rate-as-a-shit process; (4) give you (and your children by them, if you foolishly have a family with them) a continual pain in the ass in many ways; (5) in one way or another make your total relationship with them hardly worth the sex that they "give" you.

So dump on women, if you wish, in order to get them to screw you and love you. But you would much more wisely either look for those females who really accept themselves and who therefore go with you for enjoyment, rather than for ego boosting; or else choose one of the nuttier ones and help her (perhaps by encouraging her to get rational-emotive therapy!) to come to her senses and give up her dire need for approval.

6. Again as noted previously, before you make any serious passes at a woman, try to get to know something about her sex-love experiences and attitudes. Arousing her sexually, so that she balls you in spite of her basic views, may often work. But unless you seem interested only in a one-night stand, this game hardly proves worth the candle. For after she gives you her greatest favors—and I mean *favors*—she frequently tends to feel terribly guilty, thinks that she has to fall madly in love with you to show herself that she's done the right thing, demands return favors of an onerous nature, hates your guts, or otherwise tends to ruin your and her future relations. Therefore: find out her basic attitudes first and act accordingly. Either forget her because you discover that she will almost certainly turn out a DC (difficult customer) or persuade her to change some of her basic negative sex-love attitudes before you start tickling her clit.

7. Will sexual action itself help depropagandize a woman against her existing antisexual views? Often, yes. Especially if she has retained her virginity thus far and you somehow (perhaps with the help of some alcohol) get her to surrender it, many of her prior blocks against sex may suddenly vanish. Kinsey and his associates found, a good many years ago, that women who have premarital sex frequently do *not* feel guilty or ashamed after having it and make quick adjustments to their nonvirginal condition. This probably occurs because they overemphasize the desirability of chastity or the horror of intercourse in the first place, and they soon see, after a single night in bed with a suitable male, that nothing terrible happened to them and they still remain the same kind of person they felt like in their virginal state.

So sometimes you can take a chance on having sex with a reluctant woman with the hope that she will change some of her basic antisexual values *after* she has received some warmth and physical satisfaction. In this case, you'd better go out of your way to see that she does enjoy herself in bed and that you treat her nicely before, during, and after having sex with her. Particularly, in this instance, if you later show her that you still like her very much, that you have lost no respect for her whatever, that she can now have an even better life than before, and that she has gained rather than lost by this new experience, her attitudes may change remarkably for the better. However, this depends largely on her vulnerability to disturbance. Fairly healthy women will tend to accept themselves and the enjoyment of life to an even greater extent when they have had premarital sex. Fairly nutty women may not! Don't think that all your bedmates will emerge in the same category in this respect.

8. Shall you tell the truth and nothing but the truth about your own sexual experience and prowess when you try to have sex with a woman? That depends on various conditions. Most women will not wax enthusiastic about your inexperience and ineptness but will prefer a partner who at least knows what to do to satisfy them sexually—and preferably one who will teach them a thing or two. So the more you indicate that you know the ropes sexually, the easier you may find it to bed them.

Inexperience, however, also may prove advantageous. A woman with little knowledge herself, and with great fears that she will fail sexually, may feel relieved if you know just about as little as she does—just as a fifteen-year-old female on her first date may feel confortable with a sixteen-year-old companion who has also had little dating experience. At the same time, however, an experienced woman (including an older or a married woman) may delight in showing you the sexual ropes if she knows that you have had practically no prior activity yourself and will willingly learn.

In general, when you have had little sex practice at least cram up on a reasonable amount of theory. Read some modern sex manuals (such as my own *Art and Science of Love* and Alex Comfort's *The Joy of Sex* and *More Joy*). And once you get into bed with a woman, don't pretend that you know everything when you really know very little. Admit your inexperience and your possible errors. But let her know that you have the ability to learn fast!

9. As ever, don't exaggerate to yourself the disadvantages of failing—of failing to get anywhere with a woman, failing to get her to ball, failing to continue the relationship. So you may easily fail—tough! But never *awful,* near *catastrophic.* No matter how desirable this particular woman may seem to you, remember that she remains only *one* individual out of many possibilities. Sure, you will find it sad and regrettable if she thinks you a poor lover. Certainly, you won't like it if she never wants to see you again. But her refusal won't mean the end of your world, and you may even learn a lot by it. Try, therefore, as you talk to her and make passes at her, to enjoy and act yourself—and not to *prove* yourself. If you fail, you fail. But at least you can open your mouth, get closer to her if you can, and give yourself an honest try!

You may find some more tips on the art of arousing and sexually persuading a woman in *The Art of Erotic Seduction.* Again, we point out in the book that you had better go for modified seduction, so that the woman you want to lay will highly enjoy the process herself, will thereafter view it in a good light, and will feel more inclined than ever to repeat it with you and with other males. Not that you have to act as a humanitarian in this connection. But in your own self-interest, remember that if you help women to enjoy sex-love relations *generally,* and not merely with you, they will feel better about this kind of activity, will propagandize their women friends to engage in it more, will help show males how it can lead to good results, and will thereby help to create the kind of a society in which more people ball zestfully. This, naturally, will make things easier for you and probably get you into many more women's beds than otherwise. Just as you would like your society to include more political, economic, and philosophic liberals, if liberalism or libertarianism sends you, why should you not try to help promote sexual permissiveness?

Some additional rules for making things physically easier for you to have sex with women of your choice:

1. Read the chapter in this book on the sexuality of women. Although we now know that women, in thought, fantasy, and action, hardly turn out significantly less sexual than men, some significant differences in these respects still hold true. Find out what

most women tend to want sexually, and since individual differences in this area abound, find out what *this* particular woman in whom you have interest really wants—and doesn't!

2. Don't give up too easily! This doesn't mean that if you persist long enough, every woman you try to have sex with will give in and finally enjoy herself immensely. False! But lots of females require a long time to warm up sexually; and many of them take even longer than they normally would, because they don't want to put their partners to too much trouble and would rather stop themselves short before they get males to make too much effort on their behalfs. Persist, then! And show your partner that you really don't mind going to a good deal of trouble to arouse and satisfy her.

3. At the same time, don't *demand* female arousal or orgasm. I have seen hundreds of women who have got turned off to sex mainly because their lovers or husbands insist, for egoistic reasons, that they get completely excited and satisfied. These women rarely rise to great sexual heights or do so only periodically, at certain times during their menstrual cycles, or require special conditions to reach the peaks of desire and fulfillment. If they think that their mates *must* have them perform "adequately," they intently monitor themselves, worry endlessly about how long it takes them to come, and seriously interfere with their own satisfaction. So don't *require* full arousal and world-shattering climaxes from your partner. If she can have this, fine; if not, she may still distinctly enjoy sex and highly enjoy your enjoyment of it. Behave reasonably in this connection!

4. Sometimes, move onward from one sex phase to another, even if your partner seems to lag somewhat behind. Usually, if she likes kissing, you can go on to breast manipulation; if she likes that, reach for her genitalia; and so on. But sometimes you could wait forever to "naturally" progress from one stage to another. And your politeness won't get either of you anywhere! So as long as she doesn't seriously object to what you do, you had better go on to the next step, then the next—until you end up, probably, with intercourse. If her genitalia give off a real moistness during your trying to get her aroused, fine. But not necessary! Sometimes she just doesn't lubricate copiously no matter how aroused she may feel. And sometimes she does so only *during* intercourse, but hardly before that.

5. A good general rule—go as far as you can go, without

unpleasantly forcing her to do anything. Even if, today, you go too far and get to her genitalia when she'd rather you not do so, don't think that you have made a fatal error. On the contrary, just because she let you do this much today, she may much more easily let you do as much or more tomorrow. Left to her own devices, she will frequently do much less than you—and she—would really like. If you push and force things a little, she may later feel very happy that you did.

6. This particularly goes for intercourse itself, in many instances. A woman will frequently pet for hours—and for days, weeks, or months on end—without seeming to want to go beyond that. But once your cock enters her vagina, she may really start grooving on the intercourse that she previously could easily live without. And whether she does or not, she may well assume it as one of the facts of your sex life with her—and after a number of times she may consider coitus fabulous. So don't think that she has to *want* it to enjoy it. Even after you have gone together for months or years, your starting to copulate with her may often *make her* enjoy it and later want to "submit" to it. Assertiveness on your part may therefore help. Your going in may help bring her out!

7. Women differ enormously, especially in their sexual readiness. Dean divides them into several major categories: (1) those who honestly dig sex; (2) those who would like to develop into Honest Diggers but who now merely remain experimental Students of Sex; (3) those (whom he considers the majority of the female populace) whom you can look upon as Sexual Barterers—those who really want love, money, attention, status, or something else but who will willingly give sex for what they want; and (4) those who have hangups about sex (or who enjoy it but feel guilty about their enjoyment).

You may, from your own experience, add to these categories or refine them. Anyway, a woman in one group hardly responds the same way as a woman in one of the other groups. You can often, for example, get to bed with an Honest Digger by showing her that you honestly dig her and by getting to her hot box as quickly as possible and arousing her and bringing her to orgasm. For one of the Sexual Barterers, on the other hand, who really couldn't care less for sex but wants you to love her madly or to keep entertaining her every Saturday night, your honest technique can work quite differently. Merely show her that if she wants what she wants from you, you'd better get what you want from her—sex. For one of the sexually hung-up women, hours or days of therapeutic conversation may have to take place before you get to her nether regions. And then you may have to go through hours or days of post-sex therapy!

So get information and try to judge whether the woman you want fills the EC (easy customer) or DC (difficult customer) bill. If the former, great. If the latter, you may not even want to bother. DCs can certainly prove most interesting and give you a thrilling game. But how much time and energy have you available for the depropagandization they usually require? Make some overt and careful hedonic calculations in this regard!

8. Can you use other tests or signs to predict how much trouble you will have in engaging in a full-blown sex-love relationship with a woman? Will Harvey, in *How to Find and Fascinate a Mistress,* recommends what he calls the SYNAM (*So You Need A Man*) test. A woman presumably passes this test if you discover that (1) she has had, or now has, a teenage lover or one who behaves like a teenager; (2) she has decided against marriage and a family for the next two years; (3) she enjoys the mental and physical comforts of a man but fears the hangups of a heavy relationship; and (4) she feels she has to experience more sexually than she's experienced so far.

I don't doubt that many or most women who would pass this test might well make themselves available to you sexually, particularly for an ongoing relationship. But many who do not pass it would also prove quite eligible. When I think of all the long-term sex-love relations I have had with women, I find that most of the females I had them with flouted some or all of Harvey's requirements. Few of them had teenage lovers or some reasonable facsimile thereof; many of them had not decided against marriage and a family for the next two years (though they usually did not feel desperate to enter such relationships); few of them feared the hangup of a heavy relationship; and most of them had already experienced great sex relationships and looked forward to something equally good, but not necessarily better, in the future. So there! Harvey's SYNAM test may have its advantages, but don't view it too seriously.

9. Another way of categorizing women you want to have intimate relationships with consists in determining whether they date males mainly for recreational and companionship purposes or for mate selection. Many women fit into one of these categories at some time in their lives—particularly when they remain young—and in the other category at a different time. The two groups may give highly different sexual responses.

Thus, a woman who dates you mainly for recreation and companionship frequently assumes, that you will engage in sexual intimacy, especially if you keep seeing each other. She may well want it herself; and even if she doesn't, she knows that you do and that you will hardly keep seeing her if you don't find some kind of sex satisfaction. But a woman who dates you mainly for mate seeking may either deliberately avoid sex, because she fears that you will not respect her as a future mate or that you will get what you want without marriage if she goes to bed with you; or she may eagerly have sex, all right, but much more to convince you that she would make a good wife than to enjoy the sex itself.

With the first type of woman, you will tend to have few sex problems, but with the second type, you may have many, and you may even decide not to have sex, lest you lead her on to thinking of you seriously as a prospective mate when you have no intentions in this direction.

Physical Techniques of Persuasion

If a woman refuses even minor contact, such as hand holding and good-night kissing, consider something awry. Either she just does not care for you physically or she has some problem that interferes with intimacy with almost any man, including you. In either of these cases, you may wisely conclude that the hassle doesn't merit your efforts and that you'd better peddle your amorousness elsewhere.

Assuming that she seems fairly normal and has no known bias against you, often make *some* kind of physical advance early in the relationship. Hold her arm on the street. Take her hand in the movies. Put your arm around her when sitting together on a sofa. Try to kiss her good night when you leave. Sound her out physically, to see how she responds.

Don't, incidentally, *ask* her whether you can hold or kiss her, since she will often, for the sake of propriety, say no. Rarely say, "May I kiss you good night?" Kiss her! Don't ask, "May I take your arm?" Take it!

As soon as you make contact, carefully observe her response. When you hold her hand in the movies, does she let her own hand rest limply, lifelessly in yours and perhaps pull hers away after a short while? Or does she warmly press your hand and almost pull it off your arm? Does she snuggle up against you closely, when you place your arm around her? Or does she lean forward in her seat and somehow manage to slip away? If she seems cooperative, try to go further. If she seems uncooperative or neutral, you may wisely withdraw for a later attempt.

In any event, *watch* your partner's responses and responsiveness! Don't barge ahead blindly, assuming that she will go along with you, just because she does not kick or bite. For even if she does not resist, she may give in grudgingly and without enjoyments and you will get your "way" while really getting nothing.

Aim for a *warm* responsiveness. As females turn on, you can often literally *feel* them warming up—a kind of heat radiates from their bodies, their skin becomes flushed, and their breathing quickens. Look for and guide yourself by these signs. If entirely absent, it usually means that your date remains unready for further approaches —though she may, of course, constitute an exception to this rule.

From the first time you make any passes at your woman friend —which may well fall on the first day you meet her—try to go as far as you can. Why? Well, first, she may let you go all the way right at the start. Second, the farther you get this time, the farther you may well get the next. So keep progressing, if you can!

Starting with kissing, hand holding, and light embracing, go on, after a reasonable amount of time, to much firmer and deeper kissing and embracing. If she responds in kind, go the full gamut—including French kissing, with your mouths wide open, your tongue playing madly on her lips, jutting into her mouth; with your teeth and lips deeply enmeshed with her lips, tongue, and mouth, and nipping fiercely at various other parts of her body.

The same thing goes for your embraces. Starting lightly, let them get firmer and more impassioned. If she permits, press her close to you and vigorously massage her face, neck, and body with your incessantly moving hands, gently and sensuously kneading your fingertips on every square inch of her exposed surfaces. Use your hands to loosen her clothing and to get as much of her body bare as you can. Deftness and speed often pay off in this regard, because once you have fully bared a woman's breasts, taken off her skirt, or removed her undergarments, she probably won't immediately get up and cover herself again.

Feeling that she has got sort of unmasked, and that you still continue passionately to kiss and caress her, she frequently accepts the inevitable and may even volunteer to take off some more of her own clothes. But don't, normally, *ask* her to undress herself. Do it for her! And do it firmly, vigorously, in spite of some resistance on her part. Show her you feel determined to have her as nude as possible, even though you will not literally rip the clothes off her back and rape her.

Mind you, now, in this undressing process, you keep doing *two* things (at least!)—kissing and embracing her intently and getting to her skin. Don't just go about the second of these tasks while neglecting the first, since she then often remains undistracted enough to resist your divesting her. Moreover, you don't have to remove all her garments while making love. Frequently, even when her clothes remain on technically, you can get to her skin with your lips, and especially with your hands.

Thus, you can slip your hands underneath her brassiere or down the top of it, without literally removing it. And you can get to a woman's genital region without removing her skirt, slip, or underpants. If you insist on staying your attempts to get at her breasts or genitalia by fully undressing her, you will frequently defeat your amorous ends, for she will then forcibly stop you from going farther, and that will end that. If, on the other hand, you get to her vital erotic zones while her clothes still mainly cover her and you massage and kiss these zones effectively until she gets truly aroused, she will *then* often offer little resistance to taking off her clothes completely.

In all kissing, caressing, and massaging, make sure that you constantly indicate that you remain intent on pleasing *her*, not merely yourself. If she thinks that you want only to rip off her garments so that *you* can insert your penis into her vagina and have your *own* delicious orgasm, she will often show no enthusiasm. But if she can plainly see that whether or not you get satisfied that evening you seem bent on pleasing her and bringing her to the best of orgasms, she will more probably render herself cooperative. Arousing *her* remains the main issue, whatever your own state of desire and wish for ultimate fulfillment.

Because of the advisability of showing your partner your absorption in her pleasure, do relatively little about baring your own body until she gets pretty well denuded. Don't think, with peculiarly masculine arrogance, that she will get a terrific thrill by seeing your naked torso or the size and contours of your sacred genitalia. Most probably, she won't. Females much less often get excited by the sight of the male body than males do by the sight of female charms. So keep yourself out of the picture at first, and don't, for a while, expect her to do anything special to satisfy *you*.

If she spontaneously does give you bodily tit for tat and kisses and caresses you in virtually every region, you have really hit the jackpot. But this kind of behavior when you first go to bed with a woman rarely occurs. Much more commonly, she will do little more than kiss you on the lips or hold you tightly to her. Very frequently, she will not give a hoot for your satisfaction and will let you do practically anything to satisfy her, with little or no reciprocation. No matter. At this stage of the game you can well bear this lack of reciprocity and not resent it. Much later, after you have really shown her your great talent as a lover, you can indicate that you, *too*, would like satisfaction.

Even in this respect, actions often speak louder and better than words. Don't make the mistake of saying to your friend, once you have shown her how pleasurable sex can feel, "Will you please hold me here or kiss me there?" Like as not, she will shyly or resentfully or lackadaisically refuse. Instead, firmly but not ungently *put* her hand or lips where you prefer and help them make the motions you want. This kind of request she will less likely deny; and she may see that she enjoys a sex act, such as oral-genital relations, that she would previously have believed she never could enjoy and that she would have balked at had you verbally asked her to try.

Don't make the mistake of forcibly attempting intercourse with your woman too early in the game, just because she appears quite aroused—and because you know full well that *you* feel sufficiently hot to copulate with an orangutan! There exists no reason why, the first time you approach a date, she *has* to have coitus, and you'll frequently find it better for future relations if you never *do* get around to penile-vaginal intercourse.

What I have just said about kissing, embracing, and petting remains a bare (no pun intended!) outline. I could easily take an entire book to fill in the relevant details. Later, I shall give some of these details in chapters on petting and bedmanship. The main thing to emphasize here—discretion does *not* usually prove the better part of valor in making the first overtures. As noted above, you hold back from going too fast or too far at the outset; however, don't unwisely refrain from trying at all!

Take some risks. Try and in some measure keep trying—if just to *see* how and where you fail. As long as you keep trying, you can correct many erroneous details, since you learn by trial and error, and the more errors you make, the more you can see what *not* to do next time.

You can talk your goddamned head off with a woman, and she may seem highly receptive to your going farther than just plain talk. But she will rarely make actual physical overtures herself. Even if she wants to make them, she may feel deathly afraid of how *you* will react if she does. She may think it too soon. Or she may think you will deem her overassertive. Or she may feel that you will get the wrong ideas about her sexiness and mistake her affection for imperious sexuality. Or she may believe that you want to take the "manly" prerogative and make the first passes yourself.

So don't wait for her! Normally, make the first physical approach yourself. How? Well, an unpublished manuscript by N. D. Mallary, Jr., of Atlanta, Georgia, who has written a long epistle to his son, "On Sex and Making Love," contains some excellent ideas about approaching a woman sexually. Although Mr. Mallary's pointers may not serve you at all times in all conditions, his views on approaching kissing and other forms of sex stimulation contain some excellent advice. Listen to this:

> Now, since most men wait till they park to try to kiss—you want to change that. Of many techniques, I'll illustrate a few.

1. *The car exit approach*. No woman expects a man in his right mind to kiss on a public thoroughfare. Fine! Do just that! You take her to supper on the second night. You park. You go around to open the door. As she puts her feet on the ground her head remains down. Judge the distance accurately and arrange to have your lips poised when she looks up. Then kiss her. Do it gracefully and exert care not to bump mouths. Do it gently and don't hold it. Don't hug her. Dart in and out but make it good while you stay there. This gives you the opportunity to verbalize the "goodness" of the kiss (at the right time and place) and simply proceed to kiss her again.

2. *The standing approach*. (a) Sudden. You walk her to the car (or anywhere else). You take her upper arms in each of your hands. Her head remains down or level. You hold her with "restrained intensity" (but really very gently) and mutter some sentimentality—only part of which she catches. You know she will look up. As she looks up you move down such that your lips meet. She'll never know what hit her. (b) Gradual (same circumstances and position as above). With a sudden flood of "controlled intensity" you start kissing her hairline—lightly with loose lips. Pluck gently at her skin and hair. Make the movements of the tickling kind apt to produce goose bumps. Sooner or later she will turn her face up. Kiss down her face until you reach her lips. If she never turns her face up—back off. You have lost nothing.

3. *The stop-light approach*. (a) You stop for a light. Start to reach in the glove compartment, stop midway, put your left hand on her jawbone and kiss her. (b) Use the hairline approach at one light and take it to the lips at the next.

4. *Drive-in or hamburger approach*. Note: Almost everyone has sensitive skin. Almost everyone can get goose bumps. Goose bumps constitute a mild shock and the instant they occur the woman's reflexes get slower. Learn to produce goose bumps and to judge the exact instant of shock. (a) Tickle the back of her neck. Watch her face. At the instant of shock— kiss. (b) Stroke the hair and face with your *outside* hand on the *outside* of her face. When she gets goose bumps or when she closes her eyes and sighs—pull her gently to you and kiss. (c)

Cradle her face with both your palms. Women frequently interpret this as a "tender" gesture. Hold her eyes with your eyes, hold her face until you feel her body relax, throw in an intimate remark, then gently kiss her. (d) The Happy Warrior. Here you share a joke and both laugh. Reach out and cradle her against your shoulder in a spirit of camaraderie. At the split second the laughter stops she will inhale deeply. Place your hand under her chin, coincident with her inhaling, and kiss her in one motion. (e) Pick up her outside hand in your outside hand. Turn it palm up and kiss the palm, first with lips, then with tongue. Holding her hand out from but in front of her face, *start* down the wrist but go directly into her mouth.

5. *The Louise Lift approach.* Pick her up (she will grab you around the neck and giggle), wait until she stops giggling—then kiss her.

As you can see, Mr. Mallary has given careful thought and imagination to the seemingly simple problem of preliminary kissing. Taking a leaf from his book, you too can devise methods of your own. As long as you remain *active* and *undiscouraged,* very little will stop you. With any particular woman, perhaps no technique, no matter how beautifully devised or well executed, may succeed. But in general, the more you try the more you will likely achieve at least partial success.

CHAPTER 6

How to Arouse a Woman: Psychological Methods

OBVIOUSLY, IF YOU want to persuade a new woman to have sex, you had better arouse her—as I have already noted in the chapter on sexual persuasion. But sex arousal has an even greater importance than for seduction purposes, for even a woman who cares for you and has gone to bed with you many times may require renewed urging *this* time. As I showed in the chapter on women's sexuality, females often do not get as easily aroused as males—or do so on some occasions and hardly on others. You may easily find them relatively passive unless you resort to active stimulation, including psychological and physical methods.

In this chapter, let us consider some of the former.

Antisexist Attitudes

Some women, as we shall later note, get turned on by having an assertive, "manly" attitude toward having sex, but this doesn't necessarily mean that they want to feel downed or degraded. More and more, intelligent women want to get treated as individuals in their own right, not merely as sex objects. They want you to respect them as *people* and to enjoy knowing *them* and not mainly their asses and tits. Just as males frequently achieve a Ph.D. in egotism and require an enormous amount of flattery to help them feel truly interested in a woman (and sometimes sexually excited by her), so do women just as frequently require the ego-bolstering game of your paying them strong attention, showing that you have a special interest in them, and placing them paramount in your affections, and not merely your lusts.

So show your partner, if you want her to arouse herself to a maxi-

133

mum pitch, real eagerness to go to bed with *her,* not just because she happens to look and feel female but because she represents *herself.* Wax enthusiastic about her sexual and nonsexual assets and show that you can easily and gladly ignore her liabilities—especially those she puts herself down for having. Actually, if you have developed into a typical sexy male, you could sometimes screw a baby panda, in addition to her, and enjoy it. But maybe you'd better keep quiet about that as you prepare to hop into bed.

Liking and Loving

Indicate to your partner, if you can do so with any reasonable degree of honesty, that you don't merely *want* her but also *like* her —and that you will continue to do so *after* your sex appetites get appeased. This provides one reason for you to stress afterplay—and to show her kindness, consideration, and love subsequent to your achieving orgasm. A caring relationship doesn't have to go with sex, but it certainly helps! It not only aids initial sex experience but often leads to growing compatibility between the partners—as Dr. Robert Harper and I emphasize in *A Guide to Successful Marriage.*

If a single virtue existed, said Lloyd McCorkle, that would in itself make a man a lover, it would consist of tenderness. "In the developed lover, the man who has ceased trying to prove something, tenderness [gets] woven into every phase of his love-making, even the wild violence that sometimes emerges. It carries through as a certain sensitivity to the other, a constant, almost automatic awareness of the delicate structure of the loved one, both physically and psychically, and the terrible nearness brought about through sexual contact."

Dorothy Baruch and Hyman Miller add, "Talking during intercourse can also bring the partners into fuller sharing. Admiring each other's bodies. [Feeling] appreciative of each other's responses. Reiterating love. Recapturing out loud the wonder of [getting] granted these occasions of coming together. For two people never grow too old to relive the gratefulness of having found each other. They never grow too old to renew the sense of sharing that comes with feeling sexually one."

Dr. Ruth Reyna points out that both men and women, but particularly the latter, want more than just "sex" to make themselves feel fulfilled. "When sex gets pursued only for pleasure or gain, it [turns] elusive, impersonal, and ultimately disappointing. Many sensitive persons feel the need to reaffirm the spiritual meaning of sex as the means to a new depth and joy in relationship between husband and wife." Notice that Dr. Reyna here doesn't define "spiritual" in godly or mystical terms, but in terms of the deep relationship between a man and a woman. Even this practical definition of "spiritual" may not move you, since that may just not seem your cup of sex. But if your partner finds it hers, you may wisely lean over backward to provide her with this kind of "spirituality"—if just to enhance her carnality!

I have often stressed the desirability of specific communication between you and your companion if you want to achieve maximum sex compatibility, since neither of you probably has any great mind-reading skill, and *telling* each other your likes and dislikes holds up as the best way of getting what each of you truly wants. As I noted in *The Art and Science of Love,* "No man or woman proves a mind-reader. Even individuals passionately in love frequently misunderstand each other; and husbands and wives certainly do. Your sex proclivities develop so personally and uniquely that another member of the same sex has difficulty understanding them. A member of the other sex, startlingly different from you in many ways, has even greater difficulty. The best way, therefore, to know what sexually arouses and satisfies your mate? In unvarnished English—ask her! And the best way to get your mate to understand what sexually arouses and satisfies you? Tell her!

"Shame, in this connection, seems utterly silly—just as silly as a husband's feeling ashamed to tell his wife that he likes eggs scrambled instead of sunny-side up and then getting angry because, somehow, she does not fathom this. Why the devil should she? And why on earth should he feel ashamed to tell her?

"If, then, you like your sex with the lights on, with music playing, in front of mirrors, rolling on the floor, slow or fast, orally or manually, by land or by sea, for heaven's sake *say* so. And do your very best to discover, by *words* as well as deeds, what your mate likes, too."

Partially following my lead, many other authorities have stressed the importance of down-to-heart, and sometimes ruthlessly honest, communication as an aid to arousability and satisfaction. Dr. Ben Ard, Jr. notes, "I have had to tell many clients that husbands cannot read their wives' minds, that the proverbial 'gleam' in anyone's eye, male or female, may very easily [get] misread or missed entirely. Sexual partners need to talk quite explicitly to each other and tell each other what the nonverbal signs [mean]. But they must not [feel] afraid to use their lips for more than mere kisses, and tell their partners how they want their loving done, as well as when and where."

Conversation, after all, remains the heart of interpersonal relations. Some lovers can continue prolonged silence with each other and still feel fine. But not too many! And yet, as Edward Carpenter pointed out many years ago, we all have limitations in regard to our conversational ability and the amount of repetition that we inevitably employ. Don't, therefore, feel ashamed of using props. The Herrigans, in their book *Loving Free,* show they used a marriage manual to stimulate talk—and kept asking each other what he or she got out of the book and what they could do along the lines they kept reading about. But other kinds of writing can serve too—novels, plays, even books on economics! The more you have to discuss with your partner, the more alive both of you may well feel and that aliveness may lead to sexuality. This doesn't mean that you make every session in bed a full "marriage encounter"—for sometimes you just want to rest, sleep, or hold each other silently. But if you vitalize yourselves by using reading material, a film or TV show that you have seen, or anything else that proves interesting to talk about, you then go back to the kind of courtship pastimes you had when you first met each other. And let's face it—didn't some of them prove highly interesting!

Back to love! If you can work love into your sex acts with others, and they feel a unity with you and themselves as a result of having sex with you, they view their orgasms quite differently than they otherwise would; and, more importantly, they tend to *remember* what has ecstatically occurred, predict that it may well reoccur, and consequently look forward to more sex with you. This kind of remembrance and prediction of future joy really turns them on again.

Aside from your acting in a hostile fashion to your partner, you had better try to help her assert herself more forcefully and vigorously to ask you to do what she would like sexually. Masters and Johnson, in *The Pleasure Bond*, note that our double standard prevents women in our culture from asking for the kind of sex that would bring them the most pleasure; this standard encourages them, in a sense, to act *too* loving and not sufficiently self-interested. To have your mate care for you and look out for your pleasure seems fine; but to have her "lovingly" do so at the expense of not asking you to do *her* thing, leads to her defeating herself—and, in the final analysis, defeating you. Do your best, therefore, to help her assert herself—and forthrightly to ask you for the kind of sex she wants and doesn't want. Help her to feel loving *and* self-accepting; then both of you will tend to benefit!

Considerateness

Considerateness, which doesn't quite mean the same thing as love, comprises the essence of good bed manners. Don't expect your partner utopianly to want exactly the same thing you want. Often she will wish you to hold back when you'd like to rush ahead, or vice versa. Often, too, she will get much more aroused if you vigorously caress her, when you perhaps feel more gentle and tender, or if you monotonously stick to one form of stimulation, when you would prefer a more varied approach. If you show her that you *want* to do what she desires, and rarely to hang her up, she will more likely want what you want, too.

The good lover, as Rhoda Winter Russell indicates, *actively looks for* ways to please his inamorata. Without masochistically surrendering his own pleasures, he really *desires* to find ways to satisfy her, and he *communicates* this. The reason why he does not prove masochistic? Because he realizes that pleasing her also pleases him —directly, because he enjoys giving and satisfying, and indirectly, because he wants her, at various times, to reciprocate and to *want* to please him. Don't forget that in sex we normally remain somewhat at the mercy of another's kindness. So we'd *better* behave encouragingly and kindly ourselves!

Confidence

Perhaps the two main psychological aspects of arousing a woman sexually and helping her *want* to have sex with you consist of displaying a good deal of confidence yourself, in both your sexual and

your general prowess, and showing her that you have great confidence that she can behave competently with you and enjoy herself
immensely. Of the two, you will have difficulty in deciding which to
give the greater importance.

Let us look at the first, having confidence in your own sexual and
general ability. Right off the bat here, let me make clear that I do
not mean what we usually call self-confidence. Self-confidence consists of a concept that we now try to avoid in rational-emotive therapy (RET) because it implies certain exaggerated or false things. If
you have confidence in yourself (or self-esteem), this generally
means that you feel that you have worth or rate as a good person,
because you do well in various respects, including sex-love affairs.
Such a concept can lead to very dangerous results, since if you later
decide that you do poorly, you will tend to view yourself as a bad
person and will despise yourself and feel worthless. Better—don't
rate yourself, your entire person, at all, but only have self-
acceptance, meaning that you accept your aliveness and strive to
remain alive and make yourself as happy and as free from needless
pain as you can while you live.

You can quite legitimately, however, have confidence in any of
your abilities, such as your sex abilities. This merely means that you
have observed yourself in this area, noted that you have often succeeded in it in the past, and concluded that you have a good chance
of succeeding again in the future. This kind of confidence really
arises from statistics, from the term *degrees of confidence,* which
means that you assess the probability of a certain outcome when
you have certain facts about the history of past events in that area.
Thus, if you toss a coin in the air a hundred times and discover that
it turns up heads forty-nine times and tails fifty-one times, you say
that you have around .50, or 50 percent, confidence that the next
time you toss up a similar coin it will turn up heads. Similarly, if
you try sex many times and you usually succeed, you have confidence that you will mostly succeed in the present and future.

The more confidence you have and show, the more your partners
will tend to feel that you *can* handle yourself sexually; therefore,
they will want to give you a chance. Similarly if you have true
self-acceptance—meaning, again, that you give yourself the right
to live and enjoy *whether or not* you succeed sexually or amatively

—you will have one of the rarest and most treasured of all characteristics. For women, in particular, tend to like men who have *strength*, who know what they want in life and feel determined to get it; and strength very much involves self-acceptance. This kind of strength remains so rare in our society that ten zillion women will probably want to love you and screw you if they think you have it.

So also with your helping others to accept themselves and to have confidence in their sex-love abilities. One of the main reasons a woman will not go to bed with you results from her own feelings of inadequacy, her belief that she will not measure up to your expectations and desires and that she will therefore rate as a slob. Once she discovers that she *can* act as something of a sexpot with you or that she can accept herself even if she doesn't measure up sexually, she will often drool at the idea of bedding you. So show her, if you possibly can, that she *has* notable sexual prowess—and also that you value her and that she can accept herself, even if she doesn't amount to the greatest thing since Cleopatra.

Open your big mouth and show her that you have *special* thrills, pleasures, sexiness with her. Show her that you *know* she will look and behave beautifully. If she thinks you know it, she will probably know it too. If you want her to do the raping, pave the way with well-chosen words. Then watch out for your cock!

Confidence, on both your part and that of your woman friend, largely arises from realistic attitudes. When you down yourself, you usually say, "I *should or must* have an eternally erect organ, capable of three or four powerful orgasms a night, and the ability to use it so as to enormously satisfy my partner." And she tells herself, "I *must* go wild in the hay, bring my lover to the most supreme ecstasy imaginable, and easily have multiple orgasms." Well, lots of luck! This goddamned kind of unrealistic thinking, of expecting and demanding the superhuman of oneself, leads to the concomitant conclusion "Since I keep failing to do what I *must,* I obviously rate as a lowly shit, and I might as well kill myself!" Or, as I tell my clients much of the time: *Shouldhood* leads to *shithood!* If you think you *have to* perform well, at sex or at anything else, you set yourself up for lingering death.

Sexual scorekeeping, or what I call self-spying, was observed by Masters and Johnson in the great majority of their cases of sexual inadequacy. As Dr. John Eichenlaub points out, this kind of score-keeping seems automatic on the part of most of us, since we think that we have to measure up to others' performances. As we teach in RET, you don't! It would feel nice if you could do as well as Julius Caesar and Mark Antony in bed, but it hardly rates as horrible or awful if you don't. Your and your partner's pleasure remains the issue—not what Julius, Mark, or anyone else in human history feels or does.

So if you want to help a woman feel *eager* to have sex with you, don't put too much stress on either her or your performance. If either of you thinks he or she *has* to perform, woe! Here, for example, runs the story of a female nurse, thirty years old, instructively reported in Morton Hunt's study of sexual behavior. "A man I [went] with got me to read several books on peak experiences and joy and that kind of thing. I had thought I [had] a fine sex relationship with him, but this made me think differently—it made me feel inferior. I went through months of trying to feel aware, and to let it all go—to blow my mind, to reach those peaks. Well, the sad truth [remains] that I thought I [got] somewhere but it all [amounted to] a lot of bullshit. That affair [turned out] no good anyway. The man I see now likes the way I act, and so do I, and our sex life [appears] just fine, without any effort to make it bigger than Bingo." Bully for this woman's changed viewpoint! What can you do to make your own more realistic?

Sex Fantasies

We have already considered women's sex fantasies in the chapter on the sexuality of women, so let us briefly consider fantasy as a sex arouser here. Considerable recent research has shown that women can get turned on, or turn themselves on, by fantasizing about love or sex—that they do it while masturbating, while going through foreplay, and while having actual intercourse. The women on the *Oui* panel on female sexuality almost universally admitted and endorsed sex fantasy, and one of them, Margo St. James, even reported that "I used to get off reading Albert Ellis!" Barbara Hariton and Jerome Singer, Nancy Friday, J. Aphrodite, Manfred de Martino, and other researchers have shown that during intercourse about 65 percent of their respondents indicated moderate to high levels of erotic fantasy with "imaginary lover" and "submission" representing the most common themes.

Dr. Natalie Shainess holds that fantasies during sexual relations show that the fantasizer has some problems, but most authorities differ vociferously with this view. Dr. Harold Greenwald thinks fantasies "nice. If they feel like it, why shouldn't they have fantasies? I can't see where having fantasies [constitutes] a crime, and I think women have as much right to have fantasies as men, including visual fantasies, if that [seems] what they want to do."

G. and C. Greene point out that even sadomasochistic fantasies have real value in many instances, as this mode constitutes "a way of love based on the most intimate knowledge of the human soul." They show how imagination constitutes the most human of traits and how people can use it to their greatest sex-love advantage.

All of which means—what? That you and your mate can well take advantage of all kinds of fantasy, so that both of you can get maximally aroused. Use sexual imagining in your own head and encourage her, at times, to do so too. Try to admit your fantasizing, and if you find this feasible, mutually tell your fantasies aloud. In regard to intercourse, don't forget that for great sex you usually keep largely within yourself. As Dr. Richard Robertiello shows, if you focus mainly or only on pleasing your partner, you will lose much of your own sexual enjoyment—and arousal! But fantasy, most fortunately, allows you to do what you can to please your mate—while thinking some of your own private, arousing thoughts and satisfying yourself at the same time. Similarly for your partner and her inner thoughts and feelings.

By sharing fantasies with your mate, you can have them and communicate about them at the same time. As Myron Brenton points out, "When sex partners share their sex fantasies the result can [prove] fantastic in terms of adding fun, pleasure, and intimacy to the relationship."

Terry Garrity ("J.") also notes, in her famous book *The Sensuous Woman*, "If you can coerce your man into revealing his secret sexual imagery to you, bravo. Not only [will it seem] extremely interesting, it will also [prove] helpful to you to know what goes on in his head sexually." As a man, coaxing your partner to reveal her fantasies to you may have the same beneficial effect.

Does knowledge of your partner's sex fantasies have its drawbacks? Definitely—if you have ego problems. Bill Manville, the lover of Nancy Friday, reveals that when other males discover that he knows Nancy's sex fantasies, including those about other men, they feel anxious and upset, knowing that they themselves could not "take" the knowledge of their partners' thinking about others when having intercourse with them.

He deplores this fact. "I think the notion that we must control and own each other's minds [seems] crippling and impossible; the idea that we must think only of the other when fucking [seems] the kind of thought control that can make even fucking a bore. It [constitutes] the same kind of debased, degraded romanticism that enabled *McCall's* to put the noose of 'togetherness' around the throats of an entire generation (with the results we see in their kids today—and in them too). It [equals] the philosophy of Fucking Only for Love and bubble-gum pop lyrics, the sex hygiene of Billy Graham, one of the reasons divorce [constitutes] the booming growth industry [of] today, and why so many new people never want to get married at all; in a word, it [turns into] the suffocation: the death of marriage, the death of love."

Strong words! Anyway, if you want to use your own and your partner's sex-arousing fantasies to good effect, give her and yourself full leeway to have them—and, quite possibly, to communicate with each other about them. Humans, unlike lower animals, think and imagine themselves into the heights of sex-love passion. Feel free to do this with your mate, to enhance your sex pleasures.

Sex Fetishism

Richard von Krafft-Ebing, one of the earliest and most famous of sexologists, called the preference for certain particular physical characteristics in sex partners fetishism: "because this enthusiasm for certain portions of the body (or even articles of attire) and the worship of them, in obedience to sexual impulses, frequently call to mind the reverence for relics, holy objects, etc. in religious cults."

Extending Krafft-Ebing's usage, other kinds of devoted sex interests—such as semiaddiction to cross-dressing, members of the same sex, young members of the other sex, and sadomasochistic pursuits—have also at times acquired the label of fetishism. As Krafft-Ebing himself pointed out (and he easily labeled a sex act "abnormal" or "perverse"!), some form of fetishism occurs so commonly among normal humans that we find it almost impossible to say where "deviated" or "disturbed" fetishism begins.

He noted, "It would seem reasonable to assume, as the distinguishing mark of pathological fetishism, the necessity for the presence of the fetish as an indispensable condition for the possibility of performance of coitus." In other words, he tended to see fetishism as pathological when it involves obsessive-compulsive interest in a fetish and precludes adequate intercourse without its presence. But he freely admitted that any clear-cut line between "normal" and "abnormal" fetishism remains very difficult to draw.

One thing seems clear—innumerable people of both sexes, and especially males, get sexually aroused and satisfied much more quickly and intensely if they think about or engage in fetishistic activities. For example, people who cannot easily get excited or come to orgasm through interpersonal sex can do so when they think of an article of clothing, don that article, concentrate on certain parts of a partner's body, engage in specific sadomasochistic acts, or otherwise employ, in imagination or in reality, objects or body parts to which they give an especially notable significance. Some of them virtually worship fetishistic objects or acts, as Krafft-Ebing points out, and others value such fetishes highly but do not literally worship them or absolutely require them to enjoy themselves sexually.

As long as your or your partner's fetishistic preoccupations do not take on too compulsive or self-defeating character, I see no reason why you cannot use them to heighten your sex desire and fulfillment. Over the years, I have seen literally scores of transvestites—most of them male and a few female. They usually have a conventional history and have a wife or husband to whom they feel affectionately attached and with whom they have satisfactory sex. But they greatly enjoy dressing in the clothes of members of the other sex and frequently want their mates to know about this interest and, to some extent, cater to it. As long as it does not go to disturbed, compulsive lengths, I frequently speak to their mates—who at first often feel horrified at learning about the cross-dressing—and encourage them to give in, at least to some extent, to their partners' transvestite leanings, and thereby enhance sex with these partners. Usually, if I convince the mate to try this, it works out quite well, and the transvestite feels even closer and more attached to his or her mate.

This doesn't mean that if your partner insists on going to bed with you and a boa constrictor, you have to agree! Fetishes and fetishistic acts vary widely, and you may find some of them rather disagreeable. In general, however, you can try to discover whether your mate has some innocuous fetishes that you can go along with. If you do so, you will probably find her most grateful. By the same token, if you can get her to agree to let you indulge yourself in some of your own harmless fetishes, you will feel closer to her—and you probably will feel considerably more stimulated than you otherwise would. Particularly if either of you has certain sex problems (as we discuss later in this book), the use of fetishistic enjoyments may prove desirable for the achievement of maximum adequacy.

Various authorities these days take a much more permissive attitude toward fetishism than they did in Krafft-Ebing's day. Dr. S. G. Tufill, in *Sexual Stimulation*, describes and endorses several fetishistic pursuits, including bondage, unusual dressing, and mild sadomasochistic enjoyments. He quotes one of his correspondents, a minister's daughter, who calls herself a physical coward but gets aroused by her husband's caning. "The thought of anyone else caning me fills me with revulsion, so that this behavior must [get] linked to my love for my husband. Naturally, the caning my husband gives me never [proves] excessively hard—it always precedes our lovemaking, and consists simply of my husband giving me as many strokes as I want on my buttocks and thighs, while holding me bent over an easy chair, until I ask him to stop, usually after twelve to eighteen strokes, sometimes less and sometimes more. In this way I always achieve complete satisfaction and at the same time a deep feeling of contented happiness."

G. and C. Greene point out that in sadomasochistic fetishism the decisive factor consists of the presence of love—and this factor makes the s-m acts meaningful. This seems true. As I wrote some years ago, in a preface to one of the editions of the famous novel, *The Story of O,* this book seems, on the surface, like a sex book but actually revolves around love. O lets her lover, and his friends, treat her sadistically not because she enjoys pain but because she has a dire need for her inamorato's love—and will do virtually *anything* to receive it. Many people, especially women, likewise relish masochistic pursuits—especially when they keep them only in their imaginations—and use them as sex fetishes because they give them a great love significance.

Ernest Becker also indicates that even extreme fetishists garner sexual advantages. "The fetishist, then, as someone who [remains] severely limited in his behavior, [doesn't] get deprived of resourcefulness. On the contrary, limited in behavior, he tasks himself to create *an extra charge of life-enhancing meaning in a more limited area* than that necessary for the rest of us. . . . He must fix on some perceptual detail, and derive the *full justification for drawing himself to the object* from this very narrow focalization. . . . This very resourcefulness appears to the outsider as 'abnormal.' "

J. D., a female journalist, in her article, "Further Freak-outs and Fetishes," endorses everything from fabric, rubber, and leather fetishism to bondage and domination. She includes among her own possible enjoyments urination sports, coprolalia (obscene talk), gerontophilia (sex acts with the aged), and pygmalionism (fetishism directed at statues and mannequins). Some of these sound extreme, and few will amount to everyone's cup of bouillon. But if you and your partner can communicate openly with each other, discover what moderate fetishes please either or both of you, and use these constructively and creatively, you may well aid and abet your sex lives with each other.

Erotic Materials

You may sometimes find it highly desirable to use special materials, such as pictures, films, or stories, to rouse your mate to the greatest heights of desire. For many centuries, Oriental peoples have employed "pillow books," or illustrated erotic texts, to stimulate each other. The famous seventeenth-century erotic Chinese novel *Jou Pu Tuan,* by Li Yu, shows in detail how the hero instructs one of his wives by reading with her the well-illustrated *Han-kung yi-chao,* or traditional portraits from the imperial palace of the Han dynasty, which leave nothing to the imagination.

In our own day, many writers, includuding Brisson, Caprio, Kaye, Knox, Kronhausen and Kronhausen, Maddock, Sagarin, Stoctay, and Tabori, have echoed my view of erotic erotica and have enthusiastically recommended it for helping the arousal of normal lovers. Dr. Frank Caprio, for example, writes, "Pornography and erotic bedroom conversation have their place in a happy marriage. Going to an X-rated movie with your husband [appears] normal. . . . I predict that in the near future erotic movies will [get] evaluated by censors on their *scientific* and *therapeutic* merits, and will [emerge] free of sexual-emotional exploitation."

Dr. James L. Mathis points out that sex magazines provide a highly normal outlet for people who find them erotically stimulating. "Some believe that exposure to this form of literature [represents] a healthy part of growing up."

Although Masters and Johnson play down the use of erotic materials in helping couples to overcome symptoms of sexual inadequacy, many other noted sex therapists, often find them very helpful for this purpose. In one case of a male with complete inability to come to orgasm, I helped him to achieve such orgasmic potential by using sexual fantasy and erotic pictures that he later began to worry somewhat about spending too much time masturbating, since he found it so orgasmically pleasurable. In another instance, I helped a totally nonorgasmic woman to ultimately achieve several orgasms a week, also by using sex imaging and photos of attractive nude men (which she obtained largely from homosexual publications!).

Many research studies such as those by Athanasiou and Shaver, Byrne and Lamberth, Griffitt, Levitt and Brady, Mann, Sidman, Starr, Mosher, Routh and his associates, Sandford, G. Schmidt and his associates, and Zuckerman, show that both men and women can get exceptionally aroused by viewing erotic or so-called pornographic material. These studies tend to show that films, photos, drawings, reading matter, and other erotic materials all can serve sexual arousal but that for many couples such arousal lasts for only a relatively short period of time after they view the material and requires repetition for prolonged effectiveness.

Dr. G. Lombard Kelly, one of America's pioneer sexologists, recommended a good many years ago that if you want to arouse yourself and your partner to maximum heights, you can place a fairly large mirror at the foot of your bed, while one of you holds a hand mirror, and can thereby watch yourselves copulating. Although erotic stimuli have different effects on different individuals, you can unhesitatingly and unabashedly employ whatever stimulates you and your woman friend. You make your own decisions in this respect. But in certain instances, don't hesitate to make some!

As a sign of the times, we can note with interest that since the beginning of the 1970s, when erotic materials began to appear more liberally in the United States at public presentations, a series of "adult motels" has gone into business. These establishments specialize in the display of hard-core erotic films to those who register for a night or more in their rooms. According to an article, "Motels with X-rated Films Thrive on Coast," in *The New York Times*, the owners of these motels report that from 50 to 80 percent of the patrons of these rooms consist of married individuals, most of them highly respectable couples who have lived together for a number of years. They seem to thrive on the X-rated films, which they can view privately in these special motels, and often report that the films spark up their sex lives—at least for a while! However, single couples, some of whom know each other for relatively short periods of time, also patronize highly erotic films in this manner—proving that they have a distinctly arousing quality, at least for some of the people some of the time.

Don't think that women's interest in pornography, though at times equal to that of men, runs along typical male channels. Sometimes it does, but frequently it doesn't. Lois Gould, in an article on "Pornography for Women," reports her intensive research on this subject and shows that women can feel aroused by sex representations but that they often get sent more by total-body sensual focus than by direct genital depictions. She concludes that "if the sex therapists succeed in teaching men that caressing, massaging, and nongenital touching can afford intense erotic gratification for both sexes, then perhaps there [remains] hope that everyone—including pornographers—eventually will stop thinking of these movements as mere time-wasting 'foreplay' leading up to the main coital bout. Once men [get] 'turned on' to the idea of sex as a bigger picture than a closeup of genitals on the peep-show Movieola (and once women [feel] free enough to *include* the genitals in their fantasy images), we may all get a totally new kind of 'human' porn— or better still, no porn at all, because we'll [try] acting out all our own best erotic fantasies."

A word of caution, then—try "conventional" pornography at times if you will, to see if your woman friend likes it and gets aroused by reading or viewing it. But don't force it on her! And let her have her own choices. You may well discover that certain materials turn her on that have little effect on you; and vice versa. Male-produced erotic materials may not do the trick. The erotic art of Betty Dodson and other female "pornographers" may serve much better. Try to help your partner's arousal through *her* desires and tastes, and don't let your male prejudices get in the way!

Novelty and Variety

Novelty sometimes helps sex arousal. Many women feel jaded when sex always proceeds in the same manner and under similar conditions and settings. They don't always want radical change, but sometimes they do! Many authorities—such as Barrel; Sartre; Wallace and Wehmer; and Stephan, Getscheld, and Walster—have pointed out the important place of novelty and variety in stimulating both men and women.

This means what? That you try, at least at times, to arrange to have sex at unconventional or unusual periods—such as during the midafternoon or early evening. Have it in novel places—such as in the forest or on a deserted beach. Have it under different conditions —for example, with your clothes partly on or while you and your partner listen to symphonic music. As Brian Boylan points out, you only occasionally tend to make passionate love to your mate before you enter a steady relationship or live together. When the novelty passes, she frequently requires an elaborate romantic or novel setting before she wants sex at all or before she lets preliminary play lead to coitus. You, too, may find that novelty, which at first seemed entirely unnecessary, helps build up your excitement and your orgasmic pleasure.

Dr. Robert A. Harper notes that you can design "the general emotional atmosphere . . . to improve sexual focusing. . . . Select a time when there [exists] a minimum of strain and hostility between the mates, when both [feel] relaxed, rested, and unhurried, and when children and other obviously distracting influences [seem] least likely to inferfere."

Lois Bird agrees that most couples tend to have sex not necessarily at the wrong times, but definitely not at the best times. And you can correct this with a little thought and planning.

Dr. Paul Gillette and Frederick Massey also emphasize carefully chosen settings and point out that bathrooms, parlors, and other parts of the house can serve just as well as, if not better than, the proverbial bedroom. As for the bedroom itself, quite a bit of thought can go into making that a more suitable place for sex. B. C. Kaye writes about a couple who found that in a room with deep, passionate red walls and a mirror in the ceiling, they got turned on "Like nothing we've ever experienced before." Another couple reported that waterbeds provided "the best thing that's ever happened to our sex lives." Kaye adds from his own experience, "For real swinging, nothing [works] like a hammock. Who says they have to limit themselves to outdoors? Just put hooks (the kind that expand behind plaster) into the walls. But get a hammock that [proves] wide enough for two people."

John and Mimi Lobell fight sex boredom by talking, when they make love, about new things that happen every day, so that their psychic climate never feels the same twice. Bach and Wyden show how sex rituals, no matter how comfortable, can always remain "open for revisions, repeals and amendments."

You can, of course, go to great extremes to arrange for novelty and variety, such as organizing orgies or swap parties. But with most partners, especially young and not too sophisticated women, this will rarely pay off. While still keeping within the more usual range, you can often devise novel ways of having sex that will prove especially stimulating to your mate and encourage her to have it more often and more excitingly.

Talking to Yourself

One of the best ways to arouse another, of course, consists in getting yourself aroused to an almost fever pitch. Usually, if your partner sees that she really sends you and that you enjoy her immensely in various ways, including sexually, she will tend to take more fire herself. And you can frequently arouse yourself by telling yourself the right things: first, by getting rid of your emotional blocks against sex; and second, by convincing yourself, by self-talk and intense sexual fantasy, that you can get aroused, will get aroused, and, in fact, right now actually feel aroused.

Rachel Copelan's *The Sexually Fulfilled Man* includes that rarity among sex books, a fairly adequate section on self-talk. Some of her material seems to follow that previously outlined in my own writings, but she also has a good bit of information on autosuggestion. As she notes, "You may not realize it at this moment, but, awake and asleep, you constantly tell yourself things about yourself, both good and bad. The most forceful voice that we can hear [consists of] our own commanding voice. It can [prove] a tyrant or a savior." She then advises that if you want to get maximally potent, you relax yourself and repeat autosuggestions such as, "I have everything that it takes to satisfy a woman. . . . I have no trouble getting an erection when I want to. . . . Each sexual experience [proves] better than the last one. . . . I [feel] free of shame, guilt, and fear of failure."

Such positive thinking certainly has its advantages and will often work. But watch it! Positive thinking tends to cover up rather than really rid you of negative thinking, which you can still stoutly hold underneath. It also çan easily boomerang, because if you tell yourself quite vigorously, "I have no trouble getting an erection when I want to," and then you do have trouble, you easily lose faith in your own suggestions and may actually lose all faith in what you tell yourself. So if you use autosuggestion at all, you'd better use reasonable forms, such as, "I can usually get an erection when I want to," or "New sexual experiences often will prove better than previous ones."

The more effective kind of self-talk that I have recommended for quite a while now consists in noting very clearly what you do say to yourself when you feel sexually blocked or inadequate, seeing exactly why these self-statements make little or no sense, and then changing them for different internalized beliefs that do make sense and that will help you function far more effectively. When you do not easily get aroused sexually, for example, you usually tell yourself, "I *must* get an erection. Wouldn't it prove awful if I didn't! I'd not only demonstrate that I behave incompetently as a lover but also reveal myself as a lousy person!"

You can rid yourself of this kind of pernicious self-talk by disputing and questioning it, by seeing that it makes no sense, has no evidence behind it, cannot get validated. Similarly, if your partner commonly fails to get aroused sexually, doesn't enjoy sex, or feels revolted by certain kinds of acts, she probably tells herself similar *musts* and savagely berates herself when she doesn't achieve them. You can try to understand what kind of self-talk she has, get her to look at it closely, and help her vigorously dispute and challenge it. This kind of conversation with yourself will turn out much better results than plain autosuggestion, self-hypnosis, or positive thinking.

Assertiveness

As I keep emphasizing in this book, women (fortunately for some of us frail-looking "weaklings") rarely go too much for physical strength but do frequently turn themselves on to emotional strength or assertiveness. To help arouse a partner, therefore, you can show her that you really *want* her and will persist until you get her fully aroused and wanting you. As McCorkle notes in this connection, "In the Bold Approach the man comes on very strong. He assumes the attitude that he [rates as] king and [will] take exactly what he wants, whether she likes it or not. The woman will seldom [feel] awed by this prospect, for she knows full well that he can have only what she [feels] willing to give." This kind of highly assertive approach may also boomerang, since the woman may consider it a form of coercion and withdraw completely. But McCorkle has something of a point—*some* women under *certain* conditions really like strong assertiveness and actually feel sexually excited under its influence.

How can you make yourself more assertive? By pushing yourself to try for what you want and standing up for what you don't want— as Fensterheim and Baer, Manuel Smith, and Alberti and Emmons have shown. For a combination of AT (assertiveness training) and RET, see the excellent book by Lange and Jakubowski.

The Buildup

Lois Bird recommends a buildup approach if you want to satisfy a woman or make your wife your mistress. If things get too cut and dried, she thinks, and your partner *knows* in advance what will happen, she may not get too aroused. But if you gradually lead up to it, with sexual and nonsexual overtures, you may help turn her on. She recommends that you start with the woman's clothes on, not off, and preferably undress her yourself. "The most satisfying lovemaking [comes on] something like the *1812 Overture;* it builds in a crescendo until, at its peak, cannons fire and the tensions which have built explode. In lovemaking, the tensions [consist of] a big, big part of the satisfactions. It [remains] too good ever to rush, especially for a woman. And if you look at it from your standpoint, you have everything to gain by going slow. The more time and care you put into building her fires, the more she will contribute to the explosions when they come."

Again, don't make this sort of thing a general rule, to use rigorously with all your women all the time. Some want no goddamned buildup and would feel quite irritated if you wasted their time with one. But many follow the desire for a buildup pattern. Give it to these many, if you possibly can!

Using Moods to Advantage

Humans, especially women, have variable moods. One day, they sparkle and appear ready for anything; the next day, they sink into the doldrums, and practically nothing turns them on. Watch for your partner's moods, and sometimes take advantage of them—particularly when she seems lively, cheerful, energetic, and daring. At these times, your passes may well arouse her much more easily than at other times, especially if you use a little imagination and try to get them to match her mood. When she feels silly and playful, for example, you can act like a child with her, and the games you play can work into sex arousal and satisfaction. In her more somber moods, making love to her seriously and tenderly, with very little of the childish quality, may work more appropriately.

You can, of course, often create different moods—or at least, help to do so. Joan Herrigan tells how her husband hired a hotel suite for the two of them, had flowers waiting when she got there, had a bellhop bring two drinks before the husband arrived, and generally treated her so that she felt, "Now, nobody does this for his wife! It has to [represent] some broad with her lover! Did I feel great!" She got herself so sexually and emotionally ready, under this kind of stimulation, that they had a most fantastic weekend.

Play and Games

Many lovers spontaneously invent games to play with each other in bed—word games, touch games, risk-taking games, and other kinds of games. You may invent your own, with your partner, or may adapt those which others have invented. Sometimes, for example, women like to play strip poker, Scrabble, or some other game that leads to sex if they "lose." Or they like to romp in the shower with their lovers before they get around to sex. Or they take certain roles—act the way various stage or screen stars would presumably act.

Joseph M. Rizzo shows how to adapt some regular "children's" games to adult sex. In Follow the Leader, you let your partner start off petting; then you have to follow, on her body, every motion that she makes on yours. In Statue, one of you remains still while the other engages in heavy petting. In Looking Glass, you and your partner examine your sex acts, as you engage in them, in several well-placed mirrors. In Feeding Time, you place food in or on various parts of your partner's body, then nibble this food from its "dish."

Jim Deane adds some other sex games: In Blind Man's Buff, you and your partner start blindfolded at opposite ends of the bedroom and make your way to each other, relying on touch alone, and make love. In Strip Darts, you both throw darts at the silhouette of each other's figure; then, whatever section of the other's body you hit, immediately gets bared and enjoyed. In Tell Me a Secret, you, your partner, and perhaps another couple write descriptions of sex acts on pieces of paper and throw them anonymously into a bowl or hat. Whatever acts appear on the slip that you and she draw, you have to go into a bedroom and perform.

Individual Differences

As I particularly note in *The Sensuous Person,* each human in some ways seems quite different from the rest of the race—just as each also has distinct similarities. Therefore, any given set of rules of arousal, including many that appear in some highly respectable sex books, work only to the degree that your partner personally accepts and likes them. You can't tell her what she likes—and I can't tell you either!

Watch, then, for individual differences. Discover, by experimentation and questioning, what *your* partner really enjoys—and disenjoys! Throw away your preconceived notions of how she *should* respond in this respect and find out how she *does.*

As usual, you and your partner's *attitude* counts more than your basic sexuality, if you really want to enjoy sex as much as you can yourself—and truly to please the other. You can almost always adjust to any individual differences in levels of desire, capability, or capacity. If you want to! You can, of course, decide that the differences between the two of you amount to too much of a handicap and that you can seek more "naturally" acclimated partners elsewhere. But if you feel willing to stay together and to seek out your own and the other's satisfaction, you can almost always find it to some high degree—if you will accept the differences between you philosophically, stop putting yourself or the other down for having such differences, and collaborate in exploring ways of compensating for your or her idiosyncracies.

CHAPTER 7

How to Arouse a Woman: Physical Methods

EVER SINCE THE 1920s, when books like Marie Stopes' *Married Love* started appearing and turning into bestsellers, educated people have read scores of marriage manuals in order to help themselves turn on and satisfy their partners. Undoubtedly, these manuals have helped considerably in many instances. But even liberated ones like *The Sensuous Woman,* have their distinct limitations, and I have written one book, *The Sensuous Person,* that includes some severe criticisms of them.

Although descriptions of sex have their limitations, let me now go on to some of the more effective physical methods of arousing a woman. Mind you, I merely intend to explain some of these methods and how they work—or how you can use them. I do not claim that they work equally well with most of the people most of the time, for I strongly honor individual differences. And I certainly do not hold that you *must* use these methods and do so to good effect. *It would seem nice,* in many instances, if you do find them useful and use them. But you never *have to!*

With these warnings in mind, let me return to the theme that even if you employ the best psychological means of arousing a woman, she often will require considerable physical arousal before she truly wants to screw. Mechanicalness certainly has no magic about it, but it does often work! Also, you can use mechanical means *un*mechanically—with imagination, with variation, and embedded in a highly emotional context. But physical means of arousal definitely have their place in lovemaking, and they may cover a wide variety of techniques—which partly overlap with the psychological methods but also have some substance in their own right. Let us now look at some of these main physical means of arousal.

155

Erogenous Zones

As noted previously in this book, and in my own works and those of many other sexologists and psychologists, females normally have erogenous zones, certain parts of their body you can easily stimulate, not only leading to sensuous or tactile pleasure in these places, but frequently causing more specific genital or sexual arousal. In the old days, only a few such erogenous zones got listed in the textbooks, but today we realize that many such areas may exist, especially in certain individual women. As usual, no two females respond identically in this respect. But a good number of them feel sexually aroused if you properly stimulate the clitoris, the inner vaginal lips, the vestibule of the vagina, sometimes the vagina itself, the lips of the mouth, the ear lobes, the scalp, the neck, the armpits, the breasts, the buttocks, the anus, the thighs, the small of the back, the spinal column, and the shoulders.

As Richard Stiller indicates, some of the most "unsexy" parts of the body may prove unusually erogenous in special cases. Thus, the Kinsey investigators found that a few of the thousands of women they questioned had achieved orgasm "by having their eyebrows stroked, or by having the hairs on some other part of their bodies gently blown, or by having pressure applied by teeth alone." Quite a feat—if you can arrange it!

Normally, erogenous zones have good supplies of nerve endings, and that basically makes them excitable. Consequently, stimulation of primary sex organs, such as the penis and clitoris, easily leads to arousal. This can occur also with the mouth, lips, and tongue—because again, they have many sensitive nerve endings. On the other hand, the walls of the vagina and the tip of the womb, which juts into the vagina, have relatively few nerve endings, may get pressed or stretched without pain, and frequently respond poorly to stroking. But they do tend to respond to pressure, which adds to sex stimulation of many women during intercourse.

Also, humans may condition themselves so that virtually any parts of their bodies get sensitized to touch and lead to sex arousal and orgasm. Therefore, when a man actively penetrates a woman with his penis, and she actually receives relatively little sensory stimulation from this contact, she may convince herself that such penetration feels so stupendous that she may immediately and intensely arouse herself.

Some erogenous zones get tabooed in our culture and others. For example, the urethral tract, the anus, and the perineum all seem well supplied with nerve endings and sexual excitability, but we often prefer to ignore this fact. As Sentnor observed: "Although seldom discussed, of great importance in erotic stimulation in both male and female [remains] the perineum, the region from the base of the genitals to the anus. . . . In many men and women it [proves] highly responsive to caresses." Some other areas of the body that do not ordinarily get tabooed but that seldom get mentioned as highly erogenous zones include the palm of the hand, the sole of the foot (in some not too ticklish individuals!), the bend of the elbow, the outer side of the thigh, the inner side of the upper arm, the hairlines, the dimple behind the ear, the upper part of the back, the waist, the hips, and the buttocks.

What kinds of caresses seem most appropriate to stimulate your partner's erogenous zones? Many kinds, but particularly patient and gentle ones at the beginning. It may take her quite a while to get fully aroused, and if she thinks that you demand quick and intense response, she may turn herself off and never really get aroused at all. As Dr. Karl Wrage notes, "The sort of contact that can stimulate both the active partner and the recipient varies greatly. Hands and mouth [remain] the principal means of contact, but any contact of skin with skin can have a stimulating effect. With increasing excitement, the desire for more intense and energetic contact usually grows and finally leads to involuntary and intense orgasm."

Dr. Ben Ard, Jr., recommends a gentle, not too direct "attack" on a woman's erotic zones. "Many women prefer a gradual, gentler approach, with lots of kissing, fondling, and tender caresses. This foreplay should range over many parts of the body, with the male touching lightly and lovingly his partner's hands, face, neck and head *first*. Then he may extend his caresses to the breasts and thighs before finally approaching the genital area and clitoris. . . . Most important, the caressing of each of the erogenous zones has to [get] 'checked out' with the partner."

A point that you may easily miss about erogenous zones consists of the knowledge that they frequently *change* in their sensitivity. As Masters and Johnson point out, the very size of the sex organs, such as the breasts and vagina, may radically change, sometimes enlarging and sometimes growing smaller, during the various stages of stimulation. The clitoris, when you arouse a woman sufficiently, flattens immensely and gets "lost" for a while, and various other organ changes take place. These may cause that particular zone to increase or lose its sensitivity—depending on the vagaries of the individual woman. The genital organs may turn too exquisitely sensitive and painful during or after orgasm, and you may therefore wisely stop massaging them at such a point and return to less erogenous zones of your partner's body—which can at that time help her turn on again. So the timing and the changing of your stimulation can add to—or, alas, detract from—your arousing your bedmate. Watch how she reacts, physically and verbally, in this respect, and guide yourself by these reactions.

The Sensate Focus

As the pioneer sexologists like Havelock Ellis, Auguste Forel, Iwan Bloch, and Walter F. Robie pointed out a great many years ago, and as Masters and Johnson have more recently reaffirmed, sensory modalities emerge as the main ways to stimulate most women to heights of passion. And the main modalities here, as we have noted in previous chapters, consist of kissing and touching. As Dr. Robert Kolodny has written, the sensate focus as used by Masters and Johnson consists of several sessions "in which each partner, in turn, uses the touch and feel of physical contact to 'pleasure' his or her mate. The couples [avoid] the genital regions and breasts during this first phase, but as sensate focus develops on subsequent days, these areas [get] included as well. Stroking, patting, massaging all [get] employed by one partner in an attempt to give pleasurable sensations to the other and to learn the satisfaction of tactile sensations and physical expression as well."

These, mind you, constitute techniques employed by couples who have a great deal of difficulty arousing and satisfying each other. If they work so well there, you can imagine that they will also tend to work in your normal sex relations with your woman friend. So use, if you will, every possible touch and kissing modality. Your touch can range from extreme gentleness (delighted in by most females) to very firm massage (enjoyed by many).

The sensate focus can also include various other kinds of sensory stimulation besides caressing, massaging, and tonguing. Some women get turned on by sounds—such as cooing, gurgling, moaning, laughing, sucking, or other sounds. Some like music, ranging all the way from symphonic classics or string quartets to strident jazz or rock 'n' roll. I have found women—though not, I admit, too many—who like harsh sounds and the use of four-letter words. These same women—or others—may get utterly frenzied at the sound of a gentle, soothing, "Beloved, beloved, beloved!" or "Relax, relax, relax!"

As Dr. Edward Dengrove points out, some individuals get turned on by the sounds of love themselves—by hearing others performing sex acts. Naturally, you cannot easily arrange this as a "live performance"! But you can, if your woman friend wishes, get recordings of couples making love, including creaking of beds and other relevant sounds; and you can record your own lovemaking and listen to the recordings. You and your partner may get turned on by listening to your own sexual moaning and groaning. As Frank Thistle notes, "Turning on to sound sensation can [comprise] a direct route to the vast joys of sexuality."

Physical movements apart from actual sex movements can add to arousal or orgasmic response. You can frequently help a woman get in the mood by dancing with her—in fact, when you dance with her, thus legitimately holding her in your arms, she will sometimes get aroused and spontaneously want to go on to more specific sexual acts. Some individuals get aroused by merely watching dance scenes; consequently, starting the evening at a dance or a nightclub sometimes pays off. Dancing that starts off most innocently can get so arousing that before the partners realize it, they get overwhelmed with a strong urge to go much farther.

Isadora Duncan writes, in her autobiography, about a South American dance hall where upstairs rooms, always available, provided the opportunity for the dancers to continue in bed what they had started on the dance floor.

Menard notes that "the Tahitians place great emphasis on their native dances, as a form of selecting a love partner. The movements of their dances [appear] markedly erotic, and [get] used to stimulate sexual excitement. One of the basic movements of the *vahines*, a suggestive gyration of their stomach and thighs, [makes] the males esteem a particularly skilled performer in this phase of the dance, because the rotary movement [serves as] a promise of her erotic skill." Well, you don't necessarily have to go to Tahiti to test out a woman's gyrations on the dance floor!

Your penis can also serve as one of your foremost caressive organs. Normally it cannot approach your hand in this respect, because it does not have a great flexibility or staying power. But some women, perhaps mainly for psychological reasons, would much rather have their erotic zones massaged by your penis than by any part of your anatomy. Placing the penis between your partner's breasts, under her armpits, in the crack of her buttocks, and at other of her erogenous portals may lead to enormous arousal, and even orgasm, on her part.

This particularly goes for rubbing her clitoral area. As Will Harvey notes in this respect, "As usual, an enterprising young lady showed me the solution. She would make me stimulate her with my penis until I could drop it in—with no hands. Of course, she helped by moving her hips, but she would hold my hands until it [got] in."

Mechanical Aids

As I show in other parts of this book, mechanical aids can help bring a woman to organism but they can also arouse her so that she wants further sex, including intercourse. These aids vary widely, and include condoms with feathers or other stimulating objects attached to them (often called "French ticklers"); artificial penises (dildoes); small objects (such as the ends of toothbrushes) which you can insert in a woman's anus; semi-abrasive materials (such as a towel) which you can use to vigorously massage your partner's genital or other erotic regions; and almost and other kind of object you can imagine or invent that your partner just happens to find satisfying on a regular or an occasional basis. How will you know what works —and doesn't work—in this respect? Only by trial—and error!

As usual, one of the best mechanical aids available, the electric vibrator, can help turn a woman on, as well as to finally give her an orgasm. Particularly with women who have great difficulty letting themselves get aroused or coming close to climax, the vibrator can get them going. Then you have the choice of continuing to use it on their genital area, to let them come to orgasm, or stopping the vibrator after a while, and continuing with manual or lingual manipulation or with intercourse. Don't forget that a woman who knows that you will go to any lengths to arouse her, and that you do not think it wrong to use mechanical aids, will tend to let herself finally go in your presence and allow herself to feel excitable and sexy. So the use of mechanical appliances has a pronounced psychological as well as physiological value with many partners.

Intercourse as an Arouser

With some women intercourse itself seems to serve as the best possible arouser. Somehow, they do not turn themselves on with the usual kinds of foreplay, and they often do not quickly feel aroused after intercourse starts. But once it does and it continues for a reasonable length of time (varied, of course, in each case), they sometimes get exceptionally aroused and can have orgasms during intercourse or by other means. In such instances, which you can discover by experimentation, you can start intercourse even when a woman feels unaroused but still seems capable of intromission and continue it until she starts spontaneously reciprocating your motions and seems involved and working toward a climax.

Dr. David Knox notes, in this respect, that frequency of intercourse may have importance. Once a woman who has difficulty enjoying coitus or achieving a climax in the course of it gets aroused in other ways—say, by the use of a vibrator—you can include copulation as part of the sex act with her, and continue to have it regularly. The more often you have it together, the more she may train herself to respond to it and enjoy it. As Knox states, it seems important that your partner "begin to have intercourse frequently, since a positive attitude toward sex will only result from a number of enjoyable and pleasurable sexual experiences" with her mate. Practice may not only make perfect, in this connection, but lead to a gradual conditioning process.

Taste and Odors

You may consider taste and smell as a definite part of the sensate focus, although many people do not emphasize them very much. But some individuals get turned on distinctly by the taste or smell of their partner; and your woman friend may feel this way. Thus, she may get more aroused when you remained unwashed, when you use talcum powder, when you have a piece of candy in your mouth, when you have a special odor because you feel sexually aroused, or under certain other conditions. Try to discover what turns her on in this respect and use this taste or smell sensation to help her arousal.

By the same token, some partners have unusual sensitivity to various odors and think that they cannot stand you when you exude such smells. Rey Anthony suggests that "many people find body odors offensive. Cover-up products, like deodorants, [they] consider a good remedy." She also suggests that women frequently do not like the taste of semen and will therefore avoid oral sex with you, and she advises you to taste your own semen sometime, to see what objection to it may exist. If you discover that your partner finds semen distasteful, you can arrange to have her suck you off without your ejaculating into her mouth. If she objects to the taste of your lubricating fluid, which appears before ejaculation, she can even use her lips on your penis in such a manner as to avoid having the front of it in her mouth.

Tastes differ enormously, for both biological and environmental reasons. This, of course, goes for your own (literal) tastes in females. You may dote on their genital odors—or may feel quite repelled by them. Scientists have now found that the vaginas of healthy women secret pheromones, as do those of many other animals. Not all males, particularly those raised in this cleanliness-conscious culture, like vaginal odors, but some positively dote on them. This means that you may like a relatively unwashed vagina; or you may not. Also, assuming that you don't particularly enjoy vaginal odors, you may have low frustration tolerance and convince yourself that you postively *can't stand* them: or you may acquire high frustration tolerance and convince yourself that you can stand what you don't like—and may even, after a while, condition yourself to rather like them.

But humans, as always, do differ! As John Money and Tom Mazur point out, just as we get born with different hair color, we perhaps also innately acquire "different shades or degrees of turn-on by sexual pheromones. If so, then you might rate yourself as a nose-man—as well as an eye-man and a touch-man—when it comes to sexual arousal. No two people [seem] the same. You may [turn out] 20 percent a noseman, 40 percent an eye-man, and 35 percent a touchman. But your neighbor may [remain] 75 percent a nose-man, and so forth—to say nothing of how different sexual partners might rate."

An anonymous physician notes in *Forum* magazine that "a freshly washed, and worse shaved, vulva can only [get] compared with a gorgeous rose which has no scent: the experience of either [remains] a great disappointment."

One of Dr. Robert A. Harper's correspondents reports, "I like to take baths and showers with my womanfriends, but not just before we have sex. I don't mean I want to make love with a woman who's filthy—but just with a bit of natural sweat, instead of all the soap and powder smells which rob her of her natural scent."

This man complains that his woman friend thinks he's kinky in this respect, and Dr. Harper replies, "People who have one kind of preference (in smells or anything else) have a tendency to believe that people who hold to another choice [act] anywhere from slightly to terribly peculiar. . . . A suitable compromise, it would seem to me, would [consist of your] bathing consistently prior to sexual activity to meet her preference and for her occasionally at least, to forgo bathing in order to meet yours."

G. S. Stoctay points out that even anal secretions, particularly of the male, may have a strong and characteristic odor that attracts certain partners. Like various other authorities, he opposes too much genital cleanliness. He indicates, however, that although fresh human secretions may attract, yesterday's may not. So he advises couples "not to destroy that which [seems] naturally human, but to remove yesterday's and allow for fresh nature."

Women often object to your getting too close to their own genitalia, especially with your mouth, for fear that you will smell their malodorous secretions. If so, you can show them how to shower or bathe immediately before having sex, use sweet-smelling or good-tasting substances (like joy jell or whipped cream) on their genitalia, or convince them that you actually like the taste and odor of their secretions. If nothing else seems available, Rey Anthony suggests again that diluted toothpaste can enhance the taste of your partner's genitalia and make both you and her feel more comfortable about your going down on her.

Signs of Arousal

To guide you when you try to arouse a woman, many signs of arousal, both physical and emotional, exist. Masters and Johnson have indicated that women generally go through four different phases of sexuality—excitement, a plateau phase, orgasm, and a resolution phase. Naturally, your main interest lies in the excitement and plateau phase, since if your partner really feels excited and reaches her sex plateau, she will normally want to have or continue sex, including intercourse, and will achieve orgasm. According to these fine students of sexuality and the observations they have made of actual sex acts, during the excitement and plateau phases women tend to experience the following reactions.

* Erection of the nipples.
* Increased definition and extension of the vein patterns of the breasts.
* Increase in the size of the breasts.
* Marked engorgement or swelling of the areolae of the nipples.
* A pink mottling of the top, sides, and other surfaces of the breast.
* A sex flush of the breasts, lower abdomen, shoulders, and possibly other parts of the body, such as the thighs.
* Myotonia, or involuntary spasm of different body muscles, such as the musculature of the hands and feet.
* Occasional involuntary distention of the external opening of the urethra.
* Voluntary contractions of the external rectal sphincter together with the gluteal musculature.
* Hyperventilation or excited breathing, with respiratory rates sometimes increasing greatly late in the plateau phase.
* Tachycardia, or elevation of the heartbeat.
* Feelings of excessive cold or warmth, often accompanied by widespread perspiration.

Long before Masters and Johnson described these symptoms, Kinsey and his associates put out a similar list. And Lawrence Gichner noted that a woman's readiness for sex and intercourse includes several signs: close embrace with body pressure; lubrication of the genitalia; separation of her legs, with desire to have her vagina or vulva rubbed; trembling of her belly; desire for climax; trembling between anus and vagina; display of satisfaction and raising of legs with embrace; desire for deeper penetration; squeezing of the partner's body with her legs; excitement and pleasure, with moving of her body from side to side; raising of the whole body with embrace of the man; complete happiness, with relaxation of legs and arms.

Do signs exist that indicate whether a woman will get aroused easily and have little or no difficulty coming to orgasm? No, no signs of this nature seem fairly sure indicators, although men have looked for them for lo these many centuries! However, Dr. Guy E. Abraham points out that hirsute women do tend to secrete more androgen than women who have relatively little hair on their bodies. And since libido in women and men alike gets controlled to some extent by androgen levels, we find a tendency toward greater aggressiveness and sex drive in hirsute women.

Dr. Seymour Fisher, in *The Female Orgasm,* found that women who reached orgasm easily had a greater range of tones and variations in their speech style. They tended to show more expressiveness, they raised their voices for punctuation, they sighed, and seemed to have more musicality in their speech. At the same time, the low-orgasm women had more constricted, mechanical voices, speaking in narrow, overcontrolled tones. Don't count too heavily, however, on judging a woman's sexual responsiveness from either her hirsutism or the tones of her voice. You may get fooled!

Lubrication

In both the arousal and the coital process, lubrication often shows up as an important factor. Some women cannot easily get aroused, particularly by friction on their genitals, unless they have good lubrication. Others get excited but, as soon as intercourse starts, feel pain unless copious lubrication exists. Usually lubrication will commence with arousal, and, as noted above, one of the main signs that a woman feels excited consists of genital sweating or lubrication. But if this does not take place, the use of other lubricants—such as saliva, soap, Vaseline, K-Y jelly, skin lotion, special sex oils, etc.—prove valuable.

Rey Anthony personally finds K-Y jelly sticky and at times too slippery. She has successfully used a variety of things, including cold cream, mayonnaise, brilliantine, Nupercainal salve, Mentholatum, and Albolene cream. She writes, "When I use Vaseline, I rub or stroke differently than when I use nothing, or other lubricants. I find that a light touch can produce fantastic sensations. I like the feel of it. I especially enjoy it because it [doesn't dissolve] in water. Thus, that 'natural' lubricant that I produce can't interfere."

So-called Aphrodisiacs

Various foods and drugs supposedly have an arousing effect on many individuals and have got touted for their aphrodisiacal qualities for many centuries. MacDougald and other authorities, however, have shown that true aphrodisiacs seem practically nonexistent. The few drugs, such as strychnine, cantharides, and yohimbine, which sometimes do have arousing qualities, involve great dangers, and you had better avoid trying them. Alcohol frequently serves as a stimulant, partly because it allays anxiety and minimizes inhibition when taken in relatively small doses. Large quantities tend to render people, especially males, incapable of arousal or orgasm.

Marijuana has an erratic effectiveness as a sex stimulant. Many people swear by it and insist that they become thoroughly aroused when smoking pot or hashish; and they well may, since it (like alcohol) can decrease their anxiety and make them more amenable to sex participation. Other people, oppositely, almost immediately feel sleepy and inert when under the influence of marijuana and experience more or less sexual deadness. Researchers have also found that, taken steadily, marijuana tends to decrease male hormones and may lead to relative impotence. Opium and its derivatives and the synthetic analgesics (such as Demerol) may also help to reduce sex blockings temporarily and give the individual false courage to engage in activities she or he might otherwise avoid. But opiates, especially heroin, generally obliterate rather than enhance sex desire and give a *non*sexual "kick" that makes sex seem superfluous. Tranquilizers and antidepressants also make it easier for some individuals to have sex, but none has yet proved an effective and consistent aphrodisiac. Some of these drugs, especially when taken regularly, foster impotence or other forms of sex inadequacy. If you and your partner cannot excite each other without drugs, maybe you'd both better try someone else—or take up knitting!

Dealing with Difficulty of Arousal

Sometimes your partner seems entirely unarousable, no matter what you think, say, feel, or do. You can tend, under this condition, to think that you keep behaving wrongly with her and amount to a rotten lover. Not necessarily! You may do exactly the "right" thing, at least in terms of the average woman, and it may not work with her. She may just not feel attracted to you or may feel far removed from all arousal right now. Or she may even remain in a complete state of anesthesia or frigidity and let no man whatever excite or satisfy her. Find out! Talk with her about her lack of arousability and *discover* whether you have some responsibility for it.

If not, your partner may require some form of treatment. Occasionally, she may have hormonal deficiencies. In such an instance, as Dr. Herbert Kupperman has shown, she may get helped by treatment with the male hormone testosterone. Or she may have some other organic condition that requires treatment. If so, your only way of helping her may consist of encouraging her to go for some kind of therapy.

Psychologically, too, you may discover a similar impasse. Your woman friend may make herself terribly anxious about sex, feel that she doesn't deserve to enjoy it, convince herself that she absolutely cannot respond to you or to anyone else, see sex as something dirty that she has to avoid, or have some other emotional hangup that blocks her responsiveness. Again—her problem! Try to determine whether she really has such a psychological difficulty and encourage her to talk to a psychologist, marriage counselor, sex therapist, psychiatrist, social worker, or other professional about it. Later on in this book, I include a chapter dealing with sex difficulties and what you can do to cope with them. Read it. But if that or anything else does not help, see if you can't get her to accept the fact that she probably has some kind of problem and that she can go for suitable treatment.

CHAPTER 8

How to Pet and Like It

As I HAVE said to males for many years, your sacred penis hardly forms your main sex organ. Look, rather, to your hand—and to your lips! And the primary source of your own responsiveness doesn't always equal, as so many books on sex misleadingly claim, the glans, or head of your membrum virile. Rather, it consists of a large portion of your skin, ranging from the tip of your toes to your breasts, back, lips, and neck.

Don't think that penile-vaginal intercourse proves sacrosanct—though it may seem great stuff, not to get sneezed at. If you focus mainly or exclusively on inducing a woman, as quickly as possible, to grant you her "final" favors, you often miss the most of sex. Moreover, you make yourself into a poor lover—since most females tend to get more excited from petting than they do from copulation unpreceded by a considerable amount of foreplay.

Rebecca Liswood, though a sexologist of the old school and rather prim in many ways, endorses the much less prim views of the pioneering gynecologist Sophia Kleegman: "At one of our meetings of the American Association of Marriage Counselors, Dr. Sophia Kleegman told this story which I found very significant. One of her patients said to her, 'I [feel] worried because the only sexual activity we have [occurs] when my husband manipulates my clitoris.'

"Dr. Kleegman asked: 'What [seems] wrong with that?'

"The woman said, 'But I didn't marry a finger.'

" 'You didn't marry a penis either.' Dr. Kleegman told her. 'You married the whole, wonderful man.' "

I, too, heard Sophie Kleegman tell that story and many others, most of which added up to the idea that penis-vaginal copulation

168

has no sacredness and that various forms of petting—as foreplay, during play, and afterplay—satisfy women far more thoroughly than does intercourse in innumerable instances.

How can you learn to pet and like it? Fairly easily! Petting consists of any form of sex play other than intercourse itself. It includes kissing, embracing, caressing, massaging, oral-genital relations, and other extravaginal acts. You may engage in it in its own right, for its intrinsic enjoyments, or you may use it as a prelude for coitus, as what the sex books generally call foreplay.

Like almost everything else in life, petting has its advantages and its disadvantages. Much of the old-time sex literature views it as harmful when it does not lead to copulation, but little evidence exists to back this belief. As indicated previously, prolonged petting that does not lead to any climax whatever on your or your partner's part may possibly lead to pelvic or prostatic congestion in *some* instances. Dr. LeMon Clark and Nathaniel Shafer point this out. But it seems clear that vast numbers of men and women can pet indefinitely without harmful results and that women in particular can harmlessly enjoy petting in its own right. Both sexes, however, may find it safer to pet to orgasm than to stop short of climax.

As Drs. Wardell Pomeroy and Eleanor Hamilton indicate, petting can provide you and your partner with a valuable learning process. By engaging in it, you can both learn how to stimulate each other properly and learn what it feels like to get exciting and fulfilling sex excitation. This holds true particularly when you both care for and show real interest in each other; but it can also lead to good results when you use it in its own right, for pure sensual and sexual enjoyment.

As Ronald Mazur notes, "Petting without orgasm or coitus—for persons with a mature relationship and attitude—[does not prove] harmful nor does it indicate any inadequacy, physical or emotional."

Does petting before marriage enhance or interfere with postmarital satisfaction? Some controversy exists about this question. Drs. William Reevy and Carlfred Broderick showed, with some research, that couples who pet before marriage may seem to show less happiness in marriage than those who do not. But the tests and other procedures they employed tended to indicate that conservative-minded couples tend to *report* less sex before and more "happiness" after marriage than do liberal-minded couples. I pointed out this artifact of sex and marital research in a critical paper that I published many years ago. The Kinsey researchers, on the other hand, showed that women who have any kind of petting or masturbation before marriage tend to have more sex satisfaction in their marital lives.

Lip Kissing

Many people seem to think that kissing consists largely of pressing their lips, tenderly or tightly, against their partners' lips and keeping them sort of locked in that position for a while before breaking apart. Well, that does seem kissing (I guess!)—but of an exceptionally limited variety. The Hindu writer Vatsyayana, who wrote sometime between the tenth and thirteenth centuries and has given us the famous treatise *The Kama Sutra,* described a great many kisses, including:

• The nominal kiss—"when a woman only touches the mouth of her lover with her own, but does not herself do anything."

• The throbbing kiss—"when a woman, setting aside her bashfulness a little, wishes to touch the lip . . . pressed into her mouth, and with that object moves her lower lip, but not the upper one."

• The touching kiss—"when a woman touches her lover's lip with her tongue, and having shut her eyes, places her hands on those of her lover."

• The straight kiss—"when the lips of two lovers [get] brought into direct contact with each other."

• The bent kiss—"when the heads of two lovers bend towards each other, and when so bent, kissing takes place."

• The turned kiss—"when one of them turns up the face of the other by holding the head and chin, and then kissing."

• The pressed kiss—"when the lower lip gets pressed with much force."

Vatsyayana also described a dozen other kinds of kisses; and he by no means exhausted the list. Van de Velde, who has an extensive section on kissing in *Ideal Marriage,* particularly advocated marachinage, or kataglossism—a form of "soul kissing" in which the lovers' kisses turn deep and wet and where they insert their tongues into each other's mouths for long periods of mutual exploration.

Perhaps fifty or a hundred types of lip kissing exist, depending on how you divide and subtract. You and your partner can imaginatively experiment until you invent (or reinvent) special types that feel most pleasing. Mainly, *use* your lips, tongue, and even teeth in kissing. And *actively* explore your partner's lips, tongue, and mouth surface until you find mutually satisfying variations. You may kiss for long or short periods, firmly or gently, deeply or superficially, wildly or mildly—with all kinds of gradations and nuances in between! And you don't *have to* enjoy lip kissing, though you probably will learn to do so if you keep trying.

Don't give up easily. And just because you enjoy one form of kissing, don't stop there and always use that approach. Years ago, when I first started to have sex, I learned a form of closed-lip kissing that I enjoyed immensely and continued to use. But later one woman rudely interrupted me by showing me, in no uncertain terms, the distinct limitations of my osculatory activities—and insisting that I'd better wise up, open my mouth, and *really* kiss.

I learned quite a bit from this young woman and in turn used my skills successfully with many others. But more than a decade later, I came across more females who could *truly* kiss. And did I feel surprised! What I thought the end, but *really* the end, turned out somewhere around the middle. Now I kiss even better, but I realize I may still have much to learn!

So try everything in the books—and out of the books. Open your mouth and close your mouth. Kiss dry and kiss wet. Use your tongue and keep it still. Keep experimenting, experimenting, and experimenting. Forever!

Body Kissing

Kissable parts of the body include all those parts your lips and tongue can reach. "The following," said Vatsyayana, "consist of the places for kissing, viz., the forehead, the eyes, the cheeks, the throat, the bosom, the breasts, the lips, and the interior of the mouth."

But N. D. Mallary, Jr., in his unpublished manual on lovemaking, adds to these the nape of the neck, the junction of the neck and shoulder, the ear (lobes and/or inside), the shoulder, the underside of the upper arm, the inside of the forearm, the shoulderblade muscle, the palms, the waist or small of the back, the hips, the backs of the knees, and the bottoms of the feet.

And even these don't amount to all! The fingers, the knees, the buttocks, the side, the anus, the belly, and just about any other part of the body, you can kiss, tongue, nip, or bite. Not that kissing all these parts will bring equal pleasure to you and all your partners; it won't. Some women feel insensitive in certain zones that theoretically should lead to arousal. They feel nothing from having their nipples kissed or don't enjoy lip kissing, though they may go wild about some other kind of osculation.

Mores regarding kissing certainly have changed recently! In the old days, amost anything beyond lip kissing seemed strictly taboo —and many legislatures even put on the statute books severe laws against genital kissing. Today, almost anything in this respect seems to go—as Morton Hunt points out in a comprehensive survey of contemporary American sex attitudes and practices. And Dr. LeMon Clark, one of our most respected and knowledgeable gynecologists and sexologists, has come out strongly, in an article with Harry Steinberg, in favor of a comprehensive form of kissing for which a male formerly had to go to a prostitute. As Clark and Steinberg note, this act hardly ever gets "written or talked about, yet many couples have found it one of the most pleasurable of erotic experiences. Some people call it 'the trip around the world,' a form of lovemaking in which the entire body [gets] turned into an erogenous zone—a series of sex acts that can [get] done the same way each time or differently, depending on the moods and disposition of the lovers. Essentially, it combines vaginal intercourse, anal intercourse, fellatio, cunnilingus, and anilingus. If all this sounds like too much for one session, relax. A couple might do as much or as little as satisfies them. But the main feature of the 'trip around the world' [involves its] opening new vistas in a relationship that may [then develop] into a 'routine.' "

Genital Kissing

Then you have genital kissing. People once thought oral-genital relations abnormal. Now, most educated people practice this kind of sex regularly. As Allen Edwardes and R. E. L. Masters have shown, genital kissing has prevailed in various other cultures for many centuries; in our own, especially among educated people, it now seems to exist as the rule rather than the exception.

For some time, Gershon Legman has proved the outstanding authority on oral relations. The first edition of his book *Oragenitalism* appeared pseudonymously in 1940, and he updated and expanded it considerably in 1969. By all means read it!

Legman has computed that at least 14,288,400 potential positions of oral-genital sex exist. You could spend the rest of your life practicing and adding to these possibilities! In the *Art of Erotic Seduction,* Roger Conway and I boil these down to a few major positions, as follows:

1. *Woman lying on her back.* She lies on a bed or sofa (occasionally on a table or on the floor), with her legs open, preferably with a pillow under her buttocks and her thighs raised. She can raise her knees and bring her feet toward her buttocks, or she can rest her legs on your shoulders. You can assume various positions, as follows.

a. Lie on your belly between her thighs, with your legs extended or curled at your side. You can either lie flat or rise on your elbows.

b. Get on your hands and knees, making sure that she lifts her pelvis high enough to afford you good entry to her genitalia. Otherwise, your neck will remain too far down and your position will get strained. Better yet, get on your hands and knees on the floor, while she lies on her back at the edge of a bed or low table, with her legs spread wide apart and her thighs perhaps resting on your shoulders.

c. Stand and bend over her, while she lies on a high bed or table, across the arm of an upholstered chair, or across the top of an automobile seat, with her shoulders on the seat itself (and you standing or kneeling in the back seat).

d. Stand straight between her legs, provided that she lies or sits on a high bench or table, a dresser, or the crotch of a tree.

e. Squat between her legs, as in 1b

f. Sit between her legs while she lies on a bench, desk, or bed, with her feet extended over the edge (and her legs often resting on your shoulders). You can also sit on a sofa or chair while she lies on the floor with her shoulders down, and you bend forward, put your arms around her knees from underneath, and draw her genitalia up to your face.

g. Straddle the woman, with your head pointed at her feet and your elbows on each side of her body. You then approach her clitoral region from the top rather than from the bottom, and while you mouth her genitalia, she can, if she wishes, take your penis in her mouth, in the famous 69 position. Or instead, she can massage your penis with her hands or arouse and satisfy you by pressing it between her breasts. Although she may say no to these practices at first, if you ask her to engage in them while you get her hot through cunnilingus, she may do them willingly—even spontaneously. Consequently, this may turn into one of the best oral-genital positions.

h. With the woman's legs raised high and her buttocks supported by a pillow or bolster, you can lie on your side facing toward either her head or her feet and reach her genitalia with your mouth. This position will usually not feel as comfortable or maneuverable for you as some of the others, but you can use it at certain times.

2. *Woman lying on her side.* When the woman lies on her side, with her legs scissored open, you can also lie on your side and easily reach her genitals with your mouth. Or you can sit, squat, or stand yourself, particularly if you use certain pieces of apparatus (as noted under point 1), such as a bed, a sofa, a desk, or a car seat.

3. *Woman lying on her belly.* If the woman lies on her belly on a bed and raises her legs high on your shoulders, you can again reach her genitalia with your tongue and lips. This may prove a rather difficult position, and I do not recommend it under normal conditions. Better yet, if she lies on her belly on a high bed or desk, with her legs dangling over the side, you can more easily tongue her genitalia, especially if you sit, kneel, or squat.

4. *Woman sitting.* If she sits on a chair, with her thighs spread wide apart, or if she sits on the side of a bed or desk, you can sit or kneel between her legs and comfortably perform oral sex.

5. *Other positions.* If the woman kneels, squats, stands, or takes various other positions, you can engage in oral-genital relations very pleasurably. Many of these positions, however, feel uncomfortable, prove inefficient, and require special apparatus. By and large, the postures I have outlined above, with variations you may work from your own experimenting, will suffice.

In the main, try to discover what you and your partner like best, rather than merely using certain positions because others do so or because they appear novel. As ever, your *attitude* remains what counts in oral-genital sex, not merely the physical things you do. As Robert J. Rogers notes, orality functions as an important subheading for life itself; therefore, "the question for rationality and enjoyment through psychotherapy, optimally at least, has to include exploration of, and an awakening to, oral-sexual feelings."

From a woman's point of view, Dot Smith gives some down-to-earth tips on oral-genital relations. "The best possible way anyone can eat me [consists of] first positioning me prone, on my back with my legs together. Thus arranged, spread the uppermost lips exposing the clit with the fingers and madly slip the tongue in and out to the rhythm of 'Stars and Stripes Forever' as played by Vladimir Horowitz. The purpose of this relaxed position [includes removing] stress from the other parts of the body, such as elbows, knees, thighs, feet, etc. Because of this strain, I find that spreading the limbs delays orgasm, whereas the prone legs together position allows me the luxury of concentrating all my energies toward the goal—coming. . . . Nothing, but nothing, seems quite as sensational for a cunt as a willing juicy smooth tongue slipping and sliding rapidly against her slushy hot sore itchy clit. What could [seem] nicer, clit throbbing, ego bloating?"

Al Goldstein, one of the most knowledgeable of sex artists and writers, has this to say about pussy eating: "I approach a woman's cunt the way a food authority such as Gael Greene approaches a food table. Everything [gets] smelled, fondled, perceived, lapped, licked, savored, and ultimately swallowed. When I grew up in Brooklyn . . . I was upset that Van de Velde's book, *Ideal Marriage,* said that oral sex [got] occasionally permitted, but only as a preliminary. To me it [seemed] the whole pie, the total, the beginning, the middle and the end, and until I read the writings of Albert Ellis, in *Sex Without Guilt,* I [didn't] perceive that, as I passed through my adolescence, I [kept getting] inculcated with the moralistic, propagandist preachings from various sexologists. Albert Ellis thus set me free and, with an assist from Henry Miller, I [felt] able to let my pubic garden grow. . . .

"I [don't do] too good at some of the more romantic preliminaries like hickies, mouth kissing and nipple sucking, but, when I get down between a woman's legs, I [do] the best in town. Some of my admirers call me the Craig Claiborne of cunt. But almost any accolade will do, so long as my repast [doesn't get] interrupted. In fact, when I see a new woman, I don't think of fucking her, but of having her legs tightly around my head. I imagine that, as she grabs my hair and pulls me closer, I can then taste the very core, the very substance, the very warmth, and lick of her inner meaning. Some of the techniques I've developed include sucking her clitoris while moving my head up and down in a movement that [seems] probably the closest I'll ever get to cocksucking."

Notice, here, Al Goldstein's *attitude* toward genital kissing. What he does has much less importance than the *view* with which he does it. This goes for sex in general: the way you believe and feel about it directs your behavior and, in a sense, *gives* you what you get from your activity. In genital kissing you do a very specific, presumably highly physical act. But what you *think* as you do it—ah, that equals the real issue! Take a leaf—a rather poetic leaf, I must say —from this raunchy sexologist's notebook. Do whatever you do sexually—not necessarily cuntlapping, for that may not amount to your thing at all—with Goldstein's "gluttonous" attitude—and just try to do it poorly! You'll find this almost impossible. To do anything with a will instead of a whimper makes you vitally absorbed in its doing. Sex included!

Anal Petting

Anal petting constitutes one of the last sex taboos that still remains prevalent—so much so that knowledgeable couples frequently practice it today, but tend to do so, as Morton Hunt has shown, much more within the confines of legal marriage than in their premarital and extramarital relations. They somehow consider this form of sex more intimate and perhaps more "dangerous," and they therefore will only do it with a few individuals, especially with ones whom they feel pretty certain will still accept them if they ask for it.

Not that people's prejudice against anal manipulation, anal-oral relations, and anal intercourse makes no sense whatever. Some of their reluctance in this regard seems sensible, because the anus, although normally not filled with fecal matter as most people erroneously seem to believe, doesn't amount to the cleanest or most sweet-smelling area, and many lovers prefer to stay away from it out of preference and taste, rather than from irrational avoidance.

At the same time, many people have exquisitely sensitive anal areas and find that sex seems more satisfying when these areas get included in petting. Therefore, if you would train yourself as a good lover, you'd better seriously consider anal as well as genital caresses and sometimes include them as part of your lovemaking methods.

With women whom you try to get to bed for the first time, especially with young and inexperienced ones, you had better approach anal activities somewhat carefully and cautiously. If you caress or gently slap a woman's backside during sex play, she may enjoy it and even ask for more. But if you approach her anal orifice, she may feel upset, shrink back in horror, and put a complete halt to your caresses.

Watch it! Even when a woman seems to actively enjoy all kinds of petting on various parts of her body, approach her anus rather gingerly. Employ exceptional gentleness and take care that you do not hurt her in any way. Use the barest tips of your fingers, in a highly exploratory manner, and get ready to retreat quickly if she offers any serious objection or acts as if she feels pain. The anus doesn't usually lubricate as well as the genitalia, so you had better often resort to lubrication in stimulating it. And although when it has responded to a considerable amount of contact, you may find it relatively easy to insert your fingers into it for quite a depth, such penetration may take a considerable time—or a number of sessions. Using your tongue on woman's anal region, however, may prove both exciting and soothing and much less likely to lead to pain or trauma.

Once you have steady sex relations with a woman, you can broach the matter of anal sexuality in much more direct terms and can try to persuade her to experiment more fully. But at the very beginning, unless you have some reason to believe that she feels particularly receptive in this area, go easy. You'll find many a slip between the anus and the lip!

Sexual Massage

Although massage has always occupied a place in the sexual arts, manuals on the subject have neglected it until fairly recent years. In its own right, of course, it has had a respectable history. Professional masseurs have existed for a good many years, practicing their technique either as an adjunct to public bathing and gymnastics or as a health resource, particularly for individuals who have muscular and other physical problems. But then something new got added in the 1960s, when Bernard Gunther and other individuals at Esalen started making it a regular body exercise and using it as a means of loosening up individuals emotionally and sexually.

Following this lead, various writers started to espouse it for sensual and sexual purposes—including J. (Terry Garrity), M.(John and Terry Garrity), Gwen Davis, William Hartman and Marilyn Fithian, Masters and Johnson, Jack Lee Rosenberg, and William Schoenfeld. Following their lead, you can certainly give it a try. If you arm yourself, or hand yourself, with some oil or rubbing lotion, you can apply it to the body of your partner and gently or firmly rub it into her body areas, including her erotic zones. And she, of course, can reciprocate.

As a male, when your body gets massaged, you will often perceive immediate sexual results. You will feel not only generally but sexually stimulated; and if you do not after a while get an erection, that will seem odd! In fact, massage more often, in many cases, leads to sexual arousal of the male than does direct penile stimulation, since the massaged individual tends to relax and enjoy the physical sensations he gets, rather than worry about whether his cock will go and stay up. Consequently, so-called massage parlors (which really differ slightly from houses of prostitution) have gained great popularity during recent years.

Females tend to enjoy massage enormously but may or may not feel sexually aroused. Even when they don't, they often feel so nice, warm, and loving as a result of your giving them a message, that they will want to have sex with you for other than purely sexual reasons. And they may, of course, get eventually turned on by the massaging process. This particularly tends to occur when you massage not merely mechanically, but with feeling—as if you truly have a great interest in your partner and strongly wish to help make her feel good all over and to bring her to the summit of her satisfaction.

As Rosenberg notes, "The most important thing you can do for yourself is [get] with another 'thou,' with that part of the other person that shares with you this time and space dimension called 'now.' Your caring for your partner helps you get into that place." Or at least, helps the other person *think* that you have entered the same dimension as she and that the both of you share something unique.

I speak about regular massage below. But I also want to emphasize creative massage, which involves parts of the body that we ordinarily do not think of in this respect. Experiments along these lines include those like that tried by Joan Herrigan on her husband, Jeff: "Let's say that I had decided to use my breasts instead of my hands all over his back, stomach, and legs that night. How did I ease into something like that the first time? I offered to give him a backrub. I already [had donned] a nightgown that slipped off easily and the only way he would get a good rubdown [consisted of] lying on the bed with me sitting straddled across his buttocks. Using lotion, which [feels] sexy to begin with, I eventually suggested that he take off his shorts so that I could get lower down on his spine. From there nature just took its course. After a slow backrub, I leaned over and started brushing my breasts gently across his shoulders and back, then slid down to his buttocks and legs. It didn't take long before he turned over and I could continue on the front. Now what man can argue with that approach? Backrubs [prove] fantastic for starting all kinds of things. A man can use his penis as I did my breasts, or either partner can use his tongue. Even a plain backrub (and eventually front rub) with lotion can [seem] fantastically exciting."

The best way to learn how to massage, as McCorkle points out, consists in studying with a professional masseur or reading a detailed book on the subject. Nonetheless, you can start short of this and cover the main points as follows.

Usually, begin working on your partner's neck and shoulders and then her spinal column, manipulating the muscles on either side of this column; then go down to the buttocks muscles. Concentrate on your massaging and don't rush ahead; give every part of her body its real due! Use a lubricant, such as mineral oil or hand lotion. Do your partner's back, legs, and feet, then her face, arms, shoulders, belly, hips, thighs, and shins. As McCorkle notes, "One of the advantages of the amateur massage exchanged between lovers [arises because] the masseur can give free rein to his erotic thoughts and feelings. This puts something into the act that the top professionals in the field must leave out." Indeed it does!

Sexual Caressing

Everything I have said about lip kissing, body kissing, genital kissing, and sexual massage also goes for caressing. Your primary organ for satisfying a woman generally consists of your hand, because the human hand, as any anthropologist will tell you, adapts uniquely to a huge variety of tasks and manipulations.

Your fingers, moreover, easily excel your penis in many respects, since they can do practically everything it can do, whereas the reverse doesn't hold. When you stimulate the inside of a partner's vagina, for example, your fingers can remain "erect" far longer than your penis. They can reach certain parts of her vagina it can never reach. They can flexibly massage certain of her sensitive genital spots the penis can't get to, and they can "see" exactly what they do, whereas your penis cannot. Just try to bend or stretch a stiff prick and see how far you get!

Your hand can also do better than your tongue, in some respects, because it can reach parts of your partner's body (such as a clitoris deeply imbedded in surrounding tissue), that your tongue and lips cannot get to. It can exert firmer and more consistent pressure on certain areas than can your mouth. It can knead and massage parts of the female anatomy for a longer period of time than your easily tiring lips and tongue. It can make grasping and encompassing motions any normal mouth would find impossible. Your fingers, moreover, can gently caress and can imitate most of the motions of your teeth, lips, or tongue.

Therefore, if you learn to use your fingers and hands uninhibitedly, you can move most women to heights of sex arousal and satisction. I often shock people by saying that you can gain a reputation as a wonderful lover if you have no cock whatever, providing that, with your fingers, you truly carry out one key concept—*uninhibitedly* prod, pull, push, caress, and massage. For if you feel really *free* to let your hand do whatever it can do sexually, you have (literally!) at your fingertips an almost infinite variety of sex "positions." Moreover, you can maintain most of these "positions" for hours on end. A little imagination, plus a slight amount of manual dexterity, will provide you with endless titillating possibilities!

Can you feel free to use your fingers and hand uninhibitedly in sex play? You damned well can! For you can legitimately find nothig "abnormal," "perverse," or "deviant" about this, as long as you and your partner remain mutually willing and do not get completely fixated upon or obsessively-compulsively attached to a special form of caressing. Thus, if you enjoy giving a woman an orgasm *only* with your hand and can never bring yourself to kiss or copulate, or if you keep using your hands sexually because you feel terribly *afraid* of having sex in other ways—in these special circumstances, you may show signs of a sexual disturbance, and may consider getting psychological treatment. But don't worry too much. These disturbances prove rare and, for those who push themselves experimentally and flexibly, practically never exist.

Modern authorities tend to favor touching, caressing, and manipuation and massage as one of the most enjoyable and effective forms of human sexuality. Dr. James Semans invented (or reinvented) the sensate focus and the squeeze technique for sex therapy a good many years ago. Masters and Johnson and literally hundreds of their students and disciples have enthusiastically advocated it since that time.

Several authorities, such as Myron Brenton, have invented games for lovers without sex difficulties, mainly designed to increase their pleasure. As Brenton notes, "You and your partner disrobe and stand naked together in front of a full-length mirror. You point out to each other the special places where you particularly like to [get] touched and caressed—where it thrills and where it tickles; where a touch leaves you feeling blah or makes you uncomfortable. The exercise also gives you a chance to explore, to try different ways of touching and caressing. For instance, if you [feel] used to a light touch from your sex partner, how would a sudden heavy touch feel? Try not to control the situation, Hartman and Fithian caution, by rejecting a different approach out of hand. You may end up not liking it—but give yourself a chance to find out first."

Breast Stimulation

Proverbially, a woman's breasts constitute one of the most sexually arousing parts of her body; but this by no means holds true for all women all the time. I have found that some of my own partners cared very little for breast stimulation, and others even disliked it. Some, however, truly felt sent by my caressing or sucking their nipples, and if your partner has this propensity, by all means take advantage of it! As Koble and Warren note, some women even get moved to orgasm during breast stimulation. This may prove good, since they later may come to orgasm in other ways.

John Eichenlaub, in *New Approaches to Sex in Marriage,* has much to say about breast stimulation and gives some usable instructions in this connection. He notes that petting motions that start at the shoulder, nape, or back and end at the breast prove quite effectve in many instances, even more so than direct breast manipulation. Chains of kisses down the neck and chest to the nipple also work very well. To stimulate the nipple itself with your mouth, pucker your lips aound it and gently suck, then blow, then suck, so that you glide your partner's nipple in and out on the moist inner surface of your lips. You can also use your tongue to trace patterns around the nipple, placing it either inside or outside of your mouth. If you use gentle friction and simultaneously stroke your partner's arms, legs, and torso, you will frequently arouse her to a pitch of keen excitement and bring her nipple to erection—which usually indicates that she has got aroused.

When a woman's nipple gets erect, you can vibrate it with the palms of your hands or your fingers. You can also bobble it with your palm or your fingers or roll it firmly between your fingers and sometimes engage in a milking action.

Your mouth, naturally, fits nicely over the woman's nipple, and even a substantial part of her breast. You can grasp the nipple between your lips, roll it around; suck on it lightly or avidly, suck it with your tongue, bobillate it with the roof of your mouth, lightly bite it with your teeth, and otherwise stimulate it in various ways that you can easily experiment with and spontaneously invent.

Dr. Eichenlaub notes, "The most effective mouth caress of the pliable, soft nipple closely resembles an infant's feeding motions. Suction will stretch the nipple out along the roof of your mouth so that you can catch it between your palate and the body of your tongue. Suckling motions, side to side or rotary movements of the tongue, and clamping of the tongue tip on the breast so that its nipple can [get] stimulated with alternating hard suction and release give intensive stimulation. . . . If you keep the nipple in a state of firm erection, you can generally continue to build your wife's excitement and increase her pleasure with breast caresses for as long as you want without satiation effects." Certainly that often seems worth trying!

Genital Petting

Although some women remain averse to genital petting, even when they allow stimulation of other kinds, their aversion usually has psychological, rather than physical, roots. Under the proper psychological conditions, you can overcome it much of the time by stimulating these females sufficiently in nongenital areas until they feel distinctly aroused and will permit, nay welcome, more direct genital contact. In the great majority of cases, women whom you approach correctly welcome genital petting and require some degree of it to get fully aroused and to come to orgasm.

As we have noted previously, males tend to make huge errors in stimulating their partners' genital areas, since they tend to concentrate on the vagina, which has few nerve endings (except in the vestibule or entrance) rather than on the clitoral region and inner lips, which may show exquisite sensitivity. They have difficulty in accepting the fact that although the male has a single main organ, the penis, normal females have three main vulval parts: (1) the clitoris, at the very top of their sex oval, consisting of a pea-sized organ, usually the main seat of sex sensitivity; (2) the meatus, or entrance to the urethra, which lies below the clitoris and constitutes a urinary outlet; and (3) the vagina, at the lower end of the vulva, which constitutes a birth canal, an outlet for the menstrual flow, and the port of entry for the penis in intercourse.

In addition, the vulva includes the outer lips, which do not have much sensitivity, and the inner lips, which have considerable sensitivity to tactile and labial contact. Because of the multiplicity of the female organs, genital petting does *not* consist mainly of your inserting your fingers into your partner's vagina—although this will work effectively in some instances, particularly if you focus on certain sensitive spots of the vagina such as the entrance (or vestibule) or the upper wall (which lies underneath the clitoris and the urethra and occasionally has some sensitivity to excitation).

In most instances, you can properly pet your partner by locating her clitoris and massaging it and the immediately surrounding area so as to fully arouse her and eventually, in many instances, give her a full orgasm. Masters and Johnson, by actually observing females masturbate, discovered that they usually do not stimulate the clitoris itself, but finger the surrounding region. They also observed that when a female gets excited and reaches a plateau phase, before orgasm occurs, her clitoris tends to flatten out and get "lost" from sight and touch. Continued stimulation of the surrounding area, however, will usually bring her to her peak of arousal and satisfaction.

You may use several different techniques of stimulating your partner's clitoris. W. E. Parkhurst contends that a very rapid vibrato method of stimulation gives the best results with most women. But a slow, steady massage of the clitoral region may prove just as effective and, with many females, even more effective.

Berg and Street give an unusually detailed account of genital stimulation that will work with many—but, again, hardly *all*—women.

In the procedure recommended by Berg and Street you gently massage your partner's clitoral region with your finger, avoiding using too much pressure, and not increasing your touch even though she seems to want greater intensity of it as she feels more aroused. You bring her to a pitch, so that she raises her genitals against your fingers; but, as you feel her vibrations increase, you interrupt your stroking and let her sink back to her original position. You then repeat your stroking of her clitoris, noting that she more quickly feels aroused and that her vibrations appear stronger.

As she approaches orgasm, you withdraw your finger for a longer pause, trying to give her as many up-and-down sensations as possible before bringing her to a climax. If your partner wants to come to orgasm, after almost reaching it several times, fine. If she wants intercourse, she can signal you to this effect. Depending on her inclinations, intercourse can proceed in the usual conventional manner; or you can continue to stroke her clitoral area while you engage in fucking. As Berg and Street remark, "should the woman

[feel] sensitive only at the clitoris, the man must continue to stimulate it because, regardless of the movement made by the male
organ, absolutely no physical sensation will [get] induced in the
vagina by the penis alone."

In this description, Berg and Street combine clitoral stimulation
with ultimate orgasm during coitus. You can continue it, however,
until your partner receives a full climax by genital massage alone,
since you will find that many partners get diverted by intercourse
and stop feeling excited and coming closer to orgasm once it occurs.
If you would excel as a lover, try to often, but not *always,* use genital
stimulation as a prelude to or part of coitus. But if you learn to continue it in its own right, up to and including your partner's orgasm,
you will often satisfy her much more thoroughly than if you insist
on combining "foreplay" and intercourse. If your partner remains
primarily or exclusively clitoral, rather than vaginal, in orientation,
gracefully accept that fact and arrange to have intercourse or some
other stimulation of your own genitalia somewhat separate from the
act of arousing and bringing her to orgasm.

Open-minded investigation will show that female responsiveness
to stimulation of the clitoral area differs greatly. Some women seem
to like slow massage and some more rapid movements. Some enjoy
firm pressure of the fingers or tongue, and others seem to like only
very gentle approaches. Some require up-and-down or side-to-side
movements, and others want circular massaging around the outside
of the clitoris. Some women desire steady, rhythmic massage, and
others get more aroused by irregular, intermittent caresses. As
usual, experiment as much as possible, to discover exactly what
your partner enjoys; and as noted in regard to kissing and general
caressing, *keep* experimenting from time to time, to see if your partner changes her preferences or learns to respond to new approaches.

As indicated previously, oral stimulation of your partner's genital
area appears not only permissible, but highly desirable in many
instances, since your lips and tongue seem admirably designed to
excite the female genitalia. The lips and tongue can provide lubrication, whereas in manual excitation you frequently have to stop to
moisten the clitoral area with saliva, with secretions from other
parts of the women's genitalia, or with some other lubricant. Moreover, your lips and tongue work beautifully for light and tender

massaging of the genital area—which many women enjoy immensely.

Genital petting, like other forms of sex play, feels better when two-sided. Your partner may feel loath, at first, to caress or kiss your genitalia. But if you consistently and enthusiastically stimulate and satisfy her in this manner and clearly demonstrate that you consider this form of sexuality very proper and enjoyable, she will tend to reciprocate. You can particularly arrange this if you encourage her to reciprocate, not necessarily verbally, but by placing her hands and lips in the area that you want to get stimulated.

Many women, you may quickly discover, ineptly practice genital excitation. They have little experience at it and, having feminine rather than masculine feelings, just do not realize what kinds of strokings and manipulations you will find pleasing. Thus, they may grasp your penis quite harshly and try to give you an orgasm as quickly as possible. You may hardly find this approach satisfactory.

Take some time and effort, therefore, to teach your partner precisely what you would like to have her do sexually. Tell her, frankly and openly—with no resentment or hostility—what caresses and kisses you do *not* enjoy or what procedures feel, at times, *too* stimulating, since they tend to bring you to climax too quickly. Don't make yourself ashamed, by convincing yourself that it would prove awful if she didn't like what you told her and if she put you down as a person. Open your big mouth and try to get the form of stimulation you really desire! And try to help her tell you exactly what she wants you to do and to get what she desires.

A few summary points about petting:

1. You can try almost any kind of caressing and kissing and find them good—as long as you and your partner enjoy these kinds of petting, willingly participate, and do not get fetishistically or obsessively-compulsively addicted to modes that prove harmful.

2. You can often continue petting up to and including orgasm, and you don't *have to* use it as a preliminary to intercourse. Petting that does not culminate in any kind of climax may still feel good for some people under some conditions, but it has hazards and disadvantages for others. Consequently, use it with care and caution. Petting, of course, frequently amounts only to foreplay and can logically and enjoyably lead to intercourse.

3. Individual tastes in petting vary widely, and you can usually discover what both you and your partner really enjoy only by communicating openly with each other and trying various approaches until you discover mutually satisfying methods. You will find both verbal and physical communication important in this respect—as in all forms of sex relations. So practice communicating! You will almost certainly find it highly worthwhile.

CHAPTER 9

How to Help a Woman Who Has Sex Difficulties

MANY WOMEN HAVE no sex problem whatever. As long as they like you reasonably well, they get easily aroused, uninhibitedly engage in all kinds of sex activities, and soon come to full orgasm—sometimes, to many orgasms within a single session. Such women exist. But rarely! And one of the worst mistakes you can make consists of assuming that because you once went with such a woman, and enjoyed sex with her immensely, all other "normal" women act the way that she did. The hell they do!

One of my women clients, for example, had little trouble getting aroused but then took about twenty minutes to get to the point of wanting intercourse and about ten minutes of active copulation before she achieved orgasm. Finally, when she did get an orgasm, she enjoyed it greatly but hardly panted and screamed and went into great ecstasies about it. After a while her husband, who said that he cared for her greatly and exhibited other indications that he really did care, started to have sex with her in a perfunctory fashion, only spent a few minutes in foreplay, and ended intercourse after about two or three minutes. When she asserted herself and said that that kind of sex didn't work very well with her, he said that she acted abnormal—because all the other women he had had sex with before marriage got quickly aroused, easily came to orgasm, and had terrific noisy climaxes.

As I showed this husband when I saw him for a few sessions of psychotherapy, he first of all read his previous partners wrong. Some of them actually could well have lied to him about their easy arousal and orgasm—in order to' please him and get him to love them. Others acted pretty much the way he described—but mainly

188

because he had largely *selected* them for this reason. Having a great deal of impatience, he soon got rid of women, before his marriage, when they presented any real difficulties—when they couldn't get arroused easily, require him to work hard at satisfying them, or had other problems. Consequently, the three women he had lived with before he married had few or no sex problems—and *that* comprised his main reason for living with them. But he had selected them out of twenty or thirty other women who had not showed their sexual ease, and he had forgotten about how many he had rejected for acting the way his wife did. He fell in love with her for mainly non-sexual reasons—because she had unusual intelligence, pleasantness, and emotional strength—and he foolishly thought that she would "come around" sexually and act pretty much like the previous women he had lived with. How wrong his conclusion!

So don't judge all women by a few highly sexed ones. The *average* partner you have may well *not* rate as a sexpot. She can easily have difficulties of arousal and orgasm. And if you fail to note this and don't go to some trouble to get her excited and bring her to climax, she will feel reluctant to have sex with you in many instances. When you have an affair with a woman who has sex difficulties, you can do various things—some of which we shall now consider.

Discover Your Partner's Special Requirements

Some women come to excitement and orgasm mainly through one special locus of sensation, such as having their clitoral region actively stimulated. If your partner has this tendency, try to discover her special requirements—by physical experimentation and by asking her what she really wants. If you can satisfy her during intercourse, fine. But you don't have to! Your insisting that you must give her an orgasm with your sacred penis may well constitute *your* quaint notion. As long as she can get it in any way whatever, she may—and probably will—feel quite satisfied. Discover this way!

Helen Singer Kaplan notes in this connection,

"Only approximately one-half of our patients who complain of coital inorgasticity [feel] able to climax on intercourse after treatment. We do not regard those who do not as treatment failures.

Instead, we counsel such couples that reliance on clitoral stimulation may [remain] a normal variant of female sexuality."

In other words—and I agree heartily with Dr. Kaplan here—some women may *never* have an orgasm without some form of direct clitoral manipulation and may *always* require this. Does that prove that they rate as "abnormal" or "disturbed"? By no means! They may remain their special way all their lives. And if so—after, of course, a good deal of experimentation with other modalities—you'd better accept this fact and go along with it. Try to give your partner an orgasm labially or digitally; give her, if she requires it, clitoral massage during intercourse; and, if she can best or only have an orgasm when she practices self-stimulation (while you hold her, screw her, or otherwise sanction this while you stay in bed together), you can view that as perfectly all right too. Her specialness remains her specialness, and you can go along with it, even though you may not highly prefer it.

Old-time sexologists, particularly Dr. Theodore Van de Velde, insisted that unless a woman had a so-called vaginal orgasm, obtained during intercourse and achieved by penile thrusting, her climax didn't rate as "real" or "free" or "normal." Most modern sexologists, following my own early writings and those of Masters and Johnson, no longer go along with this view—as witnessed by the writings of Dr. Armando and Ms. Dorothy de Moya and Drs. Ben Ard, Jr., Milton Diamond, Seymour Fisher, Paul Jay Fink, Mary Jane Gray, Daniel Labby, Robert J. Murphy, and Irving Singer.

The case remains unsettled, however, because various Freudian and Reichian therapists still insist that clitorally induced orgasm represents an inferior mode of sex, unsatisfactory to both men and women.

Alexander Lowen states this position most vehemently:

> Most men feel the *need* to bring a woman to climax through clitoral stimulation [as] a *burden*. If done before intercourse, but after a man [gets] excited and ready to penetrate, it *imposes* a *restraint* upon his natural desire for closeness and intimacy. Not only does he lose some of his excitation through this *delay*, but the subsequent act of coitus [gets] *deprived* of its *mutual* quality. Clitoral stimulation during the act of inter-

course may help the woman to reach a climax but it *distracts* the man from the perception of his genital sensations, and greatly interferes with the pelvic movements upon which his own feeling of satisfaction depends. The *need to bring a woman to climax* through clitoral stimulation after the act of intercourse has [ended] and the man has reached climax [remains] burdensome since it *prevents him from enjoying* the relaxation and peace which [produce] the rewards of sexuality. Most men to whom I have spoken who engaged in this process *resented* it.

I do not mean to condemn the practice of clitoral stimulation if a woman finds that this [constitutes] the way she can obtain sexual release. Above all *she should not feel guilty* about using this procedure. *However I advise my patients against this practice since it focuses feelings on the clitoris and prevents the vaginal response. It [does not feel like] a fully satisfactory experience and cannot [get] considered the equivalent of a vaginal orgasm.* [Italics mine.]

Before I take Dr. Lowen to task on this statement, let me quote a rebuttal of it by the Boston Women's Book Collective.

It [seems] astonishing to us to find ourselves so totally disregarded by Lowen. In a paragraph about women's orgasms he talks exclusively about male burden, male pride, male pleasure, male resentment, and then has the audacity to tell us not to feel guilty for seeking our own pleasure. How outrageous that he can use his moral authority as a therapist to tell women *not* to go after clitoral stimulation and to write a book whose only effect [makes] us deny everything natural about what we need and [makes] us feel frigid or neurotic.

Right on! Lowen takes the fact that many men do not like the way women feel sexually, that they refuse to acknowledge that women *do* feel that way and *don't* get often much satisfaction from vaginal copulation, and that they consequently resent women for having the kind of sex reactions women do have, and he blames women for their sexuality and contends that they *must* have an orgasm during intercourse if they want to have a "normal" and "nondisturbed" vaginal response. Instead of strongly advising the men to accept reality (just as they'd better accept the reality of women's menstrual cycles) and make the best of it, in order to enhance the satisfaction of *both* sexes, Lowen insists that women have to change and that men continue just about the way they usually behave.

How unfair! How sexually self-defeating! Certainly, as a male, it would seem lovely if you found a partner who got as quickly aroused as you do and who had an explosive orgasm during intercourse in whatever brief time it takes you to have one yourself. It would also appeal to most women if you naturally *enjoyed* making love to a woman for a half hour before intercourse and you then *easily* lasted for twenty or more minutes of active copulation. But you or your partners will rarely achieve this kind of automatic, spontaneously achieved sex compatibility. Consequently, you'd better work on your low frustration tolerance—on accepting reality when it does not go exactly your way—and upon gracefully lumping, and in some ways actually learning to like, the fact that the woman you selected may well enjoy certain sex things and sex ways that you may not feel utterly enthusiastic about.

Lowen would have the man enjoy *his* relaxation after orgasm but fails to let us know how the woman gets to enjoy her lack of relaxation—if he leaves her high and dry. He assumes that the male has to satisfy the female *immediately,* when he really wants to relax and rest. He can, of course, make an effort to satisfy her later, after he has rested somewhat. And he can have sex *earlier* in the day or evening, so that he does not feel utterly exhausted and want to go to sleep after sex.

Many possibilities exist here for partners to cooperate in their sex patterns, so that both feel satisfied. But Lowen, and many other Reichians and Freudians, insist that sex follow the one main pattern of the male and female both coming in intercourse. That seems highly impractical in literally millions of instances. Women who have tried his way for years, and have in the course of their trying received long-term psychoanalytic or bioenergetic treatment, have frequently ended up only with clitorally induced orgasms—or with none at all.

Beware, therefore, of the male-chauvinist attempt to foist the masculine-oriented penile-vaginal orgasm onto women. If your partner easily falls into that pattern, or can even achieve it with some amount of effort, fine. But if she doesn't, okay—you can enjoy fulfilling her in her own sexual ways. You don't *have* to, of course; but you'll frequently find it much better if you do!

The Use of the Sensate Focus

Masters and Johnson, following the original clinical findings of Dr. J. H. Semans, especially use the sensate focus in their treatment of both males and females with sex difficulties. In the case of a woman who has trouble coming to orgasm or who doesn't achieve any climax whatever, they recognize that she largely keeps spying on herself and convincing herself that it would prove awful if she failed and that she probably can't succeed. Therefore, they try to get her to forget about orgasmic success and to focus only or mainly on sensual and sexual pleasure. She then sees that she has the ability to enjoy sex and that she may go on from there to achieve regular orgasm.

Can you employ the sensate focus yourself with a partner who has trouble getting aroused or feeling satisfied? Definitely. You merely agree with her that for a while the two of you will focus only on pleasuring each other and won't even try for climax. You then follow this kind of procedure, which I outlined for a young couple many years ago, before Masters and Johnson had begun to do any sex therapy:

> You say that you, Gloria, get close to orgasm in intercourse, but have never once achieved it, and that you, Joel, keep losing your erection and have trouble regaining it. All right, I want you to try this weekend the following: Stock the house with food, drinks, and everything else that you think you'll want so that you don't have to go out at all. If necessary, cut off the phone for the weekend. Then get into bed on Friday night and talk or listen to the radio or TV or read to each other.
>
> Whenever the spirit moves you, as often as you like, caress each other's naked bodies. Try everything in the books and out

of the books. Kiss, caress, massage, fondle, cuddle, and get in all possible kinds of body contact. But don't focus on intercourse! Forget, for the moment, about intercourse. Even forget about petting to orgasm—at least until you feel strongly urged to reach that stage. Just kiss and caress, caress and kiss—and use the entire surfaces of your body, not merely the genitalia.

Genital manipulation feels great, but don't get hung up on it! See how much sensual sensation each of you can have and don't, as Freud unfortunately did, confuse *sensual* with *sexual* —or *genital*. Caressing nongenital parts of each other's bodies may well give rise to genital feelings. But it will also lead to nongenital pleasures, which feel great in their own right.

Anyway, intermittently kiss and caress—and then, probably, return to your talking, reading, TV viewing, or what you will. As the weekend proceeds, go on to more specifically genital stimulation; but again, at first don't rush on to trying to get orgasm. See how long, in fact, you can excite yourselves without orgasm before you push ahead to get it.

Finally, when you feel ready for it, you can engage in specific genital kissing and fondling that will lead to either or both of you having a climax. Again, you don't *have* to achieve this, and you may not do so this entire weekend. But if climax appears inevitable, let it come. Not, at first, with intercourse —just through petting. Later, when you see how easily and well you can get aroused and satisfied this way, you can end up with intercourse itself.

Clear? Any questions?

This couple seemed to understand my instructions and followed them well. On Friday night, they had a great time in bed—mainly sensually. He got fully erect a few times, but she only had extremely pleasant bodily sensations, with no genital arousal. On Saturday, they both got genitally excited, and he had one orgasm. She came close to one but never went over the top. On Sunday morning, they both had orgasms by oral-genital stimulation. On Sunday evening, they screwed and he had no trouble getting and maintaining an erection and coming to orgasm. She enjoyed it but didn't quite come. Then, at 3 o'clock on Monday morning, she woke up feeling very horny, and they had intercourse for ten minutes, leading to mutual orgasm, including the first one she had ever received in this manner.

This form of the sensate focus, which I have used for years, doesn't always work that well. It often requires many weeks of homework before either partner or both succeed at achieving orgasm; and sometimes one of them never attains it during intercourse. But the method has its enormous advantages, particularly in that it takes the pressure off couples to do the "right" or "perfect" thing, and it distracts them, at least temporarily, from worrying. They consequently succeed at sex, see that they have done so and can do so in the future, and look forward to doing well and enjoying themselves again. Also, as Masters and Johnson point out, it gives couples a chance, often for the first time, to enjoy sensuality and sexuality in a *leisurely* manner.

Therefore, if your partner has difficulty getting aroused or feeling sexually satisfied, by all means try some aspects of the sensate focus with her. Arrange for a time and place when you can both devote yourself to it—as, for example, the weekend I recommend to the couple in the above illustration. And during this time emphasize, with all the verbal and nonverbal means at your disposal, the pleasure and enjoyment you can discover in each other's bodies—without stressing (and overstressing!) the accomplishment, achievement, or goal orientation of an orgasmic "result."

Some of the best sex therapists—such as Edward R. Adelson, V. Miller and Jacqueline Brockway, and Kevin McGovern and Joseph LoPiccolo—have used variations of the sensate focus in their work with people having severe sex difficulties. You can adapt some of these methods so that you and your partner may enjoy them—and so that she can see how truly interested you feel in helping her with any sex problems she may have and releasing her for her own and your own greater enjoyment.

Helping a Woman Overcome Fear of Failure and Rejection

The main reason for most of what we call emotional disturbance consists of the individual's extreme fear of failure and rejection. As I have shown in many of my books on psychotherapy and self-help —especially *Reason and Emotion in Psychotherapy, A New Guide to Rational Living* (with Robert A. Harper), *Growth through Reason,* and *Humanistic Psychotherapy: The Rational-Emotive Approach*—humans have several basic *musts* or *demands* by which they severely upset themselves, especially, "I *must* do well in all the important life tasks that I tackle!" and "I absolutely *need* your approval and *demand* that I get it!" Sexually, this gets transposed into "I *must* do well in bed, particularly with my lover!" and "If I do poorly, and I get rejected by my partner, that will make me a rotten person, undeserving of any sex-love partner, and doomed to future failure!"

As indicated previously, such a fear of failure gets partially resolved by the use of the sensate focus and similar diversion methods, since the person who feels failing and rejection gets diverted into other thoughts, such as, "Let me see how I can please my partner sensually rather than orgasmically," and "I find it great to experience such pleasure with my partner and to know that I don't have to have orgasm in order to enjoy sex." This definitely works—as the Masters and Johnson statistics show and as I and other sex therapists have seen over the years in our clinical practices.

The problem remains, however—what actually takes the place of the individual's awfulizing or catastrophizing, which constitutes his or her essence of overweening fear of failure and dire need for love? Answer—very little! Most of the awfulizing remains, though covered up. And the person still thinks something like, "Well, I have little chance of failing right now, but suppose I fail in the future? Suppose this sensate focus (or similar) technique no longer works? Wouldn't that seem awful! I never could stand it! I'd once more feel like a rotten person!"

As noted elsewhere in this book, the real answer lies in anticatastrophizing and antiawfulizing, which rational-emotive therapy has made famous. As applied to a partner who cannot seem to get very aroused or gratified sexually, you try to get her to talk to herself (or to have you talk to her) along the following lines.

"What would make it appear *awful* if no technique whatever worked and I always remained an unsexy, unorgasmic person?"

Answer: Nothing. Under such conditions, I would certainly find it inconvenient and disadvantageous. But *awful* means *more than* inconvenient. And how could 101 percent inconvenience exist? It couldn't! Also, when I say that something feels awful I mean that I find it *so* disadvantageous that it shouldn't happen that way. The world must not provide me with such a hassle! Nonsense. Of course it must—as long as it does. No matter how inconvenient or obnoxious conditions remain, I can't wish them away by calling them *awful*.

"*Could* I ever stand continuing to fail sexually?"

Answer: Of course I could. I won't die of failure. And even though I probably won't feel as happy with it as without it, I can certainly enjoy a great measure of happiness in life, even if I never succeed sexually. Moreover, sex failure, oddly enough, could lead to some good, as well as many bad, things, such as more time to devote to other pursuits, more concentration on love, and perhaps more energies. So although I will probably never *like* failing sexually, I could certainly stand it!

"What evidence can I gather to support the idea that I'd once more rate as a rotten person if I kept failing sexually?"

Answer: Not a damned bit! A rotten person, if anyone could fit that category, would mean a person who had such an essentially rotten nature that he or she *always* had to fail. But this doesn't seem provable, since at some time in the future I (or any other so-called rotten person) might very well succeed. An RP, moreover, would get viewed as so thoroughly rotten by everyone and everything in the universe that she or he would get universally damned and would deserve such damnation. But how can I prove that I would get universally damned, and remain deserving of such damnation, if I keep failing sexually? I can't! This appears a silly, unverifiable, theological assumption. I'd better give it up—especially since, if I believe it, I will tend to create a self-fulfilling prophecy by making myself continue to fail in the future.

You can, then, help your female partner to see what she tells herself to make herself have a terrible fear of failure and rejection. And you can actively help her combat her irrational ideas that cause her to have, not a reasonable fear of failing—for failing *does* engender some bad results—but an unreasonable and magical fear. You can also help her rid herself of pefectionistic, unrealistic expectations of herself. As Dr. Milton R. Sapirstein notes, she'd better not see orgasm as an *imperative* or as necessary to a good relationship.

Dr. Harold Greenwald, a pioneering psychotherapist and sex

therapist, puts it this way: "There [exists] too great a demand on people; the sexual aspect of life has [got] so played up that we transfer it to every situation. The man who [experiences] impotence feels completely hopeless and useless. Even if he [got elected] President of the United States, it wouldn't help him; he would still feel like an inadequate failure."

As for women, Dr. Greenwald finds a similar demand for success and notes that the basic rule for treatment proves simple: "If most of these women could [get] convinced that they should just let it happen, rather than trying to make it happen, the problem would [get] solved in a very short time. I knew a woman once who could have about twenty orgasms per hour, and this could go on for at least three hours. At one time she had thought of herself as frigid because she never had an orgasm. She [kept] busy trying out candidates for the job, but nothing ever worked until she gave up and said to herself, 'Okay, so I can't have an orgasm; I like it anyway.' Then she started to have orgasms and practically never stopped."

Dr. William Frosch and Dr. Arnold Lazarus both point out that our contemporary liberated society may pose a threat for some men, since they now feel that women ask that they perform better than they would have asked them to perform in the past. Consequently, the males fear failure more and perform less satisfactorily. But, of course, this thing goes the other way too: if women see that males fear failing to perform because of women's newfound assertiveness, the women get afraid to act assertive, as well as afraid of having poor sex with males. Try to show your partner, therefore, that you do not *feel* frightened of her assertiveness and that you will give her full leeway to ask what she wants of you sexually. If you give her this kind of strength, she will best feel able to let herself go sexually and to overcome blocks to performance that she might otherwise have.

In this connection, you can often teach by example. Since your partner may well have her own fear of failure, you can serve as a good model to her by minimizing your own sex anxieties. As Dr. Paul Gillette points out in *The Big Answer Book about Sex,* a male may easily get so attracted to a particular woman that, feeling in awe of her looks and her sexiness, he may fear that he will not please her and perhaps doesn't deserve her. Consequently, he may make himself relatively impotent with her—and thereby communicate some of his sex fears to her. If you have a partner who seems exceptionally attractive to you, you can still vigorously convince yourself that you do not *need* her approval, however much you would like it, and that the world *won't* come to an end if you fail to win her and keep her sexually happy. With this kind of attitude, you will tend to function much better—to have sex for pleasure and not for ego reasons—and convey to her the idea that even failing at something important does not make you (or her!) a crummy individual and does not mean that you (or she!) can never succeed again.

A form of fear of failure that many women entertain consists in their fearing the unknown—feeling afraid of what *may* happen if they let themselves go and come to climax. As Dr. Saul H. Rosenthal and Dr. Elizabeth Stanley point out, this frequently goes along with fear of loss of control. They think that if they let go sexually they will somehow lose control, act like asses, and even perhaps wind up in the loony bin. Your job, in such a case, includes showing your partner that she can well afford to lose control in your presence—that you won't think her crazy, put her down, or reject her if she acts in the "craziest" fashion in bed. Let her see, in this connection, some of your *own* let-go-ness and loss of control; and show her, verbally and otherwise, that bedtime equals the right time to let down her hair and act in whatever way she feels like acting.

Watch, of course, how you tie up a woman's sex shortcomings with the idea of emotional disturbance. As shown previously in this book, and as more and more sexologists now clearly see, even the most severe sex disabilities may have little to do with neurosis. Alexander Lowen has stated, in this respect, that when "confronted with orgastic impotence in a woman, we must suspect the presence of deep-seated conflicts in her personality. Infantilism, immaturity, and masculinization [remain] among the fixations that stunt a woman's personality." Slight truth here—and much exaggeration! I cannot too strongly insist that people, especially women, can have serious arousal and orgasmic difficulties *without* exhibiting concomitant emotional disturbance.

If your partner has trouble getting aroused or satisfied and none of the methods outlined in this chapter seems to help her, see that she sees, first, a gynecologist and, second, a sex therapist before you encourage her to visit a depth-centered psychologist, psychiatrist, or social worker. And don't, again, help her exacerbate her problem by insisting that she *must* have a severe psychological hangup. She has enough trouble already, without your adding to it!

Hormonal and Other Organic Causes of Sex Difficulties

Just as we wrongly attribute cases of sexual inadequacy to general psychological disturbances, so do we often sadly neglect organic causes of inadequacy. Although my training as a psychologist has given me relatively little background in physiology and medicine, I have seen for many years that important physical asspects of sex disability exist. Even where the primary causes seem psychological—as they do in about 90 percent of the cases seen for sex therapy—secondary physical factors often exist and get neglected. Thus, when a person easily gets "traumatized" by early sex experiences or gets "conditioned" to abhor or feel indifferent to sex because of some kind of puritanical upbringing or has low frustration tolerance and will not work very hard to overcome some of the hassles of having good sex, I often find that this individual has some additional reasons for letting these "traumatic," "conditioning," and other factors run his or her life.

Don't forget, in this connection, that some women have had the worst possible "traumas" during childhood—including rape or incest—and others grew up with the most puritanical kinds of attitudes. And yet the great majority of these women seem to have as few sex blocks and as many orgasms as women whose rearing went along much less "traumatic" lines. It seems most unlikely, therefore, that early "conditioning" holds up as the exclusive (or sometimes even the main) cause of sex problems.

At the same time, considerable evidence exists for hormonal and other organic factors in women's (and men's) dysfunctioning. Dr. John Reckless, for example, points out that in premenopausal women, "whatever interferes with physical comfort will interfere with the ability to respond with female sexual satisfaction and orgasm." And among the physical possibilities he lists "vaginal infection, vaginismus, irritation of the clitoral foreskin, urinary tract infection, or anal irritation or hemorrhoids."

Dr. Sallie S. Schumacher and Dr. Charles W. Lloyd, in their studies of men and women with sexual disabilities, have also found that "some of the significant biochemical and physiological abnormalities found in our patient population include: elevated blood sugar, alterations of thyroid function, changes in tests of liver function, hypertension, anemia, cervicitis or vaginitis, prostatic hypertrophy, pituitary tumor, and alterations in endocrine function."

Other physical anomalies can also interfere with sex functioning in women. Dr. LeMon Clark has pointed out for many years that some females have adhesions of the clitoris which can easily interfere with their sex pleasure and desire. But *some* doesn't mean *all!*

The moral of all this? If your partner has a serious sex dysfunction, it seems a good idea to have her take a complete gynecological and medical examination, to see if any organic causes of her trouble exist. In the great majority of cases, no physical anomaly will turn up. But in some instances the search for it may have distinct value.

Masturbation as Sex Therapy

I have recommended masturbation as a useful form of sex therapy for many years. As soon as I realized, by reading the pioneer sexologists like Havelock Ellis, Auguste Forel, and Iwan Bloch, and by gaining personal experience with a number of female partners, that women can often come to orgasm very easily by masturbation but not by other means, I saw that one reason for this consisted of their ability to focus upon their own sensations much better in private than "in public." When a woman masturbates, she feels concerned only about herself, she watches her own reactions carefully, she can get beautiful feedback, without any interference, she rarely worries too much about whether she will reach orgasm, and she has maximum ability to concentrate on her physical sensations and on the fantasies in her head, so that she can bring herself to passionate heights and to orgasm.

I found, therefore, that when women have sex problems, such as inability to come to climax, they frequently have not devoted sufficient time and effort to masturbation and that if they train themselves to do this, they can overcome their blockings in relatively short order. I once saw a twenty-eight-year-old woman, for example, who had petted and had intercourse with about a dozen different men, most of whom she cared for. She had married three years before, got along beautifully with her husband in most ways, and even enjoyed intercourse with him. But no matter what he, or any of the other men she had had sex with, did, she never came to orgasm. She said she had tried masturbating a few times, found it "joyless" and "boring," and had given it up.

As part of her therapy, I induced this woman to masturbate regularly, at least three times a week, and to persist until it began to feel enjoyable. I showed her how she could fantasize all kinds of sex acts—with her husband or with other men—and arouse herself thereby. At first, nothing happened, and I prepared to recommend a vibrator to her, since that often will work when nothing else will. But then she finally began to feel sexy during masturbation. At first her arousal seemed slight, but it gradually increased. Within a few weeks, she could bring herself to orgasm by clitoral manipulation —but only after thirty minutes of vigorous massage and after thinking all kinds of "wild" fantasies of getting simultaneously raped by men and apes. As time went by, she began to come more easily and quickly and with less "wild" fantasies.

At my suggestion, she tried letting her husband finger her clitoral area in the same manner that she masturbated, but at first that didn't work. She worried too much about his presence, about how long she took, and about how she inconvenienced him. It seemed as though she would take a very long time to accept the idea that she could "use" him and not feel ashamed of taking so long to come. But I meanwhile asked her why she could not get herself to masturbate while her husband watched and held her. She felt shocked at this idea, because of the "nonprivacy" of such proceedings. But I urged her to experiment, and she finally tried masturbating in his presence.

At first, again, she couldn't bring herself off, since she focused too much on his observing her. But as she persisted, on one occasion she forgot about him completely, focused only on her own sensations and images, and had a terrific orgasm while he enjoyably watched. This convinced her that she could masturbate in his presence and that she didn't have to feel any shame in so doing. Ere long, she masturbated regularly when they went to bed; and gradually she could let him hold her, kiss her, finger her anus, and participate more actively while she stimulated herself to orgasm.

Eventually, as she got totally relaxed in his presence and also began to enjoy his masturbating while she held him, she could turn on and come to orgasm as he massaged her clitoral region. Finally, much to her surprise, she even could occasionally reach orgasm during intercourse, especially if he screwed her from the side and put his arm around her and manipulated her clitoral region while they fucked.

She felt so delighted with this outcome that she talked two of her women friends, neither of whom had previously had any orgasms, into following a procedure similar to hers, and in both cases they started coming, first in masturbation and later with their lovers. I, too, spurred on by this result, tried similar methods with other non-orgasmic or rarely orgasmic women and frequently found that they worked beautifully. Some of them achieved orgasm, finally, in bed with their mates, only when they, and not their partners, fingered their genital regions.

Why? For the reason one of my clients explained to me several years ago. "Look," she said. "I always have great difficulty in reaching orgasm, and have accepted the fact that I probably always shall. If I let a man work on my clitoris, I have even greater difficulty, for I have to keep telling him exactly what to do, how to change his rhythm at certain times, and how to go faster or slower. This distracts me. If I masturbate myself, however, I have immediate feedback from my genitals and I don't have to communicate with him so much or think about what he does and doesn't do. I find that much more satisfactory. So I merely train my partners to accept my masturbating; and then I satisfy them in any way that they want. It works out fine!"

In some more difficult cases, women find that they can come only with the use of an electric vibrator—at least, at first. After coming that way, they can sometimes switch to manual stimulation, by themselves or their partner. But some of them can come, or come fully, only with the continued use of the vibrator, and that works all right too—again, as long as they train their partners to accept them, to use the vibrators on them, and to engage in other sex acts that feel good to both of them.

Well, how about you and your partner? If you find that she has difficulty getting aroused or having an orgasm, don't hesitate to suggest masturbation to her and eventually try to get her to do it in your presence. This will probably help turn both of you on. Moreover, if you can show her, by this method, that you really very much want her to enjoy herself as much as she can and that you don't find any aspect of sex shameful, you will often help loosen her up considerably and help her get to a point where she may amount to a terrific sex partner. Masturbation in the presence of another person still remains one of the least acceptable of sex acts, and the more acceptable you make it with your woman friend, the better a sex life both of you may have.

Educational Methods

I suppose that I favor educational methods of sex therapy enormously partly because of the help that I received from them myself a good many years ago. By the time I reached my twenties, I had relatively little knowledge of sex, although I considered myself exceptionally well read in philosophy, psychology, politics, economics, literature, and several other fields. Because I found myself lacking with a woman with whom I got involved when I was twenty-three, I did a considerable amount of reading in the area of sex and soon polished off scores of books on this subject (and got interested in sex research in the process). I received a great amount of help from these books and found that, first, I largely overcame my problems of fast ejaculation and, second, I turned from a poor to an excellent lover. When, a few years later, I started to do marriage counseling and sex therapy, I found that my most useful tool consisted in explaining to my clients some of the facts of life they had somehow not yet imbibed—particularly, as I had gathered from the early sexologists, that sex hardly consists only of intercourse and that women, in particular, may easily get more satisfaction from digital and oral than from penile-vaginal stimulation. Years later, sparked partly by some of my own writings on the subject, Masters and Johnson came to similar conclusions, since perhaps the most important part of their famous method of treating individuals with sexual inadequacy consists in educating them to some of the niceties of sex relations and teaching them what they may better do and not do to achieve greater degrees of satisfaction.

Dr. Walter F. Robie and Dr. G. Lombard Kelly, two pioneering American sexologists, stressed sex information even before I did. They largely *instructed* their clients and their respondents in what they could do to help themselves sexually. In their own way, psychoanalysts have often done so too, for they indirectly inform their analysands, after endlessly listening to their childhood woes, that they no longer *have* to abide by the puritanism of their parents and *can* change their own sex thinking today.

But another extremely important kind of sex reeducation exists too—the kind that we give in rational-emotive therapy.

For, as Dr. Harold Greenwald stresses, we *choose* or *decide* to listen to our early sex education in the first place—and not all of us decide to go along with it. Then, perhaps more importantly, we *decide* to retain the wrongheaded teachings of our youth and in a sense refuse to review them and to subject them to objective, scientific analysis. In Dr. Greenwald's decision therapy and my own rational-emotive therapy, we learn how to redecide our own destinies—how to reeducate ourselves emotionally, by giving up many of our irrational ideas and antiempirical premises.

If your partner, therefore, has any kind of sexual hangup, you can often help her choose to reexamine her thinking, can help her gain new information about sex, and can thereby aid her considerably in restructuring her views. She will very likely remain quite ignorant of various easily gained facts—such as that for many females clitoral stimulation will always remain paramount over other forms of sex arousal—and she will probably not see how she irrationally views certain sex acts, and perhaps her total personality, as bad, horrible, unforgivable, or shameful, when no real evidence exists that she can legitimately rate them in this self-defeating manner.

Sexual and emotional education, then, hardly remains the exclusive prerogative of the psychotherapist or psychology teacher. These days, many articles, books, recordings, films, and other informational materials exist that can help you and your partner overcome your sex problems. The more steeped you get in this material and the more you use it in the form of self-given homework assignments, the better your sex lives may prove.

Behavior-therapy Methods

Much of the Masters and Johnson technique of helping people overcome their sexual inadequacies consists of behavior therapy techniques—active-directive methods of showing the afflicted individuals how to change their thoughts, feelings, and actions, and by such forced practice to overcome their difficulties. Behavior therapy has existed for a great many years but has grown in popularity recently because of its unusual effectiveness, particularly with sex problems. My own form of therapy, rational-emotive therapy (RET), has always used cognitive-behavior methods, partly because I first got into the field of psychotherapy by doing marriage and sex counseling. In this area in particular, I soon realized, merely showing people what they did wrong and how to do better in the future rarely worked unless they also took, and actually carried out, some activity-homework assignments. Such assignments not only helped them get the necessary practice to act in new ways, but actually served to change their thinking and feeling quite radically.

I often tell the story, in this connection, of the fixed homosexual individual whom I saw a good many years ago, largely because of his general problems and not because he wanted to change his sexual orientation. I helped him get over a great deal of his anxiety and depression, and he started to do much better in life. He continued his homosexual activity but got much less compulsive at it and began to engage in some long-term relationships. At first, he never did anything sexually *for* his partners, but only satisfied himself by having them go down on him or by fucking them anally. He said that he didn't enjoy other kinds of activities and was attractive enough physically to get away with not doing them. He particularly avoided going down on another male, since he didn't like sucking a cock or having anyone ejaculate in his mouth.

As a result of his getting involved with one male, he reluctantly began to go down on this partner, and at first he took no enjoyment in it. After a while, however, he began to enjoy it and soon did it with other males as well. Finally, he began a relationship with a woman, and, ironically, she told me that he was the best mouth-genital partner she had ever had! His forcing himself, at first somewhat against his will, to engage in oral relations led to his changing his entire philosophy about such acts and to grow adept at them and enjoy them.

Various behavior-therapy methods prove effective with a woman who has sex difficulties. The main one, probably, consists of activity-homework assignments where, for example, if she has great anxiety about doing some sex act, such as having intercourse, you can set up a series of graduated assignments by which she can do it in easy stages. Since you can even suggest such things yourself and presumably serve as an encouraging partner to do them with, she may feel less averse to going through such homework with you than she would feel with some other partner. So you may help her considerably in this respect.

At the same time, you can help a partner to use operant-conditioning or self-management techniques. We usually don't go through with the retraining activities, including sexual ones, that we would better do because we at first feel terribly uncomfortable or pained by engaging in them. But if we immediately reinforce or reward ourselves for doing them and penalize ourselves when we don't, we make ourselves much more prone to go through with them and thereby decondition ourselves to our anxieties or other hangups. The famous psychologist B. F. Skinner called this reinforcement and penalizing process operant conditioning, especially the reinforcement part of it, and his followers have used it in many aspects of therapy. Before I read Skinner, I learned some of its elements from philosophic writings and mentioned it briefly in the first edition of *A Guide to Rational Living*.

Let me give an example of how self-management principles work. I saw a couple for sex therapy who had gone together for almost two years but who had not succeeded at intercourse because the woman, Vi, had had painful intercourse a few times before with males who had large penises, and she felt afraid to have it with her partner, Val, who also had a large organ. She allowed only slight penetration, but as soon as she felt a little pain she winced horribly and forced him to withdraw. Because she had had intercourse with her ex-husband for several years without pain, even though he had a moderately large penis, and because a thorough gynecological examination showed that she had no physical problems, it looked as if she had exceptionally low frustration tolerance and also kept downing herself for giving up so easily. We kept working to get her to accept more frustration and to stop damning herself when she didn't accept it.

As one of the therapeutic methods, she agreed that she would have intercourse at least once a week, even though it pained her somewhat. But then she kept copping out, used one excuse after another, and never actually went through with it. She then agreed to use self-management techniques.

"What activity do you like to do, that you tend to do every day in the week?" I asked her.

She thought for a moment, then replied, "Speak to my woman friends, either on the phone or in person."

"And about how much time do you devote to that each day?"

"Oh, at least a half hour, I'd say."

"Right!" interposed Val. "I have a hell of a time getting you on the phone on many occasions. Not that I resent your talking to your friends. But I agree that you really enjoy that and can hardly stop yourself from engaging in it."

"Fine," I said. "And what activity do you hate to do, that you keep avoiding doing if you possibly can?"

"Let me see," Vi answered. "I . . . uh . . . I don't know."

"How about visiting your mother?" Val asked.

"Oh, yes!" she laughed. "I *hate* that. She keeps wanting to see me, several times a week, if possible. And I avoid it like the plague. I see her about once a month."

"If that much!" said Val.

"Yes. I avoid seeing her as much as I can."

"Okay," I said. "Now you have agreed to try intercourse at least once a week. Today we have Tuesday. That means that by next Monday, you agree to have intercourse at least once. But no, we won't have a chance to check up that way. Let's make it Sunday. By Sunday you agree to have intercourse at least once. Okay?"

"All right. At least once."

"Fine. Now if Sunday midnight arrives and you do not allow actual penetration of your vagina for at least a couple of minutes on at least one occasion, on Monday you will not allow yourself to talk to your friends, either on the phone or in person."

"No conversation at all?"

"Right! No conversation whatever. If they call you, just explain that you can't talk to them that day. And even explain, if necessary, why you won't let yourself. Also, on Monday you visit your mother and stay with her for at least an hour."

"Really? An hour?"

"Yes. No nonsense about it! No screwing by Sunday—and you then unscrew yourself by forcing yourself to see your mother for at least an hour on Monday. No excuses! At least an hour."

"That seems hard!"

"Okay, but remember that you don't have to do it at all if you *do* have intercourse by Sunday midnight. You never have to exact the penalty, or deprive yourself of the reinforcement of talking to your friends, if you have the intercourse. Understand?"

"Yes. I see."

And to make things even more difficult for you to goof, every single day after Sunday that you do not have intercourse with Val, you again refrain from talking to your friends and you force yourself to visit your mother for another hour. For once you skip the once-a-week schedule you agreed to, you have to penalize yourself every day you refuse to reinstate it."

"Oh, but I can't do that! I don't even see Val every day of the week."

"Tough! Arrange to do so, until you have intercourse. Otherwise —no talking to your friends and at least another hour of visiting with your mother!"

"Really!"

"Yes, really."

"But that seems too hard."

"Then screw!"

With some resistance, Vi finally agreed to this plan of self-management. The first week went by and she still avoided having intercourse with Val. But after Monday passed and she didn't talk to her friends and did force herself to visit her mother, she got together with Val that very night and had intercourse for the first time in their relationship. She didn't greatly enjoy it, but she didn't find it too painful, either. Thereafter, she kept the original self-management schedule and had intercourse at least once a week—usually two or three times—and within a few weeks she had forgotten about her pain and began to enjoy intercourse.

Similarly, you can use self-management or operant-conditioning principles with your partner. You can both agree to do something that you consider onerous and that you keep avoiding and set reinforcements for doing it and penalties for avoidance. Surprisingly, you'll soon find that the "onerous" sex acts seem much less difficult, even enjoyable.

Desensitizing procedures also serve to help you and your partner over sex problems, particularly anxieties or phobias. Dr. Joseph Wolpe largely uses a gradual imaginative procedure in this connection. If, for example, your woman friend has a phobia against oral-genital relations, she can develop a hierarchy, ranging from the low risk of thinking about kissing your penis lightly and briefly to the high risk of thinking about sucking you off for ten minutes and having you copiously come in her mouth. Every time she thinks of anything in this hierarchy and feels anxious, she learns to relax herself with Jacobsen's progressive muscular-relaxation technique, with Yoga methods, or with some other relaxing procedure. If she keeps interrupting her feelings of anxiety with relaxing methods, she will gradually tend to feel she can tolerate ideas or images of having oral-genital relations with you, and she will then feel able to have, and even enjoy, such relations.

In RET, we usually employ activity-homework assignments, or what we call in vivo desensitization, instead of only imaginative procedures. Thus, in the illustration just used, we would try to get a woman with a phobia against oral-genital relations to gradually kiss the side of her lover's penis briefly, then kiss it for a longer period of time, then put the tip in her mouth for a short while, then do so for a more lengthy period, then put a greater length of the penis in her mouth, then suck on it a little, then suck on it longer, etc., until she finally felt unanxious about almost any kind of cocksucking. Frequently, in such cases, I find that if she goes through the first one or two of these procedures, she can skip the gradualism and accomplish the final process quite quickly. But sometimes a gradual, slow-moving, and even one-step-forward-half-a-step-backward approach works best.

With your woman friend, you can devise forms of imaginative desensitization or in vivo desensitization that may well help her overcome some of her sexual hangups. You can also use operant conditioning, as shown above, so that if she doesn't do one of the sex acts that she agrees to do, you help her penalize herself and you reinforce her in some pleasant manner if she does do it. So in various ways you can help her with forms of behavior modification.

Other Ways of Helping a Woman Sexually

You can use many ways of helping a woman sexually. Let me give some more suggestions.

1. Some women require several buildups before they go orgasmically over the top. If you find this true, you can try to arouse your partner to a high pitch, then let her rest awhile, then arouse her again, then perhaps let her rest again, then go back to the arousing technique—until she finally seems ready for climax. In other instances, she may have an orgasm easily enough but may not feel satisfied with this and may require three, four, or more before she wants to stop. If so, you can bring her to climax again and again—usually by digital manipulation of her clitoral area—since you will not likely have the capacity to keep up with her with your penis!

2. Watch your irritability and your anger in case your partner has sex difficulties. If you make yourself thoroughly annoyed or angry at her having trouble climaxing, she will most likely focus on your displeasure rather than on her own pleasure—and that won't work very well! Realize that innumerable women *do* have trouble getting fully aroused and gratified and stop viewing this trouble as *terrible* or *awful*. At worst, it remains a pain in the ass. And if you want to have sex-love relations with this particular woman, you can certainly put up with such a pain. The less angry and upset you make yourself with a woman who has orgasmic problems, the more relaxed she will tend to feel and the more capable of getting satisfied.

3. Some women require deep vaginal penetration to achieve climax. In such a case, you can try to penetrate deeply with your penis by using certain positions—such as when you lie on your back and your partner mounts you. If you cannot give her sufficent vaginal stimulation through intercourse, you can use your fingers—which can reach deeply into her vagina, locate sensitive spots, and keep stimulating these spots when your penis would fail. Similarly, if your partner craves powerful contact with her clitoris or some other part of her vulva, and your penis will not stimulate her adequately, remember that you have a knee, elbow, fist, and palm that you can use for such purposes!

4. Sometimes multiple contact will serve most effectively to stim-

ulate your partner to greater arousal. Thus, you can kiss her lips or breasts while copulating with her. Or massage her clitoris while also fondling her breasts or anal area with your other hand. You can devise all kinds of double and triple possibilities if you use your head (sometimes literally!).

5. Don't insist on simultaneous climax, as this will often distract your partner and help make her so fearful that she will *not* have her orgasm at the same time as you have yours. Show her that you remain willing to give her a climax either before or after your own and that you won't hesitate to satisfy her, manually or labially, even when you cannot get or sustain an erection. Show her that if she does not have a climax, you will not feel horribly put out but will gracefully accept the fact that she may just not feel up to it on this occasion—or for that matter, on any occasion. Let her know that you consider her good your good. That will tend to make you a great lover—rather than a great egotist!

6. As Dr. Henry Coffin Everett indicates, sex compatibility between two individuals largely emerges as a matter of their personal tastes. You like, for example, women who moan and sigh during sex and rip up your back with their nails, and one of your partners likes men who display extreme calmness and quietude and go through sex with hardly a murmur. Well, the two of you may never really make it together—no matter how beautifully you may get along nonsexually. However, if you reveal your tastes to each other and each gets the other to cooperate, she may do some highly histrionic sighing and moaning and you may act much calmer than you feel, and you both may make it much better in bed.

You'd better face it, however—this doesn't always work. If you like your mate to listen to your fantasies about having sex with her and a few other women and she has a devotion to monogamy, your preference may not pay off, and perhaps you'd better keep it to yourself! Anyway, if she has any sex difficulties, do try to discover her special tastes and preferences and try to cater to them to some degree. That may help a lot. In one case I know, a woman wanted her husband literally to slobber her with his semen, and get it all over her breasts and belly when he came. That really sent her! Although he felt indifferent to this kind of thing and would have much rather ejaculated his semen in her vagina, he conformed to her wishes, and she developed into a much more active and enjoyable partner.

7. Look for fatigue and energy-diversion factors if either you or your partner loses sex desire or has difficulty coming to orgasm. If your mate, for example, has a young child or two to take care of or works very long hours or has arduous academic schedules or sleeps poorly at night, she may feel so fatigued that she rarely wants or enjoys sex. Don't assume this has anything to do with you! Track down and attend to such a fatigue or energy-diversion factor. Then the sex may turn much stronger and better.

8. Again, suspect too large dosages of alcohol in some cases of sexual inadequacy. As noted before, in small doses alcohol may stimulate many women, but if they drink enough, their sex drives can easily go dead. If your partner smokes too much, takes large amounts of marijuana, or stays on other drugs that interfere with sexuality, see if you can do something to help her cut down the amounts she takes, in order to help maximize her sex drives.

9. *Action* stimulates a great deal of desire, in many instances, in seemingly "dead" individuals. If you wait for a high degree of sexuality to "spontaneously" drive your partner into your arms, you can wait forever. Often, you will do far better by throwing yourself into sex activity, even though your urges seem low, and by encouraging your mate to do the same at times. Some of the greatest fucks I have ever had have occurred when I "artificially" made myself make passes at my partner, in spite of my low sex urge at the time and my looking forward to pure rest or sleep. And some of the women whom I induced to get going when they said they really didn't feel too much like it that night finally exhibited enormous arousal and had superspecial orgasms.

This doesn't mean that you'd better never take no for an answer. Sometimes you'd damned well better! But if you can get your partner to experiment at times when both of you *think* you feel unarousable, such experimentation will sometimes pay off.

10. Although antisexual or puritanical ideas do not stop females from achieving full sex performance as much today as they did years ago, they remain potent in some instances. Your particular partner may think sex itself, certain sex acts, or acts done under specific conditions quite wrong—and even ungodly. Consequently, she

may block herself in her sex expression. If so, you can of course try to show her that we can legitimately define sex as "immoral" or "bad" only when it specifically harms people—as in instances of rape or when it gets taken to excess and interferes seriously with other life activities. And, even then, though we may say that the act seems wrong, we cannot accurately designate the person who commits it as a rotten individual or an evil person. According to the teachings of rational-emotive therapy, wrong or immoral acts constitute only parts or aspects of people—and not the people themselves. Humans act lousy, but *they* don't rate as lice for so doing.

To help your woman friend in this respect, you can get her to associate with other people who do not consider sex acts in the same puritanical light that she does, as well as with people who largely follow the RET philosophy and who forgive others for their misdeeds or "sins." You can also show her, by example, that you consider virtually all voluntarily performed sex as good and that when you do a foolish thing sexually you do not have to put your entire self down for doing it.

11. Many kinds of coitus exist—such as fast and slow, long and short, vigorous and calm. Drs. Claude and Dorothy Nolte especially espouse some of the slower, more relaxed, more extended coital methods. But some women like just the opposite—achieve so-called vaginal orgasm from exceptionally vigorous, slam-bam coitus. A good many years ago I found, to my surprise, that the very first time I fucked one of my women friends it resulted in the most intense and ecstatic orgasm she had ever had—even though that particular time seemed good but undistinguished to me. We later figured out that on that first occasion I had got carried away at the sight of her well-developed body and had put exceptional vigor into our screwing. Even though I lasted only a minute or two, she had reacted with rare intensity—and that proved the best of literally hundreds of subsequent orgasms she had with me.

Anyway—look for the mode of intercourse that seems, especially at certain times, really to send your partner. Regular modes may work okay, but not quite well enough. Dr. Helen Singer Kaplan recommends teasing, interrupted coitus, with 'rest' periods, during which you may stimulate the woman's clitoris. Even with sexually inadequate women, this technique sometimes does wonders. But whatever works, works. Positions and techniques of intercourse have a wide range. Cover that range if you have a partner with sex problems.

12. As we noted previously, women can get fully aroused by sex fantasies in many instances, and this may hold particularly true for inorgasmic women. I train a good many such women, in my sex-therapy sessions, to experiment with a range of fantasies to discover those which will work particularly well for them. As they get more adept at this kind of fantasizing, they begin to turn themselves on and get more frequent and more intense orgasms. This occurs for at least two important reasons—first, sex arousal and satisfaction largely works cognitively, through highly "sexy" images in the individual's head; and second, such images distract a woman from self-spying.

So! If you can encourage your partner to fantasize better, and perhaps help her by making up dual fantasies when you go to bed together, this will sometimes help her turn on. As usual, do not get concerned about the content of such fantasies—even if they seem weird or "sick" to you, they may well work and prove worthwhile. You can often reassure her that such fantasies do not mean that she has serious disturbances, that millions of people get them and harmlessly use them; and that you can make use of them with her. She can first fantasize while masturbating, but later can do so when having sex with you. The more encouraging you act in this respect, the better her responses may develop.

I have emphasized fantasy and imaging techniques in this book for sex arousal and satisfaction, but I can emphasize them even more in the case of some individuals with sex difficulties. In my young (and foolish) days, I could engage in sex with a minimum of fantasy—probably because I automatically thought of it as special and utterly delightful and envisioned that this particular time I would enjoy it immensely. But I noticed as I got older (and presumably wiser!) that I frequently had difficulty coming and at those times had better resort to powerful fantasy or images. Even masturbation required more powerful imaging, on many occasions, than it had when I first started doing it in my teens.

Both males and females, then, who have difficulty coming can often overcome this difficulty by powerfully and intensely resorting to sex fantasies. If you have this kind of trouble, you can think of the "sexiest" things you can imagine; and if your partner has trouble, you can help her practice fantasy too. The main block to overcome here occurs when either of you think that you *should* not have to fantasize, especially when a live partner shares your bed. You *should*—if you *do*. As I tell my psychotherapy clients, whatever exists *should* exist—because it *does*. And you may find it too bad that you have to go to some lengths to arouse and satisfy yourself, but if that holds true, you'd better take those lengths.

13. Not all women behave similarly, but many do. One of the common behaviors consists of a woman's not wanting intercourse until she reaches the plateau stage of arousal—just before orgasm. Consequently, you may find it desirable to do all kinds of things, mainly noncoital, with your partner until she feels exceptionally aroused. *Then* you can have intercourse and help her reach orgastic heights.

Some women, as I have emphasized throughout this book, require clitoral stimulation up to and including orgasm. That means that you'd better give them an orgasm with your tongue or fingers— or give them one during intercourse, by manipulating their clitoral region with your hand or another part of your body. The slightest interruption of clitoral massage may send them back to zero. If you accept this fact, you can usually or sometimes help them reach climax. If you don't accept it, and think that intercourse alone will do the trick, you and they may get very disappointed.

14. Again, don't think that your partner acts exceptional if she has trouble getting fully aroused and orgasmic. Dr. Lena Levine and David Loth reviewed the studies on women's sexuality and found that almost all researchers have reported that from one-third to two-thirds of their subjects indicate various degrees of frigidity, difficulty, or lack of pleasure in sex relations. My own clinical studies indicate that about 90 percent of females, if they have the right attitudes and keep trying, can receive distinct pleasure and occasional orgasm, but the majority of them have some kind of difficulty in these respects. Whereas the great majority of males can get an erection and come to orgasm during intercourse within a fairly short period, most women (not *all*, of course!) often do not get fully aroused, sometimes have no orgasm whatever, frequently have mild

orgasms, often come only with a great deal of direct clitoral-region massage (and *not* during intercourse), go at times from great heights of sex desire to near zero, and have various other problems.

I have had relations with a few women who almost always get fully aroused and have no difficulty reaching orgasmic heights. But damned few! Most of those with whom I have had personal and professional contacts have some problems a good deal of the time. So don't feel surprised when your partner, however sexy she seems at times, and however exciting she looks, shows little interest or pleasure on many occasions. Consider this the norm, rather than the exception!

15. Sexual inadequacy correlates significantly with lack of assertiveness in women. Because they may not easily get aroused and gratified, women had better assertively look for things that interest them and please them sexually; but they frequently don't. They let males take the lead, and for years they suffer sex acts that don't really send them, in order to please their partners. Consequently, if you can induce your mate to act more assertive, to ask herself what she *really* wants and to go after that, verbally and nonverbally, in her relations with you, she will have a higher probability of turning herself on and reaching greater heights than if she gives in to her "natural" passive tendencies and lets you run the bed routines.

Martin Obler found that active behavior-modification methods, including assertive confidence training, worked significantly better with sexually inadequate men and women than did less active psychoanalytic therapy or no therapy. I have always found that the more I can get my female clients to assert themselves sexually, the more they tend to enjoy relations with their partners.

16. Increasing a woman's sexuality often takes a long time and includes a prolonged training process. As Kinsey and other investigators have found, women may marry in their early twenties and have regular sex but reach orgasmic heights only in their late twenties.

Dr. John Eichenlaub writes, "A lot of women who ultimately prove normally responsive don't have their first climax until they've [stayed] married nine months to a year or more. Then their average starts climbing." So if your partner takes quite a while to warm up sexually, don't discourage yourself, but keep trying!

17. Dr. Arnold H. Kegel, who served as professor of gynecology at the University of Southern California School of Medicine, did a great deal of research on a major vaginal muscle that he called the pubococcygeous muscle (p.c.g. for short). This muscle acts as a kind of sling or hammock, running from the pubic bones in the front of the body to the coccyx at the back. It helps support the contents of the abdominal cavity; to hold closed the anal, urinary, and vaginal openings; and to provide sexual stimulation and the grasping of the male's penis by the vagina. Some studies seem to indicate that although the vaginal walls have few nerve endings, the p.c.g. muscle does have such endings and therefore adds to sexual and orgasmic sensations.

Dr. Kegel recommended that women tune in to their p.c.g. muscles and, if they have sex difficulties, learn to strengthen them with exercises. Thus, if they will sit on the toilet to urinate and at times stop in the middle of urinating, they can discover how to use their p.c.g. muscles and can keep contracting and releasing them. If they practice this several times a day, they strengthen these muscles and increase their sexual responsiveness.

Drs. Claude and Dorothy Nolte, students and disciples of Kegel, outline this procedure in detail in their book *Wake Up in Bed Together!* They also recommend that you, as a male, learn to locate the p.c.g. muscle with your fingers and at times stimulate it manually and that "*light* stimulation of this center with the finger tip will help awaken the woman to awareness of her internal [vaginal] response-feeling in addition to her more commonly experienced external [clitoral] response." By the same token, they say, slow intercourse movements may help you last longer sexually and increase the pubococcygeal sensations of your partner.

How about this? My experience with many women with sex difficulties tends to show that their strengthening their p.c.g. muscles may well do some good and increase their sex sensations and orgasmic capacities. But not always! Many find this procedure a dud. And those who do swear by it and help themselves sexually often seem to include a great deal of cognitive propaganda of which they may not have awareness. This means that while they exercise their p.c.g. muscles, they propagandize themselves to think something like "I can have more pleasure if I do this kind of thing. And now that I make myself aware of my p.c.g. muscle, I see that sex *has* great qualities and I *may* allow myself to enjoy it to the hilt. How great that I now feel this and that I can let myself go sexually!"

In other words, the Kegel exercises help many women accept themselves sexually and to keep practicing with their genitalia (and with their *heads*) to enjoy sex. Consequently, some of the good results they obtain may result mainly from psychological rather than physical exercises. However, as long as it works, it works! So using the Kegel muscle-contraction method may well serve many women with sex problems. At the same time, they frequently develop skill at using their vaginal muscles—which in turn helps their partners experience tighter sexual fit during intercourse and more excitement and satisfaction. So if your particular partner has sex difficulties, exercising her p.c.g. muscles and the greater awareness she thus achieves of her vaginal musculature may help her significantly.

18. As Herbert and Roberta Otto show, sympathetically listening to your partner's previous sex "traumas" may help. In this connection, I recall that several years before I started to study psychotherapy, I went with a woman who had led a highly promiscuous, semi-prostitutional life with several older men whom she did not love. She felt traumatized by these early experiences. I unmoralistically listened to her, showed her that I didn't feel shocked by what had happened, convinced her that many young women could easily let themselves do what she did, and indicated that she now could follow a quite different, nonprostitutional pattern. With this kind of "therapy," I seemed to help her significantly. She began to feel much less ashamed of her behavior and to concentrate on what she could do now to enjoy herself sexually, rather than on the horror of what she had done. Our sex life also improved amazingly as she adopted this new attitude!

19. As in all human affairs, low frustration tolerance can interfere mightily with your and your partner's sex life. Either or both of you may feel quite capable of good sex but just not go to the trouble of getting it under way. Morton Hunt, for example, quotes the case of a bright, attractive lawyer in his early thirties whose marital sex life, after eight years of living with his wife, seemed bland and colorless. "I myself [don't act] as the world's greatest lover, because I

just can't find the time or energy to work on it. I wouldn't say that
I've ever reached a zenith of sexual experience with a woman, and
[if I think realistically] I'd have to say that I [don't feel] inclined
to spend the time and effort it would require." Don't follow this
man's lead if you want good sex! Also, try to convince your partner,
if she has low frustration tolerance, that she may well find it worth
her while to exert herself to minimize it.

Low frustration tolerance (LFT) means that you keep telling
yourself: (1) "I find it hard to do this act (for example, get myself
going sexually, when at this very moment I don't *feel* like getting
going); and (2) "It therefore emerges as *too* hard to do and *must*
not feel *that* hard!" High frustration tolerance includes the philosophy: "No matter how hard I find it to do this act, I'd better look at
the difficulties of *not* doing it. If I do so, I shall often find that if I
don't get going sexually, even if I don't feel exactly like doing so, I
shall miss out on considerable pleasure, shall help disappoint my
partner, and shall probably make it, in the long run, much *harder*
for myself and her." With this latter philosophy, you can reduce the
"hardness" of certain acts, make them more pleasurable, and get
good results from them even if, at first, they have their distinct
difficulties. And as noted above, you will then serve as a good model
for your partner and quite possibly help her improve her frustration
tolerance too.

In sum, many ways exist in which you and your partner may get
to a point where she feels relatively sexless or seems unable to come
to climax. Most of these ways include psychological difficulties, and
a few have distinct physical causes. Whatever the cause, you had
better accept her with her problems and decide whether you find it
worth your while to continue the relationship. If you do, you can try
many things, particularly by discovering the specific ideas and
attitudes that contribute to her disabilities and by helping her understand and change these. In serious cases, you had better see that she
gets professional help. But in many instances, *you* can serve as her
best sex therapist—if you have enough willingness, knowledge, and
determination to do so.

CHAPTER 10

How to Handle Fast Ejaculation

NATURALLY, WOMEN do not have a monopoly on sex problems, and in many ways men have more. Practically all females can fairly easily get somewhat aroused and can have successful intercourse, at least in the sense that they get some satisfaction from it. Their main problems arise when they try to have orgasm, especially during intercourse. But they remain quite capable of satisfying themselves to some degree—and, through intercourse, of satisfying their partners.

Males frequently get themselves in another category—almost complete heterosexual (or homosexual) failure. They have great trouble getting any kind of erection when they try sex with a partner, and because they cannot get erection, they frequently cannot have pleasure or orgasm. Moreover, if their mates really want intercourse, they cannot have it at all or can have it only in a rather unsatisfactory manner. Consequently, they feel quite frustrated. Moreover, since they can usually easily achieve erection and orgasm through masturbation, they feel especially balked when they cannot do so with a partner, and they make themselves suffer the tortures of the damned.

Almost all males, moreover, have sex difficulties at some times. Even though they normally feel quite potent, occasions arise when they do not get aroused, cannot sustain their erections, cannot have an orgasm, or do not receive much pleasure in sex. If you *never* have any such problems, you can consider yourself indeed a rare bird! If you do, let me list some of the things you can do to help yourself.

221

Definition of Fast Ejaculation

The most common sex problem of males consists of fast ejacula-tion—frequently misnamed *premature ejaculation.* Why misnamed? Because, as Kinsey and his associates showed, most young males come pretty quickly—within a minute or two of active penile-vaginal copulation—and in some respects that has advantages. After all, a male who runs a race or types fast often gets considered a great athlete or a good typist; why then should we consider a man who easily gets an erection and ejaculates within a minute or two into his partner's vagina a poor sex partner?

The reason, as Masters and Johnson and other authorities show, for his "poor" rating lies in the wishes and capabilities of the average female—who not only requires a good deal of nongenital foreplay to get fully aroused, but also requires from five to thirty minutes of active intercourse if she has an orgasm coitally. Consequently, the average young male does not last long enough in intercourse to satisfy her fully, and he often leaves her frustrated and disappointed. There-fore, Masters and Johnson define male prematurity as existing when you bring your partner to orgasm in intercourse less than one-half of the time she desires it.

A somewhat pernicious view, say I! For many women do regularly take twenty or more minutes of active copulation to reach orgasm, and relatively few young males last this long or enjoy it if they do. Twenty minutes of fucking equals a hell of a lot of violent exercise! And lots of us males have poor muscles, bad backs, knees that hurt after a while, and all sorts of physical liabilities that prevent us from screwing for that long. Most of us, with practice, probably *can* last for twenty minutes, but we don't necessarily *want* to and would con-sider it onerous if we did—just as women who come to orgasm rap-idly frequently report that they find it boring and uncomfortable when their partners screw for twenty or thirty minutes.

Noncoital Solutions

The ideal of having you train yourself so that you can last twenty or more minutes in intercourse if your partner desires this amount of fucking therefore has its distinct limitations. Compromise solutions frequently had better get sought. Let us first consider some of these compromises, for if you know about them and your partner agrees to them, you can satisfy her much of the time—and can also more easily overcome your anxiety about lasting a relatively short period in intercourse, and thereby enable yourself naturally to last longer. Some of the noncoital solutions to the problem of fast ejaculation include the following:

1. As I keep emphasizing, sex does not primarily consist of penile-vaginal screwing. From the female standpoint, it largely consists of *any* method that will help arouse her fully and bring her, if she wishes, to orgasm. But many (or most) women, as Kinsey, Masters and Johnson, and most other sex authorities now agree, can more easily get excited and fulfilled by noncoital than directly coital methods. If, therefore, you will learn to use your hands, your tongue, and other nongenital parts of your body to perform whatever acts your partner most enjoys, you could literally lack a cock or have full impotence and serve as a highly satisfactory lover to most women.

More specifically, if you locate your partner's clitoral region with your fingers or tongue and stimulate it steadily and gently, and later with perhaps increasing intensity and abandon, she will normally get as good orgasms as she will get from any other means—and often much better! She can, of course, stimulate herself with her own fingers, but yours will frequently prove more exciting, and she can rest comfortably while you do the "work" of arousing and satisfying her. Moreover, although she normally can *not* go down on herself, you can use your mouth and tongue on her genitalia. This kind of stimulation will frequently prove the best, and she will appreciate it enormously.

Don't forget, too, that your toes, knees, elbows, wrists, and other parts of your anatomy can prove highly stimulating to your partner. A knee in the groin, well and firmly placed, may do wonders for her —just as, if you have difficulty coming, firmly rubbing your cock against her thigh or ass may do wonders for you. Don't limit yourself—or her—in this regard. Discover whatever part of your body jibes well with her genital region—and use that part.

2. With some women, genital stimulation hardly proves paramount. Instead, your exciting their mouths, breasts, anuses, or other parts of their bodies may prove more arousing. Usually, this kind of

stimulation serves as foreplay, or as a prelude to genital stimulation. But once in a while, a partner will require steady breast or mouth excitation, up to and including orgasm. See if your partner has this tendency, and if she does, take advantage of it!

By the same token, she may require a great deal of nongenital foreplay for genital arousal. So again, use your fingers, tongue, toes, etc., to play wth her nongenital areas *first*. Then, once she feels sensually aroused and satisfied, and it looks as if she wants genital excitation, you may go on to that part of sex. Often, you can quickly get to her genitalia and skip the "preliminaries." But often you had better not! As noted previously in this book, holding and cuddling a woman may constitute the very best form of "foreplay"—and if so, you'd better not omit this aspect.

3. Stimulating your partner externally with your penis may do a lot of good. Even though she does not seem ready for intercourse, she may feel quite willing to have you rub your (erect or nonerect) penis against her clitoral region, and you may arouse her or actually bring her to orgasm this way. No law exists that says the cock can go *only* into the vagina. It has many other pleasant resting places on and in her body, and she may find these most satisfying.

4. Never forget that your fingers can go *into* your mate's vagina! Many women, for psychological or physiological reasons, very much like intromission. It either brings them to orgasm or it adds to their orgasmic sensations, since during climax their vaginal muscles usually erupt spontaneously and have discernible contractions. If they contract around some organ that remains in the vagina, the woman frequently feels better and perhaps has a more satisfying orgasm. If your penis won't remain erect long enough in your part-ner's vagina, your fingers will do so indefinitely! Consequently, if she adores intromission, you can insert one, two, or three of your fingers into her vagina and stimulate and gratify her that way.

In point of fact, your mate may have unusually sensitive areas inside her vagina that you can reach and massage mainly with your fingers, rather than your penis. The top wall of her vagina may have nerve endings descending from her clitoral area, or her pubococcy-geus muscle may require specific pressure. And you can often utilize your fingers to get to such areas, although your penis (which has no damned sense of direction and certainly cannot bend or push itself into specific corners of the vagina) may serve you and her badly in these repsects.

Finger stimulation, moreover, can easily exist dually or triply. While fingering your partner's clitoral region, for example, you may have another finger in her vagina and still another in her anus. Remember, you have two hands and ten fingers! And only one prick! Your fingers, moreover, remain thinner than your penis and can enter certain places, such as the anal crevices, where your penis cannot comfortably go. They can easily lubricate themselves (with your saliva, with her genital secretions, or with artificial lubricants). They can continue to massage and manipulate for a much longer time than your jong can!

5. You can use intercourse combined with other forms of noncoital stimulation. Thus, you can arouse your partner with nongenital kisses and caresses, then use your fingers and tongue on her genitalia for a time, and then, when it seems that she has got quite close to orgasm, finish off with intercourse. In this way, even if it takes you only a few seconds to come yourself, you can often have an orgasm with your penis inside her. Moreoever, if you know that she feels close to orgasm when you enter her, you will normally stop worrying about how long you will last in coitus—and then you will tend to last longer.

6. Remember that whether or not you get an orgasm in intercourse, you can almost invariably get it in other ways. Don't think that you *have to* finish off with coitus. If your partner gets satisfied only, say, with clitoral manipulation, and she doesn't feel like having intercourse—perhaps because she feels too knocked out or doesn't like coitus that much—she can almost always give you an orgasm with her tongue or hands. You can also fuck her between her thighs, in her anus, against her clitoral area, etc. So don't insist on copulation; and if you don't, you will again tend to lose your overeagerness to last long during it.

A male I saw for sex therapy had never lasted more than a minute in the ten years he had been having intercourse with different women, and at twenty-nine, he still came very quickly each time. I showed him that coitus has no sacredness, and he began to satisfy his current partner with his fingers. She liked handling and sucking his organ, so she almost always gave him an orgasm that way. They didn't worry about intercourse and rarely had it. But to his surprise, when they did have it he easily lasted for up to five minutes—largely because he didn't care too much whether or not they had it, knowing that they could both get satisfied in other ways. Moreover, his having so many orgasms with her noncoitally had desensitized him somewhat to sex with her and he could last much longer, after six months of this kind of sex, than he could previously last with any other woman he had known.

7. As I show in other writings, noncoital sex need not get done simultaneously. Some women cannot reach the heights of arousal if they engage in 69 and go down on their partner while he also goes down on them. They find that too distracting and do not come to orgasm. But if they first bring him off and *then* have him stimulate their own genitalia with his tongue and lips, they have no trouble coming. Similarly, some partners can give each other orgasms manually at the same time, but others find this too distracting and have to do so separately. See what you and your partner find most satisfactory in manual or oral or other stimulation and do it either simultaneously or nonsimultaneously—as you wish.

8. Again, let me emphasize that even if you and your mate can achieve orgasm simultaneously in intercourse, you don't *have to* do so. At times it has its great advantages, but it may rarely occur. And some partners, especially those who have trouble achieving climax, want to concentrate *only* on their own getting stimulated and brought to orgasm, without at that time doing anything for the other. Later, perhaps after they have had an orgasm and rested, they feel only too glad to bring the other to climax. Even, then, if you *can* last longer and have mutual simultaneous orgasm with your partner, you don't need to feel compelled to have it that way. It doesn't make you a better person to achieve that state. And it doesn't necessarily add to enjoyment. Let it come sort of naturally when it does happen, but don't think that you have to force it to come every single time.

If, in the foregoing ways, you stop defining *sex* as *intercourse* and induce your partner to do the same, you will take an immense amount of pressure off both of you, and, not *having* to last very long in coitus, you will probably last longer than you otherwise would.

Remember, again, even women who greatly desire fucking and want to have simultaneous orgasms can get what they want much more often with a combination of coital and noncoital methods. But if you can teach your parnter not to *need* intercourse, both you and she will probably improve at having it and you will both get much more satisfied when you do.

Assuming that you learn this lesson and keep practicing it, you may still want to last longer in intercourse than you often do. For one thing, you may enjoy it more that way. For another thing, you may find it quite convenient to have your orgasm in your partner's vagina, and she may like the feel of it too.

If you do want to last longer in coitus, you can do many kinds of things to enhance your durability. Let me go into some of the more important ones here.

Having More Sex

The simplest method of retarding your ejaculation consists in having more sex. I frequently ask males who come to me because they think they come too quickly, "How many orgasms do you have a week?"

They say, "Oh, three or four."

I tell them, "Double it. Have six or seven. You'll probably come more slowly."

"And if that doesn't work?"

"Try to double that. Have as many orgasms as you can—three a day, if necessary. You'll find it surprising how slowly you'll start to come, after a while, if you have more and more orgasms. The easiest and quickest method of retarding orgasm consists of having plenty of them. Have them with your partner or with yourself, but have them! Especially if you can arrange to copulate with her once or more per day, you will tend to come more and more slowly. Try it and see!

And when they do try, they usually do see. I have had men who told me they never took more than two minutes to come tell me, a few weeks later, after they have had at least one orgasm a day with a woman, that they could easily last ten or fifteen minutes. Some of them, after a while, even had trouble coming! So first of all, try more and more ejaculations, especially with the woman you care for and especially during intercourse with her. This will, first, acclimate you to her body and her vagina, and second, deplete your sex drive. You will then probably come much more slowly.

Above all, don't *avoid* sex, but keep performing it if you suffer with fast ejaculation. For every time you avoid it, you tend to reindoctrinate your view, "It would prove terrible if I failed, because I *must* succeed." The more you do it, the less you will repropagate this false notion. You will also, with one mate or many mates, get used to having sex and get desensitized to it. And you can prove, in practice, that when you fail to maintain a prolonged erection and use *it* to satisfy your mate, many other ways of satisfying her exist —as she, if she behaves sanely and allows these ways, will tell you.

Don't arbitrarily see yourself as a once-a-day or once-a-night individual. As Dr. Lester Kirkendall discovered many years ago in his experiments with young males, most people can have almost twice the number of orgasms that they think they can have or "feel" like having. Once you come to orgasm, you will often convince yourself that because you can easily live without another one at that time, you *have* to. Rot! I found, many years ago, that no matter how easy it remains for me *not* to get an erection and orgasm again, that doesn't mean that I *can't*. It merely means that I won't try— and therefore won't get it.

I frequently tell a story in this connection of what happened to me a number of years ago. A highly sexed woman friend called me up at midnight and said, "You know, I feel horny tonight. Why don't you come over?"

"Fine!" I said; and I took a cab to her place, and fifteen minutes after her call we screwed and had a fine time of it.

Whereupon, somewhat to my surprise, she said, "I found that great! But I still feel horny. Can't we try it again?"

"But look," I said, "we did it only five minutes ago. I don't think I can get it up so soon."

She seemed very disappointed, so I said, "But let's try. If nothing happens, nothing happens."

So she went down on me, and, to my surprise, I quickly got a fine erection. I still didn't *feel* like having sex, but my cock certainly rose hard and straight. So I tried to screw her, but as soon as I turned over to get it into her vagina, it fell down again. Which didn't surprise me—because I knew I didn't really feel sexy.

Even more disappointed, she said, "What will we do now?"

"Don't worry, dear," I said, knowing the score. "Let's try it again."

She went down on me, and it soon rose, hard as a rock. This time, to make sure it stayed up, I thought of another woman, who looked very enticing but about whom I knew very little, since we never had had any sex play. But as I thought of her, my penis remained firm, and I not only turned over and screwed, but did a beautiful job of it. After a few minutes of screwing, I got turned on, had a little trouble coming to orgasm, but finally made it.

One of the best damned fucks I had ever had! Yet left to my own devices, I would never have attempted to copulate, and certainly wouldn't have done it successfully.

So don't merely go by your *feeling*. You can get it up, often, without any great sex urge—merely by your partner's stimulation or by your own sexy thinking. And once you do, you not only can succeed, but can last much longer, if you want to, than you normally would. This also means, of course, that if you want to last longer the "first" time with your partner, you can masturbate just before you visit her, can have her jerk you off before you have intercourse, or can make sure you otherwise come to orgasm soon before you start screwing. This won't always work, but it often will!

·The Stop-start Technique

Try the stop-start technique of intercourse. As noted previously, this method seems far better for many people than the squeeze technique. You have intercourse, in any regular position, including your getting on top of your partner and facing her. You enter her when you get an erection and then make a few pelvic thrusts until you get fully aroused and seem about to come. Suddenly, stop! Remain quiet, resting, with your penis still in her vagina. After a few seconds or a minute or two, start thrusting again. Keep stopping every time you think you approach orgasm—until you finally want to bring it on and continue until you do so.

With this stop-start method, you can often screw for twenty or thirty minutes. After a while, moreover, you finally feel that you have passed the point of quick orgasm and can hold out indefinitely. But even if you never reach this point, you can almost always stop before orgasm, then continue again. Your partner, of course, may not like this method, since it interrupts her passion and may feel onerous. But she may also like it and prefer that you last longer this way. So talk it over with her, get her cooperation, and see if you can't learn to start and stop, start and stop, until you prolong intercourse quite a bit. As long as you finally reach orgasm, this method will probably result in no particular trouble for you, but if you don't let yourself ultimately come, you may create prostate, urethral, and other irritation.

To retard orgasm you can use another physical technique that I mention in the *Art and Science of Love*:

> By having coitus slowly, with short strokes and a good many pauses in between thrusts, one can often ward off climax, sometimes almost indefinitely. Whenever one feels about to have an orgasm, one slows down coital movements or stops entirely for a while; then, when things have quieted down, one becomes more active again.
>
> In cases where husband and wife wish to have simultaneous or near-simultaneous climax, the husband can leave his penis almost motionless inside the vagina while he keeps pressing its base, with a side to side, up and down, or circular motion, against his wife's vulva and, especially, against her clitoral region, while she remains fairly still. He thus can wait until she approaches climax before he lets himself go and produces his own orgasm by active coital movements.
>
> If the male moves his penis in a circle instead of a straight in-and-out way, he also may vary his sensation so that it does not become too overwhelming and lead to climax. Also: by pressing against the vaginal wall with the *upper* side of his penis, instead of using the pressure of its lower side against the lower vaingal wall, the male may reduce his sensation and last longer in coitus.

As usual in these respects, you'd better find out which kind of motion serves you best—both for delaying and, at times, for bringing orgasm on. Every person behaves a little differently from others and you can find your and your partner's proclivities only by exploring and experimenting.

Notice that several ways exist of your retarding orgasm by copulative means, and some of them actually seem contradictory. As noted above, you can employ stop and start motions of intercourse, or you can thrust very vigorously and powerfully and concentrate on pressure rather than sensual excitement. Or you can use slow-paced, minimum thrusts, or you can withdraw completely and later resume intercourse; or you can give yourself a complete rest from intercourse for a while.

Coitus Reservatus

Still another technique of intercourse that often retards orgasm consists of the extreme one of coitus reservatus, sometimes called karezza. This has existed for many centuries and got popularized in the nineteenth century by the Perfectionist John Humphrey Noyes. Some of the Tantric yoga and other Oriental techniques include it. Coitus reservatus consists of your trying to have intercourse without any orgasm whatsoever. For the most part, you allow your penis to remain in your partner's vagina, with little or no movement. She may come to orgasm, but you attempt not to do so. You may get all kinds of other sensations, including a good many feelings of love, closeness, harmony, union, etc., but you train yourself, sometimes over a period of weeks or months, not to come to orgasm.

Does this method prove very practical or harmless? I doubt it. Studies at Oneida Community in New York State, many years ago, showed that many males practiced coitus reservatus unharmfully. But this may well have consisted of a highly selected group of individuals, and the average person might well develop blue balls, prostate trouble, and other difficulties if he continually practiced it.

Dr. W. F. Robie pointed out that coitus interruptus or reservatus sometimes leads to fast ejaculation. For if you worry about withdrawing your penis from your partner's vagina before ejaculation (usually as a birth-control measure) or about having to perform intercourse without coming to any orgasm whatever, you may lose your pleasure in intercourse, get imperfect erections, and precipitate fast ejaculation. The antidote consists in letting yourself ejaculate in your partner's vagina and refusing to concern yourself with coitus reservatus.

Robie also recommended modified coitus reservatus, where you can at first remain relatively passive and unorgasmic in your partner's vagina, until she reaches orgasm; but then you start active copulation or she brings you to climax with her hand or her mouth. As

Robie notes, using this kind of procedure, you can make orgasm mutual but not necessarily simultaneous—and both of you can thereby reach full satisfaction.

The Squeeze Technique

Masters and Johnson highly recommend the squeeze technique, originally invented by Dr. J. H. Semans. Using this method, you usually have your partner massage your penis until you come to erection, then continue fondling it till you near orgasm. As this occurs, you tell her you feel very excited, and she grasps your organ firmly and squeezes it with her thumb, on the underside of the penis, just below the head. This will tend to cause you to lose 20 percent of your erection. She waits a short while, then brings you to full erection again. Then, as you approach orgasm, you again signal her, and she squeezes and prevents you from actually having one. After a while, you get trained or conditioned to react less to her caresses, and you tend to take longer and longer to have an orgasm.

Once you get to this point, you can have intercourse with her, especially in a position where you lie on your back and she faces you and squats or lies on top of you. She inserts your erect penis in her vagina and moves for a while, until you approach orgasm. You then signal her, and she quickly dismounts you and squeezes your penis until you partially lose your erection. Then she mounts you again. This process continues until you can stay in her vagina for a fairly long period and have intercourse without coming.

A variation consists in your squeezing your own penis, during masturbation, just before you reach orgasm, so that you train yourself to feel less sensitized and to increase your capacity for stimulating your penis for a longer time before you climax. Another variation consists in your having sex with your partner but squeezing your penis yourself when you approach orgasm, instead of letting her do it. The squeeze technique works very well when done regularly but proves awkward and unlikable by some individuals, who would prefer the stop-start technique discussed above.

Breathing Methods

Breathing methods will often serve you well to retard orgasm. If you focus on your breathing, rather than on how stimulating the sex you keep having, this serves as a form of distraction. But the muscular activity involved in the breathing may also interfere with some of your excitement and help you come more slowly. One technique of breathing involves inhaling deeply at the point where you think orgasm may likely occur, and taking a deep breath and, after holding it a minute or two, slowly and calmly exhaling. Various kinds of breathing exercises, some of them included in yoga, may help you in this respect. Most importantly, focus on doing the breathing and stick with it, so that you definitely interrupt some of the highly excitatory sex signals you keep sending yourself.

Dr. Paul Gillette gives his own variation on breathing exercises: "Take a deep breath and hold it in your lungs as long as you can. As with the Indian breathing technique, the shift of your concentration slows excitement and thereby enhances staying power." He rightly acknowledges the essence of many sex therapy methods— things that seem physical, like breathing, actually involve concentration, a cognitive technique; and the interrupting or diverting cognition really does the trick.

Nerve-deadening Substances

I have for many years recommended Nupercainal ointment and Xylocaine ointment, both obtainable in drugstores without any prescription (since lots of people use them for painful hemorrhoids). Masters and Johnson and various other authorities think these kinds of nerve-deadening ointments pretty worthless, and I agree that they hardly constitute panaceas. But I find that some males use them effectively; and once they see, with the use of such ointments (or equivalent nerve-deadening sprays), that they can last longer, they stop worrying about coming too quickly and often tend to last longer without them.

Use of Drugs and Alcohol

Professor Sexus, columnist for the now defunct *Pleasure* magazine, noted that in addition to nerve-deadening ointments, "several other things come to mind, if you want to play around with them: take one of your wife's diet pills about two or three hours before fucking, it should slow you down sexually a bit . . . but that [seems] a little risky and may backfire. Personally if I have one or two or three strong belts of Scotch, I can usually fuck forever—not to brag, it just turns out that way."

Although alcohol, as I state elsewhere, may affect some people as an excitant when taken in moderate doses, it also serves mainly as a depressant. Dr. Jorge A. Viamontes, who has done research with alcohol at Washington University School of Medicine, St. Louis, writes, "The available studies on the effect of alcohol on sexual potency show without exception its depressant effect. In a recent study on the effect of alcohol on the sexual potency of male alcoholics and nonalcoholics in Malcolm Bliss Mental Health Center, [we] found that alcohol impairs sexual performance, affecting both ejaculation and erection. In this study the effect of alcohol [proved] temporal. Other clinicians, only on the basis of their clinical observations, have reported permanent impairment of sexual function by the chronic use of alcohol."

As Dr. Viamontes shows, alcohol may serve to depress sexual function severely in some males; however, other males may have such high sexuality and quick ejaculatory ability that they may consider this kind of depressing or suppressing effect *good*. Some individuals, in fact, seem to turn alcoholic because they first use liquor to retard their orgasms and then later find that it boomerangs because it renders them impotent.

Dr. G. Lombard Kelly, one of the pioneers in treating sex disturbances, sometimes recommended mild sedation for serious cases of fast ejaculation. He also advised a rest from sex activity. The theory here says that if you get yourself too anxious about coming rapidly, you will overexcite yourself and actually come more quickly. Therefore, temporary measures like sedation or rest may distract you or slow you down. Once you see that these measures work, you may then feel more confident that you *can* come more slowly, and your increased confidence will interrupt your anxiety and actually help you in this regard.

Powerful Thrusting

What seems like the opposite of the stop-start technique consists of the "power play" method, recommended in some cases by Dr. Paul Gillette: "Raise yourself until your penis [rests] almost outside the vagina: only the head remains inside her. Then thrust forward sharply, slamming your body hard against hers and driving your penis far inside her. Withdraw again to a head-only position. Then slam into her again." Repeat till culmination.

I agree that this technique, oddly enough, may work. At times, it proves obnoxious to your partner; at times, delightful. Sometimes, it will make you come much faster, for your pelvic thrusts tend to get harder. But, possibly because of its distracting element again, it can get you to concentrate on the hardness of your thrust and on various pressure sensations rather than more directly arousing ones. Consequently, you may last longer in this position—and your partner, if she likes it, may come more quickly.

Antiawfulizing

As in other sex therapy and general therapy, antiawfulizing seems about the very best technique that you can use to help yourself with rapid ejaculation. For one of the reasons you come quickly consists of your making yourself very anxious *about* coming. You can easily trigger off orgasm through worrying about it—and worrying how much you will satisfy your partner.

You can achieve nonvulnerability in this respect by not *needing* to win your partner's love or approval, not *having* to do well to show how great you rate as a person, and fully realizing that the world won't come to an end no matter how many times you fail to last very long in intercourse. The general techniques of RET prove exceptionally valuable in this connection, and the more you antiawfulize and anticatastrophize about the possibility of your coming quickly, the longer you will tend to last in intercourse, if that remains your goal.

Antiawfulizing proves such a powerful technique in this as in most other sex problems, that I'd better go through it in more detail, to make sure that you understand it fully. Awfulizing, or catastrophizing, springs from your irrational Beliefs—from the sentences you tell yourself or the vivid pictures in your head that go beyond reality. Thus, if you suffer from fast ejaculation of a primarily psychological nature, you first tend to have some sane or rational Beliefs (rBs): "I hope to hell I don't come too quickly, since I and my partner might enjoy that less. If so, that would prove unfortunate or frustrating, and I wouldn't like it!" These rational Beliefs make you *concerned*—and you consequently try to last longer.

At the same time, you have a set of awfulizing or irrational Beliefs (iBs): "How *terrible*, if I come quickly! I *couldn't stand* that! I *must* come more slowly, and if I don't do what I *must*, I rate as a no-good slob who will *always* fail and can *never* satisfy my partner or any other normal woman!" By having these nutty, unrealistic Beliefs, you make yourself anxious and self-downing and you frequently *create* fast ejaculation and other forms of sexual inadequacy.

How can you eliminate this type of sex anxiety? By asking yourself:

"*Why* would it prove terrible if I came quickly?"

Answer: It wouldn't! My partner and I would merely, at worst, find it highly *inconvenient* and *frustrating*. To rate as *awful* or *terrible,* I would have to find a sex (or nonsexual) performance around 100 percent bad. And fast ejaculation hardly belongs in that class! *Terrible* really means, moreover, at least 101 percent bad—or *more* than bad. And having a rapid orgasm cannot possibly rise to that nonexistent summit!

"What evidence exists that I *can't stand* coming quickly?"

Answer: None whatever! I'll never *like* failing sexually, but if I do fail, I can certainly stand or bear what I don't like.

"What proof do I have that I *must* come more slowly?"

Answer: Zero! It *would seem better* if I lasted longer, but just because I would find it *preferable* to have a trait doesn't mean that I *should* or *must* have it. The universe hardly commands what I want!

"How do I rate as a slob if I fail sexually?"

Answer: I don't. My *behavior* may prove slobbish but that hardly proves that I turn into a hundred-percent failure. A slob would have to *only* and *always* act slobbish—sexually and nonsexually; and it appears most unlikely that I rest in that category! A person who rates as *a* slob or *a* shit, moreover, deserves to fail. The universe singles him or her out for eternal *damnation* because he or she fails. Does it seem probably that for the sin of coming quickly the fates have thus damned me forever?

"What evidence exists that I could *never* satisfy my partner or any other normal woman?"

Answer: There doesn't exist, nor probably ever will, such evidence! For no matter how many times I fail to satisfy her, I may still do so in the future. And if I never do please this partner sexually, I can most probably turn on and satisfy many others. *Never* appears an overgeneralized, foolish word that I had better never—well, hardly ever!—use.

If you forcefully Dispute your irrational Beliefs in this manner, you will soon see them as magical and false. You will see that sex failure doesn't prove *you* a total loss; and that you will most likely not fail *forever* because you have done so the last several times. You will then wind up with a new philosophy or Effect (E) regarding sex failure in general, and fast ejaculation in particular. Such as: "I would certainly prefer to last longer at intercourse; but if I don't, I don't. I can almost invariably find ways to satisfy myself and my partner, no matter how quickly I come. But even if the worst comes to the worst, and I just cannot make it successfully with this particular mate, I still can fully accept myself and look for sex satisfaction elsewhere. As long as I live, I have the right to enjoy myself as best as I can, without needlessly doing in others; and if I do worse at sex (and nonsexual) affairs than other people often do, that again won't kill me. In fact, I can live as quite a happy human, in spite of such failings, and in spite of the fact that certain enjoyments rarely or never come my way."

This kind of a rational-emotive philosophy will tend to help you mightily with almost any kind of a sex problem. You can learn it yourself, by reading various RET books, listening to recordings, attending courses and workshops at the Institute for Advanced Study in Rational Psychotherapy in New York and other parts of the world, and by various other educational modalities. If you cannot get sufficient help with your emotional problems in these ways, try a rational-emotive therapist or therapy group, or some other form of effective psychotherapy.

Awfulizing and antiawfulizing about sexual inadequacy frequently get recognized, though not under the same names, by various authorities on sex failure. Sam Julty, in his excellent book *Male Sexual Performance*, sees very clearly that "impotence still reflects, or connotes, a judgment of the entire person. . . . The man without the erection sees himself as less than a man, as an unworthy, as a fraud. . . . The flag of his manhood must remain furled for lack of a mast. Thus the terror, the shame, the withdrawal spurred by the dysfunction far exceed the reaction to almost any other medical condition, such as cancer, multiple sclerosis, or amputation."

Masters and Johnson, in *The Pleasure Bond*, also see that antiawfulizing remains the real issue if you want to function well in bed. As Linda Wolfe notes, in reviewing the book, their answer shows "that breaking new bed barriers and inventing new sexual positions will prove less effective than simply not [proving] hellbent on orgasm." Correct!

The Myth of Simultaneous Orgasm

Particularly surrender the myth of the necessity of simultaneous orgasm if you want to prolong intercourse. For when you believe that you *must* come at the same time as your mate, and come during intercourse, you put enormous pressure on yourself to achieve this relatively rare feat. You don't really enjoy sex in the process; you tend to make yourself anxious about coming too quickly; and you view with enormous displeasure, and possibly horror, your coming before your partner does. Once you fully believe that it may prove *nice* but never *necessary* to have simultaneous orgasm, you will tend to enjoy sex more fully and let yourself have it in a much more relaxed, longer-lasting manner.

As Dr. John L. Schimel notes in this connection, "The myth of the mutual orgasm leads to difficulties for many sexual partners. Many consider anything less or different to [amount to] a failure, defect, or defeat. This attitude may contribute to hostility, depression, and/or secondary sexual symptoms such as impotence or premature ejaculation." Right! You may well try for mutual climax—meaning that both of you come at *some* time during your lovemaking—but not for *simultaneous* orgasm. That often proves deadly!

Use of the Urinary Muscle

Dr. John Eichenlaub points out that you can sometimes cut down on the amount of semen you ejaculate each time you have an orgasm by using the muscle with which you normally cut off your urinary stream and which you would usually not employ during intercourse. As he states, "If you clamp down with this muscle during ejaculation, you can cut the flow of semen by between one-quarter and one-half, increasing proportionately the number of sexual episodes you can manage."

Let me warn you, however—this works only some of the time for some men. Either you may have difficulty performing this or you may succeed and still not achieve a greater number of sexual episodes. Dr. Eichenlaub advocates practicing interrupting your act of urinary voiding many times for about ten days in a row, then you will feel able to clamp down the urinary muscles during intercourse. Some men actually enjoy intercourse *more* with seminal retention than without, he reports. But *some* doesn't mean *all*. Personal experimentation will show whether you remain in this "some" category.

A semihumorous aside, taken from Alex Comfort's translation and interpretation of the old Indian classic *Koka Shastra:* "One may delay ejaculation if at the time of congress one presses hard at the root of the vas deferens, thinks of other matters, and controls the breathing by the kumbha-exercise: or by firmly closing the anus and signing oneself from head to foot with the syllable Om, and with the dark-bodied, tortoise-throned Vishnu . . . likewise by tying on the buttock a bone from the right side of a black cat and taking a saptacchadda seed in the lips." Here, we have the mental and physical diversion techniques, which do work if you practice them, linked with superstitious, magical nonsense, which you can damned well forget!

Contracting Anal Muscles

For centuries we have known that contraction of the anal sphincter and the perineal muscles will control and serve to interfere with fast ejaculation. As I note in *The Art and Science of Love,* "Once a human gets to a certain point in sex arousal, he or she finds it almost impossible to control orgasmic contractions voluntarily. Nonetheless, just before this point of uncontrollability occurs, some measures of self-control can often get effectively employed. The same muscles you employ to control defecation and urination (the anal spincter and the perineal muscles) have some connection with the muscles that importantly influence orgasm and ejaculation. If, therefore, you will practice tightening or relaxing your anal or pelvic muscles when orgasm approaches, you will often find it possible to head off climax. The more you practice conscious relaxation or tightening of the muscles in the anal and perineal areas, the more likely you can achieve a certain amount, and sometimes an excellent amount, of control over having an orgasm."

Dr. Arnold Kegel assumes that males as well as females have a pubococcygeus muscle and that the anal and perineal control described in the previous paragraph acts to strengthen and control this muscle. As Allen and Martin note, "Once you have learned to contract the pubococcygeus muscle you have also learned how to make it relax. Ejaculation always [gets] accomplished by involuntary, spasmodic contraction of the smooth muscle of the prostatic urethra. If you cause the pubococcygeus muscle to relax, you will remove the muscular pressure from this area—and stop emission. If you increase the pressure of the pubococcygeus muscle, on the other hand, you will hasten and heighten the ejaculatory process. [You'll find it] so simple, so easy, and automatic to form the rest of the loop. Once the pressure for performance [gets] taken away, the pressure from the pubococcygeus muscle will go away. The process [proves] identifical to the woman's anatomical control over the vaginal muscles."

Using Sexual Surrogates

As we noted in the case of women who have sex difficulties, a male too can often make use of sexual surrogates—if he can find suitable ones. Patronizing prostitutes sometimes serves this purpose, but not too well in many instances, since the interest of the whore consists in getting through with sex as quickly as possible, and not mainly in having her partner last longer. But special women, or sex surrogates who have had training under a professional sex therapist, may prove very helpful in this respect—as several books and articles written by and about such surrogates have shown.

When asked about the value of using surrogates, Dr. Alex Comfort replied, "We clearly have to use them, unless you believe that sex can [get] taught by a correspondence course. Obviously, you don't use surrogates when there [exists] a regular partner. But you can't tell a patient who [has anxiety] about his potency or about his change of role to go and get married or pick up a stranger."

So in severe cases of fast ejaculation, where the afflicted individual does not have an available partner, the use of a sex surrogate may well prove highly valuable.

Cognitive Diversion

Techniques of cognitive diversion have served millions of men as orgasm retarders for many centuries. Orgasm usually gets triggered off by various kinds of thoughts: (1) thoughts of how attractive your partner appears and how sexy certain parts of her body seem; (2) thoughts of what great pleasure you will have in sex relations; (3) thoughts of a loving nature—of how great you find it to love your partner and share this great sexual experience with her; (4) thoughts of having sex acts of an exciting nature with your partner, even though at the moment you really go through standard, perhaps monotonous routines; (5) thoughts of having sex with other partners, of performing sex acts that your present partner might not even allow; (6) thoughts about your bodily sensations, and particularly your genital sensations, as you fuck; (7) thoughts about how frustrating and "terrible" you would find it if you came too quickly and didn't satisfy your partner fully; (8) thoughts that perhaps someone keeps observing or listening to you perform with your bedmate; (9) thoughts that the acts in which you engage rate as wicked or evil, and hence unusually exiciting; or (10) thoughts that you'd better come very quickly, or else you will lose your erection, or your partner will tire, or prolonged sex will prove wicked or harmful in some way.

All these kinds of thoughts can get temporarily or even permanently blocked by various kinds of diversion. You can deliberately think of nonsexy things (such as arithmetic sums or political events). You can focus almost exclusively on your partner and her reactions, rather than upon your own. You can get so absorbed in the mechanics of what you do sexually that you lose some of your excitement thinking abou it. You can perform some violent activity, such as vigorous petting or embracing or even fucking that will distract you from some of the penile pleasure you feel. You can focus so intently on your love feelings for your mate that you actually block off some of your sex feelings. You can create nonsexual images in your head—such as images of a house, a map, a landscape, a sports game. You can compose things, such as the words or music of songs. You can devote yourself to some distracting nonsexual activity—such as smoking, doodling, or playing with some object—while you copulate.

These various kinds of diversions have their distinct disadvantages. As Massad F. Ayoob notes, "Standard methods [consist in] 'doing multiplication tables in your head,' mentally reciting the batting averages of the Boston Red Sox—anything to get your mind off the task at hand. This basic theory [constitutes] also, of course,

the basic flaw in the method. When you have intercourse, you don't
want to get your mind off it. You [stay] *there* to enjoy a sexual
encounter, and feeling that you have to block it out [seems] bru-
tally self-defeating. 'Mind-blocking' [proves] best used as a stop-
gap approach to prolonging intercourse. Use it only while developing other ways. It [constitutes] dreary sex, and will poison any
sexual relationship if carried on long enough."

Ayoob states the case against mind-blocking too strongly. Yes, it
certainly has its limitations. But a great many people find it works
beautifully, even though it *somewhat* interferes with desire and
enjoyment. The net result, for them, seems easily worth it. So if you
feel you come too quickly, you can think of various kinds of nonsexual things to help yourself come more slowly. Don't take this
kind of diversion to foolish extremes, but do use it to the extent that
you find it comfortable and effective.

Brian Boylan, in his excellent book, *Infidelity,* tells how one of
his male respondents learned about cognitive diversion from one of
his female partners. "She described a technique that one of her previous lovers used. He mentally put himself somewhere else while he
[kept] screwing. . . . When he felt his body taking over from his
will, he immediately imagined himself stretched out on an isolated
beach in the West Indies, listening to the waves lapping around his
ankles. That way, he [could] delay his orgasm until after she had
come. Well, I tried it and it worked! Ever since, I've taken trips to
the Caribbean or the Rockies at a crucial moment, but I've held off
until Fiona [got] ready."

Use of Condoms

Most sex authorites, including Masters and Johnson, do not particularly espouse the use of mechanical deadeners, such as condoms,
to retard orgasm, but in many instances they seem wrong. I have
known quite a few males who would wear a condom, or even two
condoms, to deaden their penile sensations and make themselves
come more slowly. These days, condoms usually feel thin and silky,
not like the old-style thicker types, and therefore may not serve this
purpose well. But some individuals still find them desensitizing and
can last longer in intercourse when they wear them. Naturally, they
have other disadvantages—such as the hassle of putting them on

before intercourse. But you can don them before you even start to pet, and you can also find that they have clear-cut advantages, especially in regard to protecting you and your partner from the transmission of most venereal diseases that you or she may have. So, again, by all means experiment with them if you think that you come too quickly.

Lubrication

One method of lasting longer consists in trying to make sure that your partner feels so aroused that she lubricates copiously. If you have difficulty entering her vagina, or if she feels very tight after you enter it, your penis tends to have too much friction applied to it, and you may come rapidly. The more lubrication, the more you may find it easy to continue prolonged coitus. One warning, however—some males come quickly in intercourse, as against having their penis massaged by their partner's hand, because the vaginal secretions feel very good and hence add to their sensation. If this proves true, lack of lubrication may aid you. Also, if your partner will use her hands to massage your penis, but make sure that she employs adequate lubrication, she may help desensitize you to lubrication, so that when you later feel her moist vagina around your cock, it does not feel *too* stimulating and lead you to have a quick orgasm.

Precoital Stimulation

Dr. John Eichenlaub has an interesting view of fast ejaculation that may well include some truth. He notes that rapid change in stimulation, rather than the amount of stimulation, trips the male trigger as a man goes from getting stimulated in petting to placing his penis in his partner's vagina. Consequently, the less stimulation he gets before intercourse, the more change will exist, and the faster he will come when he enters her vagina. Dr. Eichenlaub therefore recommends that you arrange to get *more* stimulation with your partner *before* intercourse.

This has its advantages and may well work with some individuals. But many others discover that the more the man gets stimulated, the closer to orgasm he gets; consequently, as soon as he enters his partner's vagina, he comes. With these individuals, it works better either when he arouses his mate but *doesn't* let her handle his penis or when he has intercourse with her when she has not got too aroused by him, and then lasts longer and *later* satisfies her or makes sure that he somehow brings her to orgasm. So Dr. Eichenlaub's method may or may not work for you. Experiment with it and see.

Mystic Experiences

A special kind of concentration that sometimes leads to slower ejaculation goes along with some of the yoga or mystic-minded techniques that Oriental teachings often include. As far as I can tell, these techniques definitely can work; but the big question exists: "Do they not go together with so much claptrap and have so many inherent disadvantages that they hardly prove worth the effort?" My own answer: Yes, they normally do!

Nancy Phelan and Michael Volin, for example, outline the Tantric path in their book *Sex and Yoga*. They quote from the *Siva Samhita,* presumably containing the words of the god Siva: "First with the help of in-breathing (Puraka) draw in the mind with the breath to the basic Centre (Adhara) and maintain it there firmly. Then try to contract the *yoni* place between the male organ and the anus. Then concentrate on Lust (Karma), which, in the shape of an arrow shining like a thousand suns but cool like a thousand moons, lies in the centre of the principal *yoni*. Above it [shows] a subtle tongue of light which [represents] Consciousness, the Supreme Energy (Kala), and in union with it [exists] the one Supreme Self on whom one should meditate."

It seems obvious from passages like these that the Tantric yoga methods include physical techniques like breathing and exercise of the urinating muscles (like those techniques outlined previously) and concentration techniques, with the individual focusing on other things than sex arousal and satisfaction. No evidence exists that they really have anything to do with the mystical, unverifiable, and often pretty senseless philosophy that Yoga and other Oriental teachings include. If you want to benefit from them, therefore, you could use the sensible parts and omit the mystical claptrap in which they get embedded.

CHAPTER 11

How to Handle Your
Other Sex Problems

MALES FREQUENTLY SUFFER from other forms of sexual inadequacy
than fast ejaculation—particularly from the inability to achieve or
maintain an adequate erection. For the most past, these disabilities
stem from psychological causes, but as the researches of Dr. Sallie
Schumacher and Dr. Charles Lloyd show, a good many physiological reasons add to, and sometimes even lead to, these psychological
problems. Let us first discuss some of the organic difficulties.

Organic Factors in Sexual Difficulties

Dr. David S. Janowsky mentions several important hormonal
influences on adult sexuality in women and then adds that in men
hormonal factors also may regulate sexuality.

Dr. Philip R. Roen, a leading urologist, advocates a complete
medical history when a male shows loss of libido, to discover
whether he exhibits overt signs of gonadal deficiency, seems to fall
in the class of the tall fine-skinned eunuchoid type of individual who
has Klinefelter's syndrome, possesses scars of repair of bilaterial
hernia with testicular atrophy, or appears afflicted with some early
neurologic disease.

Professor Jan Raboch of the Sexological Institute of Charles University, Czechoslovakia, did a study of coital activity of men and
levels of plasma testosterone and found in all age subgroups of
impotence men lower average values of male sex hormones in the
blood than he found in nonimpotent men. Patients with primary
impotence showed "a striking low level of male sexual hormone in
the blood." He concluded that "a distinctly subnormal level of plas-
matic testosterone in some cases of primary impotence could [indi-

cate] an expression of insufficiency in physiologic mechanisms whose adequate course enable a man to successfully perform coitus."

Dr. Luis I. Kobashi notes that the so-called male climacteric stems from physiologic and psychogenic causes. There seems "no question that the aging process will bring about a gradual decrease in bodily functions possibly including the sexual drive even without actual decrease in testicular function." Normally, he holds, barring poor health or an unwilling mate, men will continue to perform indefinitely in a satisfactory manner. But they have distinct physical limitations and these may make them at times perform inadequately.

Dr. Max Ellenberg reports that his studies clearly implicate neuropathy as "a highly signicant and very common factor in the pathogenesis of impotence in diabetes." When rendered impotent by diabetes, not even testosterone (the male sex hormone) does some males any good.

Dr. Lajos Koncz and Dr. Sandor A. Friedman agree with Dr. Ellenberg about the physical factors that render some diabetics impotent; and Dr. Koncz points out that "potency depends as much on the integrity of the vascular system as it does on the autonomic nervous system."

Dr. Richard Amelar and Dr. Lawrence Dubin, two outstanding urologists, include among the causes of impotence prostatitis, lumbar disc disease, circulatory disturbances in the region of the lower aorta and Leriche's syndrome, surgical sympathectomy when the lumbar ganglia get removed, brain and spinal cord tumors or injuries and their sequelae, trauma to the perineal nerves, as in straddle injuries, and after perineal prostatectomy or perineal prostatic biopsy, severe system disease of any nature, whether acute or chronic, priapism commonly associated with sickle cell disease and with leukemia. Among drug agents that may cause or exacerbate impotence they list heroin, large intake of alcohol, chronic barbiturate intoxication, long-term use of anticholinergic agents, tranquilizers derived from phenothiazine, monoamineoxidase inhibitors, and some drugs used in the treatment of high blood pressure that prove sympathetic blocking agents.

Dr. Bruce Belt adds to this list of organic causes of impotence various herbicides, such as Dieldrin; estrogen treatment; stenosis or thrombotic occlusion of the abdominal aorta; pelvic fracture, especially when the nerves get damaged and the urethra gets ruptured; Peyronie's disease (single or multiple plaques of the cavernous sheath of the penis); fracture of the penis.

Dr. Howard Weiss discusses spinal-cord injury and its effect on erection and notes that "Bors and Comarr observed that patients with complete destruction of the sacral spinal cord could still have erections in response to erotic psychic stimuli but not in response to genital manipulation. Conversely, they found that in patients with complete transection of the spinal cord above the sacral level, erections could occur in response to manipulation of the genitalia but not in response to erotic psychic stimuli. Theoretically, spinal cord trauma should not cause complete impotence unless both the sacral and the thoraco-lumbar erection mediating centers [gets] destroyed, or unless the psychological sequelae to the trauma inhibit the intact erection center."

Although aging itself does not necessarily cause lack of sex power or erectile ability, it does have at least a partial influence on impotence in some instances. The so-called male climacteric has psychological as well as physical causes—and does not seem to afflict many men to any considerable degree. When it does occur, it may or may not affect potency. But Dr. Jan Raboch found that whereas fast ejaculation constituted the most frequent complaint of young males seen for sex therapy, "weak sexual appetite [got] mostly reported by men aged 46 to 50 years. Disturbances of erectivity with increasing years continuously increased."

Dr. Martin Goldberg, discussing physiologic factors in loss of libido in males, states that there exist "four major physiologic causes that contribute to an absence of libido. These [include] endocrine disturbances; senescence; severe debilitating diseases and/or malnutrition; and congenital abnormalities." He also notes that "men go through cycles of sexual desire, somewhat akin to the cycles in women. There [exists] a periodic waxing and waning of the intensity of libidinal drive, but this varies with individual men and [can get] predicted only on an individual basis."

As physical and psychological information accumulates, various solutions to organic impotence arise. Even psychological impotence can sometimes get solved by physical means. For years, physicians have experimented with implanting plastic substances in the male's penis, to enable him to have a sort of permanent erection; but so far, none of these works very well. More recently, however, Dr. Brantley Scott of the Baylor College of Medicine in Houston, together with Dr. William Bradley and Dr. Gerald Timm, both of the University of Minnesota Hospital, have developed a technique where two collapsible silicone-rubber cylinders get implanted into the penis and connected to a tiny hand-operated pump implanted inside the scrotum. As Aaron Latham notes, in reporting on their work, they connect the pump to a reservoir filled with fluid, implanted behind the stomach muscles.

An impotent or semi-impotent male who has this operation done and the apparatus fixed inside his body produces an erection "by reaching down, locating the small pump in the scrotum, and pressing it a half-dozen times. This action pumps the liquid from the reservoir into the cylinders in the penis."

Dr. William Bradley says that the result doesn't *seem* like a real erection—it *consists of* a real erection. "The real thing. It has all the characteristics of an erection—enlargement, growth in diameter. It [feels] great!"

If this and other types of physical procedures work out, they prove that physical factors in impotence *do* have real importance. So keep that in mind, whatever the source of your problem, psychological or physical.

Assuming that some of your sex problems do not have serious physical components but stem largely from psychological causes, let me list some of the things you can do to help yourself in this respect.

Retarded Orgasm

Occasionally, you may have the problem of *ejaculatio retardans,* or retarded ejaculation, and not feel able to come to orgasm for a long period of time, or even to come to it at all. As Dr. Harold Kenneth Fink notes, this "can create fear and panic! The man may [make himself] tense and depressed. He may begin to fantasize that his wife [goes about] considering other partners to make up for his ineffectiveness in bed." Such anxiety, of course, will tend to exacerbate your problem—since you largely bring on orgasm by thinking vigorously of exciting things and images, and if you worry enormously about coming too slowly, you will most probably take even longer to come.

I have sometimes had unusual success with males who cannot come rapidly enough by using some of the techniques outlined previously with regard to female inadequacy. Mainly, I get them to stop awfulizing about their coming and to focus on pleasuring themselves and their partners as much as they can. Obsession with coming had better go—and get replaced by a desire for sensual and sexual satisfaction, but not necessarily with orgasm. And I help them to stop defining themselves as strong, manly, or "good" people in terms of their sexual success. They learn to accept themselves *whether or not* they come to climax and to think of orgasm as *desirable* but not in the least *necessary*.

If you have trouble coming to orgasm, focus intensely on exciting stimuli. You can concentrate on your own sensations, especially your genital sensations when you engage in intercourse, or upon thoughts, images, or fantasies that you find notably exciting. As usual, the kind of fantasy you use doesn't particularly matter—as long as it works! If you find that it has to include masochistic, sadistic, or other "bizarre" elements, no matter. If you come too slowly, you usually require special kinds of mental stimulation; and since your mind can wander over an enormous range of possible excitants and use them selectively, don't hesitate to employ whatever works best.

In addition, you may require unusually vigorous or powerful physical stimulation. Some men have trouble coming because they had better exert real pressure on their genitals, and may not do so when their penis merely rubs against the relatively soft, expandable tissues of the vagina. Consequently, they find it better to use other parts of their partner's anatomy for friction—her buttocks, anus, thighs, or even knees. In masturbation, too, thrusting their organs vigorously against a mattress, a pillow, a towel, or some other firm object may serve better than rubbing it with their own hands, in the more common manner.

Sometimes, during intercourse or masturbation, large amounts of lubrication, constantly reapplied, prove desirable for persons who have trouble coming. One of my clients stays away from K-Y jelly in this connection, because it evaporates quickly and is too slick. He likes Vaseline much better. On the other hand, I have seen some males who avoid practically all lubrication and jerk off or fuck without it, because they then feel more penile friction and come to orgasm more easily.

A vibrator sometimes helps. Most vibrators of the kind that females use give the male too little stimulation. But a few work more powerfully, and some even enclose the penis, like a mouth or a vagina, and bring a man to orgasm by their sucking motions. Average males find these devices not particularly good, but some men with orgasmic difficulties can use them effectively. Also, as noted by one of the prostitutes interviewed by J. W. Wells, a vibrator can sometimes bring a man to orgasm even though he doesn't get a full erection. So if little else works, this sort of thing may prove useful.

Lack of Erection

Males frequently complain of not having the ability to get or maintain an adequate erection, and most of the time they have psychological reasons for this, although there also may exist some physical predisposition. In cases of this sort, I again find that a combination of antiawfulizing and intense imagining usually helps considerably. In the antiawfulizing, you thoroughly convince yourself that if you do not get it up and keep it up, that would prove highly inconvenient—but no *more* than that. You would lose pleasure; your partner might or might not lose some satisfaction too; but you both could get greatly satisfied by various noncoital, sensual techniques (such as the ones outlined elsewhere in this volume). Consequently, you obviously don't *have* to have a firm erection and to keep it for any length of time. Nice—but not necessary!

The imaging and fantasizing comprise the same kind of sensual focusing that you can use for other sex problems—letting yourself thoroughly enjoy all aspects of petting your partner and getting petted by her. You don't, in this kind of concentration, focus on your cock and its sensations—for you then tend to worry about your erection. Instead, you focus on sensual feelings—on those received through kissing, caressing, massaging, kneading, anal penetration, etc. As you do so, you frequently will spontaneously begin to get aroused, and sometimes to achieve an unusually firm erection. Even so, you *keep* focusing on your sensual pleasures, because if you start wondering about *how* firm your erection feels, you will easily interfere with it and may lose it.

Usually, you fantasize about some attractive partner you know. You can use the body of the woman with you—especially aspects of her anatomy or state of dress that you find highly arousing—or you can use the image of any other woman you know, including those you have had little or no sex with. In fact, in some instances, thinking of women you *don't* really know physically works better than thinking of those you do—since you can imagine a perfection in them which they really don't have. But frequently you can use images of women that you have known—and, again, especially those who have proved exceptionally pleasing to you in some part of their body or personality or with whom you have enjoyed terrific sexual satisfaction.

If you have trouble in maintaining an erection, you can sometimes place a rubber band or some similar constricting object at the base of your penis, and that will temporarily stop the blood that has engorged it from flowing out again and will help you stay erect. Dr. G. Lombard Kelly at times recommended this solution, but it has its dangers as well. In an article on African and Asian methods of prolonging sex, Robert Elliott writes, "A finger pressed down at the base of the member during erection demonstrates the effective principle which Hsi-men used to advantage in an almost forgotten era. Many men today use a rubber band about the base of the organ to achieve this effect. Doctors warn, however, that the band should not [get] too tight, lest the constriction of the blood supply [make it] a medical problem. We also [learn] that over-zealous use of the rubber band can lead to ulceration of the penis. As in all matters pertaining to sex, moderation [seems] the solution."

For individuals with sex difficulties, various kinds of fetishes sometimes help. If, for example, you have trouble getting or keeping an erection and you can get the cooperation of your partner, her use of special kinds of "sexy" clothing—such as high-heeled shoes or ultrafeminine garments—may serve you well. One of my clients trained himself, while young, to get excited by masturbating with female underthings. When he later had difficulty getting sufficiently aroused with his wife, and she would manipulate his penis with her underpants, he easily obtained a full erection and had great sex with her. Most fetishes of this nature do no harm—though addiction to them as an absolute requisite of sex sometimes may prove constricting and limiting. But used in moderation, they may enhance arousability and sex compatibility.

Dr. G. Lombard Kelly discovered that in some males who have trouble with erection, deep and continued pressure on their perineal region may help them change a partial into a complete erection. He advocated, for those males who tend to lose their erections easily, that they have intercourse in a sitting position, with their partner sitting astride on their laps, while they press on their perineal areas. Sometimes a special perineal support or brace can prove helpful in this respect.

For males who have great difficulty getting or keeping an erection, some kind of penile splint or support sometimes proves desirable. Various kinds of such supports exist. First, a plastic tube that fits over the penis and allows an individual with a flaccid penis to enter the vagina of a woman and to copulate with her. This kind of arrangement would allow little or no physical satisfaction for the man and would often prove unsatisfactory for the woman. The main advantage consists in the man's knowing that he can have some form of intercourse, consequently stopping a lot of his worrying about impotence, and therefore perhaps succeeding at it later.

Second, another kind of device, like the Loewenstein coitus-training apparatus, consists of a set of metal or plastic splints that fit over the penis and get held together by a rubber band or some similar device. This has the advantage of allowing the penis more contact with the vagina, so that both the male and the female get real physical contact, even when the man's penis stays limp. Again, knowing that he can perform in this manner, and feeling his penis rubbing against the woman's vagina, the man can sometimes achieve an erection and gain confidence that he can continue to do so. So this kind of apparatus sometimes works reasonably well and leads to better future results.

Third, a male can use a dildo, or artificial penis, that he holds in his hands, and can satisfy the woman with this object if she wants penile intromission. His own organ does not have contact with her, but if she gets excited and satisfied this way, he feels better about having sex with his penis limp. And in some cases, he can get aroused by seeing her get aroused and knowing that he can satisfy her, so that he may get erections and realize that he has the ability to do so. Similarly, if he uses a vibrator to satisfy her, both of them may gain pleasure in the process; and with the heat taken off him to perform with his penis, he may start getting erections and may perform better.

A great advantage of all these kinds of penile aids consists of the fact that the individuals using them come to realize that intercourse does not have a sacred character and that they can satisfy a woman in many ways. Once two partners start feeling this, they tend to relax and to look for whatever ways they find satisfactory, to lose their shame about their inadequacies, and to widen their sex horizons. Later, without any aids or artificial appliances, they may have a good sex life.

Although most people think that a male has to have a pretty firm erection in order to have intercourse and to succeed at it, this often proves false. You, for example, can learn to enter your partner's vagina with your penis when you have little or no stiffness. As Roger O. Conway and I write in *The Art of Erotic Seduction,*

> In many instances, you'll find it possible to introduce your limp penis into your partner's vagina and to obtain enough of an erection to copulate. After you have had a full erection and orgasm, you can frequently continue intercourse with a flaccid organ, particularly if you clasp your partner's buttocks with one hand and hold her hips firmly to your body. But even with no erection whatever, you may have coitus; and sometimes in the course of such coitus, you will get aroused and will actually achieve a completely erect state.
>
> To achieve intercourse with a flaccid penis, you can first see that your partner's genital region gets quite moist, either from her own natural secretions or with your saliva or with lubricants such as K-Y jelly. Place her on her right side, but slightly more on her back than her side. Have her draw her right leg up toward her breast, while it lies flat on the bed. Get between her legs, rest on your left side and elbow, and place

your waist across her right thigh, so that your hip bone lies beneath and touches her leg.

By moving her left leg with your right hand, you can control the angle of opening of her legs and the angle her hips make with the bed, and the total bend of her body. With a little experimentation, you can find a position that proves restful and relaxed to both of you and which puts her vaginal orifice, wide open, beneath your penis. She will tend to feel her left leg as the most unrelaxed part of her body; and you can support it in a variety of positions: on your shoulder, in the crook of your elbow, with your hand, or balanced in a vertical position.

By placing your left loin against the under side of her right thigh, you can so roll your penis up to her vaginal opening that, by using your finger as a "shoe horn," you can force your perfectly limp penis into her vagina. It sort of "pops" in like a grape forced into a narrow neck of a bottle. Once in, slow, careful movements will often produce enough of an erection to permit you to copulate. You can also achieve this kind of intercourse when you lie on top of your partner, or use other positions where her vaginal opening spreads widely and you "shoe horn" your limp penis into it. You may never get more than slightly erect during the whole process, but this frequently will prove enough to produce a climax in both you and your partner.

Another technique: You can sometimes use a nonsexual erection for purposes of coitus and with this kind of erection maintain active copulation longer than you might otherwise do. Thus, you may get morning erections and may not feel particularly desirous when you do. If, however, you copulate at this time, you may do so quite adequately and get aroused in the course of intercourse even though you may not have felt excited when you began.

Perhaps the most serious problems you will have with a partner, if you cannot easily get an erection and maintain it, will consist of communication difficulties. Because you make yourself feel ashamed and self-downing about your inadequacies, you tend to shut up and try to hide them from her. But you always worry, naturally, that she will find out the score and will tend to despise you. Thinking this, rather than of sex itself, you will almost always tend to act more inadequate; and of course, you will remain noncommunicative, and she may hate that much more than she hates your "failings."

A typical case: I saw a male for sex therapy who often failed to get a stiff erection and felt thoroughly ashamed of doing so. Consequently, he avoided having intercourse with females and only petted them to orgasm. If he happened to get erect in the process, he let them handle his penis and give him a climax, but he rarely copulated, for fear of losing his hard-earned erection.

My dialogue with him during our first session included the following:

THERAPIST: Do you let any of your partners know that you have sex difficulties?

CLIENT: Of course not! As soon as they found that out, they would despise me, and we would never hit it off.

THERAPIST: How do you know?

CLIENT: Oh, I know! I once told a woman, right at the start, that I might not succeed in screwing her, and she got turned off and refused to have anything to do with me. She thought of me as something of a real nut.

THERAPIST: A sample of one! Did you ever try acting honest with any other women?

CLIENT: Hell, no! Once seemed enough!

THERAPIST: I don't go along with that. Certainly, some women will turn themselves off if they think you have sex problems—often, because they feel inadequate and fear that they won't help you with the problem. So they cop out, even if they like you, and stay away from sex. Well, obviously such women don't fill your bill, and you'd better find them out quickly—and stay away from them.

CLIENT: But I'd feel terribly ashamed if they found me out and rejected me.

THERAPIST: Because you'd keep telling yourself—what?

CLIENTS That . . . uh . . . if they act like that, *no* women will ever like me.

THERAPIST: Prove that statement!—that if *this* woman feels turned off by your not getting an erection, *no* woman will ever like you.

CLIENT: Doesn't that seem obvious?

THERAPIST: Not to me! Show me some evidence of that hypothesis.

CLIENT: Well, uh . . . Well, I guess I do exaggerate somewhat. *Some* woman might accept me that way. Though wouldn't she have her own crazy reasons for doings so?

THERAPIST: Not necessarily. She might like *you* and not merely your stiff cock. Or not really care for intercourse very much but feel satisfied with your doing other things with her. Or know that you will probably get stiffer later, if she first accepts you the way you behave at the start. She might have several good reasons for "putting up" with your difficulty.

CLIENT: Well, uh, maybe so. But I don't like to risk it.

THERAPIST: Exactly! Which I find very funny. You don't like to risk failing with her—so by withdrawing, you ensure that you *will* fail. Do you see?

CLIENT: I guess so. You'd advise, then, that I tell a woman right from the start that I have trouble getting an erection?

THERAPIST: Why not? If she absolutely won't accept you with such trouble, obviously she doesn't seem the one for you. And if she does accept you, and you know that you don't *have* to get it up to satisfy her, then you take most of the pressure off yourself, feel able to focus on enjoying yourself with her, and most probably will sooner or later succeed.

CLIENT: But suppose she laughs at my problem or lets me try and then puts me down for failing?

THERAPIST: Suppose she does. Again, this will mainly prove that you'd better not think *her* the woman of your choice. For she puts you down for having an unfortunate trait—and will probably put you down in various other ways for other traits that she doesn't enjoy. Who needs a woman like that?

CLIENT: But how about me? How will *I* feel if she treats me that shabbily?

THERAPIST: Not great, of course! But actually, you'll feel the way you *choose* to feel. You have the wise choice of feeling that, sadly enough, she doesn't seem right for you, and that that again proves unfortunate and inconvenient. Or you have the choice of making yourself feel that everything turns horrible because she doesn't care for you enough; that you can't stand such a state of affairs; and that you amount to a terrible shit if she thinks that way. In which case, you'll almost certainly feel depressed, anxious, worthless.

CLIENT: I can *choose* to feel either of these ways?

THERAPIST: Of course you can! Anyone can. You can choose to accept the grim reality that you lose out *somewhat* if she puts you down and leaves you or choose to accept the horrible fiction that you lose *everything* in life, lose your *entire essence,* if she looks upon you as a worm.

CLIENT: How can I make this choice?

THERAPIST: By making it! By *deciding* that you don't like, and never will like, misfortune but that you damned well can stand it. By deciding that losing her represents the loss of one individual and not the loss of the world. By convincing yourself that even if you behave badly, as in failing to get erections, your bad behavior never makes *you* bad, never designates you *totally* as rotten. Only you do that. And that would consist of your nutty decision to do it, to view yourself that way.

CLIENT: Sounds good. Great, in fact. But can I really believe that way? Can I ignore her rejection of me, if I fail, and go happily on?

THERAPIST: You'd better not! You'd better face your undesirable trait, lack of erection, and try to *do* someting about it. And you'd better not feel happy if you lose out on her—and perhaps on other women as well. But you can make yourself feel appropriately sorrowful and regretful rather than inappropriately depressed and self-downing. And yes, you can do that—if you work your goddamned ass off—or, rather, your head off—to do it, and do it, and do it.

CLIENT: In other words, I have to keep convincing myself that I can take it if I fail and get rejected, keep seeing that it doesn't mean the end of the world.

THERAPIST: Not *have* to—would better! If you want better results, in terms of accepting yourself and working for firmer errections than you now keep getting.

After going over this several times with this client and getting him to do graduated homework assignments of letting women know that he had some sex difficulties, trying sex with them even when he felt pretty sure that he would fail, and continuing to face the same women with whom he had previously failed in bed, he finally began to see that he could accept the hassle of failing without putting himself down and could even take it when a couple of the women he saw actually did criticize him for doing poorly. As he saw this, he gradually succeeded on more and more occasions, and within a few months he had only slight difficulty in getting and maintaining erections. And, even better, he still enjoyed himself sexually and emotionally when he failed!

In general, the more openly you can behave with your partner, the less you will fear failing with her, and you will tend to earn her cooperation in working with you on any problem that you may have. Communication brings fine results in normal human intercourse—including sexual intercourse. When problems exist, it has even more importance. If you learn to behave openly with your partners, to listen to them and their concerns carefully, and to try to help them as they help you, both you and they will probably prove more able to minimize your sex-love hassles.

Several authors, especially Jack Litewka, have noted that a male tends to have maximum potency when he objectifies sex and really focuses on a woman as a sex object; when he fetishizes certain parts of her anatomy, such as her breasts, buttocks, and sex organs; and when he sees something exceptionally challenging and somewhat risky about winning her sex favors. This process, which we might label acute (and sometimes chronic) sexualization, tends to lead to pronounced excitement, interest, and virility on the part of most men, and it may get interfered with by too much concentration on civility, love, collaboration, and consideration.

Does this mean that a male chauvinist pig, who sees women primarily as sex objects and has a pronounced interest in screwing rather than in relating to them, will likely prove more potent than a nicer, more liberated man? I doubt this in most cases, since the male sex drive tends to have such power that it doesn't easily get interfered with and doesn't require special "masculine" spurs. I sometimes suspect, however, that males with relatively low drive, particularly those who have some trouble getting aroused and orgasmic, require a good deal more challenge and fetishism than some of us higher-sexed men. I have noticed, for example, that males who compulsively run after pornographic collections, fetishistic journals, orgies, and other very "sexy" interests may, oddly enough, have distinct sex difficulties. And they may have some special reasons for adopting their obsessive-compulsive sex games and preoccupations.

Whatever the truth of my suspicion—and I hardly have full evidence to back it—you may sometimes find, if you have trouble getting and maintaining erections, that the practice of sex objectification, fetishism, and challenge may help. You can practice thinking of women in particularly sexy ways and focus on their genital parts or other parts of their body that you find arousing. And you can seek adventure, novelty, and challenge in your contacts, to add to your excitement.

Does this mean that you have to turn into a typical male chauvinist, who thinks of women only in sex-object terms? Not at all. You can often do so in your head, to excite yourself; but in real practice, you can act as kind, considerate, and unchauvinistic as possible with your actual women friends and lovers. You can also, in practice, do your best to carry on long-term, stable, loving relationships with women (not to mention with other men and with children), while in your head, you can let your varietistic tendencies go full blast. You can love your partner, for example, and take great care to satisfy her when you have sex together. But in your imagination, while you copulate with her, you can literally have a different woman every night of the week. If she can take it, by all means communicate some of your fantasies to her; and if she can't, discretion may well remain the better part of valor!

You can also, if necessary, have two different kinds of sex partners—highly sexed, attractive women who have varietist inclinations like your own and with whom you can have ephemeral or intermittent affairs, and normally sexed, and possibly less attractive, women with whom you mainly have love and sharing relationships, which tend to last for a long time. Just because you have some of the former kind of women in your life, you may actually relate better sexually to one or more of the latter kind.

My main point—what goes for other people sexually does not have to go for you. If your bent really follows the fetishistic, competitive path, don't think that you have to squelch it completely and settle for the everyday routines that satisfy others. Either do what you really want to do, and sacrifice some of the levels of interpersonal relationship achieved by others, or keep your interpersonal goals quite high, but allow yourself more varietistic outlets either in side practice or in your imagination. See what truly works for you —even though others may find your paths "shallow," "immature," or somewhat "deviant." As long as you do not obsessively-compulsively sabotage your long-range best interest in the process, some degree of sex "kinkiness" may work well for you.

CHAPTER 12

Techniques and Positions of Intercourse

ONCE YOU START having intercourse, you may have a good deal to learn about coital technique. Practice will help enormously in this respect, and so will open-minded experimentation. But some of the lore amassed through the ages about intercourse may help, so let me outline it in this chapter.

General Conditions of Intercourse

Even the most highly sexed individuals do not want to have sex at *all* times, and many partners want it only at specific times or when you make them *feel* that they would like to have it. Some considerations you can keep in mind in this respect:

1. Try to have sex under conditions your partner finds most desirable. Although you may feel relatively insensitive or invulnerable —and can copulate successfully on a park bench with the curious squirrels looking on—she may have several sensitivities. Try to discover her preferences and to cater to them to some extent. You, for example, may prefer having coitus in a lighted or semilit room, but if she, even for silly or neurotic reasons, prefers it in the dark, you may find it wise to give in to her prejudices.

2. Look for signs of readiness in your partner and try to regulate your coital relations accordingly. She may feel more desirous at certain times of her monthly cycle, particularly before, during, or immediately after menstruation. Or she may prefer copulating during the day, rather than at night, or on weekends, instead of during the week. Try to arrange whatever times or conditions she finds especially satisfying.

261

3. Try to regulate your coital and noncoital relations to fit your and her anatomic and mechanical preferences. A slim, wiry, and acrobatically inclined partner may like certain positions (such as the female surmouting the male) that a fatter, heavier, and less acrobatic partner will not necessarily enjoy. A partner with a large mouth may enjoy certain kinds of oral-genital sex, which one with a small mouth may not. Some women—though relatively few—adore anal-genital relations, and some feel completely turned off by that sort of thing. Discover your particular partner's coital and noncoital preferences and act accordingly.

4. If your mate has orgasm difficulty, you may favor certain positions that help her (in more ways than one!) keep coming. Thus, you may find the male-surmounting-the-female position great for you, since it may enable you to come quickly and efficiently. But if she wants prolonged intercourse, you and she may favor her getting on top of you or a side-by-side copulatory technique.

5. Although you may prefer to get to and through fucking as quickly as possible, your partner may prefer a slower approach and coital timing. One woman may actually delight in your imperiousness and quick, savage coital thrusting, whereas another may find it disturbing and require slower-paced, gentler movements. Individual differences prove so important that the main rule to adopt amounts to *no* one rule!

6. Variety may or may not please your mate. Some females get bored with a single coital position and demand continual change, but others find maximum satisfaction in one conventional mode. If you can induce your partner to try a number of positions, and to try them for a sufficient length of time, you will probably both discover variations that you will want to keep repeating. But you also may not!

7. As previously noted, great numbers of women do not notably enjoy coitus, since their physiological disposition prevents their achieving sufficient clitoral or labial stimulation while fucking. For females of this type, you can often best stimulate their clitoral regions while coitally engaged. G. Lombard Kelly and Edwin Hirsch, along with old-time sexologists, recommend that you do this by "riding high" during intercourse, so that the shaft of your penis bends over against your partner's clitoris and you maintain clitoral

pressure while screwing. But practically no males seem able to assume or maintain this position during copulation. So don't kill yourself trying!

Another technique of clitoral stimulation, as recommended by Dr. Bernard Greenblatt, advocates pressing the head of your penis against your mate's clitoris prior to intercourse, and withdrawing it from time to time to reapply it to the clitoris. This technique can work, but you and your partner may not feel like interrupting coital contact to perform it.

A preferable method consists in manipulating your partner's clitoral region with your fingers during intromission. You can do this when she mounts you or sits opposite you in a face-to-face position or, better yet, when you lie on your side behind her and, after entering her vagina with your penis from the rear, put your arm around her and stimulate her clitoral region with your hand. If this doesn't help her come, nothing but nonfucking methods may. Back to your naked fingers or a vibrator!

8. Once you have your cock in your partner's vagina, you may make your strokes gradual or sudden, shallow or deep, vigorous or gentle, depending on her and your desires. Sometimes begin with short strokes and slow movements, then work up to longer and more rapid ones. You may find powerful, penetrating thrusts more exciting but painful to your partner, or you may discover that they make either of you come too fast. As noted in the chapters on sexual inadequacies, one kind of thrusting may serve a particular partner well or badly and help or hinder her in her search for arousal and orgasm. As ever, experiment and communicate to discover the most pleasing patterns for you and your bedmate.

9. Kissing and caressing, as you might expect, may madly continue *during* screwing. Not very easily, naturally, in some of the conventional positions—as when you mount the female and lean upon your hands. But if you lie on your back or side, you may keep your hands and lips quite free to engage in additionally stimulating activities while you copulate. Try it and see!

10. Normally, as we have noted before, wait until your partner adequately lubricates until you try penetration. If she has trouble lubricating, has a narrow vagina, or complains about painful sensations during coitus, artificial lubrication may save the night. You

may use saliva, K-Y jelly, most contraceptive jellies, or other water-soluble jellies and creams. Some lubricants—such as petroleum jelly (Vaseline), hand lotions, cold creams, and soaps—have distinct limitations but still prove serviceable under certain conditions. If you have prolonged intercourse, new applications of lubricants may help from time to time. If you employ a condom, you can purchase lubricated ones or can apply jelly, especially contraceptive jelly, to them yourself.

11. No special rules regarding the frequency of intercourse exist, since this varies widely from couple to couple. In general, fuck as often as you and your partner feel arousable and enjoy it. As a male, you'll find it fairly impossible to copulate too frequently, since you will not normally get an erection when you feel satiated. And when a woman has too much sex, she normally loses desire and stops having orgasms. But if you keep pushing yourself, largely for ego reasons, you may find it possible to keep fucking without real desire, and then you may get into some physical difficulties, such as, irritation of the genitals, urethritis, and prostatitis. If so, you may find it wise to cut down your coital frequency (while still satisfying your partner as much as she wants with your tongue or fingers) or may resort to more gentle methods of penile stroking or briefer periods of intercourse. Even worse than a limp cock, you may find a stiff, sore one. Don't think yourself superman—in or out of bed!

Two noted sexologists, Dr. Donald W. Hastings and Dr. Robert A. Harper, lay to rest the concept of "excessive" intercourse by healthy individuals. Asked about an individual's psychotherapist who told him that his sex life—coitus twice a day—had great dangers, Dr. Hastings replied, "One can only raise the question as to what damage the psychotherapist has in mind. If he refers to some magical norm about sexual relations, he obviously does not know what he [talks] about. If he [talks] about sexual relations twice a day with the wife of the national karate champion, he may have a point."

Dr. Harper writes that a number of false beliefs exist "about sex 'excess.' One commonly held by males [includes] that they have only a certain number of orgasms or ejaculations built into their systems. They fear that if they have sex too often, they will 'use up' their supply and not have any pleasures left for a later time in their life. It would make as much sense for these men to believe that they had a predetermined number of times they could take a walk, hit a golf ball, or eat a steak. In fact, the repetition of any of these acts, including sexual intercourse, improves rather than reduces one's powers.

"Closely tied in with the false notion that there [exists] a limited reservoir of sex experiences available, [we have] the equally mistaken idea that a male ejaculation and/or the sex act itself causes some vast drain of energy. An ounce of semen does *not* equal an ounce of blood, a man need have no fear of draining himself by frequent ejaculations, and the loss of semen in no way harms the body."

So there! Heed Dr. Hastings and Dr. Harper—and not some silly superstitions about sex "excess."

Positions of Intercourse

Theoretically, hundreds of coital positions exist, and we can list many variations. But most of them boil down to minor variations on a few major themes. Let me briefly describe the main positions you may find useful and enjoyable.

Face to Face, Man on Top

Your partner lies on her back, spreading her legs and flexing her knees or (sometimes) placing her feet on your shoulders. She may raise her buttocks, if she wants, by putting a pillow under them, or she may put a pillow under the small of her back. You lie *over* (rather than *on*) her, supporting the weight of your body on your own hands or elbows. She may keep her legs apart and flat, place them between your knees, put one of them between your legs, bend her thighs backward toward her chest, raise one of her legs while keeping the other flat, wrap one or both legs around your legs, or wrap her legs around your waist.

This face-to-face, male-above position has several advantages. It makes for easy entry, allows you to set the pace and to slow or hasten your orgasm, facilitates intimacy, enables you sometimes to continue intercourse after you have had an orgasm, allows you and your partner to caress each other actively, may lead to an interlocking position that enables you to roll over into other positions without disengaging yourselves, and enables you to give way to powerful pelvic thrusts, which may greatly satisfy you and your partner and help you bring on orgasm for both of you. If you use this position with what Dr. John Eichenlaub calls the "pillow trick," by placing a pillow under the small of the back of your partner, you may raise her clitoral region so that it tends to receive more indirect or direct friction during intercourse.

This position has distinct disadvantages for some individuals, especially since the man tends to thrust more vigorously and may come more quickly, and if he thrusts vigorously, the front of his penis may push against his partner's cervix and may cause her pain. At the same time, your mate may like this kind of pressure on her cervix, and she may like the fact that you can manipulate her anal region while you fuck and can give her considerable satisfaction that way. Also, as noted previously, if you use the stop-start technique to impede your orgasm, you can do it quite well if you lie on top of your partner. You can also easily use different kinds of stroking—such as slow or rapid stroking—in this position.

Face to Face, Woman on Top

You lie on your back and your partner squats over you and guides your penis into her vagina. Or she sits down in an astride position on your erect penis and loins, resting her back against your flexed knees and raised thighs. Or you penetrate her in some other position, such as a side position, and then gently roll around until she gets on top. Once you effect entry, she can keep squatting, sit astride, or straighten out her legs and lie between or outside your legs. You can lie prone, raise yourself on your hands or elbows, or raise your knees on the side or in back of her.

The face-to-face, woman-on-top position gives your partner maximum freedom of action and allows her to rub the sensitive parts of her vulva (and especially her clitoral region) directly against your genital area and pubic bone. It enables you to rest quietly, without too much movement, so that you may last longer in coitus. It frees your hands so that you can caress your partner's body and manipulate her clitoral region, and it similarly frees her hands to hug and caress you. It enables her to experience deep vaginal contact with your penis and to arouse herself, if she wishes, with strong pelvic thrusts.

Kwami Lundola notes that "aside from the variety it offers, this [proves] a useful position in that it allows you, the man, to rest yourself. It requires little effort on your part, allowing you to take it easy while preparing yourself for greater things to come."

Dr. Betty Cox agrees that "a physically weak man can maintain this position for a long time without getting tired," and also observes that "the wife can regulate the depth of penetration. If she enjoys deep penetration or contact of the penis with her cervix, this [proves] an ideal position for maximum penetration."

Richard Stiller gives some more advantages of your using the face-to-face, woman-on-top position. If your penis seems rather large or your partner's vaginal orifice small, she can regulate the depth and intensity of penetration to minimize pain or friction. When you have much more weight than your mate, she might feel smothered by your lying on top. At times during pregnancy, she might find it inadvisable to support your weight on her swollen abdomen. In cases where she has difficulty achieving orgasm during intercourse, she may use powerful thrusts and deep penetration, which may help bring her to climax.

Face to Face, Side by Side

You and your partner lie on your sides, facing each other. You may both have your lower legs on the bed, with her upper leg over both of yours, or her lower leg may rest on your lower leg and your upper leg may rest between her legs, so that you get interlocked. As Edwin Hirsch notes, in the so-called side positions, either you actually remain largely on your back or she does. If you stay largely on your back, you support her with your chest.

You will often find the face-to-face, side-by-side position restful and easy—one of the easiest of the various sex positions. It may provide maximum contact between your genitalia and your partner's clitoris. You can regulate your pelvic thrusts and sometimes last longer in intercourse that way. Both of you have relative freedom of movement and may attain a steady coital rhythm. You can withdraw and reinsert without a drastic change in your position. This represents one position in which you both can sometimes go to sleep after coitus while still remaining interlocked. Because of these advantages, some couples consider this one of the most intimate positions and frequently favor it.

Other advantages: If you want to pause during intercourse, so that you don't come too quickly, you can easily do it in this position, and you can sometimes learn to last almost indefinitely by pausing and resting this way. Sometimes, as when your legs remain straight and those of your partner get drawn up and flexed, you can achieve better contact between your penis and her clitoral region. Since both your movements may remain relatively free and unhampered, you may both obtain orgasm, and even simultaneous orgasm, during intercourse.

Rear Entry, Man's Face to Woman's Back

In this position, you have several main possibilities:

1. Lie on your side behind your partner's back (she, too, lying on her side), with her buttocks somewhat above your penis and her body slightly curved inward, her legs bent at her hips. Enter her vagina between her legs. After intromission she may press her thighs together, providing additional friction for your penis and preventing it from slipping out.

2. She kneels on her hands and knees, with her head and breast almost on the bed or sofa, with you kneeling behind her. Enter her vagina between her legs and press your pubes against her buttocks.

3. She lies on her belly with her pelvis raised and you on top of her. Most couples find this awkward.

4. Sit on the edge of a bed or chair, while your partner, with her back to you, sits down on your penis and your lap or the lower part of your belly. Open your thighs somewhat and lean back while she opens her thighs as wide as possible and leans forward.

In the rear-entry position, you have the advantages of feeling your partner's gluteal region with your legs, scrotum, and pubic area—which you both may find satisfying. You can also put your hands around her during copulation and play with her breasts, clitoris, or other parts of her body. In this position, she ends up with foreshortened vaginal areas, an advantage if she has a wide and slack vagina or if you have a relatively small penis and you both desire vaginal-penile friction.

Although you cannot obtain very deep penetration in most of the rear-entry positions, and your penis may keep slipping out of your partner's vagina, you can sometimes stimulate the front part and the anterior (upper) wall of her vagina that way—both of which may prove highly satisfying to her. Rear entry may sometimes aid impregnation and may serve a couple well when the woman undergoes pregnancy.

As Dr. Cox notes, "The kneeling rear entry position proves psychologically exciting to some individuals who seem to feel its mammal-like nature more novel and excitingly unusual than face to face positions."

Dr. S. G. Tufill also points out that rear entry may serve well when a male has a great deal of desire "but the wife lacks desire, as he can attain his climax quickly with little effort by the wife. It can [remain] a passive inactive position for her as she [does] not really [get] exposed to her husband if she kneels down supporting her chest on her arms over a bed or chair, and yet she complies with his wishes for intercourse."

Sitting Positions

You and your partner may employ several major sitting positions.

1. Sit on a chair or on the edge of a bed or sofa, with her facing you, her legs astride yours. With your legs apart and her legs around your waist, pull her toward and away from you and raise and lower her pelvis, thus effecting copulatory movements.

2. If you have a chair or bed suitably high, sit on it while she, facing you with her legs somewhat apart, stands. Pull her hips back and forth to you, between your spread thighs.

3. Squat between your partner's thighs, while she lies on her back facing you, with her legs on your hips. Make pelvic thrusts or pull her pelvis back and forth toward and away from you. Or she can squat between your thighs while you lie on your back with your legs apart and she moves her pelvis in a circular fashion, making churning movements around your penis.

4. Sit on a bed or chair while she bends over, in a doubled-up

position, with her back to you. Using the rear-entry position, pull her pelvis back and forth over your penis.

In the sitting positions, you can both move your hands freely. You can sometimes retard your orgasm, especially if you pull her to and from you, rather than using sharp pelvic thrusts. You can deeply penetrate your partner's vagina if you want this kind of penetration but can also enter more shallowly if you want that. You will often find the sitting positions restful and relatively free from exertion, and in these positions you can easily stimulate your mate's clitoral region if, when you face each other, she leans over backward.

Standing Positions

If your partner has long enough or you have short enough legs, you may stand and face each other and have intercourse. Or she can lie with her legs dangling over the edge of a table or bed while you stand between them. Or you can stand while she, with her arms around your neck, clasps your hips between her thighs and holds on to you. You will usually find these standing positions difficult, except in special instances. They do, however, have some advantages—since you and your partner may find them varied, exciting, and unroutine. They usually leave both your hands free for caresses. And you can combine them with dancing, taking showers together, and other standing activities.

Although, as noted above, at least half a dozen major and hundreds of minor sex positions exist, you will probably enjoy most of them only occasionally and largely stick to the few that you and your partner experimentally determine work best for you. This partly depends on your and her physical build, facility for arousal, ease of coming in intercourse, propensity to tire or feel uncomfortable in certain positions, psychological mood, state of physical health, and many other factors. Literally millions of couples, after experimenting with a number of different coital positions, wind up generally trying only one or two different ones most of the time. Why not? If you have simple tastes in sex and no difficulty with arousal or orgasm, you and your partner can concentrate on ease and comfort more than anything else. But if you want to go to various lengths to derive additional enjoyment, go! Just don't think that you *have to*.

Anal Intercourse

Only recently has anal intercourse begun to seem a legitimate part of heterosexual relations, although it has of course always had a popular appeal to homosexual individuals. Kinsey found it so rare that he published no data on its incidence. But Morton Hunt found that "today, over one-sixth of the single males and the single females under 25 who have ever had coitus have tried anal intercourse, and 9 percent of the males and 6 percent of the females used it at least occasionally in just the past year." Hunt also found that sex acts like anal intercourse tend to exist more commonly in married than in single couples, since the former apparently feel more free to experiment, at least after they have stayed together for a while, with a variety of sex outlets and positions.

This doesn't mean that women uniformly enjoy anal intercourse, for most of them do not. As Jennifer Olson notes, "Ass-fucking has not generally [proved] a favorite recreation of women. In fact, women by and large despise the idea of anal sex, because in most cases it [got] originally suggested to them by some guy who proceeded to introduce them to it forcibly, clumsily and without the aid of any lubricant. The resulting discomfort and embarrassment turns most women against anal fucking for life." But, she goes on to say, anal intercourse provides a powerful sensation of extreme penetration for women and can prove highly sexy. If only people rightly *learn* how to do it!

Some important aspects of anal fucking, if you want to engage in it with your woman friend, include the following.

1. A woman can best start anal eroticism, in many instances, by masturbation—just as she can often best start vaginal stimulation. If your partner will gently, and with some lubrication, play with her asshole, and gradually penetrate it with her fingers, she can learn how to arouse herself and pave the way for later fuller penetration.

As Jennifer Olson says to receptive women. "Some evening when you happen to [feel] alone and a little horny, play with your ass a bit. Rub it. Jiggle it. Lick your finger and press gently against your sphincter, relaxing it. When the sphincter muscle [feels] relaxed, push your finger inside. The use of a vibrator [I] also recommend. But, in order to gain the best sensations out of it, a lubricant [seems] definitely in order. . . . Of course, you will naturally masturbate your clitoris at the same time. Unlike men, women don't have a prostate gland that can qualify as an erogenous zone when prodded up through the ass-hole. But the sensations of fullness and contraction [feel] definitely erotic and, when a woman has an orgasm while something's up her ass, it can [feel] really spectacular."

2. See that nothing very large goes up your partner's anus. Her sphincter muscle may easily, and even permanently, get damaged. Putting large objects, even including a huge cock, up a woman's anal orifice may lead to injury, hemorrhoids, and loose bowel movements. Don't try it!

3. Bacteria can easily get transferred from the anus to the vagina and can cause itching and other disorders when so transferred. If you use a finger or your penis in your partner's anus, don't insert it subsequently into her vagina until you have washed it thoroughly.

4. Push your finger or penis into a woman's anus gently and slowly. Don't *poke* her with it. Even a fairly large penis, when slowly inserted, may feel fine, wheras a small one, when poked in and out, may do damage.

5. Especially in the beginning phase of ass fucking, the woman had better control the situation and sit on your cock, instead of kneeling on all fours and letting you put it into her. If she sits with her back to you and lowers herself onto your penis, she can go as slowly and gently as she wants. She also will feel less fear that you will take over and roughly jam her with your cock. Even if, at first, it takes many minutes for the insertion, let her do it the way she wants. Once she relaxes and gets used to it, it will tend to take much less time.

6. Your partner can learn to relax and to accommodate you even if you have a very large penis. A physician, with his hand or with a proctoscope, can get a lot of material up almost anyone's, even a

small person's, rectum. But he knows how to do it, and he has the recipient relax as he makes his insertion.

7. Usually, the anus remains free from feces and fairly clean. So you and your partner need not worry about your cock getting dirty from anal intercourse. But if any trouble arises, or you want to make sure that your partner's anus has a minimum amount of bacteria or fecal matter, she can take a small enema just before intercourse.

8. Once a woman has had anal fucking a few times and has got used to it, she can rest on all fours and you can crouch over her, introducing your cock into her ass from behind. Or you can both lie on your sides, with her back to you, and you can penetrate that way. In both these positions, you can reach round her with your hands to caress her breasts and her clitoral region.

She will only rarely come to orgasm by anal fucking alone, but if you manipulate her clitoral region while screwing her up the ass, she may frequently come to climax and may even enjoy it more than she does in penile-vaginal copulation. As one woman, J. D., writes, "Properly practiced (slowly, gently, very gradually penetrating, and with adequate lubrication), anal copulation [proves] every bit as stimulating and as satisfying as regular vaginal fucking. Plenty of erogenous zones there. I feel sorry for men who have such strong masculinity hangups that they have continued to deny themselves the very delightful pleasure of getting fucked in the ass; if only they knew what they [kept] missing!"

Masters and Johnson also write, "When conducted with the consent of both partners and with the routine precautions we've outlined, anal intercourse can afford great pleasure. Indeed, many women report that it provides them with overwhelming orgasmic response."

9. You may find anal intercourse with your female partner particularly delightful because of the extra stimulation you usually receive from her anal sphincter and the tightness of her asshole. Especially if you have trouble coming in intercourse—which many males do, particularly with a partner who has a large vaginal orifice or whom they have fucked for many years—you may find some amount of anal intercourse more pleasant than regular coitus. This doesn't

mean that your partner will find it equally pleasant. But she may like it from time to time or may engage in it in order to please you. All the more reason to treat her gently and considerately when you have it!

10. Anal penetration can make regular intercourse more stimulating and satisfying. While you screw, you can insert your fingers into your partner's anus, and she can do the same thing to you. As the Boston Women's Health Book Collective notes, "Some enjoy a finger or candle in the anus during regular intercourse. Some enjoy having the anus licked. You will want to use a lubricant when inserting anything in the anus."

11. When your partner sticks her fingers or some other object up your anus (or, in homosexual relations, a male inserts his penis there), you can aid your enjoyment in various ways. As Randy Wicker, a pioneer of gay liberation, notes, relaxing consists of "your passport to enjoyment. Masturbation can usually enable you to reach climax simultaneously with your partner. If a male, you'll probably enjoy [getting] screwed. (Whether you particularly like to admit it or not; it [remains] part of your inborn sensual physiology. However, unless your emotional preferences [turn] homosexual, you probably won't prefer it over conventional heterosexual intercourse.) Some heterosexual men get a yen for this particular delight and buy their womanfriends dildos."

12. If you have your partner penetrate you anally with her fingers, let her at first do so easily and gently, and with lubrication, just as you would break in a woman anally. Later, she can penetrate more deeply and learn to massage your prostate gland—which can give you an orgasm even if you have no erection. As Marco Vassi instructs, "If you want to go all the way, she can suck your cock and stimulate the gland at the same time, and when you come it will [bring on] an orgasm probably unrivalled in your life for the sheer exquisite balance between pleasure and pain." Vassi also recommends the use of a dildo by your partner. "If you really want to swing out, she can strap on a dildo and fuck you in style. For a finishing touch, you might try a double-cock dildo, such as lesbians use, and she can [get] fucked in the cunt while she fucks you in the ass."

Vassi thinks that full-fledged anal relations truly bring out the best in men and women. "When you have worked through whatever you must in order to accept your asshole as part of yourself, your lovemaking [turns] extraordinarily free. The woman can insert her finger during a moment of passion without your freaking. And you can lie on your back, your legs in the air, while she [goes] face deep between your cheeks, her tongue driving you to peak after peak of sighing contentment as it invades and laves and tickles and fucks your asshole. And this won't [seem] some form of putdown or a sniggering titillation, but simply a straightforward giving of pleasure by one person to another. Then all the shit traumas and anus fears will [seem] so much childish, smutty irrelevancy. And there will [exist] no part of you which you hold [as] unclean or forbidden. You will have [emerged as] whole."

13. Vibrators and other mechanical devices may please both you and your partner as you use them anally. A vibrator with a small head can go into your or her anal passage and provide stimulation, and sometimes the massaging of your prostate. Dildos, as indicated above, can serve a similar purpose. Tuppy Owens, a female sex scribe, enthusiastically endorses anal beads, which seem to stem mainly from the Orient but also get stocked in British and American sex shops. She reports that when her resident sex object used them in her anus, it didn't add much to her orgasm. But then she used them on him. "We put them in and he walked around the bed wagging his new black tail (use them and you'll know what I mean) like a proud dog until I grabbed his swelling dong and we got it on. He said it felt fine having them up all tight and full, maybe the way a woman feels when she's got a hot, throbbing cock up her cunt (latent little faggot!). As instructed, I pulled out the beads as he reached his climax and, with a groan, he shot his come all over the room. After a while, he gasped, 'That [felt] *great!* and, since we still [keep] scraping the come off the ceiling, I guess the beads work fine."

14. Does anal sex have its real disadvantages and dangers? Indeed, yes. As Dr. Robert Turell, a proctologist and clinical professor of surgery at Albert Einstein College of Medicine, notes, when people get too gung ho about anal sex and keep inserting large bodies into the anus, in some instances abrasions result which prove "the harbingers of acute abscesses which in turn eventuate chronic abscesses

—anal fistulas. Anal fissures, with adjacent and subjacent indura-
tion causing severe pain and bleeding at or after defecation, frequently require surgical intervention." Dr. Turrell lists other hazards
of anal intercourse, including hematomas, condylomas, polyps,
veneral diseases, proctocolitis, and possible anal cancer.

Dr. E. Schoenfeld ("Hip Pocrates") takes a somewhat more opti-
mistic view of injuries and diseases that may result from anal intercourse but also notes that "when performed frequently (and don't
ask me to define frequently) there may [exist] a tendency for the
passive partner to develop earlier in life conditions usually found a
decade or two later—such as hemorrhoids and a loosening of the
anal sphincter or muscles controlling the anus." Obviously, therefore, if you do employ and enjoy anal intercourse, do so with care
and caution. You may thereby save you and your partner considerable pain and trouble!

Varieties of Thrusting and Stroking

Innumerable people, especially males, feel that once a given
position gets used and penile entry occurs, the best or only thing to
do consists in exerting quick, powerful coital thrusts, so that both
partners fairly easily come to orgasm. Wrong! For some individuals,
this kind of fucking seems ideal, and they frequently or always
resort to it. As far as I can tell, this works best with highly sexed
couples who want to achieve quick orgasms, have no difficulty
doing so, and can frequently have several more in the course of an
evening. But all of us, alas, do not enter this category!

Instead of this kind of procedure, you can use several others.

1. Go slowly! You can at times enter your partner's vagina fairly
rapidly and then, before deep penetration takes place, change your
stroke to a slow one; or you can enter slowly and continue easy,
rhythmical movements; or you can start slowly and then suddenly
end up with a very vigorous thrust. But slow and steady often wins
the race!

2. Short, powerful strokes have their distinct advantages—especially to bring you to orgasm and perhaps to arouse a female partner who really likes that sort of thing. But long strokes really send
some females, and you can enjoyably experiment with them.

3. Especially when you lie on top of your partner, you tend to exert your main pressure against the bottom or lower wall of her vagina, which may have relative lack of sensitivity, and to keep it somewhat away from her upper wall, which may have much more sensitivity. Even in this position, however, you can push your body forward or manipulate your penis in such a fashion as mainly to press it against your mate's upper vaginal area.

4. You can make circular and side-to-side motions with your penis, in addition to in-and-out thrust. Such motions may prove arousing to your partner, and at times they may save you from getting too aroused. Thrusting the sensitive underside of your cock against the lower wall of a woman's vagina tends to bring you to orgasm most quickly, and almost any other kind of motion than this will often help you come more slowly.

5. Males, probably for ego reasons, tend to feel great when they batter a woman's cervix and the back part of her vagina with their ram of a prick. But she may not particularly like this and may even experience discomfort. Frequently, you would do yourself and her greater good if you concentrate on massaging her inner labia and the front part of her vagina with your penis. As Dr. John Eichenlaub points out, "Moderate penetration often proves more effective than full depth. In the maximum legs-up posture, for instance, you will probably find that strokes which carry the tip of the penis from just within the vagina to about half or two-thirds of full insertion stir more response than deeper ones."

Masters and Johnson note that the thrusting of your penis can easily hurt your partner for several important reasons: She may have tears in the ligaments that support her uterus; she may have infections of the cervix, uterus, or fallopian tubes; she may have endometriosis; and she may have cysts or tumors on her ovaries. The Boston Women's Health Book Collective indicates that even without these kinds of difficulties, a woman may suffer painful intercourse merely because the male's penis bangs up against the cervix —particularly when he has a large penis or she has a relatively small vagina. In any of these instances, if your partner suffers pain, a more shallow penetration on your part will usually help relieve it.

6. Since you and your partner generally both move and thrust during intercourse, you can arrange things so that you both do so at

the same time—or, better yet in many instances, so that the end of her movement coincides with the middle of yours. You may thereby bring about more intense and "syncopated" movements. Also, if you take one long stroke, she may take two or three shorter ones during the same period, and you may "swing" together much better this way.

7. Depending on your and your partner's size, physical condition, muscular agility, and other factors, you may want to arrange various aids to thrusting. Sometimes a bedboard or a wall at the foot of the bed will help you make more powerful and steady thrusting movements. Sometimes pillows placed under your or your partner's ass or back will help appreciably.

8. You had better acclimate your strokes and thrusts to the individual partner with whom you have sex, since what may please one individual may harm or displease another. Berg and Street indicate that the vulval region of a good many women, perhaps as many as one-third of all females, has only a moderate degree of sensitivity, exclusive of their clitoral region. Although, as we have noted above, violent and deep penile strokes during intercourse may well not suit the average woman, this subgroup that Berg and Street describes may actually thrive on it.

Afterplay

Sex by no means necessarily ends when coitus and orgasm occur. Some couples prefer to drop off to sleep immediately, but others feel wide awake, eager to suck or fuck some more. Most females want to feel loved and appreciated after sex and resent the male's lack of continued interest, since they interpret it as his *only* wanting them sexually and not really caring for them at all once he has come to orgasm. Watch yourself in this connection!

Also, intercourse may well not lead to orgasm even though it fully arouses your partner. And after you have come, she may get left unpleasantly hanging and may require a considerable amount of extra digital or labial stimulation to bring her to climax. At times, she may even have to bring herself to climax—since she often knows how to do so better than you do—and if so, you might wisely encourage her to do this.

Even when a woman has a full orgasm during intercourse, her feelings may ebb only slowly, while yours may ebb quickly, and you may feel immediately ready for sleep. As usual, however, individual differences remain prominent. Maxine Davis notes, "Some women fall asleep as quickly as pulling down the curtain while their husbands turn on the bedside lamp and read a while."

Individual tastes also differ widely in regard to washing oneself after intercourse. Some people don't feel at all comfortable unless they wash, and some feel discomfited if they do! Men, because they ejaculate during intercourse, may more frequently want to get up and wash and urinate, but women frequently take a dim view of this. As one woman told Will Harvey, "You make me so damn mad. One of these times, I [intend to] jump up, wash out my mouth, douche, take a shower, put on all my clothes and go out the door." Apparently, she thought that he in some way felt "unclean" after making love and therefore had to run to the john and wash.

Masters and Johnson, in their researches into human sexuality, discovered that males frequently display no desire to reach out for their partners after coitus, while females do. A postorgasmic female, even if her partner gets out of bed, tends to move toward his place in the bed and often actually settle in the spot that he has vacated.

In the light of the tendency of many people, especially women, to want postcoital contact, Dr. Edward Dengrove recommends, "A most comfortable position for both partners to assume [involves their turning] onto their left sides, with the bottom of the woman resting in the lap of the man. In such a position, he can reinsert what [remains] of his erection into her vagina. With his right arm reaching over her right hip, his fingers can touch the clitoral area [if she does not feel oversensitive], or rest on the pubic area. Further play may take place in the half-dreamy state. Sometimes, tapping gently on the lower abdomen above the pubis may bring on another orgasmic response for her."

CHAPTER 13

How to Avoid Sexual Disturbance

MILLIONS UPON MILLIONS of words keep appearing on the subject
of sex "deviation," "perversion," or "disturbance." Professionals and
nonprofessionals keep debating whether certain forms of behavior,
particularly homosexuality, can accurately receive the label of
"deviation" or "abnormality." And although attitudes in this regard
seem much more open and liberal than the views of so-called
authorities a few decades ago, they still vary widely, and no consensus appears on the horizon.

How about my own views on the subject of sex "deviation"? As a
psychotherapist and sex therapist, I have published fairly widely on
this subject for more than a quarter of a century. Some of my views,
especially those originally expressed in *The American Sexual Tragedy,* have exerted a profound influence on professional and lay
thinking and have helped spark some revolutionary developments in
the field—such as the rise of the gay-liberation movement. They
have also aroused enormous opposition, especially among conserva-
tive psychiatrists and psychologists, and they have received denun-
ciation from some radical theorists who think that no deviations
whatever exist and that sexual disturbance arises only as a fiction in
the minds of clinicians who have a stake in inventing and preserving
its "reality."

What about my present views? Do I think that sex deviation or
disturbance truly exists? If it does, do I think that writers and clinicians can help ameliorate or cure it? Does it constitute a disgrace or
a horror? Let me, after many years of research and clinical experience, answer these questions.

Defining Sexual "Deviation"

Many authorities and legislatures have tried to define sex deviation—most of them confusingly and illegitimately. Some of their main contentions? That so-called deviates:

1. act peculiar or engage in statistically abnormal pursuits;
2. flout laws or cultural rules;
3. behave unnaturally;
4. behave animalistically;
5. go against God's laws;
6. harm other humans;
7. behave neurotically or self-defeatingly.

Do any of these definitions seem plausible or legitimate? No—except, to some extent, the last two. Let us review them, to see why.

1. Although we may logically label anyone who has peculiar or unusual sex as "deviant," this seems silly. For *deviant* has at least the connotation of bad, wrong, or self-defeating. And *peculiar* or *unusual* merely means *different* and not necessarily *bad*. People who enormously enjoy rococo music, ticktacktoe, rattlesnake meat, or screwing in a wheelbarrow may act quite different from the majority of us. But they hardly defeat themselves, kill themselves, or behave badly or wrongly. What makes their idiosyncratic or statistically abnormal behavior immoral or perverted? Answer: nothing, except pretty arbitrary *definition*.

If society wants to define eating rattlesnake meat as bad or wrong and to condemn and punish people who thoroughly enjoy it and frequently engage in it as wrongdoers, it can certainly do this. But wisely? Accurately? Scientifically? Unbigotedly? Hardly! In fact, if a group of vociferous anti-rattlesnake eaters got together and insisted that the government of their country ban all ingestion of rattlesnakes and damn and jail all those who indulged in it, we might well wonder about the mental health of the members of this group. Not because they disliked snake eating and not because they tried to persuade others to give it up, but because they dogmatically *insisted* that it brought only bad results and arbitrarily tried to *force* everyone else to refrain from eating snakes.

2. If you flout cultural laws or legal statutes, you may indeed get into some social and personal difficulties. But sometimes you may find it worth your while, in spite of these hassles. Rules and laws do not prove *always* good for *everyone* or even for most of the people most of the time. Rules and laws against masturbation and adultery, for example, have existed since time immemorial—and many wise humans have sanely and happily flouted them.

If the state in which you reside bans your eating snakes, and you happen to love their taste, you would probably defeat your own ends if you went to your local grocer and ordered a tin of rattle-snake meat or if you ordered such a tin by mail. For you then could very well get caught, and even if you considered this anti-snake-eating law the most ridiculous statute ever passed, perhaps you had better publicly adhere to it and not bring on any prosecution or per-secution.

But suppose, on your own land, you happen to catch a snake and can kill it and eat it without letting anyone else know about it. Would you then foolishly defeat yourself if you did this and forever-more kept your mouth shut about your illegal act? Probably not. Because you generally want to remain a law-abiding citizen, you might well decide not to do this; and even if you kill a snake (which your community might still allow), you might refrain from eating it.

But if you decide to take a risk and flout what you consider a silly law against snake eating, can we legitimately call you "deviant" or "perverse"? I doubt it. You may behave abnormally, in a statisti-cal sense—assuming that practically everyone else in your commu-nity abides by the law and refuses to eat snake meat. But the terms *deviant* and *perverse* imply more than engaging in behavior of a sta-tistically peculiar bent. Consequently, I normally will not label you that way.

By the same token, suppose your community bans your having any kind of sex except with your legal mate, and suppose you then engage in premarital or adulterous sex relations. Even though such nonmarital acts may then harm you and your partners (because of their legal banning and because they may include other harmful ele-ments) can we still legitimately call them "deviant" or "perverse"? Only, again, statistically, since few people, under these conditions of illegality, may have nonmarital sex and most of them may harm themselves (or others). But you, personally, may never get into any legal or social difficulties by performing these statistically peculiar acts, and, in fact, you may do yourself a great deal of good thereby.

3. "Unnatural" sexual (or, for that matter, "unnatural" nonsexual) behavior can practically never get precisely defined. Some people think it unnatural to eat ants and grasshoppers; others think it unnatural *not* to do so. Whatever a given person does and harmlessly enjoys seems obviously natural to him or her—and, in part, to the race as a whole. Even if we could show that a certain kind of sex act, such as homosexual behavior, rates as unnatural because it cannot very well lead to procreation and because the human race would die out if procreation ceased, we would still have to demonstrate that the human race *has* to continue to exist and it *cannot* in any way exist if homosexuality becomes widespread or even universal.

The second of these propositions seems definitely wrong, since even if every single human engaged only in homosexual behavior, and in no heterosexuality whatever (which appears, to say the least, highly unlikely!), if these homosexual humans wanted to perpetuate themselves they could still do so by artificial insemination. The first proposition seems absolutistic and unprovable, since why *must* humans continue to perpetuate themselves? And if they decide to die out rather than to go on living, why does their decision not rate as an eminently human, and therefore natural, process?

In other words, I find it difficult to think of any act that humans can and do fairly consistently perform as unnatural. Whatever they do, they naturally do. Much of what they do definitely seems childish, irrational, and self-defeating—such as when they obsess themselves with any kind of sexuality (including heterosexual fucking in the missionary position!) and neglect other important aspects of their lives or ruin their health or potential for greater enjoyment. For *if* they want to survive for about seventy-five years and if they want to experience maximum happiness and minimum pain during their life span, they'd better follow certain sensible rules of conduct. But of course, they don't *have to,* and we have lots of data showing that they often do not. Consequently, it seems natural and human for them to sabotage what they say they hold as fundamental values or preferences. If so, to call any of their sexual (or nonsexual) behavior "unnatural" ("subhuman") appears inaccurate, and to label them as "deviant" or "perverse" for performing this "unnatural" behavior seems even sillier.

4. When we call a sex act "deviant," "perverted," or "abnormal" because of its "animality," that seems particularly illegitimate, for we *do* exist as animals—and certainly not as gods or spirits. Moreover, what we call the "lower" animals rarely turn compulsive, exclusive, or fixated in their sex behavior, although human animals frequently do. Sex compulsions stem largely from highly cognitive, often complex views—particularly the beliefs that we *must* or can *only* engage in a special kind of sex or *must not* participate in another kind. These cognitive overgeneralizations (deification of one act and devil-fication of another act) appear notably human and rarely subhuman or animalistic. We can sometimes *train* "lower" animals, in our laboratories, to act in rigid, compulsive, neurotic sex ways. But they rarely get that way on their own!

5. As for sex deviations flouting God's laws, no one has ever defined these laws for certain—or probably ever will. If an all-powerful God truly existed and proclaimed a sex act ungodly or against His law, how could a mere human actually flout that law? Not very easily! Since one God, Jehovah, supposedly labels one sex act "unnatural" and "ungodly"; since another God (or son of God), Jesus, singles out other sex acts as "abnormal"; and since still another God, Allah, has quite different definitions, it seems highly probably that "God's laws" of sexual deviation vary widely in accordance with the beliefs of those who subscribe to them and that they have no proved objective or general validity.

6. Sex acts that needlessly harm others—such as rape and seduction of a minor—and that frequently remain against the law as well may certainly appear immoral or antisocial, and we may legitimately label them as such. Usually, however, we do not call a crime—such as robbery or bribery—a *deviation* or a *perversion*. So it seems strange that we put only sex offenses in this category. If you lie in a major way, especially to one of your friends, and you needlessly harm this person thereby, we can again legitimately say that you have behaved unethically or immorally. But deviantly? Perversely?

Hardly! Many immoral acts, such as stealing and lying, occur so frequently that they cannot get called "deviant" by almost any normal standard, for deviance implies unusualness, deviation from a common norm. But even those immoral acts, such as rape, which occur only rarely seem deviant statistically, but not in any other way. As for labeling them "perverse"—on what grounds would we give them that kind of appellation?

7. If any legitimate meaning of the term *sex deviation* exists, I think we could use it as a kind of synonym for *sexual disturbance*. And even in this case, one could object on the grounds that a disturbance in other areas—such as a phobia, a nonsexual obsession, or a deep-seated feeling of worthlessness—hardly ever gets labeled a "deviation" or a "perversion." Why, then, use the term almost exclusively about a *sex* disturbance?

Why not merely say, instead, that individuals who needlessly or foolishly interfere with their own survival or happiness by engaging in some sex act (such as compulsive exhibitionism) or by refusing to engage in certain acts (such as heterosexual intercourse in a rear-entry position) because they arbitrarily label these acts "bad" or "wicked" act in a distinctly disturbed manner? And why not forget about terms like *deviation, abnormality,* and *perversion* entirely?

In other words, although the use of the term *sex deviation* may have once served some purpose, I doubt whether it does today. It means different things to different people—including to different authorities. It tends to cover, quite vaguely, a multiplicity of sex behaviors—by no means all of which we can agree produce bad results. It springs, often, from enjoyable and harmless idiosyncracies, rather than from truly self-harming or people-harming conduct. Even when it seems clearly harmful—as when an individual obsessively-compulsively engages in voyeurism and·thereby sabotages a large segment of his life—it often constitutes much more of a vice than a crime—like addiction to alcohol or to cigarettes.

I would tend to recommend, therefore, that we stop speaking about sex deviations at all, that we drop the nasty, pejorative connotations that almost invariably go with the use of such terms, and that instead we merely try to distinguish between sexual (and nonsexual) behavior that occurs in an emotionally disturbed and in a nondisturbed manner. Even then, we may have difficulty defining the term *disturbance*. But not as much as we seem to have with *deviation, perversion,* and *abnormality!*

Sexual Disturbance

How would I define the term *sexual disturbance*? Exactly the same way I would define *any* form of emotional disturbance, even though it had no sexual underpinnings or overtones. And general disturbance, as indicated in rational-emotive theory and practice, stems from three major kinds of *musts, demands,* or *whinings.*

Personal Demandingness.

Sexually disturbed individuals most frequently make inordinate personal demands on themselves. They begin with the basic philosophy, "I must do very well, or at least moderately well, at practically all times and must win others' approval for performing adequately. And if don't, I rate as a terrible, worthless person. Sexually, I must perform competently and win the approval of whatever partners I find attractive and interesting. I therefore cannot risk certain acts (such as intercourse) if I think I will do them poorly or will get condemned for performing them; I can allow myself only less risky acts (such as masturbation or peeping), at which I feel pretty sure I will perform well or which others will not know that I perform."

This type of sexual perfectionism frequently results in feelings of anxiety, depression, and inadequacy; in withdrawal (including abstinence); and in participation exclusively in various acts, ranging from normal intercourse to sex with animals or corpses, which the disturbed individual arbitrarily defines as "safe," "good," or "enjoyable." Sex perfectionists tend to overrestrictedly narrow down the many-faceted field of sex to one or a few limited aspects, because they predict that they will fail in other ways or get criticized for succeeding in these other ways and that failure or criticism would prove *awful* and *horrible*. Thus, the sexually disturbed male commonly says to himself, "If I attempted to have intercourse with highly attractive females, I would very likely fail to please them and they would probably despise me. That kind of failure and despising would make me a total shit!" Rather than risk the possible shithood he has dreamed up for himself, this individual remains abstinent, lets himself have sex only with other males (with whom he knows he *can* succeed or believes he doesn't *have to* succeed), or restricts himself to young children (whom, again, he feels safe with and knows he can easily "conquer").

Perfectionism, however, can also lead to various kinds of compulsiveness. Thus, the male who strongly feels that he would turn into a shit if he tried sex-love relations and failed may also believe that he can succeed unusually well at certain kinds of sex—such as giving women orgasms orally. He may therefore addict himself to this activity and compulsively look for one woman after another with whom to have oral relations. He doesn't so much enjoy the *sex* with these women, as the notion that he has *proved himself* by successfully having it. In this respect, he may somewhat resemble a tycoon of industry who occupies himself most of his life making large sums of money, not because he really wants the money—he actually may keep so busy making it that he has practically no time to spend it— but because he has to prove how "brilliant" or "manly" he rates by making it.

Demandingness of Others

In addition to or instead of demanding great performances of himself, a man can have unrealistic demands of others. His philosophy then runs, "You must treat me kindly and lovingly and help me sexually in any way I want, else you rate as a horrible, lousy person. I therefore will have little or nothing to do with you or with people resembling you and will devote myself to avoiding or harassing people like you and to restricting myself to sexual pursuits that I have without you or that I direct against you."

This type of sexual demandingness results in feelings of hostility, rage, unlovingness, and self-pity; in withdrawal from certain forms of sex; and in obsessive-compulsive focusing on other sex acts. Thus, a man who hates the first woman who rejects him—who happens to have dark hair and brown eyes—may thereafter allow himself only to act potent with blue-eyed blondes or with butch-type males. He may make himself just as exclusively devoted to blondes as another male who doesn't have anything against dark-haired women but who finds himself so enormously attracted to brunettes that he therefore greatly fears failing with them—and fixates himself on blondes or on men.

Compulsiveness may also stem from sex hostility. For example, a man may hate his mother, because she acted rather badly toward him during his childhood or adolescence. Because he crazily over-generalizes and places all or many women in the same hateful category with her, he may compulsively act sadistically toward most of his female partners or may pursue them, in a Don Juan manner, to prove that some women *can* love him and thus show that he has worthiness (even though his mother did not think so) or may make himself into a compulsive homosexual, exhibitionist, or child abuser, or even (in extreme cases) a compulsive sex murderer, to "get back" at his mother for treating him badly and to make her feel ashamed of his aberrant sexuality.

Demandingness of the World

Like most disturbed individuals, the sexually disturbed person tends to demand inordinately that the world treat him kindly and make things easy for him. He may hold the view, "I *must* find sex acts easily and immediately enjoyable, because it remains not only hard but *too* hard for me to learn how to succeed at them. The world *has to* provide me with an easier way; else I refuse to find sex, or life itself, truly enjoyable." He also may believe, "When I finally manage to find any form of sex enjoyable, even if it proves highly disadvantageous (as, for example, sadism or masochism may prove), I simply shouldn't have to retrain myself to have other sex enjoyments but will pigheadedly stick to this mode even though it defeats me in the long run."

This type of sexual demandingness results in low frustration toler-ance, short-range hedonism, trying to get away with doing things the easy way, and lack of discipline. And again it may short-sight-edly and self-defeatingly lead to undue sex-love restrictiveness and failure. Thus, a man may discover, fairly early in his teens, that he can easily get to bed with unattractive or disturbed women. And even though he doesn't truly enjoy such partners, he may take the easy way out and stick with one or more of them for decades to come. Or he may get involved with a highly intelligent and sexy partner who gives him a great deal of pleasure but who also makes him toe the line in certain respects. And he may upset himself so much about her "horrible" requirements, especially her making him assume certain responsibilities, that he may acquire a lifelong phobia against other attractive and bright women and may frantically avoid all future entanglements with them.

Similarly, a man may get so hung up on the immediate gratification of having someone tell him nice things about his attractiveness and quickly go to bed with him that he may compulsively seek that kind of quick ego thrill all his life—and may find it with older women, with immature males, or with some other special kind of sex partner to whom he therefore obsessively-compulsively attaches himself.

Usually, then, sexual hangups or disturbances stem from some kind of demandingness or commandingness—from an individual's not merely wanting or preferring a certain mode of sex-love activity but from his devoutly believing that he absolutely *must* have it, that his entire life will seem rather worthless without it, and that he as a person turns into an almost complete turd if he cannot prove his value by engaging successfully in this form of sexuality.

Sex disturbance, then, doesn't mean what some person or group finds peculiar, unnatural, illegal, animalistic, ungodly, or antisocial. It truly means disturbance, or needless self-defeating thoughts, feelings, and behaviors. And we'd better not call it by pejorative, denigrating terms like *deviation* or *perversion*. When more accurately described and defined, it mainly includes sex acts performed in a compulsive, overrigid, panic-stricken, hostile, disorganized, or overimpulsive manner.

Sex disturbances, moreover, exist, not because of their sexuality, but because they involve *dysfunctional* sexuality. They almost always come under the heading of general disturbances and rarely exist without some kind of general demandingness. No act, however unusual or bizarre, seems neurotic because of its unusualness. The neurotic element in it consists in the afflicted individual's performing it in a self-sabotaging *manner*.

We can even deem necrophilia (having intercourse with a dead person) "normal" or "healthy" under some unusual conditions—

say, if the necrophiliac worked in a mortuary and had no other sex outlets available. Regular intercourse, on the other hand, can get performed quite neurotically—as, say, when a person permits himself or herself to screw only very short, green-eyed members of the other sex at three A.M. on February 29 in a public square. Sex disturbance, then, comes from a disturbed *attitude*—and rarely from the specific kind of sex act performed.

A constant difficulty in defining sex disturbances arises from our inability to tell exactly when a sex act leads to defeating behavior. The same difficulty arises in connection with love. If you fall madly in love with a rather stupid woman and utterly dedicate yourself to her for many years, even though she gives you a very hard time and exploits you in many ways, we might easily label your behavior obsessive-compulsive or neurotic, and we might think it best for you to go for some sort of psychological treatment, to help you overcome this kind of "mad" love. But suppose you genuinely love this woman, achieve immense joy from staying with her, have great sex with her mainly because you have such intense feeling for her, and always consider your relationship with her eminently worthwhile. Suppose, also, that you have many chances at other women —virtually all of them brighter, more attractive, kinder, sexier, and less exploitative than she. You may still decide to stay with her and ignore all of them.

How, then, shall we diagnose you? As utterly crazy? As at least moderately neurotic? As self-defeating? Who, exactly, can say? Certainly, from an "objective" point of view, you seem to do yourself in. But subjectively—ah, quite a different story! Similarly with sex. For many years you may remain, say, a fetishist who "madly" dotes on women wearing high-heeled shoes. You may follow them on the street, try to have affairs with them, persuade all your wives and lovers to wear very high heels, spend a great deal of time and money seeking out and reading fetishistic magazines that feature pictures of women in high heels, acquire a closetful of women's high-heeled shoes, and spend much time looking at them and masturbating while you observe them. This all would seem pretty crazy to the rest of us males who have little or no similar interests.

But *would* such a very consuming interest in high heels, and great degrees of arousal and satisfaction accompanying such an interest, prove you crazy! Yes—if you ruined your entire life because of this obsession. Yes—if you trained yourself to suffer complete impotence when you temporarily had no access to high-heeled shoes. Yes —if you kept getting yourself arrested for molesting strange women who happened to wear very high heels.

But suppose you kept yourself only moderately obsessed with women's high heels and never got into any serious trouble because of your obsession? What then? Would we still call you disturbed or neurotic? Would we recommend treatment for you?

Let us not forget, in this connection, that innumerable people— perhaps, it we really knew the score, the great majority—have some kind of obsession or other. Jane Smith, for example, spends more money than she can really afford on collecting china. John Jones obsesses, for literally hours every week, with baseball batting averages. Jim and Dora Thompson devote practically all their time to building their liquor business, and even neglect their children and their friends in the process. But all these individuals thoroughly enjoy themselves and, in fact, feel miserable when something, such as an illness, interferes with their obsessive pursuits. None of them, moreover, gets in any serious trouble, regularly feels anxious or depressed, or considers himself or herself deprived. Disturbed? Yes —according to *some* standards. But how much so? And how many psychiatrists or psychologists would think that they really need help or that getting intensive psychotherapy (assuming that it would really serve any purpose) would prove worth it for people like these?

Obsessive-compulsiveness, in other words, seems almost ubiquitous among humans and has its distinct advantages. It particularly appears a natural concomitant of much sex activity—perhaps the majority of young males in our society more or less obsess about fucking, and the great majority of females of practically all ages obsess about loving. To some degree, moreover, sex obsessiveness and compulsivity helps arousal and orgasm, since people who have real difficulty in getting themselves to the heights of sex excitement or achieving orgasm after they get there frequently resort to all kinds of sex fetishes, preoccupations, obsessions, and extreme fantasies to get themselves over the top. Millions of otherwise "normal" males and females, for example, frequently resort to intense sado-masochistic fantasies to make themselves more effective in their masturbational and interpersonal sex encounters.

The question remains, shall we view many, some, or a few of these individuals as sexual neurotics? In one way, I would say few. For if practically all of us act neurotical and do so a good portion of the time, then the terms *neurotic* or *disturbed* tend to seem unrealistic, and perhaps we'd better avoid using them for any kind of behavior that appears so frequent. On the other hand, as I have shown in *Reason and Emotion in Psychotherapy,* if some form of disturbance seems to exist as the human condition, and if virtually all of us foolishly and childishly defeat ourselves in several significant ways, perhaps we had better acknowledge this fact, stop putting ourselves down for having emotional disturbances, and devote a good deal of our time and energy to various techniques of making ourselves less disturbed.

In regard to sex, I tend to take a middle-of-the-road position. On the one hand, I believe that the *tendency* toward disturbance reigns quite inclusively among humans. For if we investigate the number of people who turn up with fairly serious sex disturbances—including behaviors such as compulsive homosexuality, exhibitionism, peeping, and sexual assault that actually led to their getting into overt trouble (such as arrest) or institutionalization—we find that perhaps 10 percent of our citizens have distinct problems for a large part of their lives. But we could well add to this list of people who commit overt sex acts that get them into some kind of difficulty perhaps three or four (maybe five or six) times that number who rigidly and self-defeatingly *abstain* from various kinds of sex for highly arbitrary reasons.

Take, for example, the large number of people who often engage in regular petting and intercourse but who rigidly and bigotedly abstain from ever trying oral relations or anal sex. If these individuals practiced *only* orality or anality, we might designate them as having a sexual problem or disturbance. We would tend to say that they had fixated themselves upon this monolithic form of sex and had rigidly refrained from all other modes. But what if they rigidly, fixatedly *abstain* from oral or anal sex—and do so without ever trying it, to see how they would or would not like it? Does not their rigidity *then* constitute a problem?

If we consider all the various sex acts that humans never try, that they studiously avoid trying, and that they feel disgusted about when they consider trying, it would appear that perhaps the great majority of them have some kind of hangup. Does this mean that you have to try *everything* in the sex books to prove your normalcy? Not at all! If you honestly believe, after giving the matter some careful thought, that screwing a corpse, a goose, or a knothole just doesn't seem your cup of tea and that you'd prefer to keep away from that sort of thing, fine. No reason why you *have* to try it!

The fact remains, however, that most of us seem to avoid many kinds of sex activities—not a few of which we feel revolted about even though we have had zero experience with them. And even those which we do occasionally try—like homosexuality—we attempt in such a half-hearted manner, and on so few occasions, that we never really give them a chance, though we "honestly" feel that we don't like them for the rest of our lives.

All of which means—what? That sex bigotry or prejudice exerts a mighty influence on most of us much of the time. And since emotional health in virtually any area—from food to sex to politics—largely consists of open-mindedness, of the ability to at least *consider* viewpoints other than our usual ones, my conclusion tends to remain. A vast amount of sexual disturbance still exists, even though much less than existed a number of decades ago. Lots of things have changed for the better in this respect. Whereas in the old days, practically every member of our society seemed to abjure the possibility of appearing nude in public places, attending "pornographic" movies and shows, living in a nonmarital union with a member of the other sex, coming out of the closet if he or she led a homosexual life, openly engaging in adulterous affairs, and participating in various other forms of unconventional sex, a sizable minority (and sometimes the majority) of us participate in some of these kinds of activities today.

So our sex life has significantly changed, emerged as much more open, in some of these ways. Good! But sexual closedness, prejudice, and anxiety still remain the rule, rather than the exception. The sex revolution marches on—but slowly, and with many regressions. Therefore, I say again—sex disturbance in one form or another still exists pandemically. Less, I think, than it ever did before in our culture. But still very widely!

Preferential and Disturbed Homosexuality

To understand whether sexual disturbance exists, or what kind of behavior truly rates as "normal" and as "disturbed," we might well consider fixed or exclusive homosexuality. For a good many years I have contended that confirmed homosexuals, both male and female, mostly merit the diagnosis of "neurotic" and that in fact we can often diagnose them as "borderline psychotics." I took this stand many years ago in several articles that I wrote for homosexual publications, and I repeated it in my book *Homosexuality: Its Causes and Cure*. I tried to make very clear in these writings that although we cannot accurately see homosexual *behavior* as disturbed, we cannot say the same thing about *fixed* or *exclusive* homosexuality, since that generally tends to take on a nonpreferential, rigid aspect; and all sexual rigidities and exclusivities tend to have their distinctly neurotic aspects. The main reasons I gave for most—not all—homosexuals' having emotional disturbances included:

1. In our bigoted, antihomosexual culture, where we prejudicially and legally ban homosexuality and make it legally and socially disadvantageous, fixed homosexuals "get themselves into various legal, social, and vocational difficulties" and thereby act in a highly self-defeating manner.

2. Most confirmed or obligatory homosexuals in our society "have had little or no heterosexual experience and *still* vigorously contend that they could not possibly enjoy such experience and must remain one hundred percent homosexual. This kind of arrant prejudice and bigotry on their part remains equivalent to anti-Semitism, anti-integrationism, and other kinds of racial and religious prejudice, therefore proves distinctly a function of severe festishism or anti-fetishism, and consequently of emotional disturbance."

3. Although homosexuals theoretically could have a strong preferential attachment to members of their own sex, the great majority

of those I have talked with extensively, including many who did not feel themselves disturbed, had, not a preferential, but a highly compulsive, attachment to members of their own sex. The main irrational fears that sparked their compulsiveness included fears of rejection by members of the other sex, fear of heterosexual impotence, fear of intense emotional involvement, and fear of marital responsibilities.

4. In addition to feeling exceptionally anxious about the possibility of their failing sexually with members of the other sex, most confirmed homosexuals I have encountered have a high degree of low frustration tolerance, or "goofing." Having discovered that they can perform homosexually and have trouble doing so heterosexually, they give in to doing things the "easy" way and refuse to try to overcome their sex limitations and self-restrictions. Those I have talked with can definitely learn to enjoy and function well at heterosexual relations, and many of them do. But the great majority give up because they find this hard and, in typical neurotic style, define it as "too" hard and try half-heartedly or not at all. Most of them follow this short-range hedonism in their nonsexual as well as their sex lives and function on an academic, work, and self-discipline level far below their capacities and their wishes.

5. A very high percentage of confirmed homosexuals that I have talked with—and this again includes scores who have not come to see me or any other psychotherapist for help and many who do not consider themselves disturbed—have the typical symptoms, not merely of serious neurosis, but of borderline psychosis. They have what Dr. Paul Meehl calls cognitive slippage, in spite of their high intelligence, and find great difficulty making some of the finer discriminations required for adequate social relations. They have exceptionally low opinions of themselves, think negatively a good deal of the time, and constantly damn themselves and others. They frequently feel depressed, have low energies, act in a disorganized fashion, feel unspontaneous and anhedonic, feel woefully dependent upon others, constantly upset themselves over little things, and have relatively little fun in life except when under the influence of alcohol, drugs, or other stimulants. For the most part, they act in a highly obsessive-compulsive manner, particularly in regard to cruising for sex partners and for love partners, and have great difficulty

finding the latter on any kind of steady basis, because they mainly obsess themselves with receiving love and proving how worthwhile that makes them, rather than with loving.

These, I have found in the past, tend to remain the characteristics of the average—though hardly every single—homosexual. Do I still find this today? No, not exactly. For as the gay-liberation movement rightly claims, some amount of the disturbance that has afflicted homophiles in our culture has stemmed from our persecuting them, forcing them to live underground, and telling them that they shouldn't act the way they do and consequently rate as inadequate, worthless individuals. They have frequently bought this kind of vicious societal propaganda, and a good deal of their disturbance has resulted from agreeing with it. Consequently, I find that as we—meaning heterosexual society—take more liberal attitudes toward fixed homosexuals and allow them to do what they want with their sex lives, with a minimum of interference and persecution, the happier and less disturbed they seem to feel and behave. Also, as gay liberation again points out, more homosexuals today seem to choose their way of life on a preferential, rather than on a compulsive, rigidly fixed, basis; and as I have noted above, people who preferentially choose a mode of sex behavior, even though it seems strange and different to the majority of individuals in a given culture, may have little or no emotional disturbance. They may merely behave peculiarly rather than aberrantly.

The question still remains, do confirmed homosexuals today, even when they live in permissive environments—such as they can find in New York, San Francisco, Los Angeles, and various other parts of the world—have inherent emotional disturbances linked with their fixed homosexuality? Most authorities would tend to agree with gay liberation and answer, no, their homosexuality does not *necessarily* amount to a severe emotional problem. They *can* choose to engage in same-sex and same-love relations preferentially, and the fact that they do so does not mean that they *have to* act disturbed in the rest of their lives or that they cannot behave as maturely and effectively as the average heterosexually inclined man or woman.

Although this opinion would have rarely got voiced a few decades ago, it tends to prevail today. In consequence, the American Psychiatric Association has voted to drop confirmed homosexuality from its previous list of mental disorders. And more and more psychotherapists, most of them heterosexual, now treat homosexual clients for all kinds of sexual and nonsexual problems without considering their homophilism as one of these problems and without trying to convert them to heterosexuality.

The question whether the average homosexual has greater disturbance than the average heterosexual still remains controversial. Many outstanding authorities on homosexuality think that homosexuality, at best, constitutes something of a disorder and that gays, on the whole, definitely turn out more neurotic than straights. On the other hand, an increasing number of authorities claim that homosexuals have no more disturbance than heterosexuals or that, when they do, this results largely from societal condemnation and persecution, rather than from any other tendency to behave aberrantly.

Many of these authorities, on both sides of the fence, have their clear-cut biases—including the bias that most of those who feel that homosexuals have more than their share of disturbance tend to behave as confirmed heterosexuals, and many of those who feel that homosexuals have no more disturbance than anyone else tend to behave as confirmed homophiles.

The question of the basic origin of fixed homosexuality also remains controversial. I reviewed the evidence for the physiological causation of homoeroticism years ago and concluded that no clear-cut data existed to show that physical rather than psychological factors lead people into confirmed homosexual pathways. Most authorities, including Dr. Frank Acosta, have come to the same conclusion. But Dr. Gunther Dorner and his associates have presented some findings supporting a neuroendocrine predisposition for homosexuality in men. These findings seem more convincing than the somewhat similar findings of Kallman, Lang, Evans, and other researchers.

Drs. John Money and Anke Ehrhardt take a middle-of-the-road position, holding that "certain sexually dimorphic traits [get] laid down in the brain before birth which may facilitate the establishment of either [homosexuality, bisexuality, or heterosexuality but seem] too strongly bivalent to [prove] exclusive and invariant determinants of either homo- or heterosexuality or of their shared bisexual state."

My guess? That *some* confirmed homosexuals may well have a *slight* physiological predisposition to avoid heterosexual, and devote themselves to homosexual, relations—just as, I believe, most heterosexuals have a *slight* physiological predisposition favoring heterosexuality. But largely, I feel, humans tend to feel innately bisexual or plurisexual and can fairly easily train themselves—usually for psychological reasons—to avoid one major mode of sexuality (such as homosexuality *or* heterosexuality) and to exclusively or mainly enjoy another mode. As a result of their self-training they *feel* much more comfortable with the mode they choose, *view* it as their "natural" bent, and falsely conclude that they *had* to choose it. The more rigid they act about their main choice, the more disturbance they tend to exhibt—and that disturbance, too, has both physiological and environmental sources.

Back to the consideration of the disturbed tendencies of fixed homosexuals or gay individuals in this society—again, much controversy exists in this area at the present time.

Where do I stand on all this? Still pretty much on the side of sex *preference* rather than *compulsiveness* and still saying, as I said in the first edition of *The American Sexual Tragedy* a good many years ago: We'd better apply standards of emotional disturbance equally to straights and to gays. Disturbance does not consist of sex leanings in themselves; and contrary to the psychoanalytic hypotheses of Freud and his followers, general emotional problems rarely flow from sex problems—from castration fears or an "Oedipus complex." On the contrary, humans who have a tendency to exaggerate the significance of things, especially of making mistakes and getting criticized for these mistakes, get into sexual difficulties because they think that they *have to* do well in this respect and that they *must* win the approval of others. I see literally hundreds of heterosexual men and women who have sex disabilities or inadequacies, and virtually all of them have enormous fears of failure and a dire need to feel approved and loved. Without these fears and this need they would rarely wind up with a sex problem in the first place or would fairly easily conquer it in the second place.

My philosophy almost exactly follows, as it has for many years, that of Identity House, a counseling center in New York specifically designed to serve the gay and bisexual community. Its philosophy bases itself on "the ideal that one's sexual identity should [remain] a freely chosen expression of that which [feels] most natural to and rewarding for each individual." Well stated! If you really wanted to behave wisely in regard to sex, you would experiment during your lifetime with a fairly large variety of outlets—usually including masturbation, heterosexuality, homosexuality, and perhaps sex with animals—and would open-mindedly observe which ones seem most satisfying to you. You would also consider the practical advantages and disadvantages of these outlets—whether, for example, you have to spend much time pursuing them, how much expenditure they tend to require, whether they lead to responsibilities that you don't want to assume, what real health hazards (such as venereal disease) they tend to include, etc.

On the basis of this information, and especially on the basis of your *own* particular tastes, you would select some main forms, or even one main form, of sexual behavior that seems to suit you, and you would probably largely stick with these modes or this mode for much of your life. Not that you have to!—for you could also try a particular sexual pathway, such as homosexuality, for a time and then decide to practically abandon it for another mode, such as heterosexuality. Or you could mainly stick with one sexual outlet, such as masturbation, and from time to time engage in other outlets, such as homosexual, heterosexual, orgiastic, and other forms of sex.

In other words, I see no single, monolithic sex route that you have to follow all or most of your life. I think that, for various biological and sociological reasons, you will probably tend to favor one route rather than another—just as, in performing coitus, you may well tend to favor one position most of the time and only now and then resort to others. Most people seem to remain this way—with food, dress styles, reading tastes, music preferences, etc. They largely favor one mode and only now and then take advantage of various other modalities. So I think that you will probably do this in your sex proclivities, too.

But again, you don't have to! You can do almost anything you like sexually, especially these days, and not get into any serious trouble, as long as you don't do it too publicly or interfere with the lives of others. You can find your own way or ways and privately pursue them, especially if you live in a large metropolitan area where you can almost have your pick of different kinds of partners.

Sexual sanity (like nonsexual sanity), then, largely consists of noncompulsiveness, of personal experimentation, of open-mindedness, of sticking to pathways that do not entail too many practical disadvantages, and perhaps above all, of accepting yourself and utterly refusing to down yourself even if you do the wrong thing and indubitably behave self-defeatingly. For if you do train yourself to behave and to continue behaving in a rigid, disturbed, uncreative sex-love manner, and you perceive that you keep defeating yourself by compulsively engaging in certain forms of sex and phobically abstaining from potentially harmless and enjoyable forms, you still don't have to berate yourself or damn yourself for your unfortunate behavior. Your *acts,* under these conditions, appear foolish, but *you* never rate as *a* fool or a louse or a worm or a rotten person! For you exist as an ongoing process, an individual who, at any age, can change remarkably. And you (or anyone) cannot legitimately rate the process of your youness, your living humanity. Remember that!

The Treatment of Sexual Disturbance

As I have tried to show thus far in this chapter, sexual disturbance definitely exists, although to call it by pejorative terms, such as *deviation, perversion,* and *abnormality* and to make it completely synonymous with other kinds of more general disturbance may not appear legitimate or wise. Some people with extreme sex fetishes, for example, get along very well in their general lives—and they even manage to cater to these fetishes without bringing on themselves too many hassles. Others, like those who have an extreme fear of failure, have a general disturbance, and additionally experience it in a sexual area—as when they withdraw from sex altogether or limit themselves only to masturbation instead of experimenting with a wider range of outlets. But again, they manage to live fairly "successfully" with their handicaps and mainly fail to achieve their potential, rather than ruin their whole lives. They manage to encapsulate or limit their disturbances, and sometimes they even do better in other areas—as, for example, in art or in business—because they give up a considerable portion of their sex activity.

So don't think that sexual disturbance proves entirely debilitating or horrible, for it often doesn't. Nonetheless, it frequently has its indubitable disadvantages. For example,

1. Usually it goes with general disturbance—with feelings of anxiety, depression, hostility, or low frustration tolerance—and most people who have these kinds of disturbance hardly spend notably happy existences! Many of them, on the contrary, exist in a distinctly, and sometimes desperately, unhappy state.

2. Sexual disturbance usually evolves as a tragically *limiting* condition. Humans naturally enjoy lability, variety, and flexibility in their sex lives. When they make themselves sexually neurotic they tend to narrow down their potential circle of sexuality to a small sliver of the potential pie. And for no truly good reason!

3. As I keep trying to show in this book, sex problems usually go with various forms of irrationality—with the three major unrealistic *musts* that humans impose on themselves. They tend to involve absolutistic and magical demands that cannot get realized and that therefore lead to unfortunate, and at times to highly miserable, results.

4. Although we have liberalized our culture in recent years so that we accept people with compulsive, obsessive, and overfearful sexuality much more than previously, we still cruelly and unnecessarily penalize them to some degree. Thus, if you neurotically smoke, overeat, or refuse to discipline yourself at your work, you will tend to suffer some intrinsic penalties for your disturbed behavior, such as afflicting yourself with ill health or poor work habits. But your self-imposed penalties will frequently end right there. If you give yourself sex problems—such as making yourself compulsively homosexually or heterosexually promiscuous—you will often get scorned and additionally penalized by members of your social group. So sexual neurosis may bring on extra hazards that nonsexual disturbance may not.

Can you deal with and eliminate sex problems if you happen to have them? You certainly can, though not easily! For where many

forms of disturbance have their intrinsic pains, and therefore provide you with a strong incentive to fight against them, the opposite
tends to hold true with sex difficulties. Like other kinds of addic-
tions, they frequently provide you with so many immediate gratifi-
cations that you probably will *not* work very hard to give them up.

Take, for example, compulsive heterosexuality. Suppose you have
an inordinate or obsessive interest in screwing attractive women and
you keep giving in to it in a disturbed manner—you spend more
time than you can really afford to spend on cruising; you also
expend too much money on chasing after and going with women;
and you have something of a phobia against relating to any female
emotionally, for fear that such a relationship will interfere with your
compulsive promiscuous interests. You know that you have this
problem and that you defeat yourself in many ways by giving in to
it. But you also know that you derive a great deal of satisfaction
from it. In fact, some of the most enjoyable moments of your life
occur when you manage to seduce a new woman, and some of the
most boring moments seem to occur when you keep going with the
same partner fo. any length of time, even though she treats you very
nicely and remains consistently available sexually. You tend to
develop conjugal impotence under these conditions—you can make
it sexually with virtually any woman *except* your steady mate.

What to do? Can you, in such circumstances, actually change
your neurotic ways and begin to enjoy sex-love relationships on a
noncompulsive basis? Yes, you can—just as compulsive homosexuals can, if they really want to, work at their problem and make
themselves into enjoying bisexuals. For although sex disturbances
easily arise, usually "unconsciously," in the sense that you do not will
to bring them on, they stem largely from self-conditioning procedures; consequently, you almost invariably have the power to re-
condition yourself, if you want to take the time and trouble to do so.

Don't forget, in this connection, that so-called normal sex pleasures also originate in self-conditioning. As a human, you almost
always have innate plurisexual tendencies—you can get aroused
and come to orgasm in a fairly large variety of ways. You also may
have innate tendencies to prefer one or a few of these ways to
others. If, for example, you have trouble reaching orgasm and
usually require a good deal of pressure or friction to do so, you may

tend to prefer anal to vaginal intercourse, since that will usually provide you with a "better" kind of stimulation in your case. On the other hand, if you naturally tend to come to orgasm quite quickly, with a minimum of friction and pressure, and if you want to climax more slowly, you may "naturally" prefer your partner to use her dry hands on your penis, or you may prefer a mate with a large and slack vagina, so that you will not get so easily and quickly stimulated.

No matter what your "natural" bent remains, however, you usually can modify it significantly by thinking and stimulating yourself in various ways. As I frequently say to my clients, "Men and women obviously have an innate tendency to walk on their feet rather than to swing from trees. But if they really want to do such swinging and will practice it long enough, most of them can teach themselves to swing practically as well as monkeys. In fact, with ropes and other apparatus, they can even improve on monkeys!"

We have already discussed some of the main techniques of helping yourself with such sex problems as impotence. Let me briefly generalize these techniques to dealing with almost any kind of sex compulsion, fixation, phobia, or other disturbance.

Antiawfulizing

As a compulsive heterosexual, you most probably keep awfulizing—defining your behavior (or inactivity) as awful, terrible, and horrible. Find out, which you quickly can in most instances, *what* you define as awful and strongly and consistently dispute or challenge this definition. Start, usually, with your symptom itself— if you now compulsively cruise after women and know you defeat yourself by doing so, you may well down yourself, or feel anxious and depressed, *about* this cruising. This means that you believe, "Compulsive cruising not only proves disadvantageous and foolish, but I therefore *shouldn't* do it and must view it as *awful* if I do what I shouldn't!"

Dispute this irrational belief! "Where does evidence exist that I *shouldn't* act compulsive?" Answer: Nowhere! I can only prove that I'll find compulsive cruising disadvantageous and foolish (for several reasons). But I *should* act compulsive and foolish—if I do!

However I behave, I *should* behave—no matter how idiotic that behavior may prove. Because I remain human and fallible—and humans *do* act compulsive and foolish.

Dispute, again: "Why must I find it *awful* if I compulsively cruise for women?" Answer: Even if I do it forever, and defeat my own best ends indefinitely, I can only legitimately conclude that I behave badly, stupidly. But if I see it as *awful* for me to behave badly, then I really see it as *more than* bad, as at least 101 percent bad. And 101 percent badness hardly exists. Moreover, I really see it as awful only because I think that I *shouldn't* act that way. And, as I've just demonstrated, I should!

After disputing the awfulness or horror of your acting compulsive, see what you keep telling yourself to make yourself act that way—and dispute that. You probably devoutly believe something like, "If I don't win every woman I find attractive, I *can't stand it;* that proves *terrible! I have to* get what I want in the way of sex gratification. I rate as no-good if I lose out on desirable women." Dispute this nonsense!—Why can't I stand missing out on desirable women? What makes it terrible if I do? How do I lose worth as a total person if I keep failing to win them? Keep disputing until you come up with a rational philosophy, such as "I'll never like losing out with attractive women, and always find this kind of loss frustrating. But I can stand what I don't like and can find it merely obnoxious, and not terrible. Moreover, losing out with women never makes me a rotten person—only an individual who has lost something he wants. I never have to rate or down *myself,* even though my ability to win women may remain poor."

Rational-emotive Imagery

Using rational-emotive imagery (REI), invented by Dr. Maxie C. Maultsby, Jr., and adapted by me, you can intensely imagine or fantasize yourself trying to gain the favor of attractive women, and perhaps one that you particularly like, and consistently failing. You can then let yourself feel, as you picture yourself failing, depressed and anxious. Then you can keep this exact picture in your head and force yourself to feel *only* disappointed and sorry, and *not* depressed or angry. When you have made yourself feel only disappointed and sorry, see what you keep telling yourself to make yourself feel that way, such as, "Well, I certainly find it most unfortunate that this woman won't have anything to do with me, but that hardly means that *no* equivalent attractive woman won't. And even though I fail with her, the world will hardly come to an end. I can still find many other sexual and nonsexual enjoyments. Too bad!—but nothing *more* than that."

Every day, for the next two or three weeks, practice this rational-emotive imagery by first fantasizing your losing out sexually, then letting yourself feel hurt and depressed, then changing your feeling to one of disappointment and regret, then noticing how you changed your philosophy about rejection to make yourself have this new, appropriate feeling, then doing the same thing repeatedly, for at least ten minutes a day. In this manner, you get yourself to *practice* feeling appropriately sad instead of inappropriately depressed, and you *practice* thinking sane instead of crazy thoughts about rejection by an attractive woman.

Disputing Irrational Beliefs (DIBS)

You can take any one of your strong irrational beliefs that make you compulsively cruise for women and use the rational-emotive DIBS (Disputing Irrational Beliefs) technique to help yourself give it up. Using DIBS, you ask yourself a series of questions about your irrational belief and write down your answers to them. For example:

1. "What irrational belief do I want to dispute and surrender?"
Illustrative answer: I must keep winning every attractive woman I meet.
2. "Can I prove this belief true?"
Illustrative answer: No, I cannot.
3. "What evidence exists of the falseness of this belief?"
Illustrative answer: a. No law of the universe exists that says that I *have to* (or any male *has to*) win every attractive woman I meet. b. I can obviously survive if I lose out on many or most attractive women. c. I can clearly remain happy—though not *as* happy—if I keep failing with attractive women. d. Lots of men live happily when they get rejected by attractive women, so I can too.
4. "Does any evidence exist of the truth of this belief?"
Illustrative answer: None that I can see. Considerable evidence exists that I would find it preferable or more desirable if I kept winning attractive women. But that never proves that because I'd find it

preferable to do so, I have to. No matter how desirable anything turns out, I never *must* make it turn out that way.

5. "What worst things could *actually* happen if I don't get what I think I must (or do get what I think I mustn't)?"

Illustrative answer: If I keep failing to win the approval of attractive women, a. I would fail to get certain favors and satisfactions, such as sex and love, from them. b. I would receive extra inconveniences and annoyances, such as sex frustration. c. I might never live with or marry a woman I would truly enjoy. d. People might think me something of a worm if I continued to fail in this respect. e. Various other kinds of misfortunes and deprivations might occur. But I need not define any of these as *awful* or *horrible*. At the worst, they would remain problems and hassles—never *horrors* or *terrors*—unless I foolishly think that!

6. "What good things could I make happen if I don't get what I think I must (or do get what I think I mustn't)?"

Illustrative answer: Several good things might occur if I keep failing with attractive women. a. I could devote more time and energy to other pursuits, including working, recreation, or art. b. I could concentrate on enjoying less attractive women and perhaps have very fine relationships with them. c. I could keep trying to win with those I think attractive and improve my relating techniques. d. I could gain some very interesting experiences while failing. e. I could find it challenging and enjoyable to teach myself how to live happily with my failures. f. I could learn to accept myself fully even though I keep performing crummily—and in that matter make myself truly secure.

Again, you can practice this DIBS method at least ten minutes a day for several weeks, until you really come to disbelieve your irrational idea that you *have to* keep winning the approval of attractive women.

Homework Assignments

In RET, we almost always give activity-homework assignments to help people change their self-defeating ideas. In this case, you could give yourself the homework assignment of: (1) trying only once a week, or once every other week, to meet attractive women; (2) deliberately trying to meet less attractive women and relate to them; (3) deliberately failing with a woman to whom you feel attracted; (4) for a while refusing to try at all to meet and win the favors of any attractive women.

Self-Management Schedules

To encourage yourself to keep trying cognitive, emotive, or behavioral rational techniques, like those just listed, you can use reinforcers when you do work at them and penalties when you don't. Thus, if you do rational-emotive imagery or force yourself to talk to one attractive woman only once a week, you can reward yourself by eating a favorite food, masturbating, listening to music, or doing something else you personally find very enjoyable. And if you fail to perform the task you have set yourself, you can penalize yourself by burning a ten-dollar bill, visiting a person you dislike, cleaning the house, or doing something else that you keenly dislike doing.

Related Problems

If you compulsively run after attractive women and thereby defeat yourself, you probably act compulsive in other areas, too—such as overeating, staying out too late at night, or viewing too much television. You can use rational-emotive methods, such as those outlined in this book and in *A New Guide to Rational Living,* to work on these forms of compulsiveness. The better you do at conquering them, the better you probably will do at your sex-love compulsiveness.

Psychotherapy.

If you find that you have enormous difficulty overcoming any sex or love disturbance, you may find psychotherapy practical and beneficial. Naturally, I would recommend some form of cognitive-behavior therapy, rather than psychoanalytic, Gestalt, transactional-analysis, primal, or other therapies. I have used this type of therapy quite effectively for years, and in the realm of sexual dysfunctioning, many other therapists have found it most practicable too. Masters and Johnson use a form of sex therapy that derives mainly from informational and cognitive techniques, on the one hand, activity-homework behavioral methods, on the other, and virtually all good sex therapists today follow their example to a large extent.

In the realm of other forms of sexual disturbance, including compulsive homosexuality, cognitive-behavior therapy seems definitely the most effective method. When someone asked Dr. Arnold Lazarus, "Which type of therapist most likely [will] help a person change from homosexuality to heterosexuality?" he replied, "Leaving aside the fact that many therapists legitimately teach homosexuals how to accept and adjust to their sexual desires, the most straightforward reply to the foregoing question [states] that according to numerous outcome studies in professional journals a 'behavior therapist' [will] most likely help a person change from homosexuality to heterosexuality. To the best of my knowledge, therapists of non-behavioral persuasions seldom claim that they can readily enable a person to change from homosexuality to heterosexuality." To which I would add (and feel sure Dr. Lazarus would concur): Therapists of non-cognitive behavioral persuasion have little success enabling a person to change any heterosexual compulsion, obsession, or phobia. Effective therapy for sex problems almost always includes strong ideational *and* activity homework components.

A final word on sexual disturbances: As Dr. Edward Sagarin has pointed out for years, the mere fact that we wrongly penalize and damn sex "deviants" or "neurotics" and that we'd better stop doing this does not mean that no such thing as disturbance exists. It definitely does! And it can prove highly disadvantageous and defeating. So if you have any real hangup in this area, if you on many occasions act compulsive, rigid, phobic, or disorganized, face the fact that you have a disturbance, accept yourself fully with this disturbance, and then do your best to understand it, see how you keep creating it, and minimize or eliminate it. Don't try to change yourself just because other people think you should or because they view you as a rotten person if you remain "deviant" or "disturbed." Change because it would help *you* to do so—would increase your happiness and improve your functioning. As the theory and practice of RET states, *you* essentially create, your own emotional malfunctioning, and this has great advantages, for *you* therefore can almost always change what you have done and keep doing. What we loosely call "conditioning" actually consists of *self*-conditioning. And you can therefore do the desired reconditioning. Not that you have to. Not that you'll die or live utterly miserably if you don't. But just that in many instances, you'd better. For *your* own good!

Bibliography

Items in this bibliography preceded by a dagger (†) may prove of particular help to readers interested in additional reading in the area of rational living and sex information. You can order items preceded by an asterisk (*), from the Institute for Rational Living, 45 East 65 Street, New York, N.Y. 10021, U.S.A. The Institute will continue to make available these and other materials, as well as to present talks, seminars, workshops, and other presentations in the area of human growth, sexuality, and rational living. Those interested may send for its current list of publications and events.

Abraham, Guy E. Greater libido in hirsute women. *Medical Aspects of Human Sexuality*. 1975, 9(1), 57. •

Acosta, Frank X. Etiology and treatment of homosexuality: a review. *Archives of Sexual Behavior*, 1975, 4, 9–29.

Adelson, Edward R. Premature ejaculation. *Medical Aspects of Human Sexuality*, 1974, 8(9), 83–84.

†Adler, Alfred. Understanding human nature. Greenwich, Conn.: Fawcett Publications, 1970.

†*Alberti, R. E., and Emmons, M. L. *Your perfect right*. San Luis Obispo, California: Impact, 1971.

Allen, Clifford. *The sexual perversions and abnormalities*. London: Oxford University Press, 1949.

Allen, G., and Martin, C. G. *Intimacy*. New York: Pocket Books, 1972.

†Ansbacher, H. L., and Ansbacher, R. R. *The individual psychology of Alfred Adler*. New York: Harper & Row, 1970.

Amelar, Richard D., and Dubin, Lawrence. Impotence: organic vs. psychological. *Medical Aspects of Human Sexuality*, 1974, 8(5), 143–144.

†Anthony, Rey (pseud.). *The housewife's handbook on selective promiscuity*. Tucson: Seymour Press, 1960.

Arafat, Ibtihaj S., and Cotton, Wayne L. Masturbation practices of males and females. *Journal of Sex Research*, 1974, 10, 293–307.

†Ard, Ben N., Jr. (Ed.). *Counseling and psychotherapy*. Palo Alto: Science and Behavior Books, 1975.

Ard, Ben N., Jr. Seven ways to enjoy sex more. *Sexology*, March 1969, 508–510.

Ard, Ben N., Jr. How to stimulate the erotic zones. *Sexology*, June 1971, 4–6.

Ard, Ben N., Jr. Overcoming frigidity. *Sexology*, April, 1974, 15–19.

†Ard, Ben N., Jr. *Treating psychosexual dysfunction.* New York: Jason Aronson, 1974.

†Ard, Ben N., Jr., and Ard, Constance C. (Eds.). *Handbook of marriage counseling.* Palo Alto: Science and Behavior Books, 1969.

Arlington, Norman. Sexual starvation in the American male. *Independent,* Oct. 1958, Issue 81, 1, 8.

Arnstein, Helen S. "Marriage" manuals—helpful or harmful? *Family Circle,* September, 1965, 40–41, 107.

Arnstein, Robert L. Virgin men. *Medical Aspects of Human Sexuality,* January 1974, 113–127.

Arnstein, Robert L. Differences between men's and women's sexual drives. *Medical Aspects of Human Sexuality,* August 1974, 32–34.

Athanasiou, Robert. A review of public attitudes on sexual issues. In Zubin, Joseph, and Money, John (Eds.), *Contemporary sexual behavior.* Baltimore: Johns Hopkins University Press, 1973, 361–390.

Athanasiou, Robert, and Shaver, Phillipp. Correlates of heterosexuals' reactions to pornography. *Journal of Sex Research,* 1971, 7, 298–311.

Auerback, Alfred. Women's lesser sexual desires. *Medical Aspects of Human Sexuality,* January, 1974, 129.

Auerback, Alfred. Disinterest in marital sex. *Medical Aspects of Human Sexuality,* May, 1974, 11.

Ayoob, Massad F. How to prolong intercourse. *Sexology,* January, 1974, 6–10.

†Bach, George R., and Deutsch, Ronald M. *Pairing.* New York: Avon, 1973.

†Bach, George R., and Wyden, Peter. *The intimate enemy.* New York: Avon, 1971.

Bailey, Dee. Sexual foreplay: do unto others. *Rational Living,* 1968, 3(1), 24–28.

Barbara, Dominick. *The art of loving and making love.* Rockville Center, New York: Farnsworth, 1974.

Barclay, Andrew M. Sexual fantasies in men and women. *Medical Aspects of Human Sexuality,* May, 1973, 205–224.

Bardwick, Judith. *Psychology of women.* New York: Harper, 1971.

Barkas, Janet. New woman meets old morality. *Penthouse Forum,* May, 1974, 50–55.

Barlow, D. H. The treatment of sexual deviation. In Calhoun, K.S., Adams, H. E., and Mitchell, K. M. (Eds.), *Innovative treatment methods in psychopathology.* New York: Wiley, 1972.

Barlow, D. H., Agras, W. S., and Reymonlds, E. J. Direct and indirect modification of gender specific motor behavior in a transsexual. Paper presented at the American Psychological Association Convention, Honolulu, Sept. 1972.

Barrel, James J. Sexual arousal in the objectifying attitude. *Review of Existential Psychology and Psychiatry,* 1974, 13(1), 98–105.

Barrio, Cesareo Cubillas. Apparatus for the stimulation of human functions and the convenience of marital sexual life. Sao Leopoldo, Brasil: Author, 1970.

Bartell, Gilbert D. *Group sex*. New York: Wyden, 1971.

Baruch, Dorothy W., and Miller, Hyman. *Keeping love alive*. New York: Hart, 1962.

Becker, Ernest. *Angel in armor*. New York: Braziller, 1969.

†Beigel, Hugo. *Encyclopedia of sex education*. New York: Daye, 1952.

Beigel, Hugo. Abstinence. In Ellis, Albert, and Abarbanel, Albert (Eds.), *Encyclopedia of sexual behavior*. New York: Jason Aronson, 1973.

Beigel, Hugo. How sexual absence harms you. *Sex Guide*, 1965, 103, 40, 4–10.

Beigel, Hugo. Masturbation in marriage. *Sexology*, 1966, 33(4), 234–236.

Beigel, Hugo. The danger of orgasm worship. *Sexology*, November, 1963, 232–234.

Beigel, Hugo. The hypnotherapeutic approach to male impotence. *Journal of Sex Research*, 1971, 7, 168–176.

Beigel, Hugo. Increasing her orgasm pleasure. *Sexology*, 1975, 41(7), 6–10.

Bell, Alan P. Reasons for homosexual promiscuity. *Medical Aspects of Human Sexuality*, 1975, 9 (2), 93–94.

Bell, Robert R. Some emerging sexual expectations among women. *Medical Aspects of Human Sexuality*, October 1967, 65–72.

Bell, Robert R. *The sex survey of Australian women*. Melbourne: Sun Books, 1974.

Belt, Bruce G. Some organic causes of impotence. *Medical Aspects of Human Sexuality*, January 1973, 152–161.

Benjamin, Harry. Sex happiness in marriage. *Medical Record*, July 5, 1939. Reprint.

Benjamin, Harry. Seven kinds of sex. *Sexology*, 1961, 27, 436–442.

Benjamin, Harry. Impotence. *Sexology*, November 1959, 240–243.

Benjamin, Harry. *The transsexual phenomenon*. New York: Julian, 1966.

Benjamin, Harry, and Ellis, Albert. An objective examination of prostitution. *International Journal of Sexology*, 1954, 8, 99–105.

†Benjamin, Harry, and Masters, R. E. L. *Prostitution and morality*. New York: Julian, 1964.

†Berg, Louis, and Street, Robert. *Sex methods and manners*. New York: McBride, 1953.

Bergler, Edmund. *Homosexuality: disease or way of life?* New York: Collier, 1966.

Bergler, Edmund. *Counterfeit-sex*. New York: Grove, 1961.

Bernard, Jessie, Buchanan, Helen E., and Smith, William. *Dating, mating and marriage*. Cleveland: Allen, 1958.

Best, A. *Sex and the singular English*. New York: Taplinger, 1972.

Bianco, Fernando. Marital sexual dysfunction. Paper presented at International Congress of Medical Sexology, Paris, July 1974.

Bieber, Irving. Letter on homosexuality. *Psychiatry and Social Science Review*, 1968, 2(7), 27–32.

Bieber, Irving. Homosexuality. *American Journal of Nursing*, 1969, 69, 2637–2641.

Bieber, Irving, and others. *Homosexuality*. New York: Basic Books, 1962.

†Bird, Lois. *How to make your wife your mistress*. New York: Doubleday, 1972.

Bloch, Iwan. *The sexual life of our time.* New York: Rebman, 1908.

Boccaccio, Shirley. Sex therapy. *Sexual Freedom,* 1972, No. 11, 9–10.

Bonaparte, Marie. *Female sexuality.* London: Imago, 1953.

Bone, Harry. Two proposed alternatives to psychoanalytic interpreting. In Hammer, Emmanuel (Ed.), *Use of interpretation in treatment.* New York: Grune and Stratton, 1968, 169–196.

†Boston Women's Health Book Collective. *Our bodies, ourselves.* New York: Simon and Schuster, 1973.

†Boylan, Brian. *Infidelity.* Englewood Cliffs. N.J.: Prentice-Hall. 1971.

Bourland, D. David, Jr. A linguistic note: write in E-prime. *General Semantics Bulletin,* 1965/1966, 32 and 33, 60–61.

Bourland, D. David, Jr. The semantics of a non-Aristotelian language. *General Semantics Bulletin,* 1968, 35, 60–63.

Breedlove, William, and Breedlove, Jerrye. *Swap clubs.* Los Angeles: Sherbourne, 1964.

Brashera, Diane B. Honk! if you masturbate! Siecus Report, 1974, 3(2), 1, 14.

†Brecher, Ruth, and Brecher, Edward. *Analysis of human sexual response.* New York: New American Library, 1966.

†Brecher, Edward. *The sex researchers.* Boston: Little, Brown, 1969.

Brenton, Myron. *Sex talk.* New York: Stein and Day, 1972.

Brenton, Myron. Five keys to closeness. *Sexology,* 1974, 40(1), 54–58.

Brenton, Myron. "Hold me tight!" *Sexology,* 1975, 41(7), 30–34.

Brisson, Christopher. The erotic statues of India. *Sexology,* August 1966, 46–48.

Broderick, Carlfred B. (Moderator). Petting. *Medical Aspects of Human Sexuality,* 1969, 3(11), 82–90.

Broderick, Carlfred B. Do marriage manuals do more harm than good? *Medical Aspects of Human Sexuality,* 1970, 4(1), 50–63.

Brody, Jane. Sex attractant chemicals from women isolated. *New York Times,* December 24, 1974, 12.

Brophy, Bridget. *Black ship . . .* New York: Knopf, 1962.

Brothers, Joyce. *Woman.* New York: Pocket Books, 1962.

Bromley, Dorothy D., and Britten, F. H. *Youth and sex.* New York: Harper, 1938.

Brown, Charles. Fist fucking. *Screw,* Sept. 1, 1969, 11.

Brown, Helen Gurley. *Sex and the single girl.* New York: Geis, 1962.

Burchell, R. Clay. Self-esteem and sexuality. *Medical Aspects of Human Sexuality,* 1975, 9(1), 74–90.

Burchell, R. Clay. Coital positions. *Medical Aspects of Human Sexuality,* 1975, 9(2), 51–52.

Butler, D. R. How to make your lover come on stronger. *Sexology,* 1974, 40(10), 43–46.

Byrne, D., and Lamberth, J. The effect of erotic stimuli on sex arousal, evaluative response, and subsequent behavior. *Technical Reports of the Commission on Obscenity and Pornography, Vol. 8.* Washington: United States Government Printing Office, 1970.

Calderone, Mary. *Release from sexual tension*: New York: Random House, 1960.

Cantrell, William A. Unfulfilled sexual desires of the premature ejaculator. *Medical Aspects of Human Sexuality*, 1974, 8(10), 96.

Caplan, H. W., and Black, R. A. Unrealistic sexual expectations. *Medical Aspects of Human Sexuality*, 1974, 8(8), 8–36.

Cappon, Daniel. *Toward an understanding of homosexuality.* Englewood Cliffs, N.J.: Prentice-Hall, 1965.

Caprio, Frank S. *The sexually adequate male.* New York: Citadel, 1952.

Caprio, Frank S. *The sexually adequate female.* New York: Citadel, 1953.

Caprio, Frank S. *The modern woman's guide to sexual maturity.* New York: Grove, 1965.

Caprio, Frank S. Can X-rated movies help you? *Sexology*, 1971, 37(12), 13–15.

Caprio, Frank S., and Caprio, Louise P. Schedule your lovemaking. *Sexology*, 1970, 37(5), 56–58.

Carns, Donald E. Talking about sex: notes on first coitus and the double standard, *Journal of Marriage and the Family*, 1973, 35, 677–688.

"Carol" and "Tim". *The swinger's handbook.* New York: Pocket Books, 1975.

†Casler, Lawrence. *Is marriage necessary?* New York: Behavoral Publications, 1974.

Cawood, C. David. Petting and prostatic engorgement. *Medical Aspects of Human Sexuality*, 1971, 5(2), 204–218.

Chapman, J. D. *The feminine mind and body.* New York: Philosophical Library, 1967.

Chartham, Robert. *The sensuous couple.* New York: Ballantine, 1971.

†Chartham, Robert. *What turns women on.* New York: Ballantine, 1974.

Chesser, Eustace. *Love without fear.* New York: New American Library, 1953.

Chesser, Eustace. *The sexual, marital and family relationships of the English woman.* New York: Roy, 1956.

†Chesser, Eustace. *Unmarried love.* New York: Pocket Books, 1966.

Chevalier-Skolnikoff, Suzanne. Male-female, female-female, and male-male sexual behavior in the stumptain monkey, with special attention to the female orgasm. *Archives of Sexual Behavior*, 1974, 3, 95–116.

Chilgren, Richard A. Digital anal stimulation. *Medical Aspects of Human Sexuality*, 1974, 8(1), 115.

Chilman, Catherine S. Some psychosocial aspects of female sexuality. *Family Coordinator*, April 1974, 123–131.

Churchill, Wainwright. *Homosexual behavior among males.* Englewood Cliffs, N.J: Prentice-Hall, 1967.

Churchill, Wainwright, and Bieer, Irving. Letters. *Psychiatry and Social Science Review*, 1968, 2(7), 27–32.

Ciociola, Guido. Is chastity healthful? *Sexology*, 1961, 27, 814–817.

Clanton, Gordon, and Taylor, Barbie. The counseling perspective: "deviant dyad" and its problems. In Ellis, Albert (Moderator), Symposium, Beyond swinging, swapping, and sexual deviance. American Psychological Association Convention, Honolulu, Sept. 1, 1972.

Clark, LeMon. *Emotional adjustment in marriage.* St. Louis: Mosby, 1937.

†Clark, LeMon. *Sex and you.* Indianapolis: Bobbs-Merrill, 1949.

Clark, LeMon. A doctor looks at self-relief. *Sexology*, 1959, 24, 785–88.

Clark, LeMon. Sexual adjustment in marriage. In Ellis, Albert, and Abarbanel, Albert (Eds.), *Encyclopedia of sexual behavior*. rev. ed. New York: Jason Aronson, 1973.

Clark, LeMon. First marital intercourse, *Sexology*, 1966, 33, 241–243.

†Clark, LeMon. *101 Intimate sexual problems*. New York: New American Library, 1967.

Clark, LeMon. Orgasm: key to sexual fulfillment. *Sexology*, 1971, 37(12), 4–7.

Clark, LeMon., and Steinberg, Harry. The most erotic act. *Sexology*, 1974, 41(1), 46–48.

Clark, Thomas E. When a husband's sex desires exceed his wife's. *Medical Aspects of Human Sexuality*, January 1974, 8(1), 79–80.

Coffin, T. *The sex kick*. New York: Avon, 1967.

Cohen, Ruth C. Masturbation. *Psychoanalytic Review*, 1952, 36, 34–41.

Cole, James K. Homosexuality and homosexual love. In Curtin, M. E. (Ed.), *Symposium on love*. New York: Behavioral Publications, 1973.

Colson, Charles E. Olfactory aversion therapy for homosexual behavior. *Journal of Behavior Therapy and Experimental Psychiatry*, 1972, 3, 185–187.

Comfort, Alex. *Sexual behavior in society*. London: Duckworth, 1950.

Comfort, Alex (Ed.), *The kokka shastra*. New York: Stein and Day, 1965.

†Comfort, Alex. *The joy of sex*. New York: Crown, 1972.

†Comfort, Alex. *More joy*. New York: Crown, 1975.

Comfort, Alex. An interview with Alex Comfort. *Practical Psychology for Physicians.*, 1975, 2(1), 23–30.

Copelan, Rachel. *The sexually fulfilled man*. New York: New American Library, 1973.

†Cory, Donald Webster (pseud). *The homosexual in America*. New York: Greenberg, 1951; Paperback Library, 1963.

Cory, Donald Webster (Ed.). *Homosexuality: a cross-cultural approach*. New York: Julian, 1956.

Cory, Donald Webster. *The lesbian in America*. New York: Citadel, 1964.

Cox, Betty J. *The new sexuality*. New York: Medical Press, 1964.

Crown, Philip. Bed Talk. *Pageant*, February, 1965, 14–19.

Daniel, Ronald S. The aroused woman. *Sexology*, 1975, 41(8), 54–57.

Danielsson, Bent. *Love in the south seas*. New York: Reynal, 1956.

Davis, Katherine B. *Factors in the sex life of 2200 women*. New York: Harper, 1929.

†Davis, Maxine. *The sexual responsibility of women*. New York: Pocket Books, 1964.

Davison, Gerald C. Elimination of a sadistic fantasy by a client-controlled counter-conditioning technique. *Journal of Abnormal Psychology*, 1968, 73, 84–90.

†Dean, James. *How to win a mistress*. New York: Pyramid, 172.

Dearborn, Lester. Autoerotism. In Ellis, Albert, and Abarbanel, Albert (Eds.), *Encyclopedia of sexual behavior*. New York: Jason Aronson, 1961, 1973.

DeMartino, Manfred F. (Ed.). *Sexual behavior and personality characteristics*. New York: Grove Press, 1966.

†DeMartino, Manfred F. *The new female sexuality*. New York: Julian Press, 1969.

†DeMartino, Manfred F. *Sex and the intelligent woman*. New York: Springer, 1974.

DeMoya, Armando, and DeMoya, Dorothy. What is the basis for the distinction many patients make between vaginal and clitoral orgasm? *Medical Aspects of Human Sexuality*, November, 1973, 7(11), 95.

Denber, Herman C. B. The use of sexuality to externalize inner conflict. *Medical Aspects of Human Sexuality*, 1973, 7(9), 44–60.

Dengrove, Edward. The psysiology of impotence. *Sexology*, 1959, 25, 500–504.

Dengrove, Edward. Causes of premature ejaculation. *Sexology*, 1959, 26, 46–51.

Dengrove, Edward. Techniques for heightening sex response. Sexology Magazine, *The X report*. New York: Belmont Books, 1962.

Dengrove, Edward. The sounds of love. *Sexology*, February, 1966, 484–486.

Dengrove, Edward. Respecting your mate's feelings. *Sexology*, May, 1967, 660–668.

Dengrove, Edward. Don't stop making love after orgasm. *Sexology*, February, 1972, 27–29.

Diamond, Milton. What is the basis for the distinction many patients make between vaginal and clitoral orgasm *Medical Aspects of Human Sexuality*, November, 1973, 7(11), 98.

Dickinson, R. L., and Beam, L. *A thousand marriages*. Baltimore: Williams & Wilkins, 1931.

Dickinson, R. L., and Beam, L. *The single woman*. Baltimore: Williams & Wilkins, 1934.

†Ditzion, Sidney. *Marriage, morals, and sex in America*. New York: Twayne, 1953.

Dnowski, W. Paul. Hormonal aspects of female sexual response. *Medical Aspects of Human Sexuality*, 1974, 8(6), 92–113.

†*Dodson, Betty. *Liberating masturbation*. New York: Bodysex Designs, 1974.

Dorner, Gunter; Rohde, Wolfgang; Stahl, Fritz; Krkell, Lothar; and Wolf-Gunther, Masius. A neuroendocrine predisposition for homosexuality in men. *Archives of Sexual Behavior*, 1975, 4, 1–8.

Downing, George. *The massage book*. New York: Random House, 1972.

Drakeford, John W. Is homosexuality pathologic or a normal variant of sex? *Medical Aspects of Human Sexuality*, December 1973, 7(12), 24.

†DuBrin, Andrew J. *The singles game*. Chatsworth, California: Books for Better Living, 1974.

DuBrin, Andrew J. *Survival in the sexist jungle*. Chatsworth, California: Books for Better Living, 1974.

Duvall, Evelyn. *Love and the facts of life*. New York: Association Press, 1963.

Early, John T. How masturbation can improve lovemaking. *Sexology*, 1975, 41(7), 44–46.

Edwardes, Allen. *The jewel in the lotus*. New York: Julian, 1959.

Edwardes, Allen, and Masters, R. E. L. *The cradle of erotica*. New York: Julian, 1962.

Edwards, Marie, and Hoover, Eleanor. *The challenge of being single*. Los Angeles: Tarcher, 1974.

Eglinton, J. Z. *Greek love*. New York: Layton, 1964.

†Ehrmann, Winston W. *Premarital dating behavior*. New York: Holt, 1960.

†Eichenlaub, John E. *The marriage art*. New York: Lyle Stuart, 1961.

†Eichenlaub, John E. *New approaches to sex in marriage*. New York: Delacorte, 1967.

†Eichenlaub, John E. *The troubled bed*. New York: Delacorte, 1971.

Eisner, Betty G. *The unused potential of marriage and sex*. Boston: Little, Brown, 1970.

Elliott, Robert. African and Asian methods of prolonging sex. *Modern Sex*, August, 1964, 6–13.

Ellenberg, Max. Impotence in diabetics. *Medical Aspects of Human Sexuality*, 1973, 7(4), 12–28.

Ellenberg, Max. Futility of androgens for impotent men. *Medical Aspects of Human Sexuality*, 1974, 8(10), 115.

Ellis, Albert. A study of human love relationships. *Journal of Genetic Psychology*, 1949, 75, 61–71.

Ellis, Albert. Is the vaginal orgasm a myth? In Pillay, A. P., and Ellis, Albert (Eds.), *Sex, society and the individual*: Bombay: International Journal of Sexology Press, 1953.

†*Ellis, Albert. *The American sexual tragedy*. New York: Lyle Stuart, 1954, 1961.

†*Ellis, Albert. *How to live with a "neurotic."* New York: Crown, 1957. Revised Edition, New York: Crown, 1975.

†*Ellis, Albert. *Sex without guilt*. New York: Lyle Stuart, 1958. Revised edition, New York: Lyle Stuart and Grove Press, 1965. Hollywood: Wilshire Books, 1968.

†*Ellis, Albert. *The art and science of love*. New York: Lyle Stuart, 1960. Revised edition. New York: Lyle Stuart and Bantom Books, 1969.

*Ellis, Albert. *The folklore of sex*. Revised edition. New York: Lyle Stuart and Grove Press, 1961.

†*Ellis, Albert. *Reason and emotion in psychotherapy*. New York: Lyle Stuart, 1962.

*Ellis, Albert. *If this be sexual heresy* . . . New York: Lyle Stuart and Tower Publications, 1963.

*Ellis, Albert. *Sex and the single man*. New York: Lyle Stuart and Dell Books, 1963.

†*Ellis, Albert. *The intelligent woman's guide to man-hunting*. New York: Lyle Stuart and Dell Books, 1963.

*Ellis, Albert. *The case for sexual liberty*. Tucson: Seymour Press, 1965.

†*Ellis, Albert. *Suppressed: seven key essays publishers dared not print*. Chicago: New Classics House, 1965.

*Ellis, Albert. *Homosexuality*. New York: Lyle Stuart, 1965.

†*Ellis, Albert. Is psychoanalysis harmful? *Psychiatric Opinion*. 1968, 5(1), 16–24, New York: Institute for Rational Living, 1970.

Ellis, Albert. The role of coital positions in sexual relations. *Sexual Behavior*, July 1971, 11–12.

†*Ellis, Albert. *Growth through reason*. Palo Alto: Science and Behavior Books, 1971. Hollywood: Wilshire Books, 1974.

†*Ellis, Albert. Psychotherapy and the value of a human being. In Davis, J. W. (Ed.), *Value and valuation: essays in honor of Robert S. Hartman*. Knoxville: University of Tennessee Press, 1972, 117–139. Reprinted: New York: Institute for Rational Living, 1972.

†*Ellis, Albert. *Executive leadership: a rational approach*. New York: Citadel, 1972.

†*Ellis, Albert. *The civilized couple's guide to extramarital adventure*. New York: Peter Wyden and Pinnacle Books, 1972.

†*Ellis, Albert. The no cop-out therapy. *Psychology Today*, July 1973, 7(2), 56–62.

†*Ellis, Albert. *The sensuous person*. New York: Lyle Stuart and New American Library, 1973.

†Ellis, Albert. Rational-emotive therapy. In Corsini, Raymond J. (Ed.), *Current psychotherapies*. Itasca, Illinois: Peacock, 1973, 167–206.

†*Ellis, Albert. *Humanistic psychotherapy: the rational-emotive approach*. New York: Julian Press, 1973. New York: McGraw-Hill Paperbacks, 1974.

†Ellis, Albert. The Treatment of sex and love problems in women. In Franks, Violet, and Burtle, Vasanti (Eds.), *Women in Therapy*. New York: Bronner—Hazel, 1974, 284–306.

†Ellis, Albert. Rational-Emotive Theory. In Burton, Arthur (Ed.), *Operational Theories of Personality*. New York: Brunner Mazel, 1974, 308–344.

†*Ellis, Albert. *Disputing irrational beliefs*. New York: Institute for Rational Living, 1975.

†Ellis, Albert. The rational-emotive approach to sex therapy. Counseling psychologist, 1975, 5(1), 14–21.

†*Ellis, Albert, and Abarbanel, Albert (Eds.). *Encyclopedia of sexual behavior*. New York: Hawthorn Books, 1961. Revised edition, New York: Jason Aronson, 1973.

Ellis, Albert, and Brancale, Ralph. *The psychology of sex offenders*. Springfield, Illinois: Thomas, 1956.

†*Ellis, Albert, and Harper, Robert A. *Creative marriage*. New York: Lyle Stuart, 1961. Also published as *A guide to successful marriage*. Hollywood: Wilshire Books, 1971.

*Ellis, Albert, and Gullo, John M. *Murder and assassination*. New York: Lyle Stuart, 1972.

†*Ellis, Albert, and Harper, Robert A. *A new guide to rational living*. Englewood Cliffs, N.J: Prentice-Hall and Hollywood: Wilshire Books, 1975.

†*E'lis, Albert, Krassner, Paul and Wilson, Robert A. Impolite interview with Dr. Albert Ellis. Realist, 1960, No. 16, 9–11; 1960, No. 17, 7–12. Reprinted, New York: Institute for Rational Living, 1970.

†*Fllis, Albert and Sagarin, Edward. *Nymphomania: a study of the oversexed woman*. New York: Julian Messner, and Macfadden-Bartell, 1964.

† Ellis, Albert, Wolfe, Janet L., and Moseley, Sandra. *How to raise an emotionally healthy, happy child*. Hollywood: Wilshire Books, 1972.

Ellis, Havelock. *Psychology of sex.* New York: Emerson, 1935. New York: New American Library, 1960.

†Ellis, Havelock. *Studies in the psychology of sex.* 4 volumes. New York: Random House, 1936.

Ellis, Havelock. *Sex and marriage.* London: Williams and Norgate, 1952.

Erotic odour. Forum, 1969, 2(3), 49–50.

Evans, R. B. Sixteen personality factor questionnaire scores of homosexual men. *Journal of Consulting and Clinical Psychology,* 1970, 34, 212–215.

Everett, Henry C. Sexual demands which cause marital conflict. *Medical Aspects of Human Sexuality,* 1974, 8(9), 113–114.

Fairfield, Dick. Group dating revisited. *Modern Utopian,* 1969–1970, 4(1), 15.

Farber, Leslie H. I'm sorry dear. *Commentary,* November, 1964, 50–54.

Fast, Julius. *The incompatibility of men and women.* New York: Evans, 1971.

Feigen, Gerald M. Morbidity caused by anal intercourse. *Medical Aspects of Human Sexuality,* 1974, 8(6), 177–186.

Feldman, Philip M. Loss of sexual interest. *Medical Aspects of Human Sexuality,* 1974, 8(1), 12.

†Feldman, M. P. , and MacCulloch, M.J. *Homosexual behavior: therapy and assessment.* New York: Pergamon Press, 1971.

Fellman, Sheldon. Condom as an aid against premature ejaculation. *Medical Aspects of Human Sexuality,* 1975, 9(1), 126.

†Fensterheim, Herbert, and Baer, Jean. *Don't say yes when you want to say no.* New York: Dell Books, 1975.

Fielding, William. *Sex and the love life.* New York: Permabooks, 1961.

Final report on the task force on homosexuality. One Institute Quarterly, 1970, 8, 5–12.

Finger, Frank W. Sex beliefs and practices among male college students. *Journal of Abnormal and Social Psychology,* 1947, 42, 47–57.

Fink, Harold K. Can intercourse take too long? *Sexology,* 1971, 37(10), 54–57.

Fink, Paul Jay. What is the basis for the distinction many patients make between vaginal and clitoral orgasms? *Medical Aspects of Human Sexuality,* November, 1973, 84–88.

Fink, Paul Jay. Quality of response in masturbation vs. coitus. *Medical Aspects of Human Sexuality,* January, 1974, 8(1), 88–89.

Fink, Paul Jay. IX Understanding male and female eroticism. *Medical Aspects of Humhan Sexuality,* May, 1974, 8(5), 135–136.

Finkle, Alex L. How important is simultaneous orgasm? *Medical Aspects of Human Sexuality,* July 1969 3(7), 86–93.

Fisher, Seymour. Female orgasm: an interview with Seymour Fisher, Ph.D. *Medical Aspects of Human Sexuality,* July 1973, 7(7), 76–91.

†Fisher, Seymour. *The female orgasm.* New York: Basic Books, 1973.

Forberg, F. K. *Manual of classical erotology.* Brussels: Carrington, 1884.

†Forel, August. *The sexual question.* Brooklyn: Physician's and Surgeon's Book Co., 1922.

Forleo, Romano. Frigidity: the gynecologist's point of view. Paper presented to the International Congress of Medical Sexology, Paris, July 1974.

Franks, C. M., and Wilson, G. T. *Annual review of behavior therapy: theory and practice.* New York: Brunner-Mazel, 1973.

French Institute of Public Opinion. *Patterns of sex and love: a study of the French woman and her morals.* New York: Crown, 1961.

†Freud, Sigmund. *Collected papers.* New York: Collier Books, 1963.

Freud, Sigmund. *Basic writings.* New York: Modern Library, 1938.

†Friday, Nancy. *My secret garden.* New York: Trident, 1973.

Friedman, Henry J. An interpersonal aspect of psychogenic impotence. *American Journal of Psychotherapy,* 1973, 17, 421–425.

Friedman, Sandor A. Commentary on impotence in diabetics. *Medical Aspects of Human Sexuality,* 1973, 7(4), 25–28.

†Fromm, Erich. *The art of loving.* New York: Bantam, 1963.

Fromme, Allen. *A psychologist looks at love and marriage.* New York: Prentice-Hall, 1950.

Fromme, Allan. *Understanding the sexual response in humans.* Hollywood: Wilshire Books, 1966.

Frosch, William A. Commentary on selective impotence. *Medical Aspects of Human Sexuality,* October, 1972, 6(10), 102–103.

Frosch, William A. Commentary on men's reactions to unresponsive wives. *Medical Aspects of Human Sexuality,* November, 1973, 7(11), 23–24.

†Garrity, (Terry) Joan. See J., *The sensuous woman.*

Gebhard, Paul H. Sex differences in sexual response. *Archives of Sexual Behavior,* 1973, 2, 201–203.

†Gebhard, Paul H., Gagnon, John H., Pomeroy, Wardell B., and Christenson, Cornelia. *Sex offenders.* New York: Harper, 1965.

†Gebhard, Paul H., Pomeroy, Wardell B., Martin, Clyde E., and Christenson, Cornelia. *Pregnancy, birth and abortion.* New York: Harper, 1958.

Gichner, Lawrence. *Erotic aspects of Chinese culture.* Washington: Author, 1957.

Gilder, George. *Sexual suicide.* New York: Quadrangle, 1973.

Gilder, George. *Naked nomads.* New York: Quadrangle, 1975.

Gillette, Paul J. *An uncensored history of pornography.* Los Angeles: Holloway House, 1965.

Gillette, Paul J. *Psychodynamics of unconventional sex behavior and unusual practices.* Los Angeles: Holloway House, 1966.

†Gillette, Paul J. *The complete sex dictionary.* New York: Award Books, 1969.

Gillette, Paul J. *Layman's explanation of human sexual inadequacy.* New York: Award Books, 1970.

†Gillette, Paul J. *The big answer book about sex.* New York: Award Books, 1970.

Gillette, Paul J. Seven ways to seduce a reluctant male. *Sexology,* 1947, 37(9), 4–7.

Godwin, J. *Mating trade.* New York: Doubleday, 1973.

Goldberg, Martin. What do you tell patients who ask about coital positions? *Medical Aspects of Human Sexuality,* 1968, 2(12), 43–48.

Goldberg, Martin. When patients ask about various sex practices. *Medical Aspects of Human Sexuality,* 1969, 3(2), 54–61.

Goldberg, Martin. Selective impotence. *Medical Aspects of Human Sexuality,* 1972, 6(10), 90–109.

Goldberg, Martin. Absence of sexual desire in men. *Medical Aspects of Human Sexuality,* 1973, 7(8), 13–32.

†Goldfried, Marvin R., and Merbaum, Michael (Eds.), *Behavior change through self-control*. New York: Holt, Rinehart and Winston, 1973.

Goldstein, Al. Goldstein on pussy eating. *Screw*, February 4, 1974, 4.

Goldstein, Michael J., and Kant, Harold S. *Pornography and sexual deviance*. Berkeley: University of California Press, 1973.

†*Goodman, David, and Maultsby, Maxie C., Jr. *Emotional well-being through rational behavior training*. Springfield, Ill.: Thomas, 1974.

Gordon, D. *Sex games that people play*. New York: Ace, 1973.

†Gordon, David Cole. *Self-love*. New York: Verity House, 1968.

Gordon, Sol. *Facts about sex for today's youth*. New York: John Day, 1973.

Gould, Lois. Pornography for women. *New York Times Magazine*, March 2, 1975, 10–11, 50–62.

Gray, Mary Jane. What is the basis for the distinction many patients make between vaginal and clitoral orgasm? *Medical Aspects of Human Sexuality*, November, 1973, 7(11), 98–99.

Greenblatt, Robert B., and Leng, Jean-Joel. Factors influencing sexual behavior. *Journal of the American Geriatrics Society*, 1972, 20, 49–54.

Greenblatt, Robert B. Psychogenic and endocrine aspects of sexual behavior. *Osteopathic Physician*, 1974, 41(11), 106–111.

Greene, G., and Greene, C. *S-M, the last taboo*. New York: Grove, 1973.

Greenwald, Harold. *The call girl*. New York: Ballantine, 1957.

Greenwald, Harold. Are fantasies during sexual relations a sign of difficulty? *Sexual Behavior*, May 1971, 38–40, 49–54.

†Greenwald, Harold. *Decision therapy*. New York: Jason Aronson, 1973.

†Greenwald, Harold, and Greenwald, Ruth. *The sex-life letters*. Los Angeles: Tarcher, 1972.

Greer, Benjamin E. Painful coitus due to hymenal problems. *Medical Aspects of Human Sexuality*, 1975, 9(2), 160–169.

Griffith, E. F. *Modern marriage*. London: Methuen, 1966.

Griffitt, William. Respose to erotica and the projection of response to erotica in the opposite sex. *Journal of Experimental Research in Personality*, 1973. 6, 330–338.

Groddeck, George. *The book of the it*. New York: New American Library, 1961.

†*Grossack, Martin. *You are not alone*. Boston: Marlborough, 1974.

Group for the Advancement of Psychiatry. *Sex and the college student*. New York: Group for the Advancement of Psychiatry, 1965.

Gunther, Max. *Virility 8: a celebration of the American male*. Chicago: Playboy Press, 1975.

†Guyon, Rene. *The ethics of sexual acts*. New York: Knopf, 1934.

†Guyon, Rene. *Sexual freedom*. New York: Knopf, 1950.

Hadas, Moses (Ed.), *Essential works of stoicism*. New York: Bantam, 1961.

Hadfield, J. A. The cure of homosexuality. *British Medical Journal*, June 7, 1958, 1, 1323–1326.

Haft, Jay Stuart. Foreign bodies in the female genitourinary tract: some psychosexual aspects. *Medical Aspects of Human Sexuality*, 1974, 8(10), 54–78.

Hamilton, Eleanor. *Partners in love*. New York: Ziff-Davis, 1961.

Hamilton, Eleanor. Your wedding night. *Modern Bride*, Spring, 1962. Reprint.

†Hamilton, Eleanor. *Sex before marriage*. New York: Meredith, 1969.

Hariton, E. Barbara, and Singer, Jerome L. Women's fantasies during sexual intercourse. *Journal of Consulting and Clinical Psychology*, 1974, 42, 313–322.

Harlow, Harry. Commentary on primate sexual behavior. *Medical Aspects of Human Sexuality*, October, 1972, 6(11), 133.

Harper, Robert A. A premarital case: with two years' marital follow-up. *Marriage and Family Living*, 1952, 14, 133–149.

†Harper, Robert A. *Psychoanalysis and psychotherapy: 36 systems*. Englewood Cliffs, N.J.: Prentice-Hall, 1959.

Harper, Robert A. Petting. In Ellis, Albert, and Abarbanel, Albert (Eds.), *Encyclopedia of sexual behavior*. New York: Hawthorn Books, 1961; Rev. ed., New York: Jason Aronson, 1973.

Harper, Robert A. Sex "excess." *Sexology*, September 1964, 84–86.

Harper, Robert A. Keeping sex alive in marriage. *Sexology*, October, 1965, 148–150.

Harper, Robert A. Conflicting sex desires. *Sexology*, August 1967, 4–6.

Harper, Robert A. Ways to revive your sex drive. *Sexology*, December, 1968, 292–294.

Harper, Robert A. Sex questions and answers. *Sexology*, April 1975, 70.

†Harper, Robert A. *The new psychotherapies*. Engelwood Cliffs, N.J.: Prentice-Hall, 1975.

†Harper, Robert A., and Stokes, Walter S. *Forty-five levels to sexual understanding and enjoyment*. Englewood Cliffs, N.J.: Prentice-Hall, 1973.

†Harvey, Will. *How to find and fascinate a mistress*. New York: Pocket Books, 1973.

†Hartman, William(and Fithian, Marilyn A. *Treatment of sexual dysfunction*. Long Beach, California: Center for Marital and Sexual Studies, 1972.

†Hastings, Donald W. *Impotence and frigidity*. New York: Delta, 1963.

Hastings, Donald W. Harmlessness of frequent coitus. *Medical Aspects of Human Sexuality*, January, 1974, 8(1), 6.

Hatterer. Lawrence J. *Changing homosexuality in the male*. New York: McGraw-Hill, 1970.

†*Hauck, Paul A. *Overcoming depression*. Philadelphia: Westminster Press, 1973.

†*Hauck, Paul A. *Overcoming frustration and anger*. Philadelphia: Westminster Press, 1974.

†Hefner, Hugh M. *The playboy philosophy*. Chicago: Playboy Press, 1964.

†Hegeler, Inge and Hegeler, Sten. *An ABZ of love*. New York: Medical Press, 1953.

Helmreich, Robert. What happens when men stare at attractive women? *Medical Aspects of Human Sexuality*, 195, 9(1), 139.

Herman, Steven H., Barlow, David H., and Agras, W. Stewart. An experimental analysis of classical conditioning as a method of increasing heterosexual arousal of homosexuals. *Behavior Therapy*, 1974, 5, 33–47.

†Herrigan, Joan, and Herrigan, Joan. *Loving free*. New York: Grosset and Dunlap, 1973.

†Herschberger, Ruth. *Adam's rib*. New York: Pellegrini and Cudahy, 1948.

Hirsch, Edwin W. *Modern sex life*. New York: New American Library, 1957.

Hirsch, Edwin W. *The power to love*. New York: Pyramid, 1962.

†Hite, Shere. *Sexual honesty by women for women*. New York: Warner, 1974.

Hoagland, Robert. Quoted in *Time*, March 3, 1961.

Hoffman, Martin. *The gay world*. New York: Basic Books, 1968.

Hoffman, Martin. Homosexual. *Psychology Today*, 1969, 3(2), 43–45, 70.

Hollender, Marc H., Luborsky, Lester, and Harvey, Roberta B. Correlates of the desire to be held in women. *Journal of Psychosomatic Research*, 1970, 14(4), 387–390.

Hooker, Evelyn. The adjustment of the male overt homosexual. *Journal of Projective Techniques*, 1957, 21, 18–31.

Hooker, Evelyn. Is homosexuality pathologic or a normal variant of sexuality *Medical Aspects of Human Sexuality*, December 1973, 23.

Hooker, Evelyn. Response to the distinguished contribution award. *Clinical Psychologist*, 1975, 28(2), 18–20.

†Horney, Karen. *Collected writings*. New York: Norton, 1972.

†Hunt, Morton. *The world of the formerly married*. New York: Fawcett, 1967.

†Hunt, Morton, *Sexual behavior in the 1970's*. Chicago: Playboy Press, 1974.

Identity House. Identity House. *Radical Therapist*, January, 1975, 11.

Izard, Carroll E., and Caplan, Sanford. Sex differences in emotional responses to erotic literature. *Journal of Consulting and Clinical Psychology*, 1974, 42, 468.

†J. (pseud, for Joan (Terry) Garrity). *The sensuous woman*. New York: Lyle Stuart and Dell Books, 1969.

Janowsky, David S. Hormonal influences on sexual behavior. *Medical Aspects of Human Sexuality*, 1974, 8(7), 166.

Jensen, Gordon D. Primate sexual behavior: its relevance to human sexual behavior. *Medical Aspects of Human Sexuality*, October, 1972, 6(10), 112–133.

Jones, Warren J. Mechanical sexual devices. *Medical Aspects of Human Sexuality*, 1975, 9(1), 131.

Judy and Bill. *The love game*. New York: Pinnacle, 1973.

†Julty, Sam. *Male sexual performance*. New York: Grosset and Dunlap, 1975.

Kane, Francis J. Hormonal treatment for frigidity. *Medical Aspects of Human Sexuality*, 1974, 8(9), 171.

†Kaplan, Helen Singer. *The new sex therapy*. New York: Brunner-Mazel, 1974.

Kaplan, Helen Singer. A new classification of the female sexual dysfunctions. Paper presented at International Congress of Medical Sexology, Paris, July 1974.

Kaplan, Helen Singer, and Kohl, Richard N. Adverse reactions to the rapid treatment of sexual problems. *Psychosomatics*, 1972, 13, 185–190.

Kaye, B. C. Create a bedroom that turns you both on. *Sexology*, 1975, 41(6), 44–47.

Kaye, B. C. Porno in the bedroom. *Sexology*, 1975, 41(8), 26–29.

Kellogg, Polly. Sexual behavior in the human female: a feminist critique. *Rational Living*, 1973, 8(1), 2–5.

†Kelly, G. Lombard. *So you think you're impotent*. Augusta, Georgia: Southern Medical Supply Company, 1957.

Kelly, G. Lombard. *Sexual feeling in married men and women*. New York: Permabooks, 1961.

†Kelly, G. Lombard. *Sex manual for those married or about to be*. Augusta, Georgia: Southern Medical Supply Company, 1963.

Kelly, G. Lombard. Sexual dysfunction. In Gillette, Paul J., *Layman's explanation of human sexual inadequacy*. New York: Award, 1970.

†Kelly, George. *The psychology of personal constructs*. New York: Norton, 1955.

Kenny, J. A. Sexuality of pregnant and breastfeeding women. *Archives of Sexual Behavior*, 1973, 2, 215–229.

Kenyon, F. E. Studies in female homosexuality, VI. The exclusively homosexual group. *Acta Psychiatrica Scaninavica*, 1968, 44, 224–237.

Kenyon, F. E. Homosexuality in the female. *British Journal of Hospital Medicine*, 1970, 3, 183–206.

Kinch, R. A. H. Sexual difficulties after fifty. *Canadian Medical Association Journal*, 1966, 94, 211–215.

†Kinsey, A. C., Pomeroy, W. B., and Martin, C. E. *Sexual behavior in the human male*. Philadelphia: Saunders, 1948.

†Kinsey, A. C., Pomeroy, W. B., Martin, C. E., and Gebhard, P. H. *Sexual behavior in the human female*. Philadelphia: Saunders, 1953.

Kirkendall, Lester A. *Premarital intercourse and interpersonal relationships*. New York: Julian, 1961.

Kirkendall, Lester A. Sex drive. In Ellis, Albert, and Abarbanel, Albert (Eds.), *Encyclopedia of sexual behavior*. New York: Hawthorn Books, 1961; Rev. ed., New York: Jason Aronson, 1973.

†*Knaus, William. *Rational-emotive education*. New York: Institute for Rational Living, 1974.

Knox, David. Four ways to turn on your wife. *Sexology*, 1970, 37(4), 4–6.

†Knox, David. *Dr. Knox's marital exercise book*. New York: McKay, 1975.

Kobashi, Luis I. Sex after urologic surgery. *Medical Aspects of Human Sexuality*, 1974, 8(12), 63–64.

†Koble, W. B., and Warren, R. *Sex in marriage*. San Diego: Academy, 1972.

Koch, Leo. Sex and youth. *Eden*, 1963, No. 10, 23–25.

Koedt, Anne. The myth of the vaginal orgasm. *New York Free Press*, Nov. 7, 1968, 3.

Kolodny, Robert C. Observations on the new Masters and Johnson report. *Meical Aspects of Human Sexuality*, July 1970, 4(7), 47–60.

†Korzbyski, Alfred. *Science and Sanity*. Lancaster, Pa.: Lancaster Press, 1933.

Krafft-Ebingg, Richard von. *Psychopathia sexualis*. New York: Stein and Day, 1965.

†Kranzler, Gerald. *You can change how you feel*, Eugene, Oregon: Author, 1974.

Krantz, K. E. Physiology of female orgasm. *Medical Aspects of Human Sexuality*, 1973, 7(3), 11.

Kronhausen, Eberhard W., and Kronhausen, Phyllis C. *Pornography and the law*. New York: Ballantine, 1959.

†Kronhausen, Phyllis C., and Kronhausen, Eberard W. *The sexually responsive woman*. Rev. Ed. New York: Grove Press, 1970.

Kupperman, Herbert S. Frigidity: endocrinological aspects. In Ellis, Albert, and Abarbanel, Albert (Eds.). *Encyclopedia of sexual behavior*: New York: Hawthorn Books, 1961. Revised ed., New York: Jason Aronson, 1973.

Labby, Daniel H. Impotence. *Medical Aspects of Human Sexuality*, 1974, 8(1), 51–52.

Labby, Daniel H. Orgasm via clitoral stimulation only. *Medical Aspects of Human Sexuality*, 1974, 8(9), 35–39.

Laguardia, Robert. Seven nights that will change your lovelife. *Sexology*, 1975, 41(8), 43–47.

Laidlaw, Robert W. What do you tell patients who ask about coital positions? *Medical Aspects of Human Sexuality*, 1968, 2(12), 48.

Lamberd, W. G. The treatment of homosexuality as a monosymptomatic phobia. *American Journal of Psychiatry*, 1969, 126, 512–518.

Landis, Carney, and Bolles, M. M. *Personality and sexuality of the physically handicapped woman*. New York: Hoeber, 1942.

Landis, Carney, and others. *Sex in development*. New York: Hoeber, 1940.

Lang, Theodore. Studies in the genetic determination of homosexuality. *Journal of Nervous and Mental Disease*, 1940, 192, 55.

†*Lange, Arthur, and Jakubowski, Patricia. *Responsible assertive behavior*. Urbana, Illinois: Research Press, 1976.

Langmyhr, George. Your body, your find, your feelings. *Brides*, 1974, 40(1), 144–145, 208.

Latendresse, I. D. Masturbation and its relation to addiction. *Review of Existential Psychology and Psychiatry*, 1968, 8(1), 16–27.

Latham, A. Replaceable you. *New York*, February 10, 1975, 8(6), 37–44.

†*Lazarus, Arnold A., and Fay, Allen. *I can if I want to*. New York: William Morrow, 1975.

†*Lazarus, Arnold A. *Behavior therapy and beyond*. New York: McGraw-Hill, 1971.

†Lazarus, Arnold A. Behavior therapy for sexual problems, *Professional Psychology*, Fall, 1971, 349–353.

Lazarus, Arnold A. Commentary on selective impotence. *Medical Aspects of Human Sexuality*, October 1972, 109.

Lazarus, Arnold A. Most efficient therapy for homosexuality. *Medical Aspects of Human Sexuality*, January, 1974, 8(1), 64–65.

†Lea, Edward. Instruments for autoerotic stimulation. In Masters, R. E. L. (Ed.), *Sexual self-stimulation*. Los Angeles: Sherbourne, 1967, 315–329.

Leader, A. Quoted in Secord, H. W. Sexual frustration. *Sexology*, 1959, 25, 480–483.

Lehmann-Haupt, Christopher. Sex is just a bowl of buttons. *New York Times*, March 3, 1971, 41.

†*Lembo, John M. *Help yourself*. Niles, Illinois: Argus, 1974.

†*Lembo, John. *The counseling process*. New York: Libra Publishers, 1976.

Lesser, Kandi, and Lee, Elizabeth. What your sex fantasies tell about you. *Sexology*, 1975, 41(8), 11–14.

Levine, Lena, and Loth, David. *The frigid wife*. New York: Messner, 1962.

Levitt, E. E., and Brady, J. P. Sexual preferences in young adult males and some correlates. *Journal of Clinical Psychology*, 1965, 21, 347–354.

Lewis, Barbara. *The sexual power of marijuana.* New York: Wyden, 1970.

Lewis, Lionel S., and Brissett, Dennis. Sex as work: a study of avocational counseling. *Medical Aspects of Human Sexuality*, 1968, 2(1), 14–25.

Lewis, Robert A., and Burr, Wesley R. Premarital coitus and commitment among college students. *Archives of Sexual Behavior*, 1975, 4, 73–79.

Lewis, S. *Sex among the singles.* New York: Ace, 1973.

Libby, Roger W. Adolescent sexual attitudes and behavior. *Journal of Clinical Child Psychology*, 1974, 3(3), 36–42.

Libby, Roger W. Social scripts for sexual relationships. Syracuse: Author, 1975. Mimeo.

†Libby, Roger W., and Whitehurst. Robert N. (Eds.). *Renovating marriage: toward new sexual life styles.* Danville, California: Consensus, 1973.

Libby, Roger W., and Mazur, Ronald. Sex and the double standard. In Gordon, Sol (Ed.), *Sex and the family.* New York: John Day, 1974.

Lindenmeyer, Stratton. The manual arts. *Answers*, 1970, 1(1), 14–16, 66–68.

Linner, Birgitta, and Kand, Jur. Sexual morality and sexual reality: the Scandinvaian approach. *American Journal of Orthopsychiatry*, 1966, 36, 686–693.

Liswood, Rebecca. *A marriage doctor speaks her mind about sex.* New York: Ace, 1961.

†Litewka, Jack. The socialized penis. *Alternative to Alienation*, August-September, 1974, No. 3, 10–12.

†Lobell, John and Mimi. *John and Mimi.* New York: St. Martins, 1972.

Lobitz, W. C., and Lobitz, G. K. Primary orgasmic dysfunction. Eugene, Oregon: Authors, 1973. Mimeographed.

Loeb, Dorothy G. Building sexual confidence. *Medical Aspects of Human Sexuality*, 1973, 7(5), 82–109.

Loewenstein, J. *Treatment of impotence with special reference to mechanotherapy.* London: Hamilton, 1947.

†LoPiccolo, Joseph. Case study: systematic desensitization of homosexuality. *Behavior Therapy*, 1971, 2, 394–399.

†LoPiccolo, Joseph, and Lobitz, W. C., The role of masturbation in the treatment of Primary Orgasmic Dysfunction. *Archives of Sexual Behavior*, 1972, 3, 265–271.

Loras, Oliver. Wedding night problems. *Sexology*, July 1964, 816–818.

Lovell, Joe. I found my lover in a want-ad. *Sexology*, 1974, 41(2), 13–15.

Low, Abraham A. *Mental health through will-training.* Boston: Christopher, 1950.

Lundola, Kwame. Black sexual power. Toronto: Frontier, 1966.

Lydon, Susan. Liberating woman's orgasm. In Noveley, P. (Ed.), *The new eroticism.* New York: Random House, 1970.

Lydon, Susan. The politics of orgasm. In Morgan, Robin (Ed.), *Sisterhood is powerful.* New York: Vintage, 1970, 197–205.

M. (Pseud. for Garrity, John, and Garrity, (Terry) Joan). *The sensuous man.* New York: Lyle Stuart, 1969.

Mace, David. *Success in marriage.* New York: Abingdon, 1958.

Madison, Roger. Dig black stockings and boots? There's a bit of a fetishist in everyone. *Sexology*, 1975, 41(7), 25–29.

†Magar, Magar E. *Adultery and its compatibility with marriage*. Monona, Wisconsin: Nefertiti Publishers, 1972.

Manheim, Henry L. A socially unacceptable method of mate selection. *Sociology and Social Research*, 1961, 45, 2, 182–187.

Manis, Nancy. Inside a German sex supermarket. *Sexology*, 1971, 37(8), 4–8.

Manville, Bill. The power of the stranger. *Village Voice*, November 15, 1973, 16–17.

Marcotte, David. What sexual literature do you advise patients to read? *Medical Aspects of Human Sexuality*, 1974, 8(8), 66–85.

†Marcus Aurelius. *The thoughts of the Emperor Marcus Aurelius Antonius*. Boston: Little, Brown, 1900.

Margolis, Herbert E., and Rubenstein, Paul M. *The groupsex tapes*. New York: McKay, 1971.

Marks, Isaac M., and Gelder, M. G. A controlled retrospectible study of behaviour therapy of phobic patients. *British Journal of Psychiatry*, 1965, 111, 573–578.

Marks, Isaac M., and Gelder, M. G. Transvestism and fetishism: clinical and psychological changes during faradic aversion. *British Journal of Psychiatry*, 1967, 113, 711–729.

Marmor, Judd (Ed.). *Sexual inversion*. New York: Basic Books, 1965.

Marmor, Judd. Homosexuality and objectivity. *Siecus Newsletter*, 1970, 6(2), 1, 3.

Marmor, Judd. Is homosexuality pathologic or a normal variety of sexuality? *Medical Aspects of Human Sexuality*, December, 1973, 7(12), 10–26.

Marshall, W. L. The modification of sexual fantasies. *Behavior Research and Therapy*, 1973, 11, 557–564.

†Maslow, A. H. *Toward a psychology of being*. Princeton: Van Nostrand, 1962.

Maslow, A. H. Motivation and personality. Rev. ed., New York: Harper, 1970.

Massey, Frederick. A new look at sex toys. *Sexology*, 1973, 40(3), 6–10.

Massey, Frederick. When did you last seduce her? *Sexology*, 1974, 40(10), 6–10.

Massey, Frederick. Four myths that spoil sex. *Sexology*, 1974, 41(4), 16–20.

Massey, Frederick. Explore your lover's erogenous zones. *Sexology*, 1975, 41(8), 6–10.

Massey, Frederick. Try these movements for more sensuous intercourse. *Sexology*, 1975, 41(6), 6–10.

Masters, R. E. L. *Sexual self-stimulation*. Los Angeles: Sherbourne, 1967.

Masters, R. E. L. Forbidden sexual behavior and morality. New York: Julian, 1962.

†Masters, William H., and Johnson, Virginia E. *Human sexual response*. Boston: Little, Brown, 1966.

†Masters, William H., and Johnson, Virginia E. *Human sexual inadequacy*. Boston: Little, Brown, 1970.

Masters, William H., and Johnson, Virginia E. An interview with Masters and Johnson on "Human sexual inadequacy". *Medical Aspects of Human Sexuality*, July 1970, 21–45.

Masters, William H., and Johnson, Virginia E., With Levin, Robert. *The pleasure bond*. Boston: Little, Brown, 1975.

Mathis, James L. Psychology of "girlie" magazines. *Medical Aspects of Human Sexuality*, 1969, 3(1), 25–32.

†Maultsby, Maxie C., Jr. *More personal happiness through rational self-counseling*. Lexington, Kentucky: Author, 1971.

†*Maultsby, Maxie C., Jr. *Help yourself to happiness*. New York: Institute for Rational Living, 1975.

†*Maultsby, Maxie C., Jr. and Hendricks, Allie. *Cartoon booklets*. Lexington, Kentucky: Author, 1974.

†*Maultsby, Maxie C., Jr., and Ellis, Albert. *Technique for using rational-emotive imagery*. New York: Institute for Rational Living, 1975.

Mazur, Ronald. *Commonsense sex*. Boston: Beacon, 1968.

McCorkle, L. *How to make love*. New York: Grove, 1969.

McDaniel, Clyde O. Dating roles and reasons for dating. *Journal of Marriage and the Family*, 1969, 29, 97–107.

McGovern, Kevin, Brockway, Jacqueline, and LoPiccolo, Joseph. Case study: the behavioral treatment and longterm follow-up assessment of a primary orgasmic dysfunction. Eugene, Oregon: Authors, 1973. Mimeo.

McLennan, Holly. Positions in intercourse. *Sexology*, 1969, 36(1), 4–8.

Mead, Beverley T. The husband who does not find his wife sexually exciting. *Medical Aspects of Human Sexuality*, 1974, 8(10), 239–246.

†Meichenbaum, Donald H. *Cognitive factors in behavior modification: modifying what clients say to themselves*. Waterloo, Canada: University of Waterloo, 1971.

†Meichenbaum, Donald H. *Cognitive behavior modification*. Morristown, New Jersey: General Learning Press, 1974.

Menard, Wilmon. Sex in Tahiti. *Sexology*, 1960, 26, 344–349.

Merelo-Barberary Beltran, Juan. Orgasm during delivery. Paper presented at International Congress of Medical Sexology, Paris, July 1974.

†Merrill, M. G. There are no absolutes. *ART in Daily Living*, 1972, 1(4), 6–9.

Mill, John S. *The subjection of women*. New York: Appleton, 1969.

Millet, Kate. *Sexual politics*. New York: Avon, 1970.

Milne, Edward. Thoughts on sex. *New Statesman*, August 30, 1963, 252.

Miller, Henry. *The world of sex*. New York: Grove, 1965.

Miller, Stuart. *Hot springs*. New York: Viking, 1971.

Miller, V., and Brockway, J. Commonalities and differences in the treatment of two cases of primary orgasmic dysfunction. Eugene, Oregon: Authors, 1973. Mimeo.

Money, John. Med-school "stags." *Medical World News*, March 12, 1971, 35.

Money, John. Why are some orgasms better than others. *Medical Aspects of Human Sexuality*, 1971, 5(3), 17.

Money, John. Poronography in the home. In Zubin, J., and Money, J. (Eds.), *Contemporary Sexual Behavior*. Baltimore: Johns Hopkins Press, 1973, 409–440.

†Money, John, and Ehrhardt, Anke A. *Man and woman, boy and girl.* Balti. more: John Hopkins University Press, 1972.

Money, John, and Mazur, Tom. Follow your nose. *Sexology,* May 1974, 32–34.

Montagu, Ashley. Honeymoon blues. *Sexology,* April 1963, 580–582.

†Morris, Kenneth T., and Kanitz, H. Mike. *Rational-emotive therapy.* Boston: Houghton Mifflin, 1975.

Morse, Benjamin. *A modern marriage manual.* New York: Lancer, 1963.

Mosher, D. L. Psychological reactions to pornographic films. *Technical Reports of the Commission on Obscenity and Pornography,* Volume 8. Washington: United States Government Printing Office, 1970.

Moss, Annonna. *One hundred millions luvazoons per day.* Sherman Oaks, California: Moss Publications, 1973.

Motels with X-rated films thrive on coast. *New York Times,* February 17, 1975, 22.

Mozes, Eugene B. Married virgins. *Sexology,* 1959, 25, 412–418.

Munjack, Dennis, Reciprocity in sexual relations. *Medical Aspects of Human Sexuality,* January 1974, 156–188.

Murphy, Robert J. What is the basis for the distinction many patients make between vaginal and clitoral orgasm? *Medical Aspects of Human Sexuality,* November 1973, 7(11), 88–90.

Murphy, Robert J. Woman's inability to experience climax. *Medical Aspects of Human Sexuality,* June 1974, 8(6), 144.

†Murstein, Bernard I. *Love, sex and marriage.* New York: Springer, 1974.

National Organization for Women. *Questionnaire on female sexuality.* New York: National Organization for Women, 1972.

†Nefzawi, Mohammed al. *Perfumed garden.* Paris: Librarie Astra, no date.

Neiger, Stepehn. How to last longer in intercourse. *Sexology,* 1968, 34(8), 513–516.

Neiger, Stephen. Ways to prolong intercourse. *Sexology,* 1971, 37(8), 58–60.

Nellis, Barbara (Chairwoman). Round-table discussion: female sexuality. *Oui,* 1974, 3(6), 71–72, 81–82, 106–112.

Newton, Niles. *Maternal emotions.* New York: Columbia University Press, 1955.

Newbold, H. L. Quoted in Julty, Sam., *Male sexual performance.* New York: Grosset and Dunlap, 1975.

Nobile, Philip. Getting straight. *Oui,* 1973, 2(6), 99–100, 134.

Nolte, Claude, and Nolte, Dorothy. *Wake up in bed together!* New York: Stein and Day, 1975.

Norton, Edward. Sex-play all the way and no kidding: prof. *New York Daily News,* November 7, 1974, 4.

Obler, Martin. Systematic desensitization in sexual disorders. *Journal of Behavior Therapy and Experimental Psychiatry,* 1973, 4(2), 93–101.

O'Connor, John F., and Stern, Lenore O. Developmental factors in functional sexual disorders. *New York State Journal of Medicine,* July 15, 1972, 1838–1843; August 1, 1972, 1927–1934.

Oliven, John F. *Sexual hygiene and pathology.* Philadelphia: Lippincott, 1955.

Omega, Kane. *Cosmic sex*. New York: Lyle Stuart, 1973.

Otto, Herbert A., and Otto, Roberta. How to erase your sexual fears together. In *Total sex*. New York: Wyden, 1972.

Ovesey, Lionel. *Homosexuality and pseudohomosexuality*. New York: Science House, 1969.

Ovid. *The love books of Ovid*. New York: Rarity Press, 1930.

Pacion, Stanley J. Gandhi's struggle with sexuality. *Medical Aspects of Human Sexuality*, 1971, 5(1), 73–93.

Parlee, Mary Brown. The premenstrual syndrome. *Psychological Bulletin*, 1973, 80, 454–465.

Peles, Uri. The extremely inhibited woman. *Medical Aspects of Human Sexuality*, 1974, 8(6), 41–42.

Peterson, Gail B., and Petterson, Larry R. Sexism in the treatment of sexual dysfunction. *Family Coordinator*, October 1973, 397–404.

Phelan, Nancy, and Volin, Michael. *Sex and Yoga*. New York: Harper, 1967.

Pillay, A. P. *The art of love and sane sex living*. Bombaby: Taraporevala, 1948.

Pillay, A. P., and Elliks, Albert (Eds.). *Sex, society and the individual*. Bombay: International Journal of Sexology Press, 1953.

Poland, Jefferson, and Sloan, Sam. *Sex marchers*. Los Angeles: Elysium, 1968.

Polatin, Phillip. Postcoital sadness. *Medical Aspects of Human Sexuality*, 1973, 7(9), 12–32.

Polsky, Ned. *Hustlers, beats and others*. Chicago: Aldine, 1967.

†Pomeroy, Wardell. *Girls and sex*. New York: Dell, 1973.

Potter, Jessie. Quoted in Nellis, Barbara, *Round-table discussion: female sexuality*. *Oui*, 1974, 3(6), 71–72, 81–82, 106–112.

Potts, Richard L. How important is penis size? *Sexology*, 1968, 35, 79–82.

Proctor, E. G., Wagner, N. N., and Butler, Julius C. Differentiation of male and female orgasm: an experimental study. *Proceedings 81st Annual Convention American Psychological Association*, 1973, 411–412.

Proctor, Richard C. Commentary on men's reactions to unresponsive wives. *Medical Aspects of Human Sexuality*. November 1973, 7(11), 24–25.

Quirk, Douglas A. A follow-up on the Bond-Hutchinson case of systematic desensitization with an exhibitionist. *Behavior Therapy*, 1974, 5, 428–431.

Raboch, Jan. Causes and therapy of male impotency. Paper presented at International Congress of Medical Sexology, Paris, July 1974.

Raboch, Jan. Coital activity of men and levels of plasma testosterone. Paper presented at International Congress of Medical Sexology, Paris, July 1974.

Rainer, Julia, and Rainer, Jerome. *Sexual pleasure in marriage*. New York: Pocket Books, 1962.

Ramey, Irene G. Clitoral vs. vaginal orgasm—women dispute researchers. *Medical Aspects of Human Sexuality*, 1974, 8(5), 215–216.

Reckless, John B. Organic causes of female anorgasmia. *Medical Aspects of Human Sexuality*, July 1973, 7(7), 24.

Redmond, Anne C. When a wife's desire exceeds her husbands. *Medical Aspects of Human Sexuality*, January 1975, 9(1), 97–98.

Reevy, William R. Vestured genital apposition and coitus. In Beigel, Hugo (Ed.), *Advances in sex research*. New York: Hoeber, 1963, 27–32.

†Reich, Wilhelm. *The sexual revolution*. New York: Orgone Institute Press, 1945.

Reich, Wilhelm. *The function of the orgasm*. New York: Orgone Institute Press, 1942.

Reik, Theodor. *Of love and lust*. New York: Farrar, Straus, 1958.

Reinhard, L. *Oral sex techinques and sex practices*. Baltimore: Donti, 1968.

†Reiss, Ira L. *Premarital sexual standards in America*. Glencoe: Free Press, 1960.

Reinisch, June. *Fetal hormones, the brain, and human sex differences*. M.A. Thesis, Teachers College, Columbia University, 1972.

Reyna, Ruth. Kama Sutra: India's super sex manual. *Sexology*, 1971, 37(12), 31–34.

Rizzo, Joseph. Ten exciting hints for lovers. *Sexology*, 1973, 40(5), 11–14.

Robertiello, R. C. *Voyage from Lesbos*. New York: Citadel, 1959.

Robertiello, R. C. *Sexual fulfillment and self-affirmation*. New York: Citadel, 1964.

†Robie, W. F. *The art of love*. Ithaca, N.Y.: Rational Life Press, 1925. Hollywood: Brandon, 1965.

Robie, W. F. *Rational sex ethics*. Ithaca, N.Y.: Rational Life Press, 1927.

Robie, W. F. *Pleasure of love*. New York: Paperback Library, 1967.

Robinson, Marie N. *The power of sexual surrender*. New York: New American Library, 1962.

†Robinson, Victor (Ed.) *Encyclopedia sexualis*. New York: Dingwall Rock, 1936.

Roen, Philip R. Loss of libido in men. *Medical Aspects of Human Sexuality*, 1974, 8(8), 163–164.

Rogers, Robert J. Oral sexuality. *Voices*, Spring 1967, 65–67.

Rosenberg, Jack Lee. *Total orgasm*. New York: Random House, 1973.

Rosengard, I. Stuart. Improve your after-intercourse technique. *Sexology*, 1970, 37(5), 4–6.

Rosengard, I. Stuart. Must you reach climax together? *Sexology*, 1970, 37(7), 4–6.

Rosenthal, Saul H., and Rosenthal, Chauncey F. Commentary on women who fear orgasm. *Medical Aspects of Human Sexuality*, October 1973, 7(10), 136.

Rosenthal, Saul H., and Rosenthal, Chauncey F. Men's reactions to unresponsive wives. *Medical Aspects of Human Sexuality*, November 1973, 7(11), 12–31.

Rothenberg, R. E. *The doctors' premarital medical advisor*. New York: Grosset and Dunlap, 1969.

Routh, Donald K., Warehime, Robert G., Gresen, Rober, and Rogers, Linda. Measuring the ability to express sexual thoughts. *Journal of Personality Assessment*, 1973, 37, 342–350.

Royce, Jack R. Panel discussion on the "swinging singles scene." Paper presented at the Meeting of the Society of Medical Psychoanalysts, February 25, 1974, New York City.

Rubin, Isadore. Will sex abstinence prolong life? *Sexology*, October 1963, 158–160.

Rubin, Isadore. Unusual male and female sex devices. *Sexology*, 1969, 36(1), 10-12.

Rubin, Isadore. Helpful and harmful sex devices. *Sexology*, 1970, 36(9), 14–16.

†Russell, Bertrand. *Marriage and morals.* New York: Liveright, 1929.

†Russell, Bertrand. *The conquest of happiness.* New York: Bantam, 1968.

Ryan, M. P., and Ryan, J. J. *Love and sexuality.* New York: Holt, Rinehart and Winston, 1967.

Sadock, Virginia. Instructing men in effective sexual technique. *Medical Aspects of Human Sexuality*, 1974, 8(10), 127–128.

†Sagarin, Edward. *The anatomy of dirty words.* New York: Lyle Stuart, 1962.

Sagarin, Edward. Autoeroticism: a sociological approach. In Masters, R. E. L. (Ed.), *Sexual self-stimulation.* Los Angeles: Sherbourne, 1967, 161–171.

†Sagarin, Edward. Rational guideposts on homosexuality. *Rational Living*, 1969, 5(1), 2–7.

Sagarin, Edward. An essay on obscenity and pornography. *Humanist*, July-August, 1969, 10–12.

†Sagarin, Edward. *Odd man in.* Chicago: Quadrangle, 1969.

Sagarin, Edward, and MacNamara, Donal E. J. (Eds.). *Problems of sex behavior.* New York: Crowell, 1968.

Saghir, Marcel T., Robins, Eli, and Walbran, Bonnie. Homosexuality. II. Sexual behavior of the male homosexual. *Archives of General Psychiatry*, 1969, 21, 219–229.

Saghir, Marcel T.; Robins, Eli; Walbran, Bonnie; and Gentry, Kathye A. Homosexuality. IV. Psychiatric disorders and disability in the female homosexual. *American Journal of Psychiatry*, 1970, 127, 147–154.

Saghir, Marcel T. Counseling the homosexual. *Medical Aspects of Human Sexuality*, 1975, 9(2), 149–150.

Salzman, Leon. Effects of abstinence. *Medical Aspects of Human Sexuality*, July 1970, 4(7), 102.

Salzman, Leon. The role of coital positions in sexual relations. *Sexual Behavior*, July 1971, 10-13.

Sandford, Donald A. Patterns of sexual arousal in heterosexual males. *Journal of Sex Research*, 1974, 10, 150–155.

Sapirstein, Milton R. *Paradoxes of everyday life.* Greenwich, Conn.: Fawcett, 1966.

Sartre, Jean Paul. *Being and nothingness.* New York: Washington Square, 1968.

Saul, James R. What is wrong with masturbation? *Realife Guide*, August 1960, 22–27.

†Saxon, Robin. Learning to last. *Forum*, January 1972, 30-35.

Schafer, Leah C. *Women and sex.* New York: Pantheon, 1973.

Schmidt, G., and Sigusch, V. Sex differences in responses to psychosexual stimulation by films and slides. *Journal of Sex Research*, 1970, 6, 268–283.

Schmidt, G., Sigusch, V., and Schafer, S. Responses to reading erotic stories: male-female differences. *Archives of Sexual Behavior*, 1973, 2, 181–199.

Schimmel, John. Some nonpsychiatric factors in sexual dysfunction. *Medical Aspects of Human Sexuality*, 1975, 9(1), 95–96.

Schmidt, W. Problems related to foreplay. *Medical Aspects of Human Sexuality*, 1975, 9(1), 153–154.

†Schoenfeld, Eugene. *Dear Doctor Hip Pocrates*. New York: Grove, 1968.

Schofield, Michael. *Sociological aspects of homosexuality*: London: Longmans, Green, 1965.

Schumacher, Sallie S., and Lloyd, Charles W. Interdisciplinary treatment and study of sexual distress. Paper presented at International Congress of Medical Sexology, Paris, July 1974.

Schumacher, Warren F. A priest discusses masturbation. *Sexology*, March 1969, 516–519.

Scott, C. *Pagan sex, puritan sex*. Hollywood: Brandon, 1966.

Seaman, Barbara. Do gynecologists exploit their patients. *New York*, August 14, 1972, 47–54.

†Seaman, Barbara. *Free and female*. New York: Coward, McCann & Geoghegan, 1972.

Secor, H. W. Sex frustration. *Sexology*, 1959, 25, 480–483.

†Semans, James H. Premature ejaculation: a new approach. *Southern Medical Journal*, 1956, 49, 353–358.

Semmens, James P. Contracting gluteal muscles to enhance sexual pleasure. *Medical Aspects of Human Sexuality*, 1974, 8(12), 8.

Sentnor, Marvin, and Hult, S. Erotic zones. *Sexology*, September 1961, 77–80.

Serber, Michael. Videotape feedback in the treatment of couples with sexual dysfunction. *Archives of Sexual Behavior*, 1974, 3, 377–380.

Sewell, Hobart H. Sexual 'norms' in marriage. *Medical Aspects of Human Sexuality*, October 1974, 8(10), 83–84.

Sexus, Professor. Unfortunate husband. *Pleasure*, 1970, No. 35, 22.

Sex around the world. *Sexology*, February 1975, 36.

Sex relief. *Sexology*, January 1965, 376–378.

Shafer, Nathaniel. False gonorrhea. *Sexology*, December 1965, 338-340.

Shainess, Natalie. Are fantasies during sexual relations a sign of difficulty? *Sexual Behavior*, May 1971, 38–40, 49–54.

Shainess, Natalie. What is the psychological significance of various coital positions? *Medical Aspects of Human Sexuality*, 1971, 5(2), 8–16.

Shearer, Marguerine R. Can women enjoy sex without orgasm? *Medical Aspects of Human Sexuality*, January 1973, 7(1), 108.

†Shelton, John L., and Ackerman, J. Mark. *Homework in counseling and psychotherapy*. Springfield, Illinois: Thomas, 1975.

Sherfey, Mary Jane. *The nature and evolution of female sexuality*. New York: Vintage, 1972.

Sherman, Julia A. What men do not know about women's sexuality. *Medical Aspects of Human Sexuality*, November 1972, 6(11), 138–153.

Sherman, Julia A. Can women enjoy sex without orgasm? *Medical Aspects of Human Sexuality*, January 1973, 7(1), 108–114.

†Shibles, Warren. *Emotion*. Whitewater, Wisconsin: Language Press, 1974.

Shope, David F. Sexual responsiveness in single girls. In Henslin, J. M. (Ed.), *Studies in the sociology of sex*. New York: Appleton-Century Crofts, 1971, 29–51.

Shope, David F., and Broderick, Carlfred B. Level of sexual experience and predicted adjustment in marriage. *Journal of Marriage and the Family*, 1967, 29, 424–427.

Siegelman, Marvin. Adjustment of homosexual and heterosexual women. *British Journal of Psychiatry*, 1972, 120, 477–481.

†Singer, Irving. *The goals of human sexuality*. New York: Norton, 1973.

†Smith, Manuel J. *When I say no, I feel guilty*. New York: Bantam, 1975.

Sonne, John C. Women who fear orgasm. *Medical Aspects of Human Sexuality*, October 1973 7(10), 128–138.

Socarides, Charles W. A provisional theory of aetiology in male homosexuality. *International Journal of Psycho-analysis*, 1968, 49, 27–37.

Socarides, Charles W. *The overt homosexual*. New York: Grune and Stratton, 1968.

Socarides, Charles W. Is homosexuality pathologic or a normal variant of sexuality? *Medical Aspects of Human Sexuality*, December 1973. 7(12), 25–26.

Sorensen, Robert C. *Adolescent sexuality in contemporary America*. New York: World, 1973.

Spanier, Graham. Sexualization and premarital sexual behavior. *Family Coordinator*, 1975, 24(1), 33–41.

Spitz, Rene. Autoerotism. *Psychoanalytic Study of the Child*, 1949, 3–4, 85–120.

Spitzer, Robert L. The homosexuality decision—a background paper. *Psychiatric News*, January 16, 1974, 11–12.

Sprenkle, Douglas H. Breaking through those masturbation myths. *Sexology*, 1974, 40(12), 14–17.

Srnec, Jan, and Freund, Kurt. Treatment of male homosexuality through conditioning. *International Journal of Sexology*, 1953, 7, 92–93.

Stanley, Elizabeth. Can women enjoy sex without orgasm? *Medical Aspects of Human Sexuality*, January 1973, 7(1), 102–104.

Stanley, Elizabeth. Commentary on women who fear orgasm. *Medical Aspects of Human Sexuality*, October 1973, 7(10), 136–137.

Stekel, Wilhelm. *Frigidity in women*. New York: Liveright, 1926.

†Stekel, Wilhelm. *Autoerotism*. New York: Liveright, 1950.

Stephan, Walter, and Berscheid, Ellen. Sexual arousal and heterosexual perception. *Journal of Personality and Social Psychology*, 1971, 20, 93–101.

Stiller, Richard. Questions and answers about sex positions. *Sexology*, July 1966, 804–806.

Stiller, Richard. Erotic zones of love. *Sexology*, February, 1972, 4–7.

Stoctay, G. S., *Sex, pleasure and marriage*. San Diego: Greenleaf, 1972.

Stokes, Walter R. *Married love in today's world*. New York: Citadel, 1962.

Stokes, Walter. Wives who remain virgins. In Harper, Robert A., and Stokes, Walter R., *45 levels to sexual understanding*. Englewood Cliffs, N.J.: Prentice-Hall, 1971, 57–61.

Stone, Hannah M., and Stone, Abraham S. *A marriage manual.* New York: Simon and Schuster, 1952.

†Street, Robert. *Modern sex techniques.* New York: Archer House, 1959.

†Students Committee on Sexuality at Syracuse University. *Sex in a plain brown wrapper.* Syracuse: Syracuse University, 1973.

Sullivan, Philip R. What is the role of fantasy in sex? *Medical Aspects of Human Sexuality,* 1969, 3(4), 79–89.

Tabori, Paul. *Humor and technology of sex.* New York: Julian, 1969.

†Taylor, W. S. A critique of sublimation in males. *Genetic Psychology Monographs,* 1933, 13, 1–115.

Technology of masturbation. *Los Angeles Free Press,* October 17, 1969, 17.

†Terman, Lewis M., *Psychological factors in marital happiness.* New York: McGraw-Hill, 1938.

†Terman, Lewis M. Correlates of orgasm adequacy in a group of 556 wives. *Journal of Psychology,* 1951, 32, 115–172.

Thistle, Frank. Turning on to erotic sounds. *Sexology,* February 1975, 41(7), 16–18.

†Thornton, Henry, and Thornton, Freda. *How to achieve sex happiness in marriage.* New York: Vanguard, 1939.

†*Tosi, Donald J. *Youth: toward personal growth, a rational-emotive approach.* Columbus, Ohio: Merrill, 1974.

Trick of the trade. *Forum,* January 1972, 56.

Tripp, Clarence A. Can homosexuals change with psychotherapy? *Sexual Behavior,* July 1971, 42–49.

Tufill, S. G. *Sexual stimulation.* New York: Grove, 1973.

Tumpson, Helen. The sensuous divorcee. New York: Dell, 1974.

Turrell, Robert. Sexual problems as seen by a proctologist. *New York State Journal of Medicine,* 1974, 74, 697–698.

Ullerstam, Lars. *The erotic minorities.* New York: Grove, 1966.

Unwin, J. D. *Sexual relations and human behavior.* London: Williams and Norgate, 1933.

Valenti, Michael F. On homosexuality. *New York Times,* January 14, 1975, 33.

Vandervoor, Herbert E. Quoted in "Sex counseling gets new focus." *New York Times,* January 14, 1974, 57.

Van Deusen, Edmund. *Contract cohabitation.* New York: Grove Press, 1975.

Van de Velde, T. H. *Ideal, marriage.* New York: Covici Friede, 1926.

†Vatsyayana. *The Kama Sutra.* Paris: Librarie Astra, no date.

Viamontes, Jorge A. Sexual depressent effect of alcohol. *Medical Aspects of Human Sexuality,* 1975, 9(1), 31.

Vincent, Clark. Hidden causes of frigidity. *Sexology,* 1957, 14, 180–185.

Von Urban, Rudolf. *Sex perfection and marital happiness.* New York: Dial, 1949.

Von Urban, Rudolf. Dialogue between priest and doctor: subject masturbation. *Forum,* 1969, 1(12), 28–33.

Wallace, D. H., and Wehmer, G. Pornography and attitude change. *Journal of Sex Research,* 1971, 7(2), 116–125.

Wallin, P., and Clark A. A study of orgasm as a condition of women's enjoyment of coitus in the middle years of marriage. *Human Biology*, 1963, 5, 131.

Warren, Roger. *How to be an erotic man.* New York: Award, 1971.

Watts, Alan W. *Nature, man and woman.* New York: New American Library, 1958.

Weber, Eric. *How to pick up girls.* New York: Bantam, 1971.

Weinberg, George. *Society and the healthy homosexual.* New York: St. Martin's, 1972.

Weinberg, Martin S. Homosexual samples: differences and similarities. *Journal of Sex Research*, 1970, 6, 312–325.

Weinberg, Martin S. The male homosexual. *Social Problems*, 1970, 17, 527–537.

Weiss, Howard D. Mechanism of erection. *Medical Aspects of Human Sexuality*, 1973, 7(2), 28–40.

Wells, J. W. *Sex therapist.* New York: Lancer, 1972.

West, Donald J. *The other man.* New York: Morrow, 1955.

Westwood, Gordon. *A minority.* New York: Longmans, 1960.

Wiegold, Marsha. Sexual pleasures. *Brides*, December 1974, 40(2), 12–13, 96–97.

Wile, Ira S. (Ed.) *Sex life of the unmarried adult.* New York: Vanguard, 1934.

Wilson, G. Terence., and Davison, Gerald C. Behavior therapy and homosexuality: a critical perspective. *Behavior Therapy*, 1974, 5, 16–28.

Wilson, W. Cody, and Goldstein, Michael J. (Eds.). Pornography: attitudes, use, and effects. *Journal of Social Issues*, 1973, 29, 1–238.

Winick, Charles. *The new people.* New York: Pegasus, 1968.

Winick, Charles, and Kinsie, Paul M. *The lively commerce.* Chicago: Quadrangle, 1971.

Winston, Sam. Cruising in L.A. *Other Scenes*, April 1969, 5.

Wolfe, Linda. The question of surrogates in sex therapy. *New York*, December 3, 1973, 120–127.

Wolfe, Linda. Take two aspirins and masturbate. *Playboy*, June 1974, 21(6), 114–116, 164–171.

Wolfe, Linda, Review of *The pleasure bond* by William Masters and Virginia Johnson. *New York Times Book Review*, January 19, 1975, 2–3.

†Wolfe, Janet L., and Goldstein, Iris G. A cognitive-behavioral approach to modifying assertive behavior in women. *Counseling Psychologist*, 1975, 5, 45–52.

†*Wolfe, Janet L. *Rational-emotive therapy and women's problems.* Tape recording. New York: Institute for Rational Living, 1974.

Wolfenden Report. *Report of the committee on homosexual offenses and prostitution.* London: Her Majesty's Stationery Office, 1957.

Wolpe, Joseph, and Lazarus, Arnold. *Behavior therapy techniques.* New York: Pergamon, 1966.

Wrage, Karl. Erotic zones and intercourse. *Sexology*, 1970, 36(9), 5–8.

Wyden, Peter, and Wyden, Barbara. *Inside the sex clinic.* New York: World, 1971.

X, Mrs. *The adultery game.* New York: Stonehill, 1973.

†Yankowski, John S. *The Yankowski report on premarital sex.* Los Angeles: Holloway House, 1965.

†*Young, Howard S. *A rational counseling primer.* New York: Institute for Rational Living, 1974.

†Young, Wayland. *Eros denied*. New York: Grove, 1964.

Youngson, Jeanne. Places to meet people in and around New York. New York: Author, 1970. Mimeographed.

†Zubin, Joseph, and Money, John. *Contemporary sexual behavior*. Baltimore: Johns Hopkins University Press, 1973.

Zuckerman, Marvin. Physiological measures of sexual arousal in the human. *Psychological Bulletin*, 1971, 75, 297–329.

Zuker, Elaina. Sex is better now. *Sexology*, May 1974, 40(10), 18–22.

Zussman, Shirley, and Zussman, Leon. Keys to understanding female sexuality. *Medical Aspects of Human Sexuality*, 1974, 8(8), 125–126.

Index